THE OXFORD ILLUSTRATED HISTORY OF
THE WORLD

The historians who contributed to *The Oxford Illustrated History of the World* are all distinguished authorities in their field. They are:

PAOLO LUCA BERNARDINI - Università degli Studi dell'Insubria

JEREMY BLACK - University of Exeter

JOHN BROOKE - Ohio State University

DAVID CHRISTIAN - Macquarie University

FELIPE FERNÁNDEZ-ARMESTO - University of Notre Dame

CLIVE GAMBLE - University of Southampton

MARTIN JONES - University of Cambridge

MANUEL LUCENA GIRALDO - Centro Superior de Investigaciones Científicas, Madrid

IAN MORRIS - Stanford University

DAVID NORTHRUP - Boston College

ANJANA SINGH - Rijksuniversiteit Groningen

THE OXFORD
ILLUSTRATED HISTORY OF
THE WORLD

Edited by

FELIPE FERNÁNDEZ-ARMESTO

OXFORD
UNIVERSITY PRESS

OXFORD
UNIVERSITY PRESS

Great Clarendon Street, Oxford, OX2 6DP,
United Kingdom

Oxford University Press is a department of the University of Oxford.
It furthers the University's objective of excellence in research, scholarship,
and education by publishing worldwide. Oxford is a registered trade mark of
Oxford University Press in the UK and in certain other countries

Published in the United States of America by Oxford University Press
198 Madison Avenue, New York, NY 10016, United States of America

British Library Cataloguing in Publication Data
Data available

Library of Congress Control Number: 2018937426

ISBN 978–0–19–875290–5

Printed in Italy by
L.E.G.O. S.p.A.

CONTENTS

PART 1   Children of the Ice

*The Peopling of the World and the Beginnings of Cultural
Divergence, c. 200,000 to c. 12,000 years ago*

PART 2   Of Mud and Metal

*Divergent Cultures from the Emergence of Agriculture to the
'Crisis of the Bronze Age', c. 10,000 BCE–c. 1,000 BCE*

LIST OF MAPS

LIST OF TABLES

Introduction

IN 1928, Philo Vance, the hero of *The Bishop Murder Case*, imagined a hypothetical creature who can '...traverse all worlds at once with infinite velocity, so that he is able to behold all human history at a glance. From...Alpha Centauri he can see the earth as it was four years ago; from the Milky Way he can see it as it was 4,000 years ago, and he can also choose a point in space where he can witness the ice-age and the present day simultaneously!'

This book will not give the reader quite so privileged a perspective, but our aim is to see the world whole with objectivity hard to attain for humans trapped in our own history—to review the changes that really have taken place all over the planet, not just in parts of it—and present them in a tiny compass, such as a galactic observer might behold from an immense distance in time and space.

The erudition of Vance (the fictional detective Willard Wright created under his pseudonym, S. S. Van Dine) was affected and his science absurd. He was right, however, about the effects of perspective on historical vision. The technique of shifting to an imaginary perspective can transform the way we see our past. Even small variants in viewpoint can disclose discoveries. When painting a still life, for instance, Cézanne used to switch between vantage points, seeking to combine fleeting perceptions in a single composition. He made the curves of the rim of a bowl of apples look as if they can never meet. He painted strangely distended melons, because he wanted to capture the way the fruit seems to change shape from different angles. In his assemblages of odds and ends each object assumes its own perspective. He painted the same subjects over and over again, because with every fresh look you see something new, and every retrospect leaves you dissatisfied with the obvious imperfections of partial vision.

The past is like a painting by Cézanne—or like a sculpture in the round, the reality of which no single viewpoint can disclose. Objective reality (that which looks the same by agreement among all honest observers) lies somewhere out there, remote and difficult to find—except perhaps by encompassing all possible subjective perspectives. When we shift vantage point, we get a new glimpse, and try to fit it in when we return to our canvas. To put it another way, Clio is a muse we spy bathing between leaves. Each time we dodge and slip in and out of different points of view, a little more is revealed.

We know the advantages of multiple viewpoints from everyday experience. 'Try to see it my way, try to see it your way', sang the Beatles. We have to incorporate perspectives of protagonists and victims to reconstruct a crime. We need testimony from many witnesses to reproduce the flicker and glimmer of events. To understand whole societies, we need to know what it feels like to live in them at every level of power and wealth. To understand cultures, we need to set them in context and know what their neighbours think or thought of them. To grasp a core, we peel away at outer layers. But the past is ungraspable: we see it best when we add context, just as the bull's eye makes a clearer target when the outer rings define it and draw in the eye.

The most spectacular and objective point of view I can imagine is that of Philo Vance's 'hypothetical homunculus,' who sees the planet whole and views its complete past conspectually. The question for a global historian is, 'What would history look like to that galactic observer in the cosmic crow's nest?' I suspect that Vance's creature might need prompting even to mention a species as puny and, so far, short-lived as humankind. Grasses, or foxes, or protozoa, or viruses might seem more interesting: they all have, from a biological point of view, features at least as conspicuous as those of humans—vast environmental reach, stunning adaptability, remarkable duration. But one human feature would surely be conspicuous from any perspective: the ways in which we differ from all other species in our hectic, kaleidoscopic experience of culture, and the fact that we have more of it, of more various kinds, than any other creature. Humans have a dazzling array of contrasting ways of behaving, whereas other species—though many of them resemble us closely in bodies and genes— encompass a comparatively tiny range of differences. We have vastly more lifeways and foodways, social structures and political systems, means of representing and communicating, rites and religions than any other cultural animal—even the great apes who are most like us. That variety is the subject-matter of this book.

Over the last sixty years or so, observers have identified culture among many primate species and claimed it for many others. Human cultures, however, are different: by comparison with other species, we are strangely unstable. Communities in all cultural species become differentiated, as they change in contrasting and inconsistent ways, but the processes involved happen incalculably more often, with a perplexingly greater range of variation, among humans than among any other animals: human cultures register the constant series of changes called 'history'. They self-transform, diverge, and multiply with bewildering and apparently—now and for most of the recent past—accelerating speed. They vary, radically and rapidly, from time to time and place to place.

This book is an attempt to clasp the whole of our variety, or as much of it as possible, by seeing the themes that link it, the stories that overarch it, and the pathways through it. Some people think the big narrative, which encompasses just about the whole of history, is of progress or providence or increasing complexity, or cyclical change or dialectical conflict, or evolution, or thermodynamics, or some other irreversible trend. The galactic observer, however, would surely notice subtler, less predictable, but more compelling, tales. The contributors to *The Oxford Illustrated History of the World* muster between them five ways of tracing a path through the data. Call them master-narratives if you like, or meta-narratives if you prefer. But the storylines are objectively verifiable and can be followed in this book.

The first story is of divergence and convergence—how ways of life multiply and meet. Divergence—the single word with which, I think, the galactic observer would summarize our story—is surely dominant. It denotes how the limited, stable culture of *Homo sapiens*, at our species' first appearance in the archaeological record, scattered and self-transformed to cover the tremendous range of divergent ways of life with which we now surprise each other and infest every inhabitable environment on the planet. We started as a small species, with a uniform way of life, in a restricted environment in East Africa, where all humans behaved in much the same way, foraging for the same foods; relating to each other with a single set of conventions of deference and dominance; deploying the same technologies; using, as far as we know, the same means of communication; studying the same sky; imagining—as best we can guess— the same gods; probably submitting, like other primates, to the rule of the alpha male, but venerating the magic of women's bodies that are uniquely regenerative and uniquely attuned to the rhythms of nature. As migrant groups adjusted to new environments and lost touch with each other—so the authors of Part 1 show—they developed contrasting traditions and distinctive ways of behaving, thinking, organizing families and communities, representing the world, relating to each other and to their environments, and worshipping their peculiar deities.

Until about 12,000 years ago or so, they all had similar economies—getting their sustenance by hunting and gathering. But climate change induced a variety of strategies, with some people opting to continue traditional ways of life, others adopting herding or tillage: in Part 2, Martin Jones tells that story in Chapter 3. Farming accelerated every kind of cultural change, as Chapter 4 and Chapter 7 make clear. So, as John Brooke's contribution in Chapter 5 shows, did adjustments to the dynamics of elements of the environment beyond human control—the lurches of climate, the convulsions of the Earth, the bewildering evolution of the microbes that sometimes sustain, sometimes rupture, the ecologies of which we are part. Culture has, moreover, a dynamic of its own, partly because human imaginations are irrepressible, continually re-picturing the world and inspiring us to realize our visions, and partly because every change—especially in some areas of culture, such as science, technology, and art— unlocks new possibilities. The results are visible around us.

Tracing the divergence of humans, however, is not enough. For almost the whole length of the story, countervailing trends, which we can call convergence, have been going on, too. David Northrup's work in this book broaches the theme, which increasingly dominates the chapters from Part 4 onwards, little by little mirroring the way cultures established or re-established contact, exchanged lifeways and ideas, and grew more like each other as time went on. In convergence, sundered cultures meet at the edges of their explorations or at tense frontiers of the expansion of their territories, or in the adventures of traders or missionaries or migrants or warriors. They exchange thoughts and technologies along with people, goods, and blows.

Convergence and divergence are more than compatible: they are complementary because exchanges of culture introduce novelties, stimulate innovations, and precipitate every other kind of change. For most of the human past, divergence outstripped convergence: cultures, that is to say, became more and more diverse—more and more unlike each other—despite mutual encountering and learning. Isolation kept most of them apart for long spells. Uncrossable oceans, daunting deserts, and mountains deterred, interrupted, or prevented potentially transforming contacts. At a contested moment, however—the contributors to this book cannot agree about how or when to fix it—the balance swung away from divergence, so that convergence became more conspicuous. Over the last half millennium, convergence has been increasingly intense. Exploration has ended the isolation of almost every human community. Global trade has brought everyone's culture in reach of just about everyone else's, and global communications have made the process instantaneous. A fairly long period of Western global hegemony seems to have privileged the transmission of culture from Europe and North America to the rest of the world, 'globalizing', as we now say, Western styles in art, politics, and economics. Divergence has not been halted—merely overshadowed. Under the shell of globalization, old differences persist and new ones incubate. Some are precious, others perilous.

As divergence and convergence wind and unwind through this book, they tangle with another thread. In Chapter 7, Ian Morris calls it 'growth': accelerating change, which, with some hesitancies and reversals, has perplexed and baffled people in every age, but now seems to have speeded up uncontrollably; the sometimes faltering but ever self-reassertive increase of population, production, and consumption; ever more intensive concentrations of people—successively in foragers' settlements, agrarian villages, growing cities, mega-conurbations; increasingly populous and unwieldy polities, from chieftaincies to states to empires to superstates.

In some ways, as is apparent from David Christian in Chapter 11, all types of acceleration are measurable in terms of consumption of energy. To some extent, nature supplied the energy that accelerating human activities required, by way of global warming. Today we tend to think of global warming as the result of human profligacy with fuel, creating the greenhouse effect. But climate on Earth depends above all on the sun—a star too potent and distant to respond to humans' petty doings—and irregularities in the tilt and orbit of the planet, which are beyond our power to influence. Except for a brief blip—a 'little ice age' of diminished temperatures in the period covered by Part 3 of this book—and some minor fluctuations at other times, the incidence and results of which the reader will find chronicled in Parts 1 and 3, natural events beyond human reach have been warming the planet for about 20,000 years or so.

Meanwhile, three great revolutions, in which humans have been involved as active participants, have further boosted our access to energy: first, the switch from finding food to producing it—from foraging to farming. As Martin Jones's chapter makes clear, the switch was not solely or entirely the product of human ingenuity; nor was it a fluke (as some enquirers, including Darwin, used to think), but rather a long process in response to climate change. It was a mutual adjustment in which plants and creatures, including humans, established relationships of reciprocal dependence: humans could not survive without species that, without humans, could not exist. Insofar as human agency procured it, the inception of farming was a conservative revolution, produced by people who wanted to stick to their traditional food stocks, but had to find new ways to guarantee supply. The result was a stunning interruption of the normal pattern of evolution: for the first time, new species came into being by 'unnatural selection', crafted for human purposes by sorting, transplanting, nurturing, and hybridization.

Evolution got warped a second time in a process described in Chapter 8 and Chapter 10: the 'ecological revolution' that started when long-range voyages began regularly to cross the oceans of the world from the sixteenth century onwards. In consequence, life forms that had been diverging on mutually separate and increasingly distant continents, during about 150 million years of continental drift, began to be swapped, partly as a result of conscious human efforts to multiply access to a variety of foods, and partly as an unintended consequence of biota—weeds, pests, microbes—hitching, as it were, a ride with trading, exploring, conquering, or migrating human populations. The previously divergent course of evolution from continent to continent yielded to a new, convergent pattern. Today, as a result, climate for climate, we find the same life forms all over the world.

Not all the consequences favoured humankind. The disease environment worsened for populations that became suddenly exposed to unfamiliar bacteria and viruses; fortunately for our species, however, as we see in Chapter 8 and Chapter 11 by David Northrup and David Christian, respectively, other changes in the microbial world counteracted the negative effects, as, in response to global warming, some of the most deadly diseases mutated and targeted new, non-human niches. Overwhelmingly, meanwhile, changes in the distribution of humanly digestible food sources hugely increased the supply of energy in two crucial ways. First, more varied staples were available, indemnifying against blight and ecological disaster societies formerly dependent on a very limited range of crops or animals. (There were exceptions, as some newly available crops proved deceptively nutritious, trapping some populations into over-reliance on potatoes or maize, with subversive effects on health or the incidence of famine.) More straightforwardly, the amount of food produced in the world increased with the effects of the ecological revolution, which enabled farmers and ranchers to colonize previously unexploited or underexploited lands—especially drained, upland, and marginal soils—and to boost the productivity of existing farmland.

Supplementary sources boosted food energy: animal muscle-power, gravity, wind and running water, clockwork and gears (on a very small scale), and the combustibles (mainly wood, with some use of wax, animal and vegetable fats, peat, turf and waste grasses, tar, and coal) used to make heat for warmth and cooking. But the world resorted to no new revolutionary way of mobilizing energy until industrialization, when the use of fossil fuels and steam power multiplied muscle exponentially. The results, as we have seen, were equivocal. As Ian Morris points out, people's capacity to 'get things done' was immeasurably enhanced. But as Anjana Singh points out in her chapter, that extra capacity was exploited for destructive ends—of human life in war, and of the environment in pollution and resource depletion. In the last hundred years or so, electricity has displaced steam and new ways of generating power have begun to relieve stress on fossil fuels, but the equivocal outcomes remain unresolved.

Along with divergence and accelerating change, the third theme to emerge in *The Oxford Illustrated History of the World* is of humans' relationship with the rest of nature, which changes constantly, sometimes in response to human—or in currently fashionable jargon 'anthropogenic'—influences that form part of the story of culture, but also, more powerfully, in ways humans cannot control and are still largely unable to foresee: climatic, seismic, pathogenic. Every society has had to adjust its behaviour in order to balance exploitation with conservation. Civilization is perhaps best understood as a process of environmental modification to suit human purposes—re-shaping landscapes for ranching and tilling, for instance, then smothering them with new, built environments designed to satisfy human cravings. In some ways, environmental history is another chronicle of accelerating change, as exploitation has intensified in order to supply growing populations and growing per capita consumption. The relationship between humans and the rest of creation has always been uneasy and has become increasingly conflictive. On the one hand, humans dominate ecosystems, master vast portions of the biosphere, and obliterate species that we see as threatening or competitive. Yet, on the other, we remain vulnerable to the uncontrollable lurches of forces that dwarf us: we cannot halt earthquakes, or influence the sun, or predict every new plague.

The story of human interventions in the environment looks like a series of hair's breadth escapes from disaster, each of which, like the sallies of an adventure story, thickened the plot and introduced new difficulties. Farming helped people who practised it survive climate change; however, it created new reservoirs of disease among domesticated animals, condemned societies to dependence on limited foodstuffs, and justified tyrannous polities that organized and policed war, labour, irrigation, and warehousing. Industrialization hugely boosted productivity, at the cost of fearful labour conditions in 'infernal wens' and 'dark, satanic mills'. Fossil fuels unlocked vast reserves of energy, but polluted the air and raised global temperatures. Artificial pesticides and fertilizers saved millions from starvation, but poisoned the soil and winnowed biodiversity. Nuclear power has saved the world from exhaustion and threatened it with immolation. Medical science has spared millions of people from physical sickness, but ever more rampant 'lifestyle diseases'—often the result of misuse of sex, food, drugs, and drink—have gone on wrecking or ending lives, while neuroses and psychoses swarm. Overall, the global disease environment hardly seems benign. The costs of treatment leave most of the world outside the reach of enhanced medicine.

Technology has saved us from each successive set of self-inflicted problems, only to create new ones that demand ever bigger, riskier, and costlier solutions. A technologically dependent world is like the old woman in the song, who began by swallowing a fly and, in an effort to catch it, gulped down ever bigger predators in pursuit of each other. She ended 'dead, of course'. We have no better strategy at present than escalating recourse to technology.

The fourth theme apparent in this book concerns the one area apparently largely exempt from change: what we might call the limitations of culture—the apparently immutable background of all other stories in the stagnancy and universality of human nature, the bedrock mixture of good and evil, wisdom and folly that transcends every cultural boundary and never seems to alter much over time. While we increase our 'capacity to get things done', as Ian Morris points out, our morals and our stewardship of the world and of each other remain mired in selfishness and riven with hostilities. Anjana Singh points out how much of our enhanced capacity we divert to destructive ends—destructive of each other, destructive of the eco-systems on which we depend, destructive of the biosphere that is our common home.

We can, of course, point to some improvement, but only with subversive qualifications. Perhaps the most comforting change traceable in this book is the way our moral community has gradually enlarged to encompass almost the whole of humankind. The achievement has been astounding, because humans are not typically well disposed to those outside their own groups of kin or fellow countrymen. As Claude Lévi-Strauss pointed out, most languages have no word for 'human' beyond the term that denotes group members: outsiders are usually called by words that mean something like 'beast' or 'demon'. The struggle to induce humans to see common humanity beneath the superficialities of appearance, pigmentation, and differences of culture or priorities or abilities has been long and hard. Key moments can be traced in the chapters below by Manuel Lucena Giraldo, Anjana Singh, Paolo Luca Bernardini, and Jeremy Black, but blind spots remain. Some bio-ethicists still regard certain minorities as imperfectly human or disqualified from human rights: the unborn, the victims of euthanasia, infants supposedly too tiny to have conscious interests. Some feel our moral community will never be fully moral while it excludes non-human animals. And in practice, we behave as viciously as ever, when the opportunity arises or the perceived need occurs, persecuting and exploiting migrants and refugees, victimizing minorities, exterminating supposed enemies, immiserating the poor while increasing cruelly unjust wealth gaps, engrossing resources that ought to be common, and honouring 'human rights' in the breach. Claims of the demise or, at least, retreat of violence seem premature (though David Christian would dissent). Fears of the destructiveness of modern weapons has curtailed large-scale war, but terrorism has expanded its niche. Outside the realms of terrorism and war crimes, murder has declined, suicide grown. Abortion has replaced infanticide in some parts of the world. Spanking has dropped out of the parental armoury, while sadism has achieved tolerance, even a certain respectability. Overall, people seem no better and no worse, no dumber or brighter than ever. The effect of moral stasis is not, however, neutral, because of the way improved technologies empower evil and folly.

Finally, as this book helps to show, the story of human societies' relationships with each other can be told in terms of the shift of what I call initiative: the power of some human groups to influence others. Initiative changes broadly in line with the global distribution of power and wealth. With some exceptions, wealthier, tougher communities influence those that are less well off in these respects. As readers of this book will see, over the 7,000 years or so during which we can document the drift of initiative, it was first concentrated in southwest Asia and around the eastern end of the Mediterranean. It became concentrated, for largely undetectable reasons, in east and south Asia, and especially in China, from early in the Christian Era until a slow shift westward became discernible, in some respects, in the sixteenth and seventeenth centuries, accelerating in the nineteenth and twentieth. Western science, especially astronomy, established parity of esteem in China—a surprising achievement in the face of Chinese contempt for Western 'barbarians'. In the eighteenth century, Western European markets seem, on the whole, to have been more integrated than those of India, wages higher, mutatis mutandis, than those of India or China, and financial institutions, especially in Britain, better equipped to fund new economic initiatives. But in overall productivity and in terms of the balance of trade, China and India led the world until well into the nineteenth century. At present, Western hegemony seems to be waning and the world reverting, in this respect, to a situation in which initiative is unfocused, exchanged between cultures in multiple directions, with China re-emerging in her 'normal' place as the most likely potential world hegemon.

The global triumph of two Western ideas—capitalism and democracy—may come to seem, in retrospect, both the culmination and conclusion of Western supremacy. In the last three decades of the twentieth century, most dictatorships toppled or tottered. One form of totalitarianism, fascism, collapsed earlier in the century; its communist rival crumbled in the 1990s. Meanwhile, deregulating governments in much of the world liberated market forces. The dawn soon darkened and blight disfigured any bliss optimists may have felt at being alive. Democracy proved insecure, as many states slid back into authoritarian hands. Fanaticisms replaced ideologies: nationalism, which had seemed doomed in the increasingly interdependent world of globalization, re-emerged like vermin from the crooked woodwork of the world; religion—which secularists had hoped to see burn itself out—reignited mephitically as a justification for actions of terrorists, who generally seemed to be psychotic and incoherent victims of manipulation by criminals, but who talked like fundamentalists and dogmatists. Capitalism proved delusive. Instead of increasing wealth, it increased wealth gaps. Even in the world's most prosperous countries, the chasm between fat cats and regular guys gaped by the beginning of the new millennium at levels not seen since before the First World War. On a global scale, the scandal of inequality was frankly indecent, with, for every billionaire, thousands of the poor dying for want of basic sanitation, shelter, or medicine. Life expectancy in Japan and Spain was nearly double that of a peasant in

Burkina Faso. The global 'financial meltdown' of 2008 exposed the iniquities of under-regulated markets, but no one knew what to do about it. Economic lurches have continued, increasing the prevailing insecurities that nourish extremist politics. Capitalism has been dented, if not discredited, but no efforts to replace it, or even patch its wounds, have worked.

History is a study of change. This book is therefore divided into chronological tranches, in each of which an author who is an expert in environmental history sketches the environmental context and humans' interactions with it, before others, also experts in their fields, deal with what happened to culture—typically in one chapter on art and thought, another on politics and behaviour—in the period concerned. For early periods, up to about 10,000 years ago, the evidence of what people thought and what they did is so interdependent that contributors have to cover both in a single chapter in each part of the book. For more recent periods, the evidence is abundant enough for us to see the differences, as well as the similarities, between the way people recorded thoughts and feelings, on the one hand, and the way they behaved in practice towards each other in politics and society. Thus, the chapters multiply accordingly.

Readers will see that, although all the contributors to this book try to stand back from the world in order to see it whole, or as nearly whole as possible, and although all have in mind the themes of divergence, acceleration, environmental interactions, the limitations of culture, and the shifts of initiative, there are tensions between the authors, differences of priority and emphasis, and sometimes underlying conflicts of values or ideological tenets or religious beliefs. Still, the collegiality and goodwill with which everyone involved in the project has collaborated unstintingly is one cause for pleasure. Another, which I hope readers will appreciate, is that the diversity of my fellow writers' viewpoints echoes, in a small way, the diversity of history, and helps us see it from multiple perspectives.

PART 1

Children of the Ice

———

The Peopling of the World and the Beginnings of Cultural Divergence, c. 200,000 to c. 12,000 years ago

CHAPTER 1

Humanity from the Ice
The Emergence and Spread of an Adaptive Species

CLIVE GAMBLE

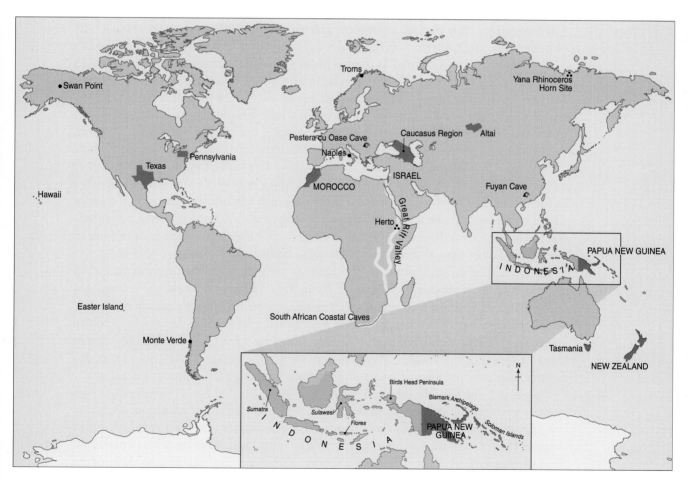

PLACES NAMED IN THE CHAPTER.

ERNEST GELLNER remarked in his philosophical history *Plough, Sword and Book* that 'primitive man has lived twice: once in and for himself, and the second time for us, in our reconstruction'. This double life has concerned archaeologists in their endeavours to fathom the clear blue water between deep history and the present. The structure of Gellner's world history, like many others, rested on three revolutions: agricultural, urban, and industrial. More recently archaeologists added a fourth, the 'human revolution', in which, some 50,000 years ago, *Homo sapiens* assembled all the cognitive, creative, and social skills subsequent civilizations required.

Humans supposedly declared their revolution ostentatiously through art, ornament, burials, persistently used places and trade in exotic stones and shells. They had big foreheads and long legs, which pointed to their African origins, as did their mothers' genes. They spoke, sang, and played musical instruments. It could be safely assumed they recognized kinship. They are often referred to as 'modern humans', an unhelpful term for the study of deep human history because it prejudices the breadth of our reconstruction. These humans were still hominins, an umbrella term for us and all our fossil ancestors. But purists argued on taxonomic grounds that hominins such as Neanderthals could not find shelter under the term we reserve for ourselves: human.

Archaeologists soon started to unpick the evidence for the parcel of skills, which, as new dating methods revealed, began to accumulate slowly at least 200,000 years ago. Markers for revolutionary change, such as beads, the use of pigments for colouring, and changes in projectile technology, were found in different parts of Africa at different times. Discoveries in the last decade by archaeologists and geneticists require a big tent to encompass the variety of our origins: one not supported by a single 'modern' pole.

Beyond Africa's borders there is another story. The trail of cultural markers goes cold as people leave the continent. The descendants of migrants from Africa are known in the rest of the Old World only from their molecular histories preserved in the genes of living people, or rare fossils, or traces of settlement of new continents, principally Australia. For example, beads and pigment use do not accompany the finds of human teeth from Fuyan Cave in southern China. These teeth are between 120,000 and 80,000 years old and the assumption in the absence of genetic information is that they represent an early dispersal of humans from Africa. However, these people did not bring with them 'modern' humans' marker artefacts, such as beads and worked ochre, which were present at this date in Africa. Additionally, no stone tools have been found in Fuyan cave. As a cultural population, 'modern humans' are invisible by conventional archaeological means. The question of when human, rather than hominin, history begins is not susceptible to investigation by using metaphors of revolution.

People did not become human because they left Africa; and over the previous two million years, many specimens of the genus *Homo* had left Africa without becoming modern. It would be wrong to class them as not-quite-modern on the grounds that they delayed their departure for what seems a very long time. Their tardiness may seem strange to us: reticence has never been a feature of what we now recognize as the modern human when it comes to broadcasting social, spiritual, and technical advances. But these humans in question lived their lives without a thought for our ability to reconstruct them. Furthermore, they lived under the selective pressures of biological and cultural evolution. These forces are my entry point to understanding deep human history.

Over the horizon

The narrative of deep human history I examine is driven neither by becoming modern in a biological sense, nor progress in technology. Developments in art and culture are dealt with in Chapter 2. My narrative will be of humans as global travellers. No hominin ever crossed a major ocean or traversed the Siberian tundra to encounter the Americas. With humans came ocean voyages to reach Australia and islands in Near Oceania. At a later date, the Americas were settled, adding almost a third of the earth's inhabitable area to the human estate. By one thousand years ago, when these travelling humans had reached the three Pacific outliers, Hawaii, Easter Island, and New Zealand, they had trekked and navigated their way to being a global species. To put the story in perspective: from the earliest hominins to the appearance of humans outside of Africa—a period of four million years—only a quarter of the world was regularly inhabited. In the last 50,000 years, less than two per cent of hominin history, the remaining three quarters were populated in one breathless rush. And by the time we had caught our breath we found we were also the lonely human species. Other hominin populations we encountered in our first travels, some of whom we bred with, some of whom we could not, fell away. Our global status came with a biological price tag where, as in the Christmas sales, variety was greatly reduced.

This chapter examines the background to this narrative and the evolutionary developments which humans underwent in Africa. Fundamental to these is the pattern of climate change and its impact on local environments and resources. Local life-spaces have to be fitted, cog-like, into the interlocking drivers of climate, the orbital rhythms of the earth, and tectonic shifts. These operate at various scales; planet, ocean, continent, and region. They display variable tempos as measured by amplitude and frequency of the regular climate cycles that their combined forces produce. The cycles combine with constant effects of latitude, longitude, and altitude on solar productivity to produce shifting ecological opportunities for a versatile and clever hominin. Such opportunities are manifest in seasons of abundance and dearth, as well as a sliding scale of the risk of starvation. They are also apparent when it comes to locating the best foods by the sex which has always borne, disproportionately, the cost of reproducing our species. This means deep human history is of necessity deeply gendered. And besides, when told as an evolutionary story, the focus is on females for the reason just given. However, when judged by the pictorial reconstructions and dioramas of a hunting life dominated by spear-wielding, male ancestors, the reader can be forgiven for thinking otherwise.

The big question for humans in deep history is if the first people we recognize as our direct ancestors *really* made that much of a break with their past. It begs further questions about how we know a human when we meet one, if they were shaped

CONVENTIONAL RECONSTRUCTIONS MISLEAD by foregrounding spear-wielding male ancestors. Female humans and hominins bore major responsibility for locating the best foods.

by changes in climate and environment, and what it was, exactly, that made us a global species.

Relevant issues include population size, the timing of global settlement, and the framework of biology and culture that can result in descent with modification; the result of Darwin's mechanisms of natural and sexual selection.

Recognizing humans

In deep history there are four routes available to identify a human; through genes, anatomy, artefacts, and geography. The lines of evidence have their own procedural assumptions, working methods, and caveats which make this interdisciplinary exercise in classification challenging.

For many years the evidence for humans was led by anatomy and, in particular, the shape of fossil skulls (Table 1.1). Sample sizes are extremely small, but this has not stopped biological anthropologists from devising evolutionary trees and applying the biological species concept based on reproductive isolation to fragmentary material. Long-standing tradition defined a biological species as groups of actually, or potentially, interbreeding natural populations, which are reproductively isolated from other such groups.

Archaeogenetics has tested this concept. The first studies, tracing female ancestry through mitochondrial DNA and male ancestry through the Y chromosome, came from the genetics of living populations to produce ancestral maps of modern human

TABLE 1.1 The anatomical criteria used by Chris Stringer and Peter Andrews to define a modern human.

1 All living humans are characterized by a gracile skeleton in comparison with that of other species of the genus *Homo*. In particular this applies to
   - longbone shape and shaft thickness.
   - the depth or extent of muscle insertions.
   - the relatively thin bone of the cranium (skull) and mandible (jawbone).

2 The cranium is voluminous, but no more so than in Neanderthals, and like the brain it contains is typically short, high, and domed.

3 The supraorbital torus (browridges) and external cranial buttressing are either considerably reduced or absent.

4 Teeth and jaws are reduced in size.

5 Probably as a result of smaller teeth, the face is tucked well under the forehead rather than sloping forward.

6 A mental eminence (chin) is present on the mandible from a young age.

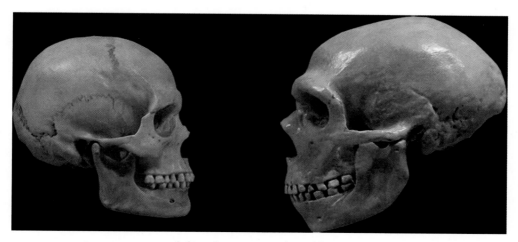

THE SKULL OF *HOMO SAPIENS* (left). When compared to older ancestors such as Neanderthal (right), it is lightly built with a high forehead and a prominent chin, features which anatomists since Huxley have held as important markers of our evolutionary status.

dispersals. However, these did not suggest any interbreeding between humans moving out of Africa and indigenous populations of *Homo* they encountered.

The second wave of studies reconstructed the genomes of extinct hominins. This breakthrough was made possible by advances in DNA extraction from ancient bones and sequencing techniques: two results are noteworthy. In the first place, the biological species concept, with reproductive isolation, does not apply to hominin populations. Eurasian Neanderthals were isolated from African humans for at least the last 500,000 years, the time when they last shared a common ancestor, *Homo heidelbergensis*. (The age estimate is based on mutation rates and varies according to assumptions in the calculation.) Yet some four per cent of genes in living *H. sapiens* is derived from Neanderthals pointing to successful interbreeding after a long period of separation. The second finding is that there are potentially many extinct lineages for which we have no fossil record. The discovery of a new hominin in Denisova Cave in the Altai region of Russia is the first example of what is likely to become a flood of genetically distinct populations in the next decade. The genetic evidence comes from a finger bone of uncertain age and which was tested in the expectation that it would provide another Neanderthal genome.

Anatomical and genetic studies of humans have much work to do to reconcile their data. As leading archaeogeneticst Svante Pääbo declares, 'My hope is, of course, eventually we will not bring turmoil but clarity to this world'. One challenge facing archaeogenetics concerns the poor preservation of DNA in fossil bones from tropical latitudes. Preservation is good in temperate regions, and best in cold climate habitats such as the Altai. When fossil finds are made, as at Fuyan Cave in southern China at latitude 25°N, the chances of recovering DNA from them are currently slight.

The third line of evidence is archaeological. A checklist, originally drawn up by Richard Klein (Table 1.2) to support a short, sharp human revolution, has been expanded to cover more time and space. The aim of archaeologists has been to match changes in the use of resources and the innovation of new artefacts on the one hand with, on the other, the appearance of modern looking skulls and the phylogeographies of modern populations, reconstructed from various lines of DNA evidence to produce maps of where populations originated and how they moved. This

TABLE 1.2 A ten-point checklist of traits of fully modern behaviour detectable in the archaeological record and beginning 50,000–40,000 years ago.

1 Substantial growth in the diversity and standardization of artefact types.
2 Rapid increase in the rate of artefactual change through time and in the degree of artefact diversity through space.
3 First shaping of bone, ivory, shell, and related materials into formal artefacts, e.g. points, awls, needles, pins.
4 Earliest appearance of incontrovertible art.
5 Oldest undeniable evidence for spatial organization of camp floors, including elaborate hearths and the oldest indisputable structural 'ruins'.
6 Oldest evidence for the transport of large quantities of highly desirable stone raw material over scores or even hundreds of kilometres.
7 Earliest secure evidence for ceremony or ritual, expressed both in art and in relatively elaborate graves.
8 First evidence for human ability to live in the coldest, most continental parts of Eurasia.
9 First evidence for human population densities approaching those of historic hunter-gatherers in similar environments.
10 First evidence for fishing and for other significant advances in human ability to acquire energy from nature.

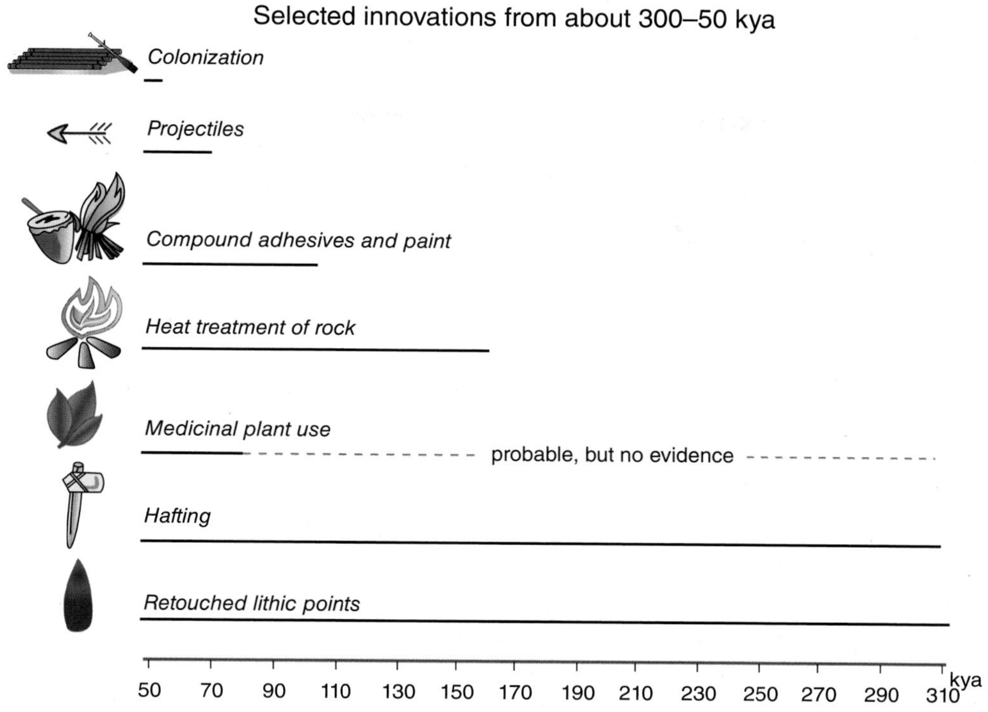

Selected innovations from about 300–50 kya

Colonization

Projectiles

Compound adhesives and paint

Heat treatment of rock

Medicinal plant use
- - - - - - - - - - - - - - probable, but no evidence - - - - - - - - - - - - -

Hafting

Retouched lithic points

| 50 | 70 | 90 | 110 | 130 | 150 | 170 | 190 | 210 | 230 | 250 | 270 | 290 | 310 | kya |

SOME IMPORTANT INNOVATIONS, *c.* 300,000–*c.* 50,000 BCE. These show that the transition to what some call modern behaviour was slow and piecemeal rather than revolutionary.

has met with limited success, as indicated in Table 1.3. Instead of a human revolution, we see a long drawn-out affair.

Evidence of the slow assembly of the various parts, genes, anatomy and artefacts within Africa has inspired the construction of another supposed ancestor, who might make us modify Gellner's dictum and say that primitive man has lived thrice, the third time for biological anthropologists. This is the 'anatomically modern human' (AMH), who looks like us, falls in the time range since the last common ancestor, and yet does not display the full suite of modern skills in key areas such as art, music, and the use of symbols to organize their worlds. This classification was first used in 1971 and has grown in popularity to the present. A good example is provided by the 160,000-year-old skulls from Herto in Ethiopia. These three skulls were assigned a subspecies status, *Homo sapiens idaltu*, on the basis of their morphology. The last name means elder in the Afar language. The stone tools they were found with could have been made at any time during the previous 300,000 years. But the skulls had been modified post-mortem: de-fleshed and partially polished in what the excavators described as a deliberate mortuary practice. Modern-looking, with novel skull modification but an ancient stone technology, these contradictory aspects identify Herto as AMH, rather than modern human, when skulls, genes, and new artefacts (Table 1.2) signal the completed deal.

TABLE 1.3 The timeframe for the appearance of *Homo sapiens,* modern humans.

Evidence	Dating method	Age, years ago
Genomes: last common ancestor between *Homo sapiens* and *Homo neanderthalensis.*	Age based on estimates of the mutation and divergence rates in the genomes of the two species.	440,000–207,000
Mitochondrial lineages point to an ancestral Eve in Africa from which all female mitochondrial lineages today are descended.		200,000
Y male chromosome lineages point to a later date for an equivalent ancestral Adam.		156,000–120,000
Cranial anatomy: the three oldest skulls attributed to *Homo sapiens* come from the Omo valley of northern Kenya.	Science-based dating techniques using the principles of isotope decay:	195,000
Artefacts and resources: an array of novel objects which change appearance, such as ornaments and pigment colours, as well as new technology using adhesives for hafting and reducing the size of stone points, and the sustained use of new resources such as shellfish.	U/Th (Uranium/Thorium) K/Ar (Potassium/Argon) C^{14} (radiocarbon), and OSL (Optical stimulated luminescence)	300,000–40,000
Geographical: first appearance outside Africa.		>100,000
China, evidence of modern human teeth at Fuyan Cave in Daoxian county, Hunan Province.		>80,000
Australia, evidence for first settlement of the continent.		60,000–50,000

The use of AMH to ascribe such evidence tells us rather more about our classifications than about the hominins. AMH was invented to resolve a contradiction; modern-looking skulls found with ancient types of stone tools. Now, archaeogenetics has added further information. It is unlikely, however, that the three lines of evidence will ever present a harmonious picture. Contradictions must be expected when it comes to biological and cultural identities. Archaeologists often build their schemes on the idea of exclusive membership, known as the monothetic set. To be classed as a modern human, or, say, a representative of an Iron Age tribe or the citizen of an ancient city state, an individual had to display overwhelming adherence to the same material markers. The reality is that identity is based on sharing some, rather than all, of the traits on offer—the polythetic set approach. The difference is between exclusive and shared elements. The AMH is a good example of identity, in this case, membership of the modern human club, which is denied if a monothetic standard is applied, but which passes under polythetic rules. And as molecular evidence increases, the expectations are high that, for the same reasons, we will start to hear of genetically modern humans (GMH).

Another complicating fact in the saga of AMH has come with the discovery of a small-brained, but stone-tool-using hominin on the Indonesian island of Flores. Dubbed the hobbit on account of their one-metre-high stature, the hominins from Liang Bua Cave appear to contradict the expected trajectory of human evolution towards larger brains for equivalent body size. *Homo floresiensis* has a brain size of 401 cms^3, whereas their contemporaries, Pleistocene *Homo sapiens*, reach 1478 cms^3. When scaled against body size, however, the small Flores hominins have an encephalization quotient (EQ) of 4.3 compared to *Homo sapiens'* EQ of 5.4. The ratio for *Homo floresiensis* is small, but still higher than all the Australopithecines and, indeed, *Homo heidelbergensis*.

The Liang Bua discoveries were unexpected and judged to fall outside the biological species concept as applied to *Homo sapiens*. Nonetheless, they were placed in the genus *Homo*. Their small brains have been compared to a much older hominin *Australopithecus africanus*, which had a brain size of 464cms^3 and an EQ of 2.81. The study of brain endocasts reveals that, although both brains were small, they were differently structured, with Liang Bua much closer to our modern form. A final reason for in their inclusion in the genus *Homo* is that these Liang Bua people became extinct between 38,000 and 12,000 years ago, whereas the last small-brained Australopithecine, *A. africanus*, became extinct 2.4 million years ago.

Let us now move from their classification and ask some questions about the earliest *Homo sapiens*. What made them distinctive beyond their chins and limb proportions (Table 1.1)? The answer: not that much. They share a physique similar to that of their close hominin relatives, the Neanderthals. Ice Age humans were robustly built and generally large bodied. Slender, more lightly built skeletons came much later with warmer Holocene climates and a change in diets to grains, starch, and carbohydrates made soft and digestible by boiling. Furthermore, the key element, a large brain, was found also among Neanderthals (Table 1.4).

Brain size is important because it can be used to infer the size of the social communities within which individuals lived. A study of communities and brain size among living non-human primates reveals a strong statistical relationship between brain and social group size: the larger the brains, the bigger the social communities in which individuals live. For example, chimpanzees have a brain size of 367 cms^3 and an individual's personal network typically has 57 other individuals in it. The smaller-brained macaque has as brain of 63cms^3 and 40 network partners (Figure 1.4). The reason for these differences is put down to the challenge of remembering and maintaining social relationships, a constraint known as cognitive load. Such a relationship between brain and group size has led to a description of the brain as a *social brain* and the following hypothesis: that in human evolution, the enlargement of our

TABLE 1.4 A comparison of three hominin species.

	Brain size	Encephalization quotient (EQ) ratio of brain to body size	Predicted personal network size (Dunbar's number)	% of daytime which would be needed in primate-style grooming
Homo sapiens Pleistocene	1478	5.38	144	40
Homo neanderthalensis	1426	4.75	141	39
Homo heidelbergensis	1204	4.07	126	35

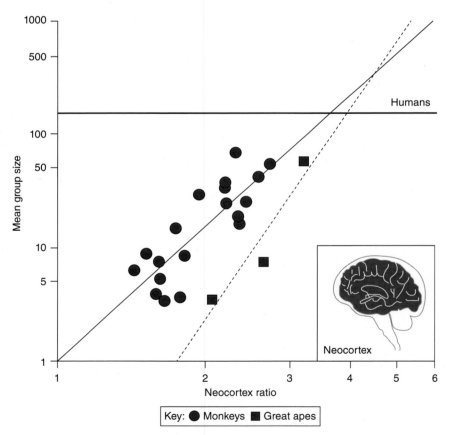

PRIMATES' BRAINS COMPARED FOR SIZE: the correlation with the numbers in typical groups is clear.

brains was driven by our social lives. The selection pressure that explains this process was supplied originally by the advantages of living in larger groups when it came to resisting predators.

If the line in the brain/group size graph is continued to include the brain sizes for hominins and humans, we discover that the predicted number of people in a community for a primate with a brain of our size is about 150. This is known as Dunbar's number, after the evolutionary psychologist Robin Dunbar, who first examined the relationship with biological anthropologist Leslie Aiello. The social brain hypothesis is about social complexity, the ability to associate with larger numbers of individuals, and to retain information about peoples' history, intentions, and the way they respond when interacting. When Dunbar's number was first proposed on the basis of the primate graph, there were no Internet-based social media. The appearance of these has confirmed his prediction. We know that the average number of friends on an individual's Facebook account is 130, a figure calculated from a dataset of 1.44 billion active users. What defines either a Facebook friend or a member of a Pleistocene human's personal network is the frequency and strength of interaction. Originally this would have been face to face, but increasingly through keepsakes and mementoes, and then technologies of separation such as letters, phones, and now the Internet, we have found ways to extend our social lives, to go beyond physical presence. That skill was an essential part of becoming a global species. It allowed us to cross oceans and enter cold continental interiors where population densities are low and social interactions infrequent.

Dunbar's number, however, remains the basic social building block irrespective of either the environment where people live or their material culture and technology. The latter can be hand-held stone tools or the haptic interfaces of the present silicon revolution; the number of people we regularly interact with in a significant way has remained constant. Dunbar's number underpins societies that range in scale from the few hundreds among hunters and gatherers to the billions of the industrial world. It is best explained by the cognitive load of personal information we can sustain before social impairment begins. Cognitively, therefore, we are still a very similar species to our direct Pleistocene ancestors, irrespective of what we see as our superior technological savvy.

Ice ages and humans

Human evolution is played out at geographical scales—of planet, oceans, continents, and regions—subject to cyclical processes and interspersed with events like volcanic eruptions. Together, these determine the pattern of local ecology to which humans are adapted and which exerts, through the distribution and reliability of food resources, important selection pressures.

Mobility and the original social network

We can see the outcome of these selection pressures in the response of mobile societies that practise a hunting and gathering economy today. The imperative of solving the seasonal cycles of dearth and abundance, wet and dry, cold and heat has led to many cultural solutions to avoid the risk of starvation. Among these are technologies that obtain food and store it in time-efficient ways. As a result, periods of abundance are spread out over the year. The solutions vary in predictable ways according to local ecologies.

Two tactics are paramount in reducing the risk of starvation and responding to local selection pressures. These are mobility and sharing. Mobility adjusts population in time and space to fluctuating food resources. The degree of mobility varies between low- and high-latitude societies. At the equator, where plant foods form a large part of the diet, people move frequently and camp sites are used briefly. Availability of water, few storage opportunities, and rapidly eating out the country around these campsites all add to the peripatetic movements along well-worn tracks. At the other latitudinal extreme, Arctic hunters move less frequently and occupy locales on a permanent or semi-permanent basis. They move greater distances from these villages than their counterparts at the equator. They have more complex technologies to catch elusive sea mammals, migrating caribou, and salmon, which they then preserve by smoking and drying and keeping in storehouses, pits, and stone built caches.

Whatever the environment, mobility is the key tactic for survival and success. Consequently, foragers' landscapes are best described as tracks and itineraries, rather than as territories. When farming is adopted in the low and middle latitudes during the Holocene, loss of mobility represented a major change and, of course, had demographic consequences. Arctic hunters practise sedentary lifestyles without population growth, unlike their farming counterparts (see Chapter 3).

The second tactic that humans practise is social networking. The tracks they travel in search of food and resources are also the trade routes, songlines, and marriage networks that extend an individual's reach across space and time beyond familiar genetic kin. Belonging to inter-regional networks of exchange and kinship is described as 'kinshipping', i.e. our human ability to make relationships that are not based on genetic kinship—the auntie who is not really an auntie, the 'son' we always wanted. Among the Kalahari in southern Africa, for instance, through kinship and alliance, individuals form part of an interregional network for the exchange of materials, artefacts, and information along with wives and husbands. The social ties that are created also act as an insurance policy. If drought hits one part of the region, membership of the network allows people to move without hindrance to areas that can support them. Comparable systems are found throughout the varied environments of Australia, which was, until the eighteenth century, par excellence the continent of hunters and gatherers. Here, a distinction is made between people's *estate*, where they were born and have their spiritual locus, and a much larger *range* over which they travel, hunt, and gather, and where they encounter other related and un-related people. Fictive kin allow us to move freely through social and geographical space and present the hospitable side of our species. In consequence, of course, we also risk being turned away from the shelter of the inn.

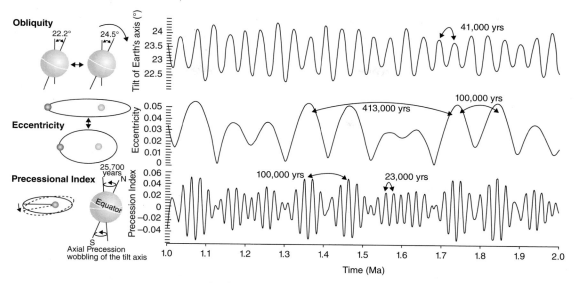

ICE AGES OCCUR WITH CHANGES in the distance from the sun and modifications of the angle at which its rays strike the Earth.

Changes forced by variations in the Earth's orbit

We can understand much about contemporary hunting and gathering societies through their responses to local ecology. However, we must also take into account a big difference between their circumstances and those of our remote ancestors: the fact that we inhabit a warm interglacial period that is getting warmer. Therefore, we now turn to the effects of the Ice Age climates of the Pleistocene, 2.5 million years to 11,000 years ago.

It has long been known that changes in the earth's orbit, rotation, and tilt around its axis, known respectively as eccentricity, precession, and obliquity, have an impact on climate. Using astronomical data, it is also possible to determine the length of these interlocking orbital cycles at 100,000 years (eccentricity), 41,000 years (obliquity), and 23,000 years (precession). These are the cycles that account for the regular pattern of climate change and which resulted, in broad terms, in the warm and cold phase of the Pleistocene. But finding evidence for the astronomers' claims of many such alternating climates once proved elusive. The breakthrough came with the deep-sea drilling programme. The study of small marine creatures recovered from these cores provided a continuous record of change measured in the oxygen isotopes contained in their tiny shells. It was found that as the oceans changed in size (large in warm periods, and small in cold) this change was reflected in the ratio between two oxygen isotopes, O^{16} and O^{18}, in the skeletons of these tiny sea creatures. One early finding was that the last 800,000 years had seen not four complete interglacial-glacial cycles as geologists once claimed, but eight. Furthermore, compared to the previous million years, when polar ice caps first started to form, the severity of these cycles has increased as part of the long-term trend towards a cooler and drier Earth. Eccentricity, changes in the Earth's elliptical orbit every 100,000 years, now dominated the climate pattern. More than 800,000 years ago it had been the shorter, less extreme obliquity cycles with a duration of 41,000 years.

These cycles drive the planet's climate, and the impact is felt in two main ways. During the warm, interglacial phase of the cycle, seas are high and ice caps small. Alternatively, during the cold, glacial phases, sea level drops dramatically and in areas with sufficient moisture huge ice sheets are built. In the northern hemisphere, ice sheets extended down to almost 52°N, the latitude today of Quebec and London. This regular global exchange between ocean and land is more important for the history of humans than the degree of cold or warmth they had to endure.

Ocean temperatures and continental shelves

The oceans play a key role in translating the orbital climate signal into changes that affect humans. In particular, attention focuses on the circulation of the currents that act as conveyors of warm and cold water, and which control sea surface temperatures and impact on terrestrial environments. The North Atlantic conveyor brings tropical water to the coasts of northwest Europe, and as a result the Norwegian port of Troms above the Arctic Circle is free of ice in winter. Any shutdown of this conveyor would have a major impact on Europe's vegetation and the composition of animal communities. At a briefer duration, such impacts can be traced with changes in the El Niño-Southern Oscillation, or ENSO, in the southern oceans that results in extreme but predictable weather events.

Ice sheets only grow at the expense of oceans. The latter provide the moisture needed to build the three kilometre-thick Laurentide ice sheet over Canada and its counterpart on Scandinavia and northern Europe. In other regions such as northern Siberia and Alaska there has never been, despite the extreme cold, enough moisture for ice caps to form.

The growth of ice sheets also brings benefits. At the height of the glacial phases, world sea level drops by up to 130 m, exposing the continental shelves in western Europe and joining Siberia to Alaska to form the palaeocontinent of Beringia. These were formerly substantial landmasses; in the case of Beringia, an additional 1.6 million km² and for the European Manche shelf, a further half million km² south of the ice cap. However, extreme cold and high winds resulting from proximity to ice sheets did not make these land gains particularly productive or attractive. Of greater interest would be the smaller area of continental shelf around the tip of temperate southern Africa. But the great bonus of any ice age when sea levels reach their lowest stands is the exposed continental shelf of Southeast Asia, the palaeocontinent of Sunda. Separated by a short ocean crossing from this new land is the palaeocontinent of Sahul which combines Tasmania, Australia, and Papua New Guinea.

As Table 1.5 shows, the land gains are significant. The two palaeocontinents together account for about one-third of all the land exposed as a result of ice sheets reducing the

TABLE 1.5 The effect of different falls in sea level on land area and, in particular, the palaeocontinents of Sunda and Sahul.

Region	Global	Sunda & Sahul	Sahul only	Sunda only
Modern land area	**150,215,941**	**14,308,427**	**9,751,168**	**4,557,259**
Additional land area revealed when sea level falls by:				
−20m	8,029,385	2,875,620	1,546,150	1,329,470
−50m	14,330,962	5,183,012	2,621,932	2,561,080
−100m	21,117,563	6,768,410	3,468,844	3,299,566
−130m	22,968,715	7,008,185	3,588,038	3,420,147

size of oceans. But more to the point is where this exposure takes place. The equator passes through Sunda and northern Sahul, and much of these palaeocontinents are between the tropics. They therefore lie in the area of maximum solar radiation and at a time when tropical rain forest is reduced and savannah habitats expand. The latter are advantageous to humans and hominins because of the readily usable animal and plant resources they sustain.

A further point about the bonanza of Sunda, and Sahul once the ocean crossing is achieved, is that lower sea levels were the norm, and not the exception, during the Pleistocene. If we examine the sea level curve for the last interglacial-glacial cycle—130,000–11,000 years ago—we see that interglacial conditions, comparable to the present, account for about eight per cent of that time. Minimum sea levels are similarly a small percentage of the cycle. The majority comprises sea levels between 100 and 20 m lower that at present and which, as Table 1.5 shows, still results in major land gains in one of the world's most productive ecological zones.

Continents and regions: tectonics and deserts

Ice and oceans provide a rhythm to human evolution. These are matched on the continents by tectonics, volcanic eruptions, and a switch in major desert habitats every bit as dramatic for humans as the exposure of the Sunda shelf.

The impact of tectonics on land forms and mountain building over the last 300,000 years is considerable. The Old World has a tectonic spine that extends for more than 11,000 kms. It starts with the Wall of Africa that extends along the south-north Rift Valley and then turns east across the Ramparts of Asia. Along this eastern arm the rate of uplift for the Tibetan plateau and Himalayas has been estimated at up to 5mm per annum allowing substantial uplift in the last 200,000 years. The importance of such mountain building in eastern Africa and South Asia comes with the rain shadows they form and the effect of high plateaus on the pattern of monsoons. Tectonic activity also fragments landscapes in evolutionarily significant ways, increasing ecological diversity and, potentially, separating populations—conditions which may lead to divergence and speciation, the process by which new species evolve.

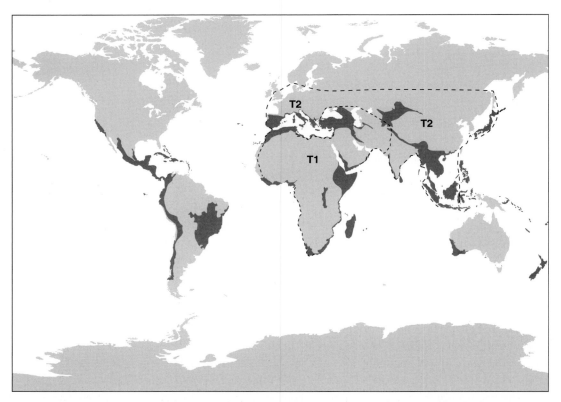

THE EARTH HAS SEVERAL AREAS where the number of species of plants and animals is high. These bio-diversity hotspots were also important centres for the evolution of hominins. T1 and T2 are the two earliest areas of the Old World that early hominins inhabited.

The impact of tectonics is shown by the location of current biodiversity hotspots. The 'heat' in any one spot is measured by the number of endemic plant and animal species. When these are plotted, it is apparent these *species factories* coincide with the tropics where solar radiation and primary productivity—measured in amounts of new plant growth—are highest, as in East Africa and Southeast Asia, and where tectonic and volcanic activity are also marked, contributing to the fragmentation of habitats and the populations which live in them. Major hotspots are found also in tectonically active areas in the mid-latitudes, notably Turkey and the Caucasus.

The last major continental habitats to consider are the Old World deserts. For many years it was assumed that the desert belt which stretches from the Sahara across Arabia to Pakistan had always been a barrier to the movement of peoples in deep history; a giant cork in the African bottle. We now know better. Fieldwork by quaternary scientists aided by satellite imagery has revealed the existence of former megalakes, rivers, and extensive inland drainage systems. Far from being a barrier to dispersal and communication, what are now deserts went through cycles of wet and dry phases. A Green Arabia and a Green Sahara regularly appeared. In green phases, the bodies of

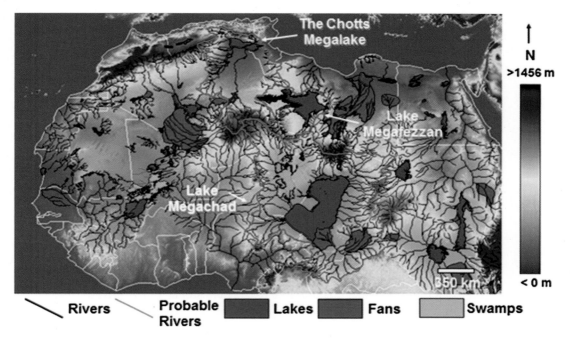

The Chotts Megalake

Lake Megafezzan

Lake Megachad

N
>1456 m

350 km

< 0 m

Rivers   Probable Rivers   Lakes   Fans   Swamps

MEGALAKES, RIVERS, AND EXTENSIVE INLAND drainage formerly made for a 'Green Sahara'.

water found within them were very considerable. During the Pleistocene, Lake Megachad in the south of the Sahara ranged in size from between 837,000 to 361,000 km² (Lake Superior in North America is 82,000 km², the Caspian Sea in Central Asia is 371,000 km²). To the north, Lake Megafezzan was smaller, but still covered 130,000 km². Scientific techniques dating the shorelines of the palaeo-lakes in Green Arabia show that moist and humid phases prevailed during the last interglacial 130,000–120,000 years ago, and then briefly 80,000 years ago; these ages correspond to high sea levels. Therefore, when Arabia and the Sahara were green, Sunda in the eastern part of the Old World was at its smallest and dominated by tropical rain forest. Across continents, consequent differences in the distribution of terrestrial food resources for humans fluctuated on a regular basis from attractive to less attractive conditions.

Habitat changes also occurred on a regional scale. Already mentioned are the biodiversity hotspots that stand out as regions with high rates of endemism—local speciation. Another large region that stretched across the northern hemisphere from Southwest France to Alaska was the mammoth steppe, named for the woolly mammoth typical of the cold-adapted fauna of glacial phases. The mammoth steppe was a highly productive grazing environment in both maritime and continental conditions as indicated by abundant herd animals—reindeer-caribou, horse, bison, and woolly rhino—as well as the carnivore triumvirate of lion, hyena, and wolf. Such productivity in animal biomass was only exceeded by the low-latitude savannahs in Africa, where greater numbers of antelope and equid species combined with the megafauna—elephant, giraffe, rhino, hippopotamus, and buffalo. Productive habitats for animals were also found in northern India and temperate China. The Americas, prior to the arrival of humans, had diverse fauna in both continents with many species, now extinct, that included mastodons and giant varieties of sloths, bears, and armadillos. The marsupials of Sahul were also extremely diverse before humans arrived. There were giant kangaroos and a rhino-sized grazer, *Diprotodon*. By comparison, the tropical rainforest of southwest Asia had greater productivity in plants with many smaller forest animals, none of which formed large herds. As in other regions, periodic transformations between forest and savannah accompanied shifts in the distribution not only of plants, but also of animals. At a smaller scale, the same pattern is visible across the continental divide in Europe. To the south lies a refuge zone, while to the north and the east is a region into which plants and animals, adapted either to cold or warmth, expanded and contracted in turn.

Such regional variation in plants and animals is to be expected and is part of deep history. It is often difficult to demarcate regions because the flora and fauna that live there are under pressure, as climate changes, either to move along with their shifting habitat or to stay where they are and adapt to the new one as it sweeps in. But on a regional scale, it is possible to see persistence in patterns of distribution which show the value of a regional approach. In East Africa the importance of lake basins in hominin evolution has been stressed. Water is often a critical constraint in Australia, where, to investigate human adaptations, the continent has been divided into regions which correspond to the major drainage basins. When the cultural patterns of language and material culture are overlaid, it does appear that people interacted more frequently within, rather than outside, these geographical regions. The approach using drainage divisions has been applied to Europe to account for differences in the archaeological evidence for the size and frequency of settlement in nine different regions. Here, the drainage basins are supplemented by latitude, longitude, and relief—constants which transform whatever solar energy there is into resources, irrespective of whether conditions are interglacial or glacial, and which applies worldwide.

Push-pull factors and species factories

Here, then is the environmental framework to understand the evolution of humans in the last 200,000 years. We see an ancestral pattern to which *Homo sapiens* conformed on leaving Africa. This pattern can be conceived of as a push-pull mechanism between two tropical areas in Africa and Southeast Asia, which are the primary species factories as indicated by the biodiversity map. Other areas of high diversity, such as Madagascar and coastal South Africa, are not factories for dispersal. Instead, they produce species for the local market—hence the high endemism rates—rather than for export. But in tropical Africa and Asia the dispersal of new taxa is never one way. Faunal exchanges between the continents and the northern centres in the Caucasus and Altai have accompanied cycles that increase the size of Sunda while changing its habitat from tropical forest to savannah; in the reverse direction, it is the wet phases of the

Saharan-Arabian deserts that pull populations in from the African savannahs to the south and then, in a dry phase, push them out. This is the basic engine of hominin population dispersal, the precise workings of which are under investigation. The push-pull factors of desert, continental shelf, rain forest, savannah, and tectonic activity are not as well understood as the interlocking cycles of orbital eccentricity, precession, and obliquity upon which they also depend.

Australia shows the model working in miniature. It has been suggested that this push-pull arrangement operated at a continental scale with population growth in the arid interior being pushed to the wetter regions around the coast. Population densities were much higher in these coastal regions because of the resources that were available, which exerted their own pull for population to cross the boundaries of the interior drainage basins. To complete the model, the higher rates of disease in the moisture-rich coasts contributed a mechanism that balanced population to resources and allowed immigration from the interior to proceed.

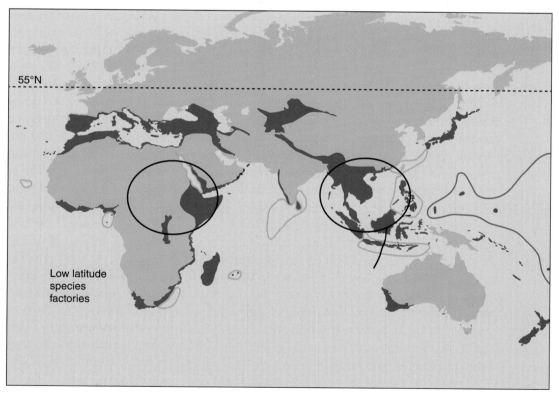

TWO EQUATORIAL REGIONS IN EAST AFRICA AND SOUTHEAST ASIA (circled) stand out as 'factories' where new animal species, including hominins, repeatedly evolved. These were also areas of high population growth and environmental changes drove frequent movements of people and animals between these two highly productive regions. This pendulum effect forms one of the geographical engines behind human evolution.

This is the pattern of human population history at the global scale. The centres of highest population increase have always been the warm temperate and sub-tropical zones irrespective of whether the economic base has been hunting and plant-gathering, or herding and plant-growing. Population has been checked by the disease belts around the equator and by environmental health issues such as deficiencies in UV above latitude 46°N. The latter does not appear to have been a problem for Neanderthals or the genetically distinctive Denisovans living in Siberia at latitude 51°N.

Versatile humans

How did hominins and humans respond to these climatic changes? They could not adapt to the future or the length of an orbital cycle. They could not anticipate a fall in sea level. It is tempting to argue that what distinguishes *Homo sapiens* from our hominin ancestors is our ability to cope with a great range of environmental challenges and opportunities, as ecological generalists, using technology to find solutions to seasonal resources, the cold, and crossing oceans. The obvious inference is that the preceding hominins, whom *Homo sapiens* replaced, were *specialists*, adapted to particular circumstances like those of the mammoth steppe. When faced with environmental change from interglacial to glacial conditions, the specialists either followed the conditions which suited them best or became locally extinct. However, the distinction between generalists and specialists ignores the flexible technological skills of all hominins and mobility, their key survival tactic.

Alongside the specialist and the generalist, a third characterization is needed: the *versatile* hominin. Hominins evolved their hallmark versatility under the selection pressure of environmental variability. As a result, hominins did not adapt to the climatic trend of the last two million years, which saw conditions becoming colder and drier. If they had, then we might well see species that were either specialists or generalists as the environment required. Instead, the argument is that environmental inconsistency, rather than the trend to drier, colder conditions, applied the greatest selection forces during the Pleistocene and caused the variability that affected hominins on the local scale—the patches of food they depended on, which shifted by season and through time. The prediction of environmental selection for versatile hominins has been tested by examining the Pleistocene temperature curve obtained from the deep-sea cores. This curve is, at the moment, the only environmental variable for which we have a continuous record that covers the timescale of human evolution. The findings are clear. When temperature was inconsistent—the measure that environments were highly variable—the hominins in the simulation with a versatile strategy out-competed the specialists and generalists.

Hominins and humans were never tied by their anatomy and biology to being either ecological specialists like Galápagos finches and the lichen-eating caribou, or dietary generalists like the omnivorous bear and pig. But why was it only versatile humans, not hominins, who became a global species? I examine this question in the last section.

Settling the earth

I have now touched on three of the routes to define humans; anatomy, genes and artefacts (see also Chapter 2). It is now time to turn to the fourth, geography, and provide an overview of global settlement in the 100,000 years prior to farming. To do this I refer to the unfolding process in terms of two of the five settled hominin Terrae. These Terrae are those parts of the earth inhabited at particular times by groups of hominin and human ancestors, and I concentrate on the period 200,000–11,000 years ago first, within Terra 2 (1.8 million–50,000 years ago) and then Terra 3 (50,000–4,000 years ago).

The aspect of geography that concerns me here is the expansion of the human range. Two stages in the process by which we became a global species can be recognized. The first was an environmental envelope formed by a part of the Old World and within which hominins dispersed on a regular basis. This is hominin Terra 2. It was bounded to the south by ocean crossings and to the north, at *circa* latitude 55°N, by environments which always had low ecological productivity, boreal forest, cold steppe, and tundra, and which were subject to extreme continental seasonality. Mobile peoples thrive in these lands today. But there are high costs in terms of maintaining social connections and curating a complex technology. The bounty of these northern regions often lies in the rivers and along the coasts. But fish and marine resources were rarely used in Terra 2, and outside of southern Africa never in great quantities.

The movements of hominins and humans within this circumscribed geography was driven by the environmental motor already described; a motor which operated at a continental scale according to wet and dry phases in the Saharan-Arabian deserts and low and high sea levels in tropical Sunda. This broad pattern was affected at smaller, regional scales by constant tectonic changes. But at the Old World scale of Terra 2 the geographical range occupied by the earliest widespread hominin, *Homo erectus*, grew

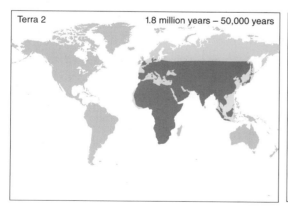
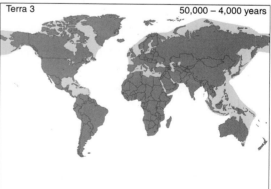

THE MAP COMPARES THE EXTENT of hominin and human settlement of the planet at the key stages known as Terra 2 and Terra 3.

incrementally only in the subsequent two million years. This was one envelope that the earliest representatives of our species, *Homo sapiens*, did not push.

The second stage of the process enters the more familiar human geography of Terra 3; familiar because it now includes Sahul as well as the unglaciated Arctic of northern Russia, the palaeocontinent of Beringia, and the varied habitats of the Americas. Exponential expansion gets underway during the last Ice Age (71,000–11,000 years ago). It was accomplished by mobile peoples living a hunting and gathering lifestyle. Ice Age humans had no domestic animals other than the dog. Expansion required technological advances: boats, winter-proofed clothes and houses, and new techniques such as the ability to store foods and de-toxify poisonous, but highly productive, plants. But above all, expansion on this global scale needed a novel social framework that permitted people to go beyond the local, rather than stay at home. The environments which the settlers of Terra 3 did not reach were the distant islands of the Pacific; their settlement would depend upon domestic crops and animals, transporting the human niche into remote Oceania. That history of global settlement happened in the late Holocene of Terra 4. Rather than adapting to conditions, settlers imposed their own.

The two-stage process, the contrast between the hominin world of Terra 2 and the human one of Terra 3, can be summed up as living within and outside the familiar envelope. Leaving Africa did not signal that humans had appeared and would soon replace the hominins-in-residence outside this continent. Instead, those anatomically modern humans (AMH), and their anticipated counterparts, genetically modern humans (GMH), were regular inhabitants and travellers in Terra 2. The recent finds of modern teeth at Fuyan Cave in China and the older skulls of AMH excavated in the caves of Skhūl and Qafzeh in Israel have been dated by science-based methods to between 80,000 and 135,000 years ago. These finds point to the traditional pattern of movement from one continental species factory to another, Africa to Sunda, and Sunda to Africa, but always staying in the envelope defined by Terra 2, boundaries that had been observed more or less for two million years.

What made global expansion possible?

The aforementioned boats and cold-weather clothing certainly contributed to global expansion, but the absence of these was not the only limitation which, for so long, applied the brake to geographical expansion. Technological advances are not limited by brain power and lack of inspiration; they need a social context within which new objects can be imagined. There was no need to tweet in the Stone Age, just as living in the Silicon Age means we have no use for a stone-tipped arrow.

The social context that stimulated these innovations as well as those regarded as indicative of a symbolic imagination—art, ornament, and burial rites (Chapter 2)—involved four cultural elements:

1. A society based on kinship categories that relate people across and between generations and enshrine rights, e.g. who you can marry, obligations involving

hospitality. These categories are not genetically proscribed and allow individuals to extend their social reach in time and space through the practice of kinshipping.

2. The accumulation and consumption of materials and goods for use at different times. This involves the storage of foods and raw materials. It also includes collecting and hoarding valuables.

3. The use of these resources to construct societies now controlled by males. Previously, it was the relationship between females and the optimum resources in their local ecology that regulated how the sexes co-operated. Males now co-operate to defend these resources and control the lines of exchange they allow by kinshipping.

4. A domestic economy that further intensifies the use of those resources and which offers the opportunity to global settlers to transport their landscapes (environmental niche) with them as they move. The movement of farmers and the settlement of the Pacific by horticulturalists are two examples.

Identifying the settlers

Neither AMH nor GMH signal they are on the move by using distinctive and widespread new artefacts. Archaeologists, however, are accustomed to clear-cut evidence pointing to people on the move. The clearest example is the spread of farmers from the Near East into Europe accompanied with a Neolithic package of long-houses, pots, querns, and polished axes, sheep, wheat, and barley. This wave of advance swept the resident hunters aside and was achieved in a few millennia. Comparable waves of advance also with a brave new cultural aspect are the farming dispersals, 5,000 years ago, into southern Africa, marked by crops, livestock, distinctive pots, metallurgy, the Bantu language, and the Lapita expansion, beginning 3,500 years ago, into the remote Pacific signalled by highly decorated pots, elaborate burial practices, and a wide range of domestic crops and animals.

But viewing deep history through the Neolithic lens of late Terra 3 has distorted the picture. There is nothing comparable to mark what must have been multiple hominin and human movements between continents within the confines of the earlier Terra 2. Stone technologies 200,000–50,000 years ago were remarkably similar across the varied habitats of this world, with flake-shaped blanks, often struck from carefully prepared cores and then retouched into a set of points, scrapers, knives, notches, and burins. Hafting, a process by which an artefact, often bone, metal, or stone, is attached to a haft (handle or strap), is known, and produces composite artefacts of wood, stone, sinew, and mastic, tools that do not occur in nature. The reality is a technological sameness over long periods of time and across large parts of Terra 2. So where are those distinctive cultural packages that trace the movements of AMH and GMH?

We see such a package in the European Upper Palaeolithic of Terra 3 with its art, ornaments, new stone technology, and modern skulls. This archaeological package bundled together two expectations; a trademark culture for 'modern humans', with the cultural signature that a human population was on the move. The European Upper Palaeolithic had stone blanks that were long, thin blades struck from prepared cores, retouched into lightweight components for hafting, and supplemented by art and ornaments made from shell, ivory, bone, and stone. The replacement in Europe of the resident Neanderthals by the incoming humans provides an earlier run-out for the Neolithic model of populations on the move.

But Europe in Terra 3 is not representative of the world of Terra 2. We do not know how many separate populations made the journey from the species factories of East Africa and Sunda. The preliminary genetic evidence suggests there were many excursions. Dating them by the notoriously inaccurate molecular clock presents a challenge. Archaeologically they are invisible.

Terra 2 Africa 200,000–50,000 years ago

On current evidence, the three routes to humans—anatomy, artefacts, and genes—coalesce in Africa. The earliest AMH at Herto in Ethiopia and Omo in Kenya are featured in Table 1.2. The artefact evidence shows widespread innovations in shell ornament, bone technology, hafting with mastics, use of pigments, and distinctive projectile technologies. Furthermore, a number of these additions to the cultural repertoire of humans in Africa can be found at the same site. In particular, the large coastal caves of South Africa, Klasies River Mouth, Pinnacle Point, and Blombos Cave contain long, well-dated sequences where the appearance of these innovations can be traced. The southern Cape is particularly rich in innovations, but so too are the caves of North Africa. Of interest is the discovery of shell beads from the Grotte des Pigeons at Taforalt in Morocco. Separated from Blombos Cave by 8400 km, it is striking that the same marine shell *Nassarius kraussianus* was used to make beads which were then threaded to form a necklace. At both caves science-based techniques date these finds to at least 82,000 years ago. When combined with the cut and incised pieces of ochre from several of the South Africa caves, it is easy to see why claims have been made that Africa saw the first non-utilitarian, symbolic artefacts (see Chapter 2).

In terms of anatomy and material culture, Africa during Terra 2 emerges as a continent of innovation. It is a huge and diverse landmass. The movement of population within Africa was undoubtedly as continuous and complex as movements outside. The appearance in southern China and Southwest Asia of AMH elsewhere in Terra 2 is not accompanied by the same innovations in projectile points, shells, or the use of pigment. Burials are known, principally at Skhūl and Qafzeh in Israel. Such deliberate inhumations within caves are relatively common in the northern pasts of Terra 2 occupied by Neanderthals.

The third line of evidence is genetic. Male and female phylogeographies, based respectively on modern Y-Chromosome and mitochondrial (mtDNA) data, are more diverse among Africans than for any other living population. Statistical uncertainties surround dates based on the molecular clock and mutation rates. The indications are, however, that the woman from whom all of today's mitochondrial lineages descend

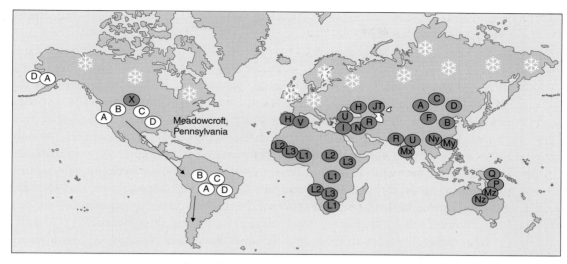

PETER FORSTER'S GENETIC map of population movements some 20,000 years ago at a time of continental ice ages (snowflake symbols). The letters are clusters of genes known as haplotypes. The L haplotypes in Africa are the oldest, while A–D in the Americas the most recent. Meadowcroft Rockshelter in Pennsylvania is one of the earliest archaeological sites in North America that lends credibility to the genetic reconstructions.

lived 192,000 years ago. These lineages have been subdivided into branches known as haplogroups and it is these which form the data for phylogeographic reconstructions. Since mitochondrial Eve, four haplogroups evolved in sub-Saharan Africa, of which the last, L3, is estimated by the molecular clock to have appeared 72,000 years ago. Populations of GMH seem therefore to have been moving around Africa when modern-looking people (AMH) had appeared and innovations were occurring in material culture. Given the propensity for human populations to interbreed, *Homo sapiens* and Neanderthals being a good example, it seems perverse not to regard everyone in Africa after 200,000 as *Homo sapiens* and hence as 'modern humans'.

But where was their homeland within sub-Saharan Africa? Modelling the data for haplotype L3 indicates population growth in the period 86,000 to 61,000 years ago. This occurs in East Africa. This same region is a biodiversity hotspot as well as the most genetically diverse region for humans. East Africa currently fits the bill.

The significance of haplogroup L3 is that it is the only one found in modern populations both inside and outside this African region. The big question is when L3 moved into other parts of Terra 2. It has been proposed that the massive volcanic explosion of Toba 71,000 years ago on the island of Sumatra precipitated a volcanic winter and facilitated the movement of people out of Africa by extirpating regional populations in Asia. But the effects have been exaggerated. It would have been devastating under the ash fall, but elsewhere mobility and low population numbers would have allowed rapid adjustment to new conditions. The Toba explosion did not, for example, lead to the extinction of another large bodied primate, the orang-utan.

Terra 3 Arriving in Sahul 50,000 years ago

The continental patchwork of anatomical, genetic, and cultural innovation is the reason Africa is regarded as the source and Sahul (New Guinea, Australia, and Tasmania) the target area for the expansion which defined humans as a global species; it started the journey which resulted in them becoming today's lonely species, the only one of its genus left. Reaching Australia, between 60,000 to 50,000 years ago, marked the transition between Terra 2 and Terra 3, a threshold moment in deep world history. As people moved through Terra 2 to reach this area, new haplogroups were founded and the genetic basis was laid for much of the phenotypic variation–skin colour, hair type, stature, and facial architecture—still seen in regional populations.

The eastward routes from source to target have been debated. A coastal route around Arabia and India to southeast Asia has been put forward in what archaeogeneticist Stephen Oppenheimer described as the great arc of dispersal, where rich marine resources assisted the population growth and budding-off that drove expansion. Alternatively, an overland northern route could take mobile populations to the biodiversity hotspot of Turkey–Iran, and from there to other parts of Terra 2 and beyond the environmental frontier at 55°N. Neither route has any supporting archaeological evidence and the timing of the archaeogenetics data is unreliable. This is why the initial settlement of Sahul is so important. There was always a water crossing of at least 70km to be made. The most probable direction was from Sulawesi to the Bird's Head peninsula in West Papua, and the earliest radiocarbon dates for archaeological evidence in Sahul come from the Ivane Valley, 2000 m above sea level, in Highland New Guinea to the east. Here, stone axes and Pandanus nutshells are dated between 44,000 to 49,000 years ago. Between 35,000 and 40,000 years ago, the major habitats of Sahul were settled. These included the highlands of New Guinea, the arid interior, the glacial landscapes of southwest Tasmania, the coastal savannahs of the Northern Territory, and the large islands of the Bismarck Archipelago and the Solomon Islands in Near Oceania, settlements that necessitated a further sea crossing. Because of the good radiocarbon chronology for Sahul, it is possible to estimate the speed of expansion. From the Bird's Head peninsula to Southwest Tasmania is a distance of 7500 km and this was covered in 5,000 radiocarbon years, a rate of 1.5 km per annum. And this rate was achieved with a hafted stone technology that used flakes, rather than blades, and a fisher-gatherer-hunter mobile lifestyle.

Terra 3 Negotiating Siberia and the Americas

The challenge facing settlement above latitude 55°N was not necessarily the cold, although that was extreme, but rather the attenuated character of human settlement. Particular emphasis would be placed on goods, and conventions such as kinshipping, that linked people together into far-flung regional networks. Population densities

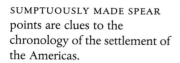

SUMPTUOUSLY MADE SPEAR points are clues to the chronology of the settlement of the Americas.

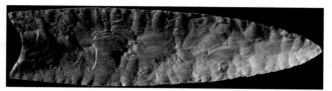

would be low and without storage of food it is difficult to see how populations could function as social units through predictable contacts and gatherings.

The source area for the settling of the unglaciated Arctic and on to Beringia is uncertain, but two candidates are the Altai and Lake Baikal regions with archaeological locales dated to between 40,000 and 50,000 years ago. One of the earliest Arctic settlements is found at 71°N in northern Siberia. This is the Yana Rhinoceros Horn Site dated to 30,000 years ago. The Yana evidence is now supported by the find of a hunted mammoth discovered at similar latitude in the Central Siberian Arctic and dated to 45,000 years ago. Yana lies 3,000 km to the west of Beringia. Here, the oldest well-dated archaeological locale is Swan Point in Alaska at 14,000 years ago. A study of the radiocarbon dates establishes a quick-slow-quick tempo to the human dispersal over almost 7,000 km from the Altai to Alaska. The overall rate of movement is 0.22 km a year. The artefacts that accompany this settlement trend do not form a distinctive monothetic set.

Cultural variety was also the case once humans got below the ice in North America and headed for the sun. The routes they took are hotly debated. They could have come overland once the ice permitted, or down the West Coast assisted by watercraft, or both. For many years the sumptuously made stone projectile points of the Clovis culture, which are found in a variety of forms throughout both continents, were seen as the markers of these first settlers. The first flush of radiocarbon dates indicated they moved very fast, occupying new territory at a rate of between 14–23 km per annum. At this pace, they had reached the tip of South America about a thousand years after entering unglaciated North America. However, it is now widely recognized that the Clovis points do not represent the first American settlers. Forensic study of the radiocarbon dates has revealed that Clovis lasted for only 200 radiocarbon years, from 13,130 to 12,930 years ago. This would give even more improbable estimates for the speed of settlement. Alternatively, with a pre-Clovis population in place, those distinctive stone points could rapidly disperse over large areas, either as an idea or as objects made for exchange and display. And this was achieved with nobody moving. Evidence from much older locales at Monte Verde, Chile, Meadowcroft Rockshelter, Pennsylvania, and the Debra L. Friedkin site in Texas supports the argument. All three locales are reliably dated to at least 15,000 years ago, and probably older. The artefacts from these widespread locales do not have any distinctive Clovis-like artefacts and they differ from each other in a polythetic way. Neither are they associated with megafauna, as is the case with Clovis. Some claimed these were the resources which fuelled the dramatic rates of expansion and led to mass extinctions among the American faunas. It would seem that interpreting Clovis artefacts is another example where the archaeology of the earliest settlement of a continent is expected to mimic the later Neolithic dispersals.

Terra 3 Europe

The last region to consider in this global overview is Europe. The long history of research has produced a rich data base, ever since the discovery in 1856 of a resident hominin species, *Homo neanderthalensis,* and the incoming *Homo sapiens* who replaced them. The nature of that replacement—genocide, assimilation, competitive advantage, regional evolution from one to the other—has been a source of literary as well as scientific examination. What we do know is that volcanic ash, tephra, which can be found as microscopic traces in many stratigraphic sequences from the caves of Central and Eastern Europe now points to when replacement took place. The ash came from a major eruption in the Campi Flegrei, Naples, when 300 km³ of ash known as the Campanian Ignimbrite (CI) was produced 40,000 years ago. Across those parts of Europe covered by the ash cloud the change-over from Middle to Upper Palaeolithic stone assemblages—a transition from flake to blade techniques of making artefacts— occurs before that date. Human skulls and skeletons are extremely rare for this period. And when they are found as at Pestera cu Oase Cave in Romania there are no artefacts in attendance. After 150 years of dedicated research in Europe, it still remains an untested assumption that humans were responsible for the technological change. It is also the case that the earliest art in the form of human and animal figurines, musical instruments, ivory, and bird bone are also found in Germany at ages greater than the CI volcanic eruption (see Chapter 2).

Neanderthals were as large brained as their human contemporaries and both populations had achieved personal network sizes of 150, Dunbar's number. Increasing numbers of significant others in your network poses problems of contact time for any primate, and hominins are no exception (Table 1.4). One inference is that both Neanderthals and humans had language. Speech processes information faster and makes effective interaction possible in these larger personal networks.

Neanderthals were also proficient in symbolic behaviour. There are some simple ornaments, ochre coloured shells and burials, but only in caves. They selected and wore black bird feathers. They made jewellery from eagle talons. Where they appear to have differed is in the underpinning social structures such as kinshipping. They were bound to Terra 2. And although they moved within it they did not go beyond it. Neither do we find evidence for the storage of materials and goods on any significant scale that might indicate males had made the break with their hominin, and indeed primate ancestry, and now controlled resources.

Humans settled Europe during a temporary amelioration in the last Ice Age. When full glacial conditions returned after 26,000 years ago, as the Fenno-Scandinavian ice sheets expanded once again, much of the area to the west of the continental divide was abandoned. A large radiocarbon data set exists to study the subsequent repopulation of this region from the long-term population refuge in the south. It begins at a small scale in a very cold phase 16,000 years ago and accelerates in the following warm intersta-dial, only for numbers to be cut back during the return to near-glacial conditions in the Younger Dryas period between 12,900 and 11,700 years ago. The rate of settlement expansion is 0.77 km per annum over a distance of 925 km from southern to northern Europe. The movement into unoccupied lands has a strong archaeological signature known as the Magdalenian culture. Using ethnographic estimates of population density, we arrive at 17,000 people in the Western European refuge rising to 64,000 during the Late Glacial interstadial when expansion northwards took place.

Conclusion

At the end of the Younger Dryas, when the world of Terra 3 now included all the continents except Antarctica, human population stood, by the best current estimates, at seven million. Over the next 11,000 years it rose to seven billion. Yet for all this growth in numbers and the wild variety of innovations, technology, economies, and societies, some aspects remained the same. The seven million had achieved a global range thanks to the use of kinship, social groupings, material storage, and co-operation between males, with the consequent changes in the control and hence realignment of resources. They were also on the cusp of the fourth requirement for global status: domestic crops and animals. They had not yet relinquished the age-old hominin tactic of mobility whereby resources were matched to flexible population units of varying size and duration. Cognitively these people had limits to the numbers they could draw into their personal networks and through which the ambitions and imaginations of human history have been realized. That limit of 150, Dunbar's number, has proved remarkably versatile since it holds together the larger social and political structures as described in the rest of this book. So, the answer to whether the first people we recognize as our direct ancestors were that much of a break with their past is 'no'. We are not the children of a revolution. We became the lonely, global species as a result of imagination, supported by advanced cognitive skills, which gave us myths, afterlives, ancestors, gods, and history—the cultural dreams of a clever, versatile biped, always good with hands, gifted with speech, and socially inventive. This imagination, validated by society and culture, saw benefit in going beyond, taking the risk, moving out of the long-inhabited hominin comfort zone of Terra 2. It is a human trait to build worlds in our imaginations, and then live in them. Settling Terra 3 provides the clearest indication of when our ancestors crossed that threshold—when hominin history became human history. We have always drawn deeply from our hominin past. Evolutionary principles still structure our lives, as shown by Dunbar's number and the pressure of population on the environment. But once those imaginative worlds were inhabited the voyages to new shores and experiments with hitherto untapped potential began.

CHAPTER 2

The Mind in the Ice

Art and Thought before Agriculture

FELIPE FERNÁNDEZ-ARMESTO

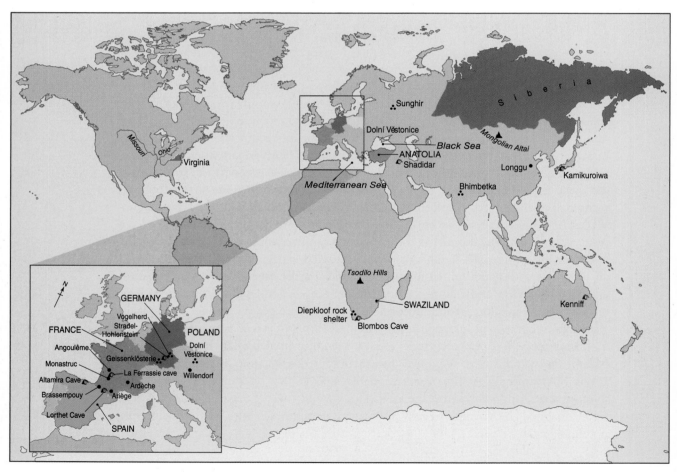

PLACES NAMED IN THE CHAPTER.

SENSING a draft from inside the rockfall, the three speleologists dug among the stones to make a passage wide enough for the thinnest of them to crawl through. It was 1996, and Jean-Marie Chauvet, Eliette Brunel-Deschamps, and Christian Hillaire were exploring the Ardèche in southern France, where caves and corridors honeycomb the limestone. When Eliette realized there was a tunnel ahead, she called the others. They shouted in the darkness to get an echo, which would give them an idea of the cave's dimensions. The noise seemed lost in vast emptiness. When they returned with full equipment, they found that the corridor led to the biggest cavern ever discovered in this part of France. Yet more astounding was what they saw in an adjoining chamber: a three-foot high, red ochre portrait of a rearing bear, preserved for who knew how many thousands of years.

It soon became apparent that Chauvet Cave—as they called their find—was one of the most extensive collections of Ice Age art in the world, and one of the most brilliantly executed by artists who lived, in some cases, well over thirty thousand years ago. The notable works that survive in almost unblemished condition include a stampede of wild horses with incised eyes, and a bison hurtling at speed indicated by the way the artist has sketched several pairs of blurred legs (a technique that anticipates futurist painting of the early twentieth century). Woolly rhinoceroses—vast and alert, with huge front horns—evoke the presence of the long-extinct species in a cold climate. Lions, whose now unfamiliar features—round ears, maneless heads, and deep jaws—match skeletal specimens from the painters' period, crouch and strain after prey. In Chauvet and the many other caves where peculiarities of the atmosphere

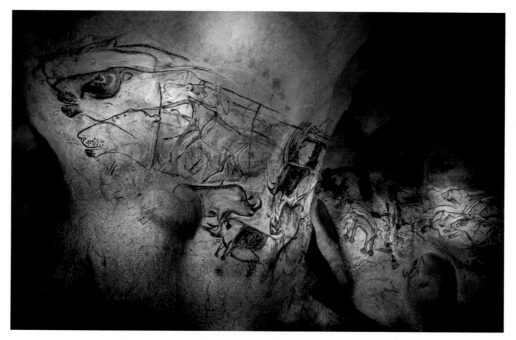

AT THE CHAUVET CAVE: Lions leap from the rock from which Paleolithic painters teased their images in charcoal sketches, perhaps some thirty thousand years old.

have preserved visions from the Ice Age, there are also puzzlingly unrepresentative works, including sprays of dots, massed hand-prints, and intriguing geometrical shapes that tempt onlookers to see them as symbols. In every period, art is the mirror of society—the images left to us by people of the past so that we can see their world as they saw it, and to invite us, as it were, to share, by inference, their thoughts and experiences. The task for this chapter is—without stretching inference implausibly beyond the evidence—to read some of those thoughts and experiences in objects of art and material culture from the Ice Age.

The birth of creativity?

The environment of the time demands examination to reveal what made it conducive to creativity, and to understand why a cold climate seems to have been mentally bracing. The period was long, and the climate fluctuated within the irregular pattern of prevailing cold. We can link the emergence of *Homo sapiens* with a cool spell at about 150,000 to 200,000 years ago. As discussed in Chapter 1, their dispersal over an unprecedented swathe of the globe, from about 100,000 years ago, coincided with another advance of the ice that stole south from the Arctic to overlap what is now the Baltic region. About 65,000 years ago, the ice cap began to withdraw, unevenly, for a period of between 12,000–15,000 years. By then, a new, intensely cold phase was under way. At its most extensive, by about 20,000 years ago, ice spread in the northern hemisphere as far south as the present lower courses of the Missouri and Ohio Rivers in North America and deep into what are now the British Isles; it covered Scandinavia. Most of the rest of Europe was tundra or taiga. In central Eurasia, tundra reached almost to the present latitudes of the Black Sea. Steppe licked the shores of the Mediterranean. In the New World, tundra and taiga extended to where Virginia is today.

The apparent paradox is that periods of the most dynamic human activity coincided with intensifications of cold—first, the extensive migration or dispersion that peopled much of the Earth in the cold millennia from about 100,000 to about 65,000 years ago, and second, the production of stunningly accomplished material culture, in the form of artworks and edifices, in the era of the cave artists, from about 40,000 to about 20,000 years ago; the focus of this chapter is on this latter period.

Food for thought

The paradox, however, is superficial. It arises partly because nowadays we think of boreal environments as hard, demanding, daunting, and costly to adapt to the kind of markedly sedentary, agrarian-dependent civilization we favour, and partly from a conviction that *Homo sapiens*, the only surviving 'naked ape' species, seems ill-designed for cold. But cold environments that house fat-rich prey, yielding magnificent quantities of calories per unit of bulk, suit the lifeways and tastes of hunters. Perhaps there was an era, long before the emergence of *Homo sapiens*, when life was 'poor, nasty, brutish, and short' for hominids who scavenged for their livelihoods without leisure for ratiocination; but as far as we know, for hundreds of thousands of subsequent years all people—all creatures, that is, ancestral to ourselves—were foragers. Many of them enjoyed 'Stone Age affluence': abundant game and wild food crops, plentiful energy sources, long days of leisure unequalled in most farming societies, and plenty of time for observing nature, thinking about the observations, and recording the results in art. Dietary fat has a bad reputation today, but for most of history, most people have eagerly sought it. Relatively speaking, animal fat is the world's most energy-giving source of food, yielding on average three times as much reward, in calorific terms, as any other form of intake. In some parts of the Ice Age tundra, concentrations of small animals could supply human populations: easily trapped Arctic hare or creatures vulnerable to the bows that appeared about 20,000 years ago could supply human populations. More commonly, however, hunters favoured species they could kill in large numbers by driving them over cliffs or into bogs or lakes. For the killers, while stocks lasted, the result was a fat bonanza, achieved with a relatively modest expenditure of effort. Average levels of nutrition, approaching those of the privileged inhabitants of industrialized or post-industrial societies today, were attainable by only two or three days' food-garnering work a week. For people who experienced it, the Ice Age was a productive time that supported specialized elites and plenty of inventive thinking and creative work.

Brain power

Over such a long period as this chapter covers, encompassing many changes of climate, not everyone saw the world in the same way or depicted, projected, or re-imagined it with the same conventions. Nevertheless, the evidence does disclose enough continuity to justify telling a single story. The most conspicuously unchanging element was the human mind, which still works with the same brain matter as our Ice Age ancestors had in their heads; the neural elements and processes, the chemistry and electricity of what happens when we think, have not changed. Synapses fire and proteins flood as ever they did. Relative to the numbers of people, the amount of human wisdom and cunning, genius and ingenuity, is unchanged since the Ice Age— although Ice Age minds had fewer data to work with, of course, less readily accessible, than our own.

Equally consistent throughout the time covered in this chapter—and, probably connected with the way human mental faculties emerged and developed—was a key element of the Ice Age way of life. All the people who are our subjects in this chapter practised much the same forager economy, and obtained substantial amounts of nutrition from hunting. Predation is, in one sense, good for the mind: it promotes faculties of anticipation—of the movements of prey and rival predators. An excellent way to confirm this is by watching hunting chimpanzees, co-ordinating their movements to trap a colobus monkey—their favourite prey—in a trajectory through treetops, adjusting routes, pace, and recalculating the point of the encounter as the

CHIMPANZEE HUNTERS TAKE A BITE OUT OF THEIR FAVOURITE PREY: a colobus monkey.

hunt proceeds. Yet chimpanzees are novices and amateurs in the hunt, with a probably short history of predation behind them when compared with the two or three million years of expertise that accumulated in the line of evolution that produced *Homo sapiens*. And predation yields for chimpanzees typically no more than a tenth—in some cases less than a twentieth—of the calories that human foragers commonly get from it. Anticipation, the key faculty of a hunter, is akin to imagination. For, while imagination is the power of seeing what is absent before one's eyes—what is not there—anticipation is the power of seeing what is not there *yet*. By the time our species emerged in the fossil record, our ancestors had been, for over two million years, par excellence, the hunting apes. Species ancestral to or cognate with *Homo sapiens* had collected ornamental objects, used pigments, and fashioned tools with élan for, at least, a substantial fragment of that period, although the evidence is too sparse to attribute meaning to it with confidence. We can say for sure, however, that *Homo sapiens* leapt into life fully armed with imagination fertile enough to create great art and think great thoughts.

Life imitating art

When the migrations began that peopled the world—about 100,000 years ago—the migrants carried artefacts associable with thoughts and sensibilities akin to our own: shell jewellery, and incised slabs of ochre. Astonishingly, shell crucibles and spatulas for mixing pigments, made perhaps as many as 80,000 years ago, were found in Blombos Cave in South Africa, an area settled by migrants from East Africa. Of the same period are objects of art too delicate to be of much practical use: fragments of ostrich eggshells meticulously engraved with geometric designs found in the Diepkloof rock shelter 180 kilometres north of Cape Town. At about the same time, at Rhino Cave in the Todsilo Hills of Botswana, decorators of spearheads ground pigments and collected colourful stones from many miles away. That the people who crafted these objects had 'a theory of mind'—consciousness of their own consciousness—is a proposition hard to resist in the presence of so much evidence of imaginations so creative and so constructive. They had the mental equipment necessary to imagine themselves in changed circumstances and new environments, and to attempt to realize the changes by targeted labour and applied ingenuity.

The artefacts left behind by Ice Age people are keys to creative minds. Material objects can be 'read' almost like documents, using techniques specialists call 'cognitive archaeology'. For example, the people who, twenty thousand years ago, hunted mammoths to extinction on the Ice Age steppes of what is now southern Russia have left daunting, but perhaps decipherable, clues. They built dome-shaped dwellings of mammoth ivory. On a circular plan, typically twelve or fifteen feet in diameter, the bone-houses seem sublime triumphs of the imagination. They are reconstructions of mammoth nature, humanly reimagined, perhaps to acquire the beasts' strength or to conjure magic power over them. Ordinary, everyday activities went on inside these extraordinary dwellings—sleeping, eating, and all the routines of family life—in communities, on average, of fewer than a hundred people. But no dwelling is purely practical; your house reflects your ideas about your place in the world.

Modern anthropological observations can provide further guidance, helping us, as we shall see, to interpret evidence of Ice Age religion, or hinting at the antiquity of very widespread practices, like totemism and taboos, for which there is no prehistoric evidence and which we can only suspect, not detect. From about 40,000 years ago and onward, we can also draw on abundant art—including a rich repertoire of symbols. Realistic depictions of people made 20,000–30,000 years ago show a lexicon of gestures and postures that recur again and again. Palaeolithic artworks often include annotations of what seem to be numbers, signified by dots and notches, and conventional marks that can no longer be interpreted, but are undeniably systematic. Neat lozenges are engraved over a brilliant scene of a reindeer crossing a ford among leaping salmon on a bone fragment found at Lorthet in France; the widely occurring mark that resembles a P has been read as a logogram meaning 'female' because of a supposed resemblance to the hooplike form with which Palaeolithic artists described the curves of women's bodies. It is hard to resist the temptation of acknowledging Ice Age people as systematic manipulators of symbolic notation. The idea that one thing can signify something else seems odd. Presumably, it is a development from association—the discovery that some events cue others, or that some objects advertise the proximity of

WHAT DO THE APPARENTLY SYMBOLIC LOZENGES mean in this scene of reindeer fording a salmon leap, carved on a Palaeolithic bone fragment from Lorthet in France?

others. Mental associations are products of thought—noises from rattled chains of ideas. No other evidence is as good as evidence we can read, but most of the past happened without it. To foreclose on so much history would be an unwarrantable sacrifice. As least in patches, we can clarify the opacity of preliterate thinking by careful use of such evidence as we have. We can no longer decipher Ice Age symbols, but they hint at how people saw, understood, and reimagined their world. The results are visible in the sublime achievements of Palaeolithic art.

Art as narrative

The cave painters of 20,000–30,000 years ago worked secretly in deep caverns, beyond tortuously twisted passages, lit by the flicker of torchlight. They strained on laboriously erected scaffolding to adapt their compositions to the contours of the rock, with a palette of three or four kinds of mud and dye, using brushes of twig and twine, bone and hair, or fingers smeared with coloured soil. They scraped the stone surfaces in preparation for painting. Typically, they sketched outlines in charcoal before applying pigments. They used bumps and blemishes in the rock face to add relief and supply details. They pierced the rock to evoke the cavities of eyes and sometimes of ears or sexual organs. Sometimes, if the surface was suitable, they carved extensive panels in relief. The result, according to Pablo Picasso and many other sensitive and well-informed modern beholders, was art unsurpassed in any later age. Some of the world's best art, indeed, is the oldest.

Even then, this artistry was a mature tradition and practised, specialized hands produced the images. Nineteenth-century explorers who discovered examples 20,000–30,000 years old in Spain and France were so impressed by the artists' genius that they could not believe the works were genuine. Even the earliest surviving works appeal instantly to modern sensibilities: the drawing is free and firm, the subjects are shrewdly observed, and sensitively captured. The looks and litheness of the animals portrayed spring to the beholder's mind. Carvings from the same sort of period exhibit similar accomplishment. Realistic images include elegant, 30,000-year-old ivory sculptures in the round: from Vogelherd in southern Germany, galloping arched-necked horses, for instance, or a dynamically sculpted water-bird of prey—duck, perhaps, or cormorant—swooping from the mammoth bone from which a carver coaxed it in Germany in about the same period. From Brassempouy in France, a portrait survives from about 5,000 years later: a neatly coiffured beauty, with almond eyes, tip-tilted nose, and dimpled chin. Perhaps even older is her counterpart from Dolní Věstonice, whose enchanting, tapering eyes are heavy lidded and downcast about a delicately snubbed nose. A kiln 27,000 years old at Věstonice fired clay models of bears, dogs, and women. In the same period, creatures of the hunt were relief-sculpted on cave walls or engraved on tools.

We have become used to admiring the output of these Ice Age artists. We should bear in mind the resistance of the learned world to acknowledging the authenticity of the evidence when it was first disclosed—not least because object-lessons in excessive scepticism are salutary when we contemplate surprising recent and new finds. The first examples of finely carved objects from the period covered in this chapter began to appear in the archaeological record in the 1830s, but it was not until some of them were included in the 1867 Paris Exposition Universelle that the notion was generally admitted that such ancient and reputedly 'primitive' people were capable of art. The fantastic paintings in the Ebbou Cave in the Ardèche were first reported in 1837, but then remained ignored and neglected for over a hundred years. In 1868, when Modest Cubillas discovered the cave painting of Altamira—one of the most glorious 'galleries' of the Ice Age—scholarly hostility dismissed the find and suppressed the evidence as fraudulent until the accumulation of similar finds elsewhere in the 1890s forced a defensive-minded academic establishment into endorsement.

The painted European artworks of the Ice Age survived because they were made in the shelters to which the climate drove the inhabitants, as well as in deep chambers evidently chosen for their inaccessibility. Other cultures of the time created proficient work, such as four painted rock slabs, as old as any art in Europe, at the Apollo 11 Cave in Namibia. But most has been lost: weathered away on exposed rock faces, perished with the bodies or hides on which it was daubed, or scattered by wind from the earth in which it was scratched. Where caves enclose suitable environments, scattered remains suggest that the art and thought of the European Ice Age were echoed all over the world, albeit not perhaps as early as in Europe. The caves of Kapoyava in Bashkhortostan are arrayed with a repertoire of images, including mammoths and shaman-like human-animal hybrids, perhaps 15,000 years old, strikingly reminiscent of their better-known European counterparts. Of uncertain, but perhaps comparable, date, paintings and carvings of deer have been reported in Turobong Cave in Korea. Representations of horses, bison, and rhinoceroses at a shallow rock shelter in Bhimbetka, India, are among the sparse proofs widely strewn across India, mainly in the form of fragments of decorated ostrich shells. Similarly, suggestive finds in caves in the Mongolian Altai may be taken into account, along with carved pebbles in Kamikuroiwa Cave in Japan and a fragment of decorated deer's antler, dated to about 13,000 years ago, from Longgu, China. More reliable assemblages are found in Australia, where a hint about the origins of the idea of representing life in art fades today from a rock face in Kenniff, where stencils of human hands and tools were made 20,000 years ago. Traces of similar stencilling are visible on some of the cave walls that bear paintings in Europe. The abundance of material in Europe looks anomalous, but may be

THE ENIGMATIC WILLENDORF CARVING, bulging with fertility, or obesity, or both.

a trick of the evidence—an exceptionally enduring and well-worked corner of a global phenomenon.

If stencilling was an early artists' technique, it seems believable that footprints and handprints inspired it. Scholars debate inconclusively the first function of art. It surely told stories and had magical, ritual uses: animal images were scored through or punctured many times over, as if in symbolic sacrifice. A good case has been made for seeing the cave paintings as hunters' mnemonics: the shapes of hooves, the seasonal habits, the favourite foods, and the spoor of the beasts were important items in the artists' stock of images. Yet the aesthetic effect, which communicates across the ages, transcends any practical function. This was not, perhaps, art for art's sake, but it was surely art: a new kind of power, which, ever since, has been able to galvanize the spirit, capture the imagination, inspire action, represent ideas, and mirror or challenge society.

The fat of the beasts that fed the artists had consequences, or, at least, correspondences in aesthetic, emotional, and intellectual life. For Ice Age artists, fat was beautiful. The Venus—the name, though ludicrous is traditional—of Willendorf—a plump little carving of a fat female—is 30,000 years old and named for the place in Germany where she was found. Critics have interpreted her as a goddess, a ruler, or, since she could be pregnant, a means of conjuring fertility. However, her slightly more recent look-alike, the jokingly so-called 'Venus' of Laussel, carved on a cave wall in France, evidently became fat the way most of us do: through enjoyment and indulgence. She raises a horn—literally, a cornucopia—which must surely contain food or drink.

The spirit world

The artists have left us sources that open windows into two kinds of thinking: religious and political. Surprisingly, perhaps, to modern sensibilities, religion begins with scepticism—with doubts about the unique reality of matter, or, to put it in today's argot, whether what you see is all you get. Spirits became part of the human world when people discovered that the invisible, inaudible, untouchable—because immaterial—realities, although inaccessible to the senses, were attainable to humans by other means.

The spirit realm, when first divined, was a subtle and surprising concept—a breakthrough from a passive submission to the constraints of life in a material world into the freedom of an infinitely plastic, infinitely unpredictable future. A living environment inspires poetry, commands reverence, and raises presumptions of immortality; the flame is extinguished, the wave calmed, the tree uprooted, the stone shattered, but the spirits live on. People who believe in spirits are usually aware of the effects of their interventions in Nature: animists typically ask the victim's leave before they fell a tree or kill a creature.

There is plenty of evidence that Ice Age thinkers knew (or thought they knew) the reality of invisible things: after all, they painted, sculpted, and carved them. By analogy with the rock paintings of hunter-gatherers of later periods, Ice Age art depicts an imagined world full of the spirits of animals that people needed and admired: a magical world, perhaps, accessed via mystical trances. We glimpse members of the Ice Age elite, people considered special and set apart from the group. Animal masks—antlered or lion-like—transform the wearers. From anthropological studies of the recent past, we know such disguises are normally parts of rituals performed to communicate with the dead or with the gods. To see and hear realms normally inaccessible to the senses, the shaman may seek a state of ecstasy induced by drugs, dancing, drumming, or playing on pipes; in Geissenklösterle, more than 40,000 years ago, someone played a flute made from a vulture's bones.

Talking to the spirits

We can still see figures that evoke or prefigure shamans at work. A carving from an ivory tusk, made perhaps about 40,000 years ago and excavated from a German cave just before the outbreak of the Second World War shows the 'Lion Man'—half man, half lion—of Stadel-Hohlenstein. He stands about a foot high, with an imperious gaze and a rigid posture that matches the glaring lions on the walls of Chauvet Cave.

The earliest known depiction of what seems to be a shaman dancing in antler-headed disguise is a freestyle smear in red ochre on a fragment of Veronese limestone, drawn well over 30,000 years ago. Mircea Eliade arrived at his theory that shamanism was the world's first universal religion while contemplating the figure of a human dancer disguised as a deer, who appeared on a cave wall painted in the depth and grip of the Ice Age in the cave of Les Trois Frères, at Ariège in the Pyrenees.

Of comparable antiquity is the bird-headed man in the cave of Lascaux. Herbert Kuhn confidently reported his exploration of the cave art of Tuc d'Audonbert that he was confronting evidence of an ancient priesthood whose magic was animal magic. He described the subterranean voyage into prehistory through the waterlogged cave, the emergence from darkness by lantern-light, at last confronted by an Ice Age view of the world. The cave ceiling was so low that the explorers had first to crouch, then lie on the deck of their punt. The rock-vaulting

> …scraped the tops of the boat's sides.…Suddenly, there they were. Pictures. Beasts engraved in the stones.…Shamans, too: men wearing breast-marks, uncanny and weird.

Even with all the evidence that has accumulated since then, Ice Age shamanism remains an inference; Kuhn's insight seems ever more convincing. By putting all the clues together, we can build up a persuasive picture of the world's first documented religion. Shamans, depicted on cave walls in divine disguises and the throes of psychotropic self-transformation, were responsible for communicating with a spirit world, imbedded deep in the rocks, where gods and ancestors dwelt in the forms of the animals the painters admired.

From there, the spirits emerged, leaving their traces on the surface of the stone, where the painters filled in their outlines and recaptured their energy. On the same

THE 'LION MAN' OF STADEL-
HOHLENSTEIN: a shaman in a lion's
head mask?

stones, visitors imprinted in ochre the images of their hands, as if leaving evidence of
their worship with the spirits, or reaching toward them. The world of the spirits was
probably also the world of the dead; perhaps the ochre that adorned burials can be
understood as 'blood for the ghosts,' such as Odysseus offered the dead at the gates
of Hades.

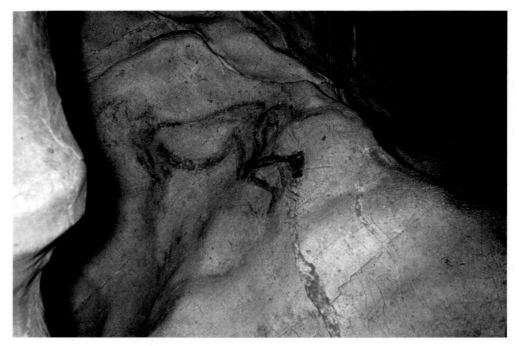

HUMAN DANCER DISGUISED AS A DEER ON A CAVE WALL at Les Trois Frères, Ariège, in the Pyrenees. The combination of dance and disguise suggests the possibility that shamanism was part of the religion of the people who decorated the caves.

Art as understanding

On balance, it seems fair to speak—albeit tentatively—of shamanic religion, but we should resist the temptation to try to interpret all Ice Age art using a single theory. Not all Ice Age artists were necessarily engaged in communicating with spirits or manipulating nature, nor were they all working under the influence of psychotropic drugs that warped their visions or swirled them into waves or spirals or shivered them into spots and specks. One of the reasons why humans make images of the objects they see is in an effort to understand them: understanding is inescapably prior to control. Like modern 'abstract' artists today, Ice Age predecessors tried to capture the key properties and patterns of the nature they observed, not to reproduce its exact appearance. Hence, the prevalence in their art of animals in boldly sketched outline, scarifications, herpetic zigzags, caracol twistings, honeycombs, and slanting, interlocking parallel lines. It may not be too adventurous to say that Palaeolithic art became more and more abstract and minimalist as time went on.

The feminine in Ice Age art

In what are generally classed as works in the last stages of the tradition, from about 14,000 to about 12,000 years ago, in widely separated sites stretching from Poland to central England, painters' and relief-makers' representations of women, in particular, seem reduced to a few sketched lines. In Monastruc, France on a chisel carved from an antler, a lozenge-shaped head emerges from other lozenges arranged to evoke a big-waisted body with generous hips, tapering thighs, and pudenda indicated by two slashes that form a V open at the top. At Nebra in the Unstrut valley, sculptors who fed on reindeer, horse, ptarmigan, and hare fashioned bones into schematic evocations of female forms on what look like little knives, with the shallow breasts and ample posteriors framing the grips and thighs tapering to a point.

Somewhere in the mental cosmos of the Ice Age, there may also have been a goddess cult, represented by the big-hipped carvings and other clues from Ice Age sculpture. Stylized, steatopygous women preponderate, like the Willendorf and Laussel images: sculptors from widely spread locations—as far east as Siberia—crafted pregnant bellies and powerful hips for many thousands of years. The oldest securely dated sculpture in the world—a mammoth-ivory pendant, at least 35,000 years old by carbon dating may belong in the same category: a bulbous female body, depicted, with a gaping vulva,

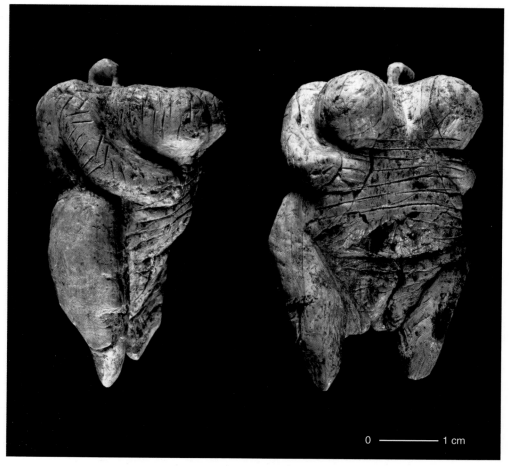

0 ———— 1 cm

CARVED IN MAMMOTH IVORY AT LEAST 35,000 YEARS AGO, the world's earliest known sculpture depicts a bodacious female body.

from neck to knees. Not much later, people in Dolní Věstonice wore pendant jewels modelled in the shape of breasts. Generic female or specifically divine representations tend to be characteristically faceless—sometimes headless—whereas the lively, human features of the beauties of Brassempouy and Dolní Věstonice are more like individual portraits of real people; however, there is no single explanation about Ice Age artists' treatments of femininity. Whether talismanic or devotional, symbolic or representative, these artefacts retain their quasi-magical power, today helping us to conjure fragments of a lost world.

Magic

Though the evidence is equivocal, scholarship has proposed magic as the origin of religion and science: certainly, all three traditions have been deeply concerned with efforts to extend human control over nature. It is too much to hope that we can ever be specific about the time or the context in which the idea of magic arose. Red ochre was perhaps the first magician's aid—the earliest substance with what seems to have had a role in rituals. At Blombos Cave, 70,000-year-old ochre objects apparently engraved with crisscross patterns form part of the assemblage. Lion Cave, about 42,000 years old, in Swaziland, is the oldest known ochre mine in the world: the vivid, lurid colour was applied to bodies at burials, perhaps as a precious offering, or perhaps to imitate blood and reinvest the dead with life. Rather than reaching for an unattainably exact chronology, helpful speculations about the prehistory of magic focus on the likelihood of a slow process, deep in the hominid past, of mutual nourishment between observation and imagination. Some apparently magical transformations happen by accident and can be imitated by experience: the effect of benign bacteria or mastication, for instance, in making food digestible; of fire in colouring, caramelizing, and crisping it, or in making clay impermeable; or the conversion of a stick or bone into a tool or

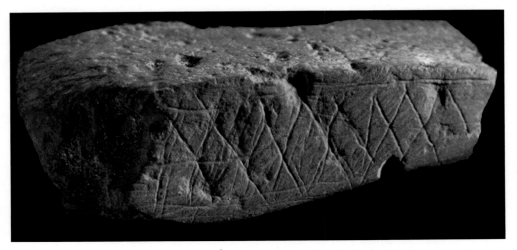

THE FIRST MAGICIANS' AID: A SLAB OF RED OCHRE, shaped and incised with a lozenge pattern to accompany a buried corpse some 70,000 years ago.

weapon. Some transformations, however, require more radical acts of imagination. Weaving is a miracle-working technology, presumably discovered cumulatively in a long history of pre-human origins, that combines strands of fibre to achieve strength and breadth unattainable by a single strand, as chimpanzees do when they twist branches or stalks and combine them into nests. Practical measures, extemporized to meet material needs, could act as 'cues', stimulating the imagination to make magical inferences. For example, the bone-houses constructed by mammoth hunters on the Pleistocene steppes, seem magical—the bones are transformed into buildings, and it is tempting to classify them as temples—and yet, they enclosed the same daily activities as those performed in unremarkable dwellings. Perhaps they served simultaneously as temples and homes? Perhaps the builders would not have regarded the functions as mutually exclusive or even different.

Art and the afterlife

Further evidence lies among graves some 40,000 years old—recent enough to coincide with *Homo sapiens*, but actually belonging to the distinct species we call Neanderthals. *Homo sapiens* has always had an equivocal relationship with its Neanderthal cousin, whose extinction in shared environments where our ancestors survived has puzzled theorists. Darwinian thinking has encouraged speculations, red in tooth and claw, that *Homo sapiens* out-competed or exterminated the presumed rival. But the more we know about Neanderthals, the more like us they seem: fully equipped with minds, sensibilities, technologies much like our own, and capacities, including language, formerly supposed to be unique privileges of *Homo sapiens*. DNA evidence is accumulating that, at the margin, Neanderthals and Sapiens could, and did, interbreed. The famous 'Neanderthal necklace'—a string of wolf- and fox-fang pendants, some 34,000 years old, found in a Neanderthal context at Grotte du Renne, Arcy-sur-Cure—was, if not a Neanderthal artefact, an acquisition from *Homo sapiens*. A Neanderthal family is buried together at La Ferrassie. Two adults of different sexes are curled into the foetal position, which is characteristic of Neanderthal burials all over what is now Europe and the Near East. Nearby, three children of between three and five years old and a new-born baby lie with flint tools and fragments of animal bones. The remains of an undeveloped foetus, extracted from the womb, are interred with the same dignity as the other family members, albeit without the tools. Other Neanderthal burials have more valuable grave goods: a pair of ibex horns are buried with one youth, and a sprinkling of ochre was strewn on another. At Shanidar, in what is now Iran, an old man—who had survived, in the care of his community, for many years after losing the use of an arm, severe disablement to both legs, and blindness in one eye—lies with traces of flowers and medicinal herbs. These cases, and many others of what look like ritual Neanderthal burials, have been challenged by sceptical scholars—'explained away' as the results of accident or fraud—but there are too many of them to discount. At the other extreme, credulity has drawn irresponsible inferences from this evidence, crediting Neanderthals with a broad concept of humanity, a belief in the immortality of the soul, a system of

NEANDERTHAL BURIALS TYPICALLY are of cadavers curled into a foetal position.

social welfare, a gerontocracy, and a political system of philosopher-rule. They may have had such things, but there is no evidence of them in the graves.

The burials do disclose strenuous thinking. Mere burial is evidence only of material concerns: to deter scavengers, to mask the odour of putrescence. But ritual burial is evidence of the concepts of life and death, and contemporary cultures still find it hard to define them. In particular cases—such as impenetrable comas and the misery of the moribund on life-support—we cannot say exactly where the difference between them lies. But the conceptual distinction we make between the quick and the dead goes back about 40,000 years, when people began to mark it by rites of differentiation of the dead. The Spanish palaeoanthropologist Juan Luis Arsuaga expresses Neanderthal gravediggers poetically as

> humans who discovered death [and then] reacted by celebrating life. Through self-adornment and embellishment, they affirmed their existence, defying the final tragedy to come. They employed symbolism to express their immense joy at being alive.

These first celebrations of death sanctified life. They constitute a conviction that life is worthy of reverence: the first evidence of a more than merely instinctive valuing of life, and which has remained the basis of all human moral action ever since.

Even ceremonial burial is not necessarily evidence that the people who practise it believe in an afterlife: it might instead be an act of commemoration, or a mark of respect. Goods deposited with the dead may be intended to work their propitiatory magic on the living and to contribute to survival in this world, rather than transition to the next. Nevertheless, when grave goods include a complete survival kit—food, clothes, negotiable valuables, and the tools of one's trade—it is hard to resist the impression that they constitute equipment for a new life. Burial goods like these became ubiquitous throughout the inhabited world by 35,000–40,000 years ago. At the very least, gifts of ochre are found in graves even of people from very modest levels of society, and the incidence of tools and decorative objects constitutes an index of social rank in societies perhaps already riven by inequalities.

Nor is the survivability of death a difficult idea to understand. Across the lifespan, we maintain a sense of the continuity of our identities despite the constant transformations of our bodies. If we survive changes as big as puberty, or menopause, or traumatic injury without ceasing to be ourselves, why should death, which, after all, is only the most radical of a series of such changes, mark our extinction?

Therefore, the idea of afterlife was probably not, in itself, of great importance: the grave goods of early burials imply that the next life will be a prolongation of this one, and they affirm the survival of status, rather than of the soul. Indeed, all grave goods seem to have been selected on this sort of assumption until as recently as the first millennium BCE—and even then, only in some parts of the world. What mattered were the (presumably) later (certainly, later-documented) refinements to the *idea* of afterlife; for example, the claim that the afterlife would be a place of reward or punishment, or that it would be an opportunity for a new life, perhaps through re-incarnation. The way an individual imagined the afterlife could then become a moral influence for living in this world and, in the right hands, a means of moulding society. For example, the Shanidar burial, and its evidence that the half-blind cripple was cared for for years before he died, seems representative of a society with a carefully considered and costly moral code that prescribed care for the weak. On the other hand, those who cared for him may have been securing access to the aging man's wisdom or esoteric knowledge in their own interests.

Ice Age art as comment on society and values

Clearly, Ice Age art could not have been produced outside a socially differentiated society with hierarchies and a leisure class: there is too much of it; it includes too much costly ornament; and it demanded a level of proficiency too practised to explain in any other way. Because the era was abundant in food resources, it was possible for communities to be much more stable than those of most foraging folk today, with sites occupied for successive seasons, over long periods, with privileged or incapacitated individuals living in one place; other people made the long journeys that led to new hunting grounds, sources of new products, or sites of trade with other human groups. Finds at Dolní Věstonice dating back 30,000 years include fragments of clay figurines that bear marks of the woven products in which they were once wrapped. That those who produced these ancient textiles—perhaps some were women—could work at their craft at length without interruption indicates that these artisans were among the privileged. Costly objects—in terms of time taken to manufacture them and the rarity of the materials from which they were fashioned—such as elaborately

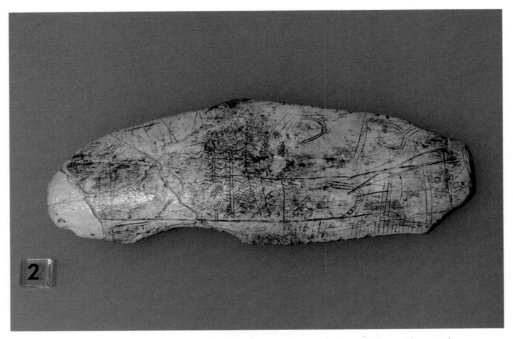

TWENTY THOUSAND YEARS AGO on this fragment of mammoth tusk from Elseevitchi, a carver depicted a fish, with fins that are still visible, scored with radiating incisions.

carved and notched ivory ornaments seem to be created for the elite of the society. A dainty slip of thin, curved ivory, between 22,000 and 26,000 years old from Kostienki, bears hundreds of mutually enfolded zigzags around a central band studded with geometrical shapes with perforations for threading and wearing it. The scales, etched 20,000 years ago onto a strip of mammoth tusk from Elseevitchi, were evidently meant to represent a fish, whose fins are still visible, scored with radiating incisions, but whose head has been broken and lost. Many other highly decorative artefacts were utensils, elevating the preparation and consumption of meals to a level beyond that of mere nutrition. As children were a valuable resource—exploitable and exchangeable in most societies for most of the past— the prevalence of images of pregnancy and fertility in the arts of the era indicates the importance of and reverence for the female in the community. As long ago as 40,000 years, items of value were evidently traded to where they were unavailable locally. The ivory that supplied the artisans of Castel Merle, in the mid-thirty-thousands BCE, travelled over 100 km, and seashells adorned people of the time who lived 300 km from the coast.

Feasts and power

Visions such as those that inspired cave art also crafted politics. The political thinking of the Ice Age is barely accessible, but it is possible to say something in turn about leadership, broader ideas of order, and what we might call Ice Age political economy. In our attempt to understand the power hierarchy in Ice Age societies, the first bits of evidence are fragments of feasts—crumbs from the tables of the rich. Ritual sharing of food, made special by cost or quantity, are ways of mediating power and forging allegiance. Some foraging peoples do not have such a practice: their special occasions happen when hunters make large-scale kills or scavengers discover a carrion bonanza. So, feasting is probably not as old an idea as those that underlie genuinely universal practices. (It is possible, however, that this is a trick of the evidence: some hunting peoples confine feasts to remote and secretive locations, which, far from their usual habitation sites, might not show up in the archaeological record.) In early agrarian and pastoral societies, however, feasting was the method by which chiefs supervised the distribution of surplus production among the community. In some instances, at a later stage, privileged feasts defined the elites who had access to them, and provided opportunities to forge bonds. In the former cases, feasts were crucial to social cohesion, and in the latter, to the consolidation of power. The earliest clear evidence, dating from about 10,000–11,000 years ago, is in the remains of deposits of plants and prey dropped by a diner at Hallan Çemi Tepesi in Anatolia—people who were beginning to produce food instead of relying wholly on hunting and gathering. Recent archaeological work, however, has pushed back the possible origins of the practice to the privileged hunting societies of the era of Palaeolithic abundance—the same period that produced surviving cave art. Additionally, at Altamira, archaeologists have found ashes from large-scale cooking and the calcified debris of food dating back 23,000 years. The tally sticks that survive from the same region in the same period may have been records of expenditure on feasts.

What were such feasts for? Because it involves a lot of effort and expense, a feast surely needs justification. It could be symbolic or magical, to celebrate times of plenty against the threat of famine. It could also be given for practical reasons: to enhance the power, status, or clientage network of a feast-giver; to create ties of reciprocity between feasters; or to concentrate labour where feast-givers wanted it. By analogy with modern hunting peoples, the most likely reason for lavish entertaining was to forge alliances between communities. Despite some scholarly opinions that feasts were male-bonding occasions, feasting occurred, in all cases so far known to archaeology, close to major dwelling sites where women and children would be present. Rather, from the moment of its emergence, the idea of the feast had practical consequences: to build and strengthen societies and enhance the power of those who organized the feasts and controlled the food.

Leadership figures

The societies of hominids, hominins, and early *Homo sapiens* had leaders. Presumably, by analogy with other apes, alpha males imposed rule by intimidation and violence. But when we turn to the political ideas of the Ice Age, cave-wall rituals are clues to political thinking, too: political revolutions multiplied ways of assigning authority and selecting chiefs. Visions empower visionaries and charisma predominates over brute force, with the spiritually gifted surpassing the physically powerful in the culture's hierarchy. In some societies, the authority of chiefs, priests, and nobles is justified on the grounds of their special access to or relationship with mana, or to some similar source of power. Paintings and carvings disclose new kinds of political thinking—the emergence of new forms of leadership.

The shaman

Priest-like figures, in divine garb or animal disguises, undertaking fantastic journeys are evidence of the rise of those who wielded new kinds of power alongside physical strength. In cases known from anthropological studies of the recent past, such disguises are normally associated with efforts to communicate with the dead or with the gods: to attain access to 'other worlds'. In states of extreme exaltation—induced by drugs, dance, or drumming—shamans can become the mediums through which the spirits talk to this world. Among the Chukchi hunters of northern Siberia—whose way of life and environment are similar to those of the Ice Age artists—the vision event is represented as a journey. The purpose of an animal disguise is to appropriate the fleetness of the creature or, in other traditions, to identify with a totem or a supposed animal 'ancestor' (which should not necessarily be understood literally as a progenitor). The power of disguise unlocked another idea: that of getting in touch with the spirits— the gods and the dead, who are the forces that are responsible for making the world the way it is—thereby obtaining inside information on what happens and will happen. The

CHUKCHI SHAMANS TODAY
REMAIN proud of the drums that
generate the mind-blowing noise that
helps to induce visions.

shaman may even influence the gods and spirits to change their plans, inducing them to reorder the world to make it agreeable to humans: to cause rain, stop floods, or make the sun shine to ripen the harvest: the shaman manipulates nature through manipulation of the spirit world.

If the dancers in animal guises on the cave walls performed shamanic functions, they must have exercised tremendous social influence, and people would be willing to pay with gifts, deference, service, and obedience to incur the favour of someone in touch with the spirits. A shaman can be a formidable source of authority: the flashpoint of a political revolution that replaces the patriarch or alpha male with the shaman. When we scan the caves, a knowledge class seems to emerge alongside a prowess class. By choosing elites who had the gift of communicating with spirits, Ice Age societies could escape the oppression of the physically powerful or those privileged by birth, effecting what might be called the first political revolutions. Shamanism replaced the strong with the seer and the sage.

Special access to the other world has been an important constituent of political legitimacy in many societies in recent times: the claims of 'prophets' to power, of monarchs to divine right, and of churches to temporal supremacy have all been based on it. As a way of identifying a ruler, feality to those with the gift of communicating with spirits was clearly an early alternative—perhaps the earliest—to submission to the most physically powerful.

Hereditary leadership
In the last millennium or so of the Ice Age, cognitive archaeology reveals the emergence of hereditary leadership. One of the biggest problems for all human societies is

how power, wealth, and rank are transferred peacefully. Early human communities did not need an idea of inequality: it came naturally to them. But how could the idea have arisen that acquired status should be transmitted by heredity? On the face of it, it seems dysfunctional, since parental excellence is no guarantee of an offspring's merit, whereas leadership won in competition is objectively justifiable. For hereditary rulership, there are no parallels in the animal kingdom, except as represented by Disney. Yet all societies have come to admit the hereditary principle in some measure; most made it, for most of history, the normal means of recruitment to high levels of command.

Although we cannot be sure about the nature of the hereditary Ice Age power class, we know it existed, because of glaring inequalities in the way Ice Age people were buried. In a cemetery at Sunghir, near Moscow, dated about 28,000 years ago, the evidence of lavish quality of life stunned readers of O. N. Bader's official report in 1970. The recorded jewellery included polar fox fangs bored with holes for stringing as necklaces, bracelets, and girdles; bracelets made of thin roundels sliced from mammoths' tusks; mammoth ivory beads sewn in rows onto fur blouses, donned by pulling them over the wearers' heads, and trousers attached by stitching to leather boots. The highest-status person seems, at first glance, to have been an elderly man. His burial goods, under a grave-marker in the form of a female skull in a pool of red ochre, include a cap sewn with fox's teeth, about twenty-five ivory bracelets, and nearly 3,000 beads. These could have been the rewards of an active life. Nearby, however, two children—probably a boy and a girl—about 10–12 years old and 8–10 years old, respectively, have even more spectacular ornaments. As well as ivory bracelets, necklaces, a pinned collar, and fox-tooth buttons and belt-studs, the boy had a carved horse and mammoth to accompany him in death and beautifully wrought weapons, including a spear or vast wand of mammoth ivory, over six feet long. Some 5,000 finely

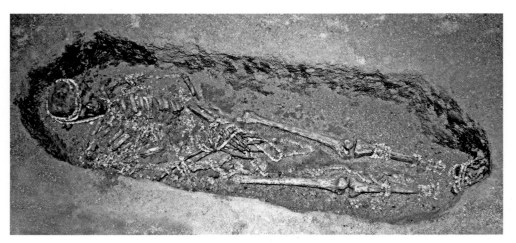

A RICHLY BEJEWELLED BURIAL AT SUNGHIR IN RUSSIA suggests the presence of a lavish elite—and perhaps a hereditary—form of leadership 28,000 years ago.

worked ivory beads had been drizzled over the head, torso, and limbs of each body. Here was evidence of a further revolution—the inception of a society that marked leaders for greatness from boyhood and therefore, perhaps, from birth. The idea of the hereditary principle supplied one of the earliest answers.

Various explanations have been suggested for the emergence of hereditary leadership: as a matter of common observation (for which genetic theory now provides sophisticated explanations), many mental and physical attributes are heritable. This creates a rational bias in favour of the children of self-made leaders. The instinct to nurture, it is sometimes said, makes parents want to pass their property, including position, status, or office, to offspring and, therefore, will to allow others to do so. By deterring competition, the hereditary principle is conducive to peace. Specialization creates disparities of leisure between elites and plebs and enables parents with specialized roles to train their children to succeed them. Some states still enjoy the advantages of hereditary monarchs (and, in the case of the United Kingdom, a partly hereditary legislature), protected from the corruption of popular politics and elevated above conflictive arenas. Heredity is, by rational standards, a good way to choose a leader.

Time to think

Specialized, privileged elites enjoying the continuity of power that heredity guaranteed had time for thinking. We can detect some of the thoughts that occurred to them, as they scoured the heavens for the data they needed in their jobs. In the absence of other books, the stars made compelling reading for early humans. In some eyes, the stars are pinpricks in the veil of the sky through which we glimpse light from an otherwise unapproachable heaven. By virtue of being mediators with the heavens, rulers became keepers of time.

Time is an elusive idea (St Augustine said that he thought he knew what it was until someone asked him). It is best understood, perhaps, as a means of measuring change by comparing one set of changes with another—noting, for instance that 'this taxing was first made when Quinius was governor of Syria', or responding to a query about the date of the birth of his son, as a Nuer father, might by recalling that it happened 'when my calf was so high'. Such methods seem to be universal. Almost equally widely diffused is the method of measuring changes against the motions of celestial bodies, which confers the advantage of providing a universal, apparently unalterable standard of measurement, as the irregularities of the cycles of the sun, moon, and stars are negligible for normal purposes. (While nowadays we have improved on them by using the rate of deterioration of a caesium atom as our universal standard, the principle is unchanged.) Like all very widely diffused practices, the calendrical system of timekeeping can fairly be assumed to be of great antiquity. In tracing its origins to the Ice Age, we can bolster inference with evidence, albeit not absolute, to make the presumption that Ice Age stargazers read the heavens and linked the motions of celestial bodies to events on Earth. The earliest known artefact that looks as though it might be a calendar was made, about 30,000 years ago in the Dordogne, from a flat bone inscribed with crescents and circles: the intervals look systematic, and have been read as a record of phases of the moon. Thereafter, during the long gap in the evidence, many sites have yielded tally sticks, or, at least, objects scored with regular incisions, but these are not securely identifiable as calendars; they are as likely to be 'doodles', games, decorative objects, ritual aids, or numerical records of other kinds.

Environmental influence on human change

Before the Ice Age was over, some of the world's best ideas had already sprung into life and modified the world: symbolic communication, the distinction between life and death, the existence of more than a material cosmos, the accessibility of other worlds, and spirits, mana, or perhaps even God. Political thought had already produced various ways of choosing leaders—including by means of charisma and heredity, as well as prowess, as well as devices for regulating society, including food- and sex-related taboos, and the ritualized exchange of goods. But what happened when the ice retreated and environments people had treasured disappeared? When global warming resumed, fitfully, between 10,000–20,000 years ago, threatening the familiar comfort of traditional ways of life, how did people respond? What new ideas arose in response or indifference to the changing environment?

It is worth recalling that our Palaeolithic ancestors were children of ice, for whom the cold phases of climate were catalysts for dispersion and invention. To understand them, we have to imagine a global climate capable of sustaining musk oxen in what is now the Dordogne. Over 20,000 years ago in Roc des Sers, near Angoulême (and not much later nor far away in the rock shelter of Laugerie Haute), sculptors captured these mighty quadrupeds' musculature, their thick, shaggy coats, and their flaring nostrils, which protected their lungs from cold by heating inhaled air. The musk ox example at Roc des Sers is a relief, bent intently as if to graze, rising from the rock as convincingly as one of Michelangelo's *Captives*. Only the head of the Laugerie Haute work survives, but, despite millennia of weathering, it is still immediately suggestive of the reality of the great beast, showing the peculiar bony forehead of the musk ox lowering between curling horns, and crowned with a dense, tufted mane. To judge from the debris of meals from that time, the artist who made the head rarely, if ever, ate musk ox; horse bones dominate the detritus. We cannot say what it meant to the maker, but we can be sure that the artist perceived more than food when he beheld his subject: a means, perhaps, of expressing emotion, and of acknowledging the beast's greatness and closeness to imagined worlds. The musk ox survives today, but roams only the northernmost, icebound fastnesses of boreal America. Reindeer that now scrape at the lichen near the Arctic circle and the extinct shaggy mammoth built for icy climates are common images in the art of Dolní Věstonice.

Climate change threatened the world the Ice Ages artists reflected and the societies they belonged to and built. In some ways, we can sympathize on the basis of our own

MUSK OXEN ARE AMONG THE FAVOURED SUBJECTS RECOGNIZABLE IN ICE AGE ART: fat, calorifically rewarding creatures, hard to capture or kill.

experience. We, too, inhabit a worryingly warming world. There have been some intervening fluctuations, and the present phase of rising temperatures is unusually intense, partly because human activities aggravate it; but we are still enduring the warming that brought the Ice Age to an end. People of 10,000–20,000 years ago did not, of course, all respond to warming in the same way. At the risk of oversimplification, we can detect two broad kinds of reaction. Some people migrated in search of familiar environments, while others stayed put and tried to adapt. These are the subjects of the next chapter.

PART 2

Of Mud and Metal

———

Divergent Cultures from the Emergence of Agriculture to the
'Crisis of the Bronze Age', c. 10,000 BCE–c. 1,000 BCE

CHAPTER 3

Into a Warming World

MARTIN JONES

BY the time the world's ice caps had substantially receded, and our current warm period, or 'Interglacial', had begun, the global journey of the human species had taken our forebears to every continent bar Antarctica. In each of those adopted continents, some communities would embark upon a novel engagement with nature, and they would do so in several distinct regions of the world. That new engagement would involve a closer association with the plants and animals in our food chain on which we depended, often in partnership with a fellow traveller across the globe, the dog. In different places, those associations would involve a range of flowering plants, to varying degrees a number of grazing mammals, and occasionally birds. This new ecology was transformative of the human condition, such that generations of archaeologists and anthropologists have demarcated a clear boundary between worlds of food procurement and food production: between a world of hunting, gathering, and foraging, and a world of agriculture.

There has been much debate over the transition between the former and the latter. Some have suggested something inevitable led between them, a pathway of development along which all societies found themselves differentially positioned. Others have situated the transition culturally and historically, exploring situations and circumstances that result in revolutionary change and active transmission of a novel idea and strategy, rather than some steadily turning flywheel of evolutionary change. Neither approach on its own has found it easy to fully account for the pattern of evidence.

The gradual evolutionary explanation is faced with the question of why the transition was so late. Our species is around 200,000 years old, and has been displaying all the cognitive attributes of modernity for at least 80,000 years. During the period that preceded agriculture, humans adapted to a wide range of climatic, geographic, and ecological circumstances around the world—circumstances which have fluctuated between a series of environmental extremes. What was so special about the subsequent period, and what were the novel challenges that led to such a radical change? Those questions have stimulated archaeological fieldwork, initially and most intensively in southwest Asia and Meso-America, subsequently in China, and many other regions of the world. Fieldwork projects have lent credence to a range of answers that relate to particular regions and particular times. Profound changes in the nature and style of human settlement in these places suggested that 'revolutions' could and did disperse new lifestyles and practices. New ideas, it seems, might account for much of the evidence. However, that same evidence resists containment within a small number of locales. The transition was clearly repeated in multiple centres, remote from each other, in a manner consistent with a global evolutionary process.

Many current accounts consequently interweave the revolutionary and evolutionary aspects of change, bringing together such themes as environmental fluctuations and cultural and demographic responses. The evidence on which such narratives are based has also been transformed. The earliest accounts drew on recovered artefacts, arrows and spearheads for hunting, stones for grinding and pots for cooking. In time, the physical remains of the plants and animals used in the human food quest complemented the data,

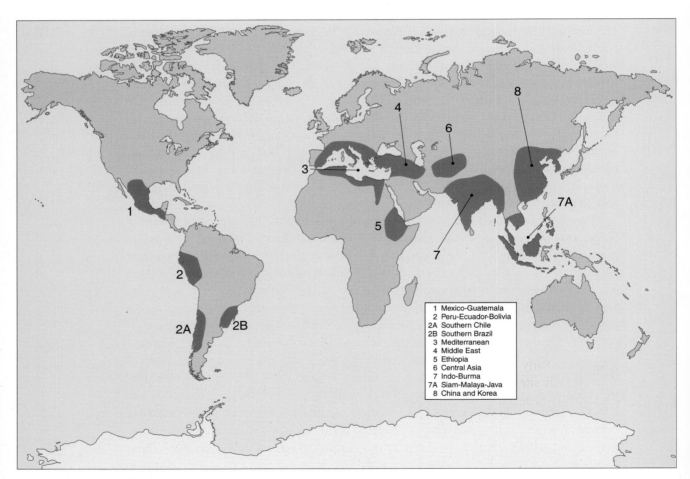

1 Mexico-Guatemala
2 Peru-Ecuador-Bolivia
2A Southern Chile
2B Southern Brazil
3 Mediterranean
4 Middle East
5 Ethiopia
6 Central Asia
7 Indo-Burma
7A Siam-Malaya-Java
8 China and Korea

NICOLAI VAVILOV'S 'CENTRES OF DIVERSITY' AND PUTATIVE ORIGINS OF DOMESTICATED CROPS.

with, most recently of all, detailed evidence of the genetic transformations at the heart of this radical change in our engagement with nature.

The environmental context of the transition is also better understood. It happened in different millennia in different regions, but in all cases after the 'Younger Dryas'—a sharp decline in temperature that affected a large part of the Northern Hemisphere between 12,900 and 11,700 ago—when a protracted series of significant climatic swings ended and the current warm epoch, which we label the 'Holocene', began. The radical temperature swings of the preceding millennia had threatened the survival of many large organisms, particularly the big-bodied terrestrial vertebrates. Several of these large vertebrates moved towards extinction during this period, and the human family was not immune. In the previous interglacial period there were at least five species of *Homo* in the world. By 10,000 years ago, only one remained and, rather than follow its closest relatives towards extinction, it bucked the trend. Across a warming world *Homo sapiens* spread more plentifully and extensively than any of its predecessors and cousins.

Knowing nature

Primates generally tend to eschew new environments but, as the case of mountain gorillas show, can sometimes shift at need. Humans are especially adept in this respect but are still very conservative when it comes to migration, often travelling a long way—across the globe, for instance, in the case of early modern European migrants in search of 'new Europes'—to find environments like those they left behind. Even in modern times, they favour familiar urban settings when they switch continents. How was our single surviving African taxon responding to the novelties of the world across which it travelled? What was it doing in environments that were at first slightly novel, and subsequently markedly distinct? By the time that taxon had travelled across four continents to reach Patagonia at the tip of Southern America, the African plant and animal species to which humans had gradually adapted were nowhere to be seen. On the journey from Africa, across Asia and the Bering Straits, through North, Central, and South America, the flora and fauna had radically changed not just once, but several times. How did humans adapt?

Fauna

The question is most easily addressed in the case of the animals we pursued and consumed. Early members of our species that hunted 40,000–80,000 years ago, around such sites as Sibudu Cave in the Cape region of South Africa, may have significantly depended on such animals as bushpig and blue duiker for food, but left them behind. Those species were not to be found in Europe, but other pigs and antelopes, the clusters of taxa to which they respectively belong, could be located and consumed. In some cases, the novel species were of very different sizes or appearances, and yet a switch was effected. It seems reasonable to conclude that early human perception was not locked into responding to what we would regard as

SIBUDU CAVE, NORTH OF DURBAN IN SOUTH AFRICA, where excavations show people sewed garments, made their beds, used arrows, and concocted glue some seventy thousand years ago.

singular taxa. They could do more than just recognize and name individual species. One thing we have learned from near-contemporary ethnographies is that, although indigenous classification systems may not coincide with ours, they are recurrently detailed and precise. We have no difficulty in inferring that in addition to names for specific species they had generic terms along the lines of our term 'mammal'. A key part of early mobility was dependent on being able to allow one type of 'mammal' to stand in for another, and to switch hunting strategy accordingly. It is tempting to extend the argument and infer separate generic terms for 'birds' and 'fish', and more speculatively, such subdivisions as 'suid' (pig relatives), 'cervid' (deer relatives), and 'bovid' (cow relatives). These generic categories may seem so intuitively obvious to ourselves that we find it difficult to think of them not being self-evident. However, such multilevel classifications are not universal and can by no means be assumed. It is notable that only a minority of hominid species made such a journey.

Flora

The manner in which cognitive abilities constrained movement out of Africa remains a matter for speculation. The challenge humans met on coming across different plant types was much greater than that arising from the different animals they encountered.

Such categories as 'animals' or 'cervids' may be reasonably clear to specialist and non-specialist alike. However, it takes some more elaborate training or instruction to identify categories of plants shared in common, for example, by elements of a rainforest and an arctic tundra. Beyond both being green, in parts, and alive, also in parts, elaboration of underlying similarities benefits from what we would all recognize as 'specialist knowledge'. Yet somehow, early humans ranged these contrasting ecosystems, drawing on knowledge of old ecosystems to find and recognize plants to eat in new ecosystems. I suggest they did so in a similar manner as they did with animals. They had generic categories that allowed them to move quite imaginatively and adventurously from one species to another until they found something to eat. Two of these categories dominate agriculture in the Old World; in our modern taxonomy, they correspond to 'legumes' and 'monocots'.

The characteristic big-seeded linear legume pods would be familiar to our species at each stage on its journey from Africa. They could be consumed as green pods before the seeds had fully hardened. They would be encountered hanging from the flat-topped *Acacia* trees that peppered the African savanna, or emerging from the bushy vines of wild cowpea in moister African environments. On the rockier, submontane slopes of the South West Asian hilly flanks, they would swell implausibly from the diminutive wild chickpea. So, in each new ecosystem, the familiar pods were not too far away, and if a more familiar form was unavailable, a less familiar one could be tried. This was probably best described as an 'acceptable-risk' strategy rather than a low-risk strategy, and a certain amount of gastric discomfort, and occasional dangers of something worse, would be a perennial feature of experimentation. But the end result is that around twenty species within ten genera of legumes featured in the different agricultural ecosystems of the Old World.

The only group in the human food chain that exceeds the legumes in diversity and scale is the monocot group. Once again, this group can be found as plants of large (coconut palm, bamboo) and small (sedge, onion) stature, but can be recognized by the

LEGUME PODS HANGING from a flat-topped *acacia* tree.

parallel veins on the leaves, and sheathing structure of the stem and tuber. Once these sheathing leaf bases are stripped away, the core stem material often comprises a proportion of accessible edible carbohydrates. That is not something that applies so generally to the other types of terrestrial plants. Dicots ('broad-leaved' plants) and conifers, for example, both make extensive use of woody tissue in their stems, inaccessible to human teeth and guts. The delicate unlignified parts of dicots may look edible, but the range and complexity of their chemical protection is less predictable. It is simply a higher-risk strategy to eat the broad leaves and pretty fruits and flowers of newly encountered and unfamiliar plants. There is growing evidence that unripe legume pods and overground and underground monocot stems were routine plant foods of a number of hominid species, as part of another 'acceptable-risk' strategy of entering new ecosystems. Among the hominids, the elaborate tool kits of our species in particular greatly facilitated the exploitation of each of these groups in another, radically important way.

Left to ripen, legumes and monocots alike (and especially one family of monocots, the grasses) could form dry seeds or grains. These are too hard to eat raw, and it is unlikely they were the first parts of the plant to be consumed by our ancestors, who instead grazed on tubers, stems, shoots, and unripe fruiting parts. However, the great diversification of the human toolkit observed in relation to our own species enabled transformation of grinding, pulverizing, and cooking technologies. The dry seeds and grains were now an important food source, with the additional advantage that they could be stored and easily transported. The agricultural legacy of monocot consumption appears in a series of stem foods in central latitudes, in particular yams and taros, and also the many tubers of the ginger family, including arrowroot. In temperate latitudes, the monocot grains predominate and indeed have dominated the diets of agrarian peoples. They comprise at least 50 species of cereals, of which three, bread wheat, rice, and maize, account for over half the biological energy entering the global human food chain today.

Classifying food in nature

These observations have related to the Old World, and more specifically, to the Sub-Boreal Old World. While our focus in this chapter is our own, singular, species of hominid, it could be said to apply to a range of hominids. As indicated previously, the majority of species in the hominid line did not make such an adventurous journey into the wider range of global ecosystems. However, at least five species of one genus, *Homo*, did at some point expand their ranges beyond Africa, and a number reached the Boreal line in the north of Eurasia, hunting animals, and balancing their meat diet with, amongst other things, legumes and monocots. It may be that only one species established itself sufficiently in the Northern Boreal zone to find itself in the American landmass beyond. In ecological terms, it may have been a challenging journey, in which that particular suite of natural categories provided insufficient flexibility to successfully exploit the stunted, waxy, woody vegetation cover of the cold north. What we can infer from the evidence of plant use they leave behind is that, having made the intrepid journey, humans moved south across the American landmass equipped with a more elaborate language of plants.

That greater elaboration can be sketched out, rather than precisely described. Take, for example, stem foods and tubers. These, in the Old World, are recurrently variations of a single theme, the acceptable risk of monocots. In parts of the New World, that monocot theme recurs in the tubers of arrowroot, American yam, cocoyam, and the highest altitude tuber of all, lleren. But alongside these, the three tubers that become most important are from some of the most dangerous plant families around; manioc is a member of the spurge family, sweet potato in the morning glory family, and potato is from that most toxic of families, the *Solanaceae*, or nightshades. In order to develop a dependable relationship with these new resources, communities would have required some sort of multi-level taxonomy that allowed groups and subgroups to be knowledgeably filtered and distinguished. By implication, this in turn might imply communicated expert knowledge, allowing experimentation and use in this manner. The confidence that knowledge instills allows users not just to avoid poisons, but also to exploit them, for hunting poisons, medicines, and psycho-active drugs.

More diversity is evident in the New World exploitation of dry grains. There are indeed monocots (maize, maygrass, little barley) and many legumes (kidney bean, lima bean, jack bean, and yam bean), but also hard seeds from the families of chenopods, amaranths, and sunflowers. None of this is to imply that subsequent generations after millennia in place, either in the Old World, or the New, did not develop considerable ethnobotanical diversity. Indeed, they did. However, in the underlying shape of how nature was recognized and utilized among the pioneering human wanderers in both the Old World and the New, a difference can be discerned in relation to these early wanderings. In the sub-Boreal latitudes of the Old World, a conservative classificatory strategy was adequate to establish a viable mode of plant exploitation. That conservative strategy had been shared and acted upon by several species of *Homo*. At some stage in the northern journey across to America, it ceased to be sufficient. The more complex language of nature that was required to negotiate harsh northern ecosystems, so strange and inhospitable to our African taxon, cannot be directly recovered. Any groups that migrated through unfamiliar biomes would have had to re-craft and re-learn classifications at successive stages. Those that passed through zones with few edible plants would have relied on selective use of animal products to make up for essential nutrients that normally come from plants, and so would be unlikely to retain their ancestors' classificatory lexicon. However, its imprint and legacy remains in the distinctive and especially elaborate nature of new world ethnobotanical knowledge, in this case enacted by one species alone.

Nature as nurture

While this chapter places great emphasis on the transition to agriculturists' production of plant foods, there are two features of modern diet that qualify that emphasis. First, if we look within today's global cuisine for what are regarded as its healthiest elements, they are likely to derive from fishing and other forms of foraging, or from horticultural traditions that have thrived along the world's watery edges, around lakes, rivers, and coasts. The Japanese Jomon culture is one of several that can be described in such a manner, and one that thrived throughout the period covered in this chapter, with a deep awareness of nature at least equal to that of agricultural communities of the time and unconsciously echoed, perhaps, in the sensibilities of fastidious modern eaters. Second, if we look within that same modern global cuisine for what are commonly regarded as the highest status elements, we may well turn to the tasty meat of the grazing herds moved by nomadic pastoralists across large tracts of continental Asia and Africa. For much of the last 10,000 years, the world's tillers of the soil have coexisted with these parallel modes of life, and in some cases interwoven them into single lives, changing practice from season to season. There is yet another ecological mode of great importance, but archaeological knowledge of it is even slimmer. The world's woodlands have shrunk, and the communities that understood and lived within them have drastically diminished, while deep woodland archaeology has gained momentum only recently.

SETTLED LIFE PRECEDED AGRICULTURE in the Japanese Jomon culture of about 12,000 years ago, represented in this reconstruction. The abundance of aquatic foods enabled people to live in permanent villages, with leisure to make—often in large sizes and elaborate styles—some of the world's earliest known ceramic pots.

Alongside the rich water's edge, the expanses of grazed grassland, and the unknown diversity of woodland human ecologies, what was the key element that raised farming to prominence? The answer is probably calories. The most notable output of agriculture is biological energy on an unprecedented scale, and with the potential to grow, to be accumulated in stores, and exchanged. That is connected with a whole new range of ways of culturally being human that is explored in the next chapter. Here, we return to how our novel relationship with nature rendered agriculture possible.

Taming life

Some of the previous section's account of the transition to a world with agriculture derives directly from primary archaeological evidence, but a great deal depends upon looking backwards into this ecological journey through the lens of its most conspicuous consequences, domestication and agriculture itself. Detailed patterns within the biology, genetics, and geography of selected grasses, legumes, and animals can lead us back to the deep history of their exploitation. A key episode in the history of those plants and animals has been that each species lost its reproductive independence, and eventually became reliant on their principal predator, humans, to produce a new generation. This loss of reproductive independence is at the heart of the concept of 'domestication'. Its extent is variable. In the process of domestication, several of our major cereals have had their natural dispersal mechanisms so disabled they will disappear completely from an untended plot after two or three years. Others, in particular some of the lesser known small-grained cereals or 'millets', may persist quite long in untended plots, and regularly interbreed with wild relatives. Animals are similarly variable. It is hard to imagine cattle persisting outside a human ecosystem, and their wild ancestors are, in any case, extinct. The relationship between pigs and wild boars is less clear cut. Looking across the human chain, the full range of dependence and independence can be seen, ranging from fish and seafood which, up until the creation of fish farms in the twentieth century, remained almost entirely wild, to the three grasses (cereals) that dominate the calorific input into our food chain. Wheat, rice, and maize are all heavily dependent on human intervention to complete their reproductive cycles, and thus, fully 'domesticated'.

Domesticated crops

Preceding chapters in this volume have followed the pathway of humans out of Africa and across the world, a pathway elucidated both by archaeology and genetics. This latter science has also been crucially important in establishing how and where domestication took place, and how agriculture spread across much of the world. Nikolai Vavilov, the Russian pioneer of crop genetics, argued that the regions in which domestication occurred, and from which agriculture spread, could be tracked down by looking at the diversity among the living wild relatives of crop plants.

His method led him to suggest eight primary foci of crop origin in the world, marked out by high diversities of wild relatives, and spanning Africa, Asia, and America. The foci he recognized were not in the heart of the world's peaks of biological productivity. The great equatorial rain forests were nowhere highlighted. Instead it was transitional zones, between high and low altitude, between wet and dry zones—marginal ecosystems acutely sensitive to the fluctuation of the seasons. Those transitional ecosystems favoured seasonal plants, in particular seed plants, which dominate those foci. While Vavilov's two Southern Centres had just a few domesticates, to each of the remaining six centres, he attributed the origins of between 38 and 138 domesticated species, approaching 700 plant taxa transformed around the world for human needs.

In the period after the World War II, Vavilov's maps inspired and guided a series of key fieldwork projects that furnished selected 'Centres of Origin' with a story and a date. His foci of crop diversity soon attracted archaeological interest, and have sustained that interest with successive episodes of fieldwork and analysis.

The most intensively studied of these foci, Asia Minor, also corresponded to an arc recognized by James Breasted, a scholar who combined archaeology and biblical history to link the lands drained by the Nile, the Jordan, the Tigris, and the Euphrates into one continuous arc he christened the 'Fertile Crescent'. Breasted's students Robert and Linda Braidwood took that arc and pushed it uphill to meet the novel

THE 9,000-YEAR-OLD SETTLEMENT OF JARMO 800 metres up from the Tigris River in the foothills beneath the Zagros Mountains.

archaeological evidence they helped reveal. Such sites as the 9,000-year-old settlement of Jarmo were to prove critical in our understanding of the emergence of farming. Jarmo was not located down in the valley of the Tigris, but 800 m up in the foothills beneath the Zagros Mountains that drained into that valley. Such was to prove a recurrent pattern leading the Braidwoods to emphasize 'hilly flanks', the interface between the exposed mountain and the accumulated foothill sediment at its base, as a primary focus for the emergence of farming, with the valley bottoms, secondary, to be fully tamed at a later date.

A shift in detecting agricultural beginnings from the river valleys to the foothills fringing those valleys is a theme that recurs in other centres of agricultural origin. The Yellow Valley that drains Northern China had been regarded as the focus of ancestral Han origins long before archaeological endeavour in China. When the first twentieth-century archaeologists began their fieldwork at such sites as Neolithic Yangshao, they confirmed the importance of the great Yellow River, and by the 1960s, in response to rich findings of early rice grains at Hemedu, the Yangtse River in the south was also recognized as a focus of early agriculture. Over the last 20 years, in both the north and south of China, finer-grained surveys have, in a manner resonant with the Braidwood's 'Hilly Flanks', shifted attention away from the valley bottom to the foothills on either side, once again at the point the exposed mountain rock becomes clothed in softer foothill sediments.

Moving to the New World, two centres, meso-America and the Andes were suggested by Vivilov. These were each goals in the mid-twentieth-century search for agricultural origins. When Richard McNeish recovered diminutive maize cobs from the Coxcatlan cave in the thorn-forested highlands above the Mexican valley of Tehuacan, the location resonated with the perched, valley flanking sites of the Old World. That elevated topography of the early sites is mirrored by the cave of Guila Naquitz above the Oaxaca Valley, which may have the earliest evidence of plant domestication in Meso-America, with domesticated cucurbits attested at 10,750 years ago.

The Andean centres of South America take the theme of elevation above the valley to an extreme, giving rise to such high-altitude crops as maca, canihua, mashwa, oca, and bitter potato, each of them adapted to altitudes up to around 4,000 metres. Much of the resource diversity of South America is vertically organized, with a rich array of domesticates at each altitudinal band.

Vavilov's centres no longer have a precise correspondence with our current archaeological evidence for regions of agricultural origin; archaeological fieldwork has led to many adjustments to the map. However, considerable geographical resonance with those centres remains, and Vavilov's approach still offers archaeologists a valuable signpost to guide our continued search for those origins. Some regions of origin, such as the Eastern United States, in which the sunflower and certain of the chenopods arose, and the sub-Saharan belt, home to several of the African millets, were not detected in Vavilov's original analysis; others, such as the Mediterranean, were overemphasized.

There is now a greater number of regions for which an intimate evolutionary engagement with plants and animals is attested. When archaeologists first attempted to find sites that related to Vavilov's maps, archaeobotanical methodologies were only just emerging, and had only become refined for the detection of seeds and fruits. The first Neolithic world geographies that emerged consequently placed a strong emphasis upon grain crops, principally cereals and legumes. Those geographies were consequently biased towards the mosaic grassy ecosystems in which wild grains flourished. It was only gradually that methods of analyses were refined to detect underground storage organs, through charred remains and plant microfossils, such that the origins of the important root and tuber agriculture of equatorial regions came more clearly to light. Such improvement in methods opened our eyes to such sites as Kuk Swamp in New Guinea, where 9,000 years ago, communities were diverting streams and digging the soil in order to cultivate taro. Within a few millennia, the site was also yielding evidence of sugar cane and banana.

Archaeological fieldwork since Vavilov's original analysis has expanded the range of agricultural origins in a number of ways. Vavilov suggested eight centres, and new evidence has enlarged that set to at least twelve. Moreover, the widespread and regular application of radiocarbon dating has scattered their dates and drawn attention to a further issue, the pace of change.

In a number of intimate associations between humans and other life forms, the biological transformation of the plant or animal is an observable consequence; wild forms become domesticated forms. Grasses become cereals, legumes become pulses, and wolves become dogs. Darwin himself made extensive use of the close analogy between ancient plant and animal domestication, and contemporary plant and animal breeding. According to common assumptions, conscious selection for improved, more convenient and more dependable forms helped to drive the transition to agriculture. However, where it has been possible to date the different stages of visible transformations, the process seems to have been slow—so slow that the human populations engaged in it would have struggled to notice that it was actually going on. The notion of 'conscious' selection becomes problematic in that context.

The 'Fertile Crescent'

The richest evidence for the pace of change still comes from the region of South West Asia that James Breasted described as the 'Fertile Crescent'. Here, the intensive use of wild cereals is documented as far back as 23,000 years ago at the Levantine site of Ohalo II. In the same region, stone mortars and pestles have been recovered from houses constructed 14,000 years ago at Wadi Hammeh 27. Wild cereal use a thousand years later is now attested in Northern Syria, and, after a further lapse of a millennium, in Northern Iraq. By 11,300 years ago, such sites as Jerf El Ahmar in Northern Syria bear witness to quite substantial stone-built structures housing intensive cereal processing activities, and varied evidence of a grain-based cuisine. At this time, a period by which evidence could be found along the full stretch of the Fertile Crescent for a

STONE MORTARS AND PESTLES recovered from houses constructed 14,000 years ago at Wadi Hammeh 27, at Pella in Jordan.

long-established engagement with a range of cereals and other plants, those same plants showed no morphological signs of domestication; they were structurally wild. This does not necessarily mean that no human intervention was under way as sedentary foragers nurtured their sources of food. If wild cereals are abundant and relatively easy to process for human food, interventions might not register evidence of modification, and conscious processes, such as winnowing, weeding, and re-planting, that can be presumed to precede hybridization will not necessarily produce detectable structural or genetic modifications.

Direct observations of the changing form of the cereal rachis (the part of the stem bearing the grains) from archaeological contexts of different dates, has allowed the pace of morphological change to be assessed. In the western branch of the Fertile Crescent, evidence for the growing prominence of tough rachis domesticated forms appears from around 10,500 years ago, and in the Eastern Branch, around 700 years later. Even then, there is a millennial time gap before these traits become 'fixed' (when the morphological change has stabilized as a persistent feature of the population as a whole). Fixation occurs at different times in different regions of the Fertile Crescent, but in each case, several thousand years after the stone mortars and pestles from Wadi Hammeh 27.

A similarly slow pace has been observed in the case of East Asian rice. Rice phytolith evidence (phytoliths are rigid, microscopic structures made of silica found in some plant tissues that persist after the decay of the plant) is indicative of rice cultivation at Diaotonghuan in Jianxi Province by about twelve thousand years ago. The fixation of domestication traits has been directly observed in fragments of chaff from rice plants preserved at Tianluoshan about five thousand years later. Between 6,900 and 6,600 years ago, the proportion of seed heads that have lost their original, wild attribute on breaking up or 'shattering' when ripe increases from 27–39 per cent, at the same time as rice remains move from 8–24 per cent of the total plant residue in the archaeological context from the site. The evidence from Tianluoshan thus provides a useful record of morphological domestication in action, which in its overall slow pace mirrors the pattern observed further to the west for wheat and barley.

We now have evidence that in several distinct regions across the world, communities moved slowly (to any contemporary human observer, imperceptibly slowly) towards an association with several plants, often with grazing animals and sometimes with birds, that led repeatedly to a biological change in the species concerned—a change we describe as morphological domestication—in each case entailing a greater dependence upon the human exploiter to complete the reproductive cycle. Within the ensuing world of agriculture, settlements and societies adopted some radically new forms, and ultimately became interconnected in novel ways.

House, hearth, and kiln

An intimate engagement with the life cycles of the plants and animals on which it feeds is invariably a driving feature of how a species places itself within a landscape. During earlier epochs in the human past, two different forms of placement co-existed. One involved an agile mobility in temporary camps that shadowed the seasonal movement of large grazing mammals, and could sometimes carry humans across vast distances. The other entailed a persistence at carefully protected points along the interface between ecological boundaries, between land and water, or between hill and plain. Emphasis on plants, particularly legumes and monocots, emerged and grew alongside a new style of placement within the landscape that reflected the ecology of humanly exploited plants, and the degree of sustained attention that was required to nurture and protect them, as their dependence on their predator increased.

The idea of a 'built space' was not new to this period. Evidence for the artificial containment of the ground surface around a managed fire, to create shelter and safety for small groups of people, may be found at least three times as early as evidence for the domestication of plants and animals, and most strikingly visible in the Palaeolithic landscape houses fashioned from mammoth bones, a building material sometimes utilized by the Gravettian and Epi-Gravettian hunters of Europe and Asia. What happened around the time of domestication was a considerable elaboration of form and diversification of materials. Two particularly versatile examples were cut stone and mud-brick. These novel products enabled the construction of a wider range of shapes, and different combinations, of rooms and cells than had been achieved in the earlier use of organic materials.

A striking early instance is the site of Ein Es-Sultan close to modern Jericho. During the tenth millennium BCE, 70 circular houses around 5 m in diameter were constructed from sun-dried bricks of clay tempered with straw. The number greatly proliferated in

HOUSES FASHIONED FROM MAMMOTH BONES were common in the Eurasian plains, from perhaps about 20,000 years ago, until construction materials made of earth replaced them. See also p. 47 Ordinary, everyday activities went on inside these extraordinary dwellings—sleeping, eating, and all the routines of family life.

AT ÇATAL HÜYÜK, NEAR KONYA IN TURKEY, about ten thousand years ago, dwellings were honeycombed closely together, and rooftop walkways served as streets.

MERHGARH, A NEOLITHIC (7000 BCE TO ABOUT 2500/2000 BCE) site located near the Bolan Pass on the Kacchi Plain of Balochistan, Pakistan, to the west of the Indus River valley, where 'a cluster of mud brick houses' grew into a settlement covering more than 29 hectares.

the following millennium, and the settlement was surrounded by a stone-built wall, enclosing four hectares and incorporating a stone tower rising to 3.6 metres. By the eighth millennium BCE, built space at Çatal Hüyük, near Konya in Turkey, reached a complexity and elaboration comparable in scale to many contemporary settlements, housing thousands of people in closely packed dwellings.

From then on, a more diverse range of built spaces in different regions of the Old World would connect communities to productive stands of plants. The built spaces and the plants around them reflected increasing investment in particular places, and increasing dependence on their security. Built structures emphasized connections and dependencies in place and, by allusion to ancestry and the deceased, in time.

As the world's climate moved into the warmest phase of the Holocene, an optimum period from around 9000 to 5000 years ago, several of the centres of agricultural origin across the Old World and the New ultimately give rise to the elaborate, densely packed built spaces that have variously been described as 'villages', 'towns', and 'cities'. To the west of the Indus River, on the Kachi plain of Baluchistan in modern Pakistan, wheat and barley farmers of the eighth millennium built a cluster of mud-brick houses and granaries at a site that would continue to flourish over the next three millennia. Three thousand years later, Merhgarh had grown to a series of settled mounds spanning more than 200 hectares. Further to the east, near Xi'an on China's Yellow River, the 'village' of Banpo emerged during the seventh millennium BP. Across an expanse of eight hectares, around 100 buildings and over twice that number of tombs, were arranged together with elaborate pottery firing kilns.

Energy and fire

Houses and kilns alike highlight a central feature of built spaces: the containment and control of energy. The circle around the hearth, as the primary focus and source of that energy, delineates community and collectivity, and the architectural boundaries around that same hearth denote separation and restriction. In this way, by endless variations in these themes, architecture and society proceed on their entangled symbiotic course. The containment of the hearth encompasses another symbiosis around pyrotechnology. Many materials with which that containment is achieved, such as hardened clay and plaster, depend upon a hearth (further contained within an oven, kiln, or furnace) for their production. There is a thermal continuum between keeping a community warm and dry, preparing its food, and fashioning its material constructions and artefacts. Moving along that continuum entails modifying the hearth, the inputs of fuel and air, and the form of containment. Hearth-centred built spaces offer a continual arena for experiments in pyrotechnology.

Temperatures employed for cooking in the period under review could also be utilized for drying mud-brick and roasting gypsum to produce a plaster. With closer containment and more oxygen, temperatures could exceed 500°C, sufficient to transform wet clay into a durable and versatile material. Further modification of the enclosed hearths and selection of charcoal as a fuel would permit the fusion of silica into glass and the smelting of copper and gold. To smelt iron, the same themes—enclosed fire, well-chosen fuel, and plentiful oxygen—would be brought together to reach temperatures hitherto unknown on the surface of the earth, not even where that surface erupted in volcanoes.

The allure of fire runs as deeply into the human past as does our enchantment with decorative materials. Both can be traced back 30,000–40,000 years at least in Eurasia, and twice as far back again in Africa. By the start of the period embarked upon in this chapter, humans in various regions of the world had, for thousands of years, modelled plaster and clay pastes into the shapes of human and animals, and furthermore used those pastes to create functional containers. Also for thousands of years they had gathered visually interesting earths, stones, and skeletal elements to their gatherings around the hearth, elaborated them yet further, strung them into beads, rendered them into paste to adorn their faces and bodies, doing something similar to the skulls of their departed ancestors.

Ancestral skulls of this kind have been recovered from the site of Ain Ghazal in Jordan. Around 7,000 years ago, the flesh on those skulls had been reimagined in lime plaster, a medium subsequently used on the site to fashion human models. Different kinds of plaster were also used from an early date to create a surface for floors and walls, and those surfaces might be further decorated with coloured pastes. Among those pastes may have been ones prepared from ground colourful stones. In the case of many such stones, including blue azurite, green malachite, and red cuprite, they owe their distinctive hue to a rich content of copper ions.

Copper was among those metals encountered from time to time in its native state. Early communities may also have encountered nodules of gold, silver, tin, and meteoric iron. When hearths reached temperatures of between 600 and 1100°C, the metals could be released from their much more plentiful ores, for example, the decorative greenstones. Smelting temperatures can be reached in an open fire, but not by accident: they require a firepit filled with quantities of well-chosen, naturally

ANCESTRAL SKULL recovered from the site of Ain Ghazal in Jordan 'with flesh reimagined in lime plaster' about nine thousand years ago.

available fuels left to freely burn for some time. On the basis of the world's earliest ceramics, we can infer that such pit fires have been in use for at least 20,000 years. Fragments of fire-hardened clay from such early periods may have derived from the enclosure of specialist hearths within firing ovens or 'kilns'.

The firing of clay objects goes back at least 26,000 years to the 'Venus' figurines of Upper Palaeolithic settlements as Dolni Věstonice in today's Czech Republic. Containers of fired clay were first recovered in later deposits from the far side of Eurasia, where ceramic containers go back at least 20,000 years at Xianrendong Cave in the Chinese province of Jianxi. By 12,000 years ago, several parts of East Asia and the Japanese Archipelago were familiar with ceramic containers, corresponding to an equally deep-seated cuisine of moist, slow-cooked food. At the same period, the open fires of West Eurasia were attached to a cuisine based on roasting and baking meat and dough-based confections, hand-held foods for which containers were superfluous either in preparation or to consumption. While pottery production had begun in sub-Saharan Africa by the tenth millennium BCE, it was not until the seventh millennium that ceramic vessels become part of the European tradition, and the sixth millennium in the Americas.

This global scatter of pottery traditions suggests multiple experimentation with clay and fire in different regions of the world. It would not be surprising, therefore, if that experimentation were to lead in several places to a wider range of pyrotechnic outcomes. In approaching the temperatures of 1,000°C that can be passed in an open bonfire, different communities may have repeatedly encountered glassy materials and native metals as a by-product of ceramic production. At present the earliest evidence of the systematic roasting of ores to release copper comes from a series of Serbian sites, dating to around 5,000 BCE. Similar evidence is encountered in Iran from a few centuries later.

The copper was sometimes fashioned into objects in a fairly pure form, though incidental impurities, particularly arsenic, could generate a harder substance. Metal-lurgists exploited this feature by actively adding hardening materials, arsenic-rich ores first of all. In the following millennium, a different mixture had a considerable impact. If copper was diluted to around nine-tenths by tin rather than arsenic, the resulting mixture would harden to a new, strong, and easily worked material. The old world was transformed by the appearance of prehistory's best known alloy, bronze.

The bronze prepared at the mid-fifth millennium Vinca culture sites in Serbia were used to make foil, which in turn had various decorative functions. In subsequent millennia the alloy was used for a wide range of utilitarian equipment, equestrian accessories, and wheeled transport, and for various blades, knives, and weapons. Successive scholars have been intrigued by the relationship between this versatile new material, the constraints on its production, and the complexity of the societies associated with it. While Neolithic communities have been envisioned as collectively working their lands and bringing forward the harvest, Bronze Age Societies have been envisioned as hierarchical, complex with elites and specialists.

Looking forward to those Bronze Age societies of the second millennium BCE, the idea of a plentiful access to metal for some brings with it parallel notions of weaponry, accumulated wealth, and elite power, and a series of highly mobile communities with wheeled transport that connect and harmonize the material culture in a region that spans the continent. In the preceding third millennium, however, a series of more loosely interconnected local communities were nonetheless sharing ideas and passing on their practical knowledge of metallurgy. As early as the fifth and fourth millennia BCE, the North Balkans and Carpathian basin were working to some degree with materials of copper and arsenical bronze. By the third millennium BCE, settlements of the Yamnaya culture stretching in a northern arc between the Black and Caspian Seas, and those of the Afanasievo culture towards the Altai Mountains in Southern Siberia, were depositing metal implements in their graves. These were stock-raising communities moving around the forest steppe interface, which offered grazing lands to their cattle, horses, goats, and sheep, and wood for their warmth and their crafts, including metalworking. Metal objects are also found during this period in hilly and montane regions across China, from Xinjiang to the south of the Altai, through Inner Mongolia and Liaoning to the east, and towards the eastern coast of Asia in Shangdong.

This series of connections along the forest steppe of northern Eurasia is traced by the metal objects, and a pastoral mode of life. Beyond that, the cultural attributes of the component communities vary; much of life, its patterns, and its cultural traits remains locally circumscribed. The reticulate movement of pastoralist communities and their herds in search of fresh pastorage has been modelled by the archaeologist Michael Frachetti, who demonstrates how extensive those networks of neighbour-to-neighbour contact can be in societies without elaborately centralized organization.

Regulating water and soil

While pastoralism and metalworking expanded along the forests, steppes, and hills of Eurasia, communities in different parts of the world were engaging more intensively with particular stretches of landscape, the water flowing through them, and the soils nourished by those waters.

Human interventions in the flow of water through the landscape have, in the past, taken a variety of forms; these can be broken down to three interconnected processes. The first entails slowing the journey from rainfall to the sea, causing the water to connect more gradually and intimately with the soils on the way. The second entails challenging gravity yet further, by physically lifting water from a lower reservoir or channel to a higher. The third is the creation of entirely artificially waterways, vertical and horizontal, above ground and below, to challenge and reconfigure the entire pattern of drainage across the landscape. Prior to 10,000 BCE, the first of these three processes was widely practised and established, as was the second in the form of water wells. The third became much more significant in periods addressed in later chapters within this volume.

Stepped terracing

The slowing of the water's journey was first achieved by the combination of a vast number of relatively small acts, rather than by major centralized works. That constellation of small acts has bequeathed to us some of the most dramatically sculpted human landscapes in the world. From the precipitous Andean slopes of Peru to the rice fields of South East Asia and the Pacific, the Loess Plateau of North China, and the great heights of the Himalayan uplift, the integrated patterns of stepped terracing are striking topographic features. It is still, arguably, the form of agriculture in which the largest number of contemporary farmers toil, yet in terms of the dynamics and history of farming systems, we know far, far less about the high terraces than the low plains. We can infer from their structure the manner in which they were formed.

It began with a banking of the river high up and close to its source, where its volume was small and modest placements of stones and earth could interrupt its flow. Then came the next terrace down, and the next, each time constraining a manageable flow from the terrace above. In time, the entire landscape was contained with topographical stripes, in turn defining a sequence of necessary social relationships in which each farmer was dependent on the choices of the farmers above, and held sway over the prosperity of the farmers working below.

Such landscapes may have come into place over 6,000 years ago in China. Grains of rice and soil organic matter indicative of paddy rice farming have been carbon dated to *c.* 4270 BCE at Chaodun in Kunshan County. Slightly younger paddy fields have been excavated at Caoxieshan in Jiangsu Province. On the other side of the world, Peru's Zana Valley has yielded evidence of water channels to support agricultural systems of over 5,400 years' antiquity. During the second millennium BCE, both wheat and barley cultivation were being cultivated above 3000 m on the Tibetan plateau. In Europe, Mediterranean agricultural terraces have been dated back to the Bronze Age. In a number of these regions, not only does the stepping of the hillside force the water to travel more gradually across the landscape, the ridge-and-furrow cultivation within each terrace softens that passage yet further, and ensures that the water flows to each tended plant.

STEPPED TERRACING STILL IN USE ON THE TIBETAN PLATEAU.

Flooding

Turning from the hill slopes to the valley bottom, the slowing of the water's journey takes place in different ways, principally by the flooding of lateral banks. This method is charted in some detail in early texts and images from Mesopotamia and Egypt. By the fourth or fifth millennium BCE, the Tigris and the Euphrates rivers in South West Asia were being managed by dams constructed at right angles to the main flow of the river, connecting with a series of canals and dykes. When the river was at its highest, the water would be diverted into lateral canals and allowed to flood the fields, the water only returning to its course after the crops had been nourished. By the third millennium BC, a similar system of irrigation basin agriculture was being practised along the Nile River. On the far side of Asia, such sites as Maoshan in the Lower Yangtze Valley also provide direct evidence of lower river management, in systems of rice paddy fields belonging to the fifth millennium BCE.

Wells

Lifting technologies are of great antiquity. Over 7,000 years ago, the first farmers to reach Northern Europe (of the Linear Bandkeramic Culture, so named after the banded decoration found on their pottery vessels) were sinking elegant timber-lined wells to depths of at least 7 m. This introduced the option of supplementing recent rains with 'fossil' water, as some of the water accumulating below ground has been there for centuries or millennia.

Soil

Regulation of water has typically been closely associated with regulation of the soils it feeds. As already indicated, the creation of furrows by cultivation contributes to the regulation of water flow. In addition, cultivation of the soil achieves a number of different things in different places, always with the aim of maintaining an amenable environment for the chosen crops. In temperate lowlands, one key aim of deep ploughing may be to destroy the extant plant cover to minimize competition with the crop. In tropical hillsides, a key aim of shallow cultivation is conversely to leave as much of the extant plant cover intact, in order to protect the soils from insolation and erosion. In prehistory, the two principal variants in cultivation technology were depth of cultivation and energy of traction. These two variables would often be interlinked.

At the lowest energy level cultivators employed a series of hand-held devices: spades, picks, hoes, in prehistory typically fashioned from wood and occasionally from animal skeletal elements, e.g. antlers or scapulae. While the latter materials have a better chance of persisting into the archaeological record, waterlogged deposits have repeatedly yielded cultivation tools of wood, the principal fabric of prehistory. In form those hand-held implements can be scaled up and combined with animal traction to generate a range of ploughing technologies.

Ploughing

A 'true plough' in the strictest sense is not a prehistoric implement. While the term is commonly also used with a more general inclusive meaning, the strictest usage of 'plough' reserves the term for a heavy implement that not only cuts into the turf, but also lifts and inverts it. It both cuts deep, and is the most effective 'weed-killer' of all cultivation implements. Such an implement, encountered in classical Europe and Han China, came to be the major agricultural implement in many regions in subsequent centuries. In prehistory, the corresponding tool was the 'ard'.

The tip of the ard bites into the ground and, according to design and mode of use, may penetrate shallow or deep. However, it does not invert the turf. The lightest ards may be pulled by a single animal, or by a person. The heaviest ards may require the energy of two trained oxen, and they may go as deep as the later 'true plough'. Some of these implements may be augmented by 'wings', which achieve a certain amount of soil turning, and if farmers had access to metal for utilitarian use—and even in the

WOODEN ARD, WITH FARMER AND TRACTION ANIMALS, painted in the thirteenth century BCE on the wall of the tomb of Sennedjem, who was himself an excavator and decorator of tombs, but who seems to have imagined himself as a farmer in the afterlife.

'metal ages' we cannot assume that the majority did—their wooden implements could be given a sharper cutting edge. The true ploughs of a later period might be entirely of metal, but in prehistory, the deployment of metal in farming was typically modest and selective. The first priority for those with access to this high value material was for harvesting tools. Marks left in the subsoil from wooden ard cultivation are known from South West Asia in the sixth millennium BCE, and in Europe from the fourth millennium BCE. By the third millennium BCE, they are in evidence in many places from North West Europe to China. By this period, they are also well documented in illustrations of various kinds, together with farmer and traction animals.

The earliest farming plots were most likely hand cultivated, and the ard cultivated or ploughed field would remain a subset within a wider, hand-cultivated horticultural tradition, going back far deeper in time, and reaching far further to the distinct corners of the world. Animal-assisted cultivation was limited by the distribution of suitable animals; horses came into domestication in Central Asia, while cattle and donkeys are Asian and African in origin. Topography and ecology limited the deployment of animals. Tropical horticulture with a focus upon tubers and tree crops is better suited to hand cultivation. In the New World, the agriculture of maize, beans and several other grain crops reached a considerable extent on the basis of the digging stick and hoe.

Putting down roots

Many elements of the farming way of life entailed a commitment to a place, to a particular patch of earth. That commitment could extend beyond the lifespan of the principal annual crops, to successive years in which soils were tended and improved. It could extend beyond the lifetime of the individual farmers tending those soils. The primary crops of farming systems in the mid-latitudes typically required a recurrent commitment during successive growing seasons, from spring to autumn. In tropical horticulture, much tending of plants was perennial from the start, and a multi-annual engagement with plants made sense. Perennial crops were eventually drawn into mid-latitude farming as well. From the fourth millennium BCE, a range of woody perennials, each with a long history of more extensive exploitation, were folded into intensive field-based cultivation for their fruits. Notable among these are the Mediterranean fruits, including date, olive, grape, fig, and pomegranate. Many Asian fruits of the Rosaceae family, including apples, pears, plums, cherries, and almonds were to gain prominence in the orchards of the historic epoch, and were widely exploited in prehistory. The intensive management of some rosaceous fruits, particularly the peach and possibly the apricot, may have been as early in China as the prehistoric orchards of the Mediterranean. Similarly, the citrus fruits of South East Asia may all have been brought into domestication before 1000 BCE. In many distinct regions of the world, productive agricultural plots were managed on many different tempos, from the fast-growing herb completing its cycle in a couple of months, through perennial vegetables and tubers, to the wizened old fruit trees whose antiquity may, in certain cases, surpass a millennium.

Though never approaching a millennial timescale, animals can also be husbanded at different tempos. While their life cycles are typically perennial, if the emphasis is upon meat, then the intensive work of fattening up livestock can take place seasonally, alongside the growth of crops. A breeding population can be maintained over the winter months, but the main productivity is of young animals, fattened from spring and culled in the autumn. It is this emphasis upon the primary product, meat, that Andrew Sherratt argued characterizes the first millennia of agriculture. We can envisage an intensity of activity during the growing season, and something quite different in the rest of the year, not necessarily agricultural in nature at all. It is not until the fourth or third millennia BCE that the archaeological record shifts from a sole emphasis on primary product (meat, at the end of an animal's life) to secondary products from the living animal managed over a longer life trajectory to supply as adults: milk, traction, and wool. The tempo of plant and animal management repeatedly comes together in these longer-term human ecosystems, in which the investment and human attachment are intergenerational. The Bronze Age system of Mediterranean polyculture is a classic example, with milk and cheese production, and the possibilities of animal traction integrated with management of orchards for olives and grapevine.

Sherratt encapsulated these elements into the concept of a 'Secondary Products Revolution'. The carcass products, especially the meat, were all 'primary', and any productive use made of animals still alive was 'secondary'. Secondary products include milking, wool gathering, animal traction (carts, chariots, and ploughs), and riding. As the name of his concept suggests, Sherratt's template for the Secondary Products Revolution, was the early Neolithic Revolution associated with Vere Gordon Childe. Both revolutions were perceived as having a particular origin in space (in each case the Near East) and time, and a subsequent episode of dispersal of the new idea. Rather like the earlier Revolution, many of the core themes of the Secondary Products Revolution persist as valuable ideas, whereas ideas of its chronology and geography have been questioned, and the overall picture understood to be more variable and patterned. The example of milking provides a clear example of how new forms of evidence have clarified the picture. Sherratt's original evidence for milking derived from specialist ceramic artefacts tentatively associated with milk straining and cheese making. This evidence base has since been enhanced, first by archaeozoological studies of herd structure, and second by directly detecting milk biomolecules adhering to ancient pots. The latter evidence in particular has pushed the earliest evidence of milking back to the seventh millennium BCE in the coastal region around the Sea of Marmara. There is still a millennial time gap between early indications of domestication and of milking, but no longer as lengthy as originally envisaged.

The geography of the Revolution, which Sherratt rooted in the Near East, has also been debated, particularly in relation to two of the Old World's major draft animals, the camel and the horse. Human engagement with both of these emerges further east, within Central Asia, and the relationship with the horse in particular has been greatly clarified by subsequent zooarchaeological study. The sites of Botai and Krasnyi Yar in

North Kazakhstan provide ample evidence that horses were of central importance to human communities of the mid-fourth millennium BCE, but the nature of the relationship remains a matter for debate. On the one hand, many among the rich collection of horse bones at the sites could be explained in terms of the culling of freely roaming animals for meat and other carcass products. Such an activity may have had a greater resemblance to the hunting of wild game than the herding of domestic animals. Excavations at both sites have, however, presented evidence of corralling and of the gathering of horse dung. Moreover, some of the Botai pots retain traces of milk fats, while some of the horse teeth evidence of 'bit-ware' is suggestive of harnessing. The artefactual evidence for wheeled transport does become widely evident across Eurasia in later periods, with slow-moving carts during the third millennium BCE, and fast-moving chariots during the second millennium BCE. The Botai evidence, however, indicates that secondary product exploitation is in evidence among central Asia horses of the fourth millennium BCE.

There is a direct connection between the harnessing and mobilizing of animal power, and the potential for cultivating the ground for crops. Most crops can be effectively grown under a wide range of cultivation methods, involving various permutations of humans, animals, and mechanical equipment. Our evidence for the earlier episode of early agriculture is consistent with cultivation using human power, and tools of wood, bamboo, and stone. During the later episode, those resources are

ACCUMULATIONS OF BUTCHERED HORSE BONES at the sites of Botai and Krasnyi Yar in North Kazakhstan provide ample evidence that horses were of central importance.

complemented by two further key resources: the harnessing of animal power and the routine production of metal items. A further feature that connects with these is an emerging emphasis on particular crops, grown singly in large fields. Field size and shape has often been associated with the pragmatic considerations of how it is cultivated, and there is indeed a limit to the cultivation tools that may be employed in the smallest of fields. The greater the harnessing of animal power for traction of cultivation tools, the greater the advantage of long fields to minimize the time and energy costs of changing direction.

Two episodes of prehistoric agriculture

The farming landscapes of prehistory have often been described in terms of two contrasting episodes, broadly corresponding to light cultivation in small fields of an earlier period, and heavy cultivation of larger fields in a later period. A difference in form, between an earlier extensive agriculture of the Neolithic and a later intensive agriculture of the Bronze Age, has been discussed since the early days of archaeological endeavour. In the absence of a today's rich data, nineteenth- and early twentieth-century scholars drew heavily from ethnographic parallels. Ideas about the extensive agriculture of the Neolithic were initially drawn from collected contemporary observations of hilly equatorial regions supporting shifting slash-and-burn agriculture. Ideas about the intensive agriculture of the Bronze Age were similarly drawn from observations of the agrarian landscapes around the heavily centralized and autocratic systems of governance in India and China. The resulting farming landscapes were put in a simple sequence, according to principles of linear social evolution. While these parallels from ethnographic observation certainly provided an early opportunity to envision prehistoric agriculture, a wealth of archaeological evidence has allowed us to develop a more robust picture. This new picture is more detailed, and also more complicated and varied, across both space and time. However, some similarities with a two-stage model remain.

The tropical slash-and-burn model may still have resonance with some of the direct evidence for early agriculture. Early farmsteads sometimes (but not always) display the impermanence that might be equated with the mobility associated with shifting agriculture. As Holocene pollen records proliferated, particularly in Europe and North America, evidence of fire episodes and temporary woodland clearances could be detected in a number of these sequences. Turning to the written record, a number of classical and historical authors seem to describe farming systems of this kind on the periphery of various civilized worlds. Thus, there are a range of plausible arguments that at least one element of earlier prehistoric agriculture was substantially dependent on fire clearance of woodland plots for temporary agrarian use. However, other Holocene sequences indicate sustained openings in the Neolithic woodland that endure for generations or centuries. The current evidence supports a global picture of Neolithic farming which is extremely diverse in resources, cultivation methods, and land use strategies across space and time.

Just as evidence of past agriculture has proliferated, so has our understanding grown of the recent slash-and-burn systems with which they were compared. Rather than being 'prehistoric relics', we are now more conscious of these systems as particular adaptations to tropical ecosystems and their hill-slope soils. Such aspects are not universally transferable to prehistoric landscapes elsewhere in the world. Nor is it the case that all agrarian ecosystems in the past may be expected to have a modern analogue in the ethnographic record. The past is proving more diverse than that.

Some general points may, however, be suggested for the world of earlier prehistoric farming landscapes. It will have been widely the case that in these landscapes, domesticated and undomesticated resources each played major roles in human subsistence. It will also have generally been the case that the key domesticated resources, while expanding beyond their point of origin, remained in the same general region of the world, retaining many adaptive traits effective in that region.

The later, intensive episode of agriculture has been similarly reimagined. Two important concepts in the development of ideas about this episode have been Karl Marx's 'Asiatic mode of production' theory, and Karl Wittfogel's *Oriental Despotism*. Each of these concepts drew upon their authors' understanding of heavily centralized and autocratic systems of governance in India and China, seen as centrally directing all key aspects of land use and management, in Wittfogel's case, with specific emphasis on the management of water. Both ideas have been critiqued in relation to how well, or poorly, the Chinese and Indian systems in question had been understood. The close relationship implied, between forms of despotic power and control on the one hand and the management of natural resources on the other, was further challenged by reference to an improved knowledge of how the Chinese and Indian systems operated, and how they came into being. Both historic and contemporary examples of complex and intricate water management systems were found which either lacked or preceded evidence of despotic elite dominance.

In a manner parallel to our reinterpretation of the earlier episode, we are now aware of a later prehistoric agrarian world which is much more diverse than that, but nonetheless displays some recurrent themes. Among those themes, the relationship between farmer and particular plots of land becomes perennial and enduring, and the commitment to the water flow, the soil, the animals, and some of the crops plants, of necessity is also perennial, with forward investment an integral part of the relationship. It is primarily intensive in terms of the energy in productive soils, which in turn is variously linked with animal power and metal technology.

Within the more varied and diverse prehistoric world we now envisage, it seems that the general theme of extensive and intensive farming episodes, each of a millennial scale, recurs in varying forms in several distinct regions of the world, in distinct material circumstances, with different scales of time, space, and ancestral lineage, and varying potential for political and social effects. While the episodes have some broad features in common, the evidence currently available indicates far more contingency from region to region than that implied in the more straightforward linear social evolutionary schemes popular in the early days of archaeology.

Home and the wanderer

Not far from the upper reaches of the Euphrates River and southeastern Turkey stands the remarkable site of Göblekli Teke. Today's visitors can admire the immaculately carved stone pillars, weighing up to 20 tonnes each, arranged more than 11,000 years ago in circles to mark a focal point in the landscape, a point to which communities returned for tens, possibly hundreds, of generations. The site lies at the heart of the most intensively studied region of early farming and the domestication of plants and animals in South West Asia, and is an emphatic early manifestation of marking a place and putting down roots. However, not only does it reveal evidence of marking a place of permanence, it coexists with parallel evidence of substantial mobility.

Dropped among the massive limestone slabs were a series of small blades fashioned from obsidian, a glassy volcanic rock. This is a material that can be chemically sourced; some of the Göbekli Teki obsidian blades are from Central Turkey, others from north eastern Turkey, but in each case they have travelled distances of around 300 miles.

ONE OF THE STONE PILLARS THAT, arranged in circles, defined focal points at Göblekli Teke, more than eleven thousand years ago, in southeastern Turkey near the upper reaches of the Euphrates River.

It might seem paradoxical that this settling down and intensive marking of particular places should facilitate greater mobility, but implicit in all human journeys is the prospect of return. The more secure that return, the more ambitious the potential journey may be. Mobile Palaeolithic hunters, travelling to follow the migrations of their prey, will return seasonally to the home base, and both that base and the seasonal camps leave archaeological traces. If the home base has the security of generations, marked out by ancestral monuments, then much longer journeys can be conceived and enacted. This may not apply to everyone, not even the majority; it is a reasonable conjecture that in prehistory, as in present, a majority of lives were lived within easy reach of many members of an extended family. Alongside these, a minority has been more accustomed to being away from home, and spending the night alone or with strangers. Such an accustomed state could enable that minority to cover vast distances, even continents, before returning home. Today that minority may be large, and the journey time measured in hours or, at most, days. In prehistory, the minority may have been smaller, and the journey measured in months, or perhaps years, but the potential to cross continents was also there.

Those two ways of being in the landscape—one putting down and affirming roots in explicit reference to lineage and ancestry, the other moving through the landscape, and following recurrent pasts—framed distinct ecological trajectories of the different communities in manners that were always intertwined, and the more secure the home, the more ambitious the potential journey.

Food globalization and the trans-Eurasian exchange

Some of the clearest signs of a new scale in cross-continental contact derive from the primary product of farming labour, the crops themselves. By the middle of the third millennium BCE, wheat domesticated in the Fertile Crescent of South West Asia had been transported through farming communities deep into central Asia, where it has been recovered from a prehistoric campsite on the slopes of Dzhunghar Mountains above Lake Balkhash in Kazakhstan. There is an enigmatic record of similar antiquity even further east at Zhaojiazhuang in the Chinese province of Shandong. Back on the Dzhunghar Mountain slopes, evidence survives of a Chinese cereal moving westwards. The earliest levels of a pastoralist hamlet at Begash, also of third millennium, conserve charred grains of broomcorn millet. A few centuries later in the Urmia Basin of Azerbaijan, the refuse deposits and hearths of the substantial settlement of Haftavan Tepe were yielding broomcorn millet grains in large quantities, and the southwest Asian cereals were widely cultivated and consumed in north and west China. Alongside the Asian millets, two species of buckwheat believed to originate from China are widely attested in the pollen records of European prehistory, suggesting that they too have crossed the continent at an early date.

Questions remain over how these crops moved over vast continental distances. As the earliest records predate the series of material cultural footprints that culminated in the 'Silk Route' of later epochs, we lack the more obvious material cues. However, that same lack may be an indication that movement did not entail the kind of elite recognized through their material wealth, and the visibility of that wealth among grave goods. Early appearances of crops a significant distance from the evolutionary home broadly coincide with the earliest appearance of metal and metallurgy in distinct cultural contexts across Eurasia. Both are phenomena repeatedly attested for the third millennium BCE and occasional possibilities of earlier dates still. However, the two patterns at this early period are geographically distinct, and within each of those patterns, there are distinct component patterns. While it is certainly the case that burials at Begash, where crops had arrived from both the east and the west, were occasionally adorned with bronze earrings or gold pendants, the metallurgists found across Eurasia's forest steppe to the north do not appear to have been supplementing their meaty diet with cereals of any kind. They may have made good use of wild plants found along the water's edge, but the northerly expansion of millet agriculture appears to be a phenomenon of the Iron Age.

If we return from the geography of early metallurgy to that of early crop movement, a distinct part of the landscape comes into view. Wheat and millet provide much of the detail, but they are not alone. By around 1600 BCE, a series of crop movements of this kind had coalesced into a continuous network of pathways linking much of Eurasia and also connecting with Africa. Prominent in the emerging pattern is a string of foothills tracing an interface between the hard geology of the high mountain, and the seasonally turbulent drainage of the plain. At the head of the intervening foothills, the soils were productive and the water flow manageable. These foothills had been critical in the fostering the cross-species intimacy of domestication. They were now critical in connecting communities and their resources over significant distances. The primary driver of movement is likely to have been the needs of grazing rather than either crops or goods. This followed the 'Inner Asian Mountain Corridor', forging a network that is subsequently used for the movement of a range of other goods and items, ultimately crystalizing into precursors of the Silk Road. In the changing phases of these networks, we can trace the spread of animals, crops, and artefacts. We can also reflect on the identities of the wanderers themselves.

Elite graves, conserving heirlooms and bounty from far and wide, are highly informative in tracing the later interconnections of the second millennium BCE, but for the earlier episodes of crop movement, we rely upon the crops themselves, and upon direct evidence of their consumption. Human skeletons from cemeteries dated to that period conserve evidence of that consumption in their bone chemistry. Differences in the stable carbon isotope balance in that bone chemistry provides us with a method to follow western crops moving east, and eastern crops moving west.

The first West Eurasians to have consumed millet (which ultimately derive from North China) on any scale were individuals living among Neolithic communities that ate differently. Such individuals have so far been identified in funerary remains in Iran, Greece, and Hungary dating to 3000 BCE and earlier; the Hungarian individual may be as early as the sixth millennium BCE. During the second millennium BCE the pattern of western millet consumption changes; in this millennium we encounter communities the majority, rather than the minority, of whom eat millet on a regular basis. Particularly in the second half of the millennium, these communities are known from Russia, Italy, and Greece. While they correspond to a time when East-West connections across Eurasia are emerging from several forms of evidence, no obvious correlation with other discernible cultural traits has thus far come to light.

The evidence for eastward movement of western crops to some extent mirrors this, in that a few records of charred grain indicate a scattered presence of western crops in third millennium China which, during the second millennium, crystalizes into a more coherent and sustained pattern. At the start of the second millennium, western crops make an emphatic and widespread impact upon the isotopic signature of human skeletal remains recovered from a key corridor between the East and West, the Hexi Corridor in Gansu Province. It appears that before 1900 BCE, no one in the Hexi Corridor supplemented millet harvests with western crops, whereas after 1900 BCE, everyone consumed substantial quantities of western cereals.

The incipient connections of the third millennium BCE that crystalized during the second into a global Old World network, most visible through the agricultural produce of ordinary communities with little legacy of visible wealth, is discernible in many different parts of Eurasia. A striking node of that global network is in North West India, which by the second millennium BCE had received crops from the Fertile Crescent, from North and South China, from various parts of South Asia, and from Africa. These all contributed to a multi-cropping system, well adapted to exploit both the winter and the summer rains.

Just as African crops, including sorghum, finger millet, cowpea, and hyacinth bean, make important contributions to prehistoric farming in India, so do Indian livestock to the ecological resilience of African Cattle. In Southern Asia, 'zebu' cattle are most easily recognized by their thoracic hump and pendulous dewlap. Among their less visible distinguishing features is a greater resilience to variable or fragmented water availability than their humpless 'taurine' relatives. Cattle indigenous to Africa are all of the 'taurine' form, whose water requirements restrict them to sufficiently moist regions of north and west Africa. At some stage during this early period of global contact and resource exchange, some Indian zebu bulls were crossed with some African taurine cows, and their drought-resilient progeny became a key resource in the southerly migration of Bantu-speaking populations, which had a profound impact on Africa's demography from the first millennium BCE.

Nature reframed

By the time *Homo sapiens* had reached the southern tip of each of the world's vegetated continents, the global climate was set upon a course of amelioration from the harsh glacial epoch and its final severe thermal downturn in the Younger Dryas. For the next few millennia, pioneer woodlands would progressively encroach upon the open grasslands and tundra landscapes that had reached their greatest expanse during the cold period. Richer, deeper, more diverse woodlands would, in turn, replace these pioneer woodlands, and the whole wooded landscape would extend to a point at which only the coldest peripheries, the driest interiors, and the highest altitude remained open and treeless.

Through that ameliorating landscape our own species spread across a remarkable array of biomes, often following the interface between ecosystems, such as along the various woodland edges. Our impact on those ecological boundaries would ultimately be considerable, through cultivation and pastoralism pushing back the edge between grassland and woodland, and that between desert and grassland. As the warming climate clothed the terrestrial surface of the planet with deeper vegetation, successive generations of farmers would render it shallow again, and populate the open spaces with domesticated plants and animals.

The Holocene climatic optimum had already ended by the time domesticated species had themselves moved far from their regions of origin, crossing vast expanses of Eurasia to contribute to the intermingling of indigenous and exotic resources. The general trend of global temperatures was one of decline.

That overall trend was punctuated on occasion by episodes of more abrupt change. The world 5,900 years ago and 4,200 years ago experienced and then recovered from sharp downturns in temperature, in many regions precipitating periods of drought. In places, the timing of that latter downturn coincides with the ending of sustained periods of settlement enlargement and elaboration. In the regions where it occurred, that ending has been interpreted and narrated as 'civilization collapse'. It indeed seems reasonable to infer the changes were associated with substantial modifications in the organization of society, and that a pronounced fluctuation in climate might be linked in time to a demise of the institutions of political organization and control. Whether or not the lowly farmers in the arena of their control were doing better or worse is less easy to determine. One thing that may be inferred is that their options for adaptation had changed.

In comparison with the first farmers, as a consequence of the global movement of food resources, communities of the third millennium BCE enjoyed an enlarged suite of strategies for mitigating the effects of the climate. The continental mingling of food resources expanded their options for response to temperature, nutrient, and water availability, even to the pattern and structure of the seasons.

The first farmers had been locked into their local seasons by the tight coupling to those seasons of the plants upon which they depended. The more crops moved around and crossed continental distances, the more detached they became from their seasonal context. A number of these crops lost their seasonal sensitivity, such that the farmer could control the timing of their growth. Multiple, sequential cropping was possible, so long as the right mix of local and exogenous crops was available, water availability could be managed, and soil temperatures mitigated by cultivation. With animals stalled over winter, and crops grown on the same land in succession, the seasons did not disappear, but were nonetheless significantly adjusted with the potential of greater, and more sustainable, agricultural productivity.

Conclusion

This chapter opened by remarking on the scale of the human journey that reached this point, a journey surpassing that previously made by any of our hominid relatives. Each preceding hominid species was at some point contained within an ecological border separating the world's major terrestrial biomes. Our own species has managed to transcend each of those borders to become a global taxon. This epoch of the global human has often been portrayed as a 'conquest over nature'. While 'conquest' may be a little too theatrical a concept for today's more nuanced ecological analyses of the past, the epoch is clearly marked out by a series of human engagements with nature whose outcome is conspicuous and enduring, marking our human action as a global force.

The first of these is the clearance of vegetation from large tracts of land. It was by no means an expectation of the first researchers to examine of deep pollen sequences that they would encounter a prehistoric pollen signal that could not be fully explained by fluctuations in climate. The recognition of a Neolithic 'Elm Decline' across many parts of northwest Europe changed that perception, and opened the way for a whole series of detections of 'anthropogenic indicators' and substantial woodland clearances of both short and long duration. Further research recognized fire and clearance as associated with some hunter-gatherers in search of game, and not confined solely to the activities of farming communities.

Throughout the period covered by this chapter, such clearances can be charted, and their considerable significance observed within particular human landscapes. If we move back, and view the world on a larger scale, we would see those disturbances coalescence into a distinct pattern of shifting boundaries between extant ecological zones. The boundaries of woodlands have retreated in the advance of heathlands and grasslands, whose own boundaries have in turn retreated with the advance of deserts, progressively more starved of life. These anthropic boundary fluctuations have many similarities to those instigated by the cooling of the climate. Human action in this case can be thought of as a change in the pace of an ongoing theme of boundary shift in nature.

The second of these human engagements has been genetic. Farming has resulted in widespread modification of the genotypes of a series of plants and animals that make an ever-increasing contribution to the world's biosphere, and extend the proportion of that biosphere that depends upon humans to complete its reproductive cycle. While the active transformation of genetic makeup is most directly seen in the exploited plants and animals themselves, the genetic consequences of farming have been manifest across the human food chain. A wide range of diseases and parasites of plants, animals, and humans underwent an evolutionary explosion in the context of animal management and settled agriculture. The diversity of humans themselves became significantly shaped by the expansion of farming communities across the globe.

The third engagement is both the least visible and arguably the most consequential. The earth's atmosphere today comprises approximately four-fifths nitrogen and one-fifth oxygen. Two gases occurring at much lower quantities are carbon dioxide (around one part in 25) and methane (around one part in 5,000). While these proportions are small, and only detectable with sensitive scientific equipment, there is much current debate about their elevation as a consequence of human action, and the dangers to which the global biosphere is consequently exposed. Much of that elevation is attributed to the industrial and modern eras, and the associated burning of fossil fuels. However, the deflection of these gas concentrations from their expected paths could have begun much earlier.

One way of assessing such a deflection is to compare the changing gas levels through time during the Holocene with the equivalent fluctuations in previous interglacials. Such comparisons have prompted inferences that carbon dioxide levels departed from its expected course around the time of the first expansion of farming and the extensive clearance it entailed. Methane levels followed that pattern a few millennia later, perhaps in association with the expansion of rice paddy farming. By the close of the period under consideration in this chapter, these gases had elevated above their equivalent levels interpolated from preceding interglacials by between 20 per cent and 50 per cent. Some have taken those elevations to mark the end of the Holocene epoch that had framed the cross-continental journey of our species. A new geological epoch, the 'Anthropocene', has been proposed in which human action becomes the primary driver of the global ecosystem.

The core theme of epoch examined in this chapter has been a novel manner in which the one surviving species of *Homo* engaged with nature. That novel engagement affected all but one of the world's continents. It impacted substantially on the planet's sedimentary processes and the formation of its soils. It radically changed the balance of plant, animal, and microbial species, reconfiguring the genetics and reproductive behaviour of many of them. Most critically of all, it began to have a measurable impact upon the gas balance within the atmosphere upon which the whole system depended. Whether or not that constitutes 'conquest', it is demonstrably the case that, from this period of prehistory onwards, the dynamics of the planet at every level would be shaped by human action.

CHAPTER 4

The Farmers' Empires

Climax and Crises in Agrarian States and Cities

FELIPE FERNÁNDEZ-ARMESTO

ACCELERATED cultural divergence—a greater number of societies increasingly different from each other—was the most conspicuous global consequence of the changes that accompanied the spread and intensification of agriculture. The history of how, in the long period covered in this chapter, agrarian peoples became increasingly differentiated from one another is best traversed in two phases. In the first phase, in widely separated places around the world between the fifth and third millennia BCE, we can track divergence through common experiences: intensified settlement; growing concentrations of population; multiplying social categories and functions of government; emerging states and, in some cases, their transformation into empires; and increasingly diversified and specialized economic activity. Developments in four areas—Egypt, Mesopotamia, and the valleys of the Indus and Yellow Rivers (in what are now Pakistan and China respectively)—claim special attention, because, albeit on an exceptional scale, they were representative of global developments. To explain the sometimes fatal, always transmutative changes that occurred in the second phase, towards or around the late second millennium, we shall have to broaden focus again, to take in comparable common experience in the regions where our world tour starts, in the Mediterranean and, first, the New World.

The spread and growth of dense settlements and large states

The Americas

The earliest known large settlements in the hemisphere began to appear in the fourth millennium BCE on alluvial plains in coastal Peru, in the region north of present-day Lima, especially in the Supe Valley. By the mid-third millennium, mounds at Aspero supported half a dozen platforms and terraces with large, complex dwellings and storehouses. Political order was tight: supervisors could measure workers' labour thanks to the uniform containers that held the rubble. In a grave under a grinding stone, an infant lay daubed with red ochre, wrapped in textiles, and scattered with hundreds of beads—evidence of inherited wealth and, perhaps, power in a grain-dependent economy, where a flour-making tool marked the difference between life and death. Covering over 32 acres, Aspero must have had a population uniquely big by the standards of the Americas at the time; but the region contained many centres of up to 3,000 inhabitants, where people exchanged the products of different ecosystems—marine shells, mountain foodstuffs, and featherwork from the brightly coloured birds of the forests east of the Andes.

About 3,500 years ago, experiments in civilization spread from alluvial areas on the Peruvian coast to less obviously favourable environments. In Cerro Sechín, only about 300 feet higher, an astounding settlement existed in about 1500 BCE on a site of about 12 acres dominated by a stone platform, where rites of victory seem to have been celebrated. Still visible in effigy, hundreds of warriors slash their victims in two, exposing entrails or severing heads. By about 1200 BCE, nearby Sechín Alto was one of the world's great ceremonial complexes, with gigantic mounds and monumental buildings arrayed along two boulevard-like spaces, each more than a mile long. The biggest mound is almost 140 feet tall. These places, and others like them, suggest new experiments to manage the environment and coordinate food production, and the violent carvings of Cerro Sechín show the price paid in blood to defend or enlarge them.

In the same period, farther up the coast, new settlements took shape around the Cupisnique gorge. Though the environment was similar, the physical remains suggest

A PLUMED FIGURE AMONG SEVERED HEADS at Cerro Sechín in Peru, *c.* 1500 BCE.

a different culture and different politics: extraordinary cultural diversity among connected communities within a fairly small space. Huaca de los Reyes, for instance, had dozens of stucco-fronted buildings and colonnades of fat pillars guarded by huge, sabre-toothed clay heads. At Pampa de Caña Cruz, a similar head stared from a 170-foot-long mosaic made of thousands of fragments of coloured rock embedded in the earth, so that a viewer could only appreciate its shape from a great height, which the humans who made it could not reach, but their gods, perhaps, could. Building on a monumental scale followed soon afterward in the nearby highlands.

Most Andean experiments in civilization were short lived. With modest technologies, they struggled to survive in unstable environments. El Niño—the periodic reversal of the normal flow of Pacific currents—was always a threat. At irregular intervals, usually once or twice a decade, El Niño drenches the region in torrential rain and kills or diverts the usually ample supply of ocean fish. Andean civilizations also faced adverse consequences of success when population levels outgrew food supplies, over-exploitation impoverished the soil, or envious neighbours unleashed wars.

Meanwhile, in Mesoamerica in the second millennium BCE, the culture we call Olmec arose in what is now southern Mexico, where the swamps of Tabasco had supported agriculture for at least 1,000 years. We can picture the Olmecs with the help of portraits they left: huge sculpted heads, carved from stones and columns of basalt, each of up to 40 tons, toted or dragged over distances of up to 100 miles. Some have

HUGE BASALT HEADS REVEAL THE FEATURES OF OLMEC GODS OR HEROES—or at least the faces the sculptors wanted beholders to see.

jaguar-like masks or squat heads, with almond eyes, parted lips, and sneers of cold command: shaman-rulers, perhaps, with the power of divine self-transformation.

The Olmec chose settlement sites near mangrove swamps and rain forest, close to beach and ocean, where they could exploit varied environments. Marshy lakes, full of aquatic prey, attracted settlers. Mounds dredged for farming from the swamp became the models for ceremonial platforms, and between them, canals flowed with fish and turtles. The earliest known ceremonial centre, around 1200 BCE, was on a rise above the river Coatzalcos. La Venta, built with stones toted and rolled from more than 100 km away, soon followed, deep among the mangrove swamps on the Tonalá River, where a mound over 30 m tall was a setting for the most important rituals. In one of the ceremonial courts the builders buried a mosaic pavement that resembles a jaguar mask. Similar buried offerings were placed under other buildings, perhaps the way some Christians bury relics from saints in the foundations and altars of churches. By about 1000 BCE, nearby San Lorenzo had substantial reservoirs and drainage systems integrated into a plan of causeways, plazas, platforms, and mounds. Dense settlements clustered around the ceremonial centres.

How and why did these ambitious attempts to modify the environment begin? Monumental building requires ample food supplies to support manpower and generate spare energy. Many scholars still believe that the Olmecs could have produced sufficient food by slashing forest clearings, setting fire to the stumps, and planting seeds directly in the ash. However, it is more likely that the transition to city-building began with the exploitation of high-yielding varieties of maize. With beans and squash, maize provided complete nourishment. The three plants together were so important to Olmec life that they appeared on gods' and chieftains' headgear. Although the evidence is scanty, it looks as if a determined, visionary leadership energized by shamanism drove Olmec civilization forward. Archaeologists found buried in sand—perhaps as an offering—an exquisite scene of what seems to be a ceremony in progress, in which carved figures with misshapen heads, as if with skulls deliberately deformed, stand in a rough circle of upright stone slabs. They wear nothing but loincloths and ear ornaments. Their mouths are open, their postures relaxed. Similar figures include a small creature, half jaguar, half human. Others carry torches on phallic staffs, or kneel or sit in a restless posture, as if ready to be transformed from shaman into jaguar. For the rites of transformation, Olmecs built stepped platforms—forerunners or perhaps early examples of the angular mounds and pyramids typical of later New World civilizations.

Rulers were buried dressed in ritual garb as fantastic creatures: caiman's body and nose; jaguar's eyes and mouth; feathered eyebrows that evoke raised hands. They lay in pillared chambers with bloodletting tools of jade or stingray spine. We can still see their images carved on benchlike thrones of basalt, where they sat to shed blood—their own and their captives'. One of the carvings shows a throne with a submissive figure roped to an eagle-crested character, who leans outward as if to address an audience.

Those who believe in the diffusionist theory of civilization have hailed the Olmecs as the mother civilization of the Americas. Diffusionism states, in brief, that

AN OLMEC RITUAL AS A SCULPTOR SAW IT: naked figures with distorted—perhaps deliberately deformed—heads gather before monoliths.

civilization is such an extraordinary achievement that we can credit only a few gifted peoples with creating it. It then diffused—or spread by example and instruction—to others who were less inventive. The theory is almost certainly false. Nevertheless, Olmec influence seems to have spread widely in Mesoamerica and perhaps beyond. Many aspects of Olmec life became characteristic of later New World civilizations: mound building; a tendency to seek balance and symmetry in art and architecture; ambitious urban planning around angular temples and plazas; specialized elites, including chieftains commemorated in monumental art; rites of rulership involving bloodletting and human sacrifice; a religion rooted in shamanism with bloody rites of sacrifice and ecstatic performances by kings and priests; and agriculture based on maize, beans, and squash.

Eurasia

The New World pattern can be summed up as that of the emergence of agrarian states and cities. Compared, however, with similar changes across Eurasia, the process in the Americas was tardy, patchy and, in most cases, modest. The best available explanation

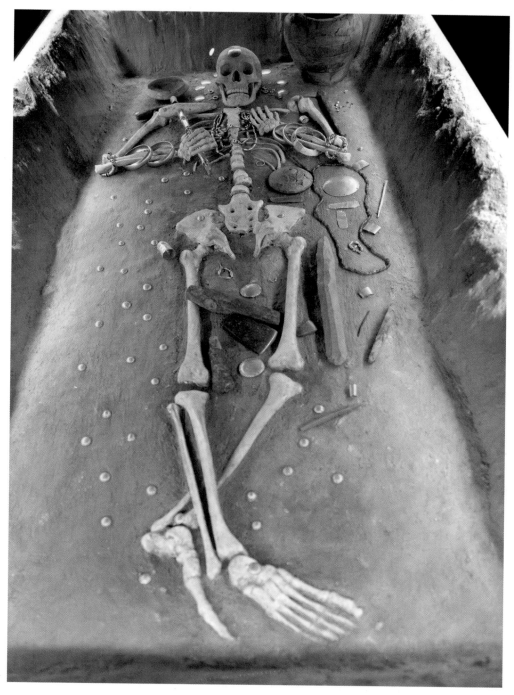

THE FABULOUSLY RICH COPPER-AGE CHIEF, buried at Varna in Bulgaria, with many hundreds of gold ornaments, including a sheath for his penis.

is that isolation—a consequence of the untraversable geography that separated New Word centres of civilization—retards change, whereas continuities of climate, navigable seas, and long-range land-routes encouraged cultural exchange and stimulated development across much of Eurasia.

However that may be, in parts of eastern Europe around the turn of the fifth and fourth millennia, innovations in technology and government appeared without, as far as we know, any influence from outside the region. In the shadow of the Carpathian Mountains, Europe's oldest copper mine at Rudna Glava, above the middle Danube River in modern Serbia, was a centre of early metallurgy. In Tisza, in what is now Hungary, smelters worked copper into beads and small tools—a 'magical' process that made smiths mythical. In Bulgaria, in gold-rich hills, trenches and palisades surrounded settlements with gateways exactly aligned at the points of the compass, as in later Roman army camps. No place in prehistoric Europe gleams more astonishingly than Varna on the Black Sea, where a chief was buried clutching a gold-handled axe, with his penis sheathed in gold, and nearly 1,000 gold ornaments, including hundreds of discs that must have spangled on a dazzling coat. From nearby Tartaria in Romania, markings on clay tablets look uncannily like writing.

Also around 5000 BCE, a little to the east at Sredny Stog on the middle Dnieper, the earliest known domesticators of horses filled middens with horse bones. As if for use in an afterlife, in graves five millennia old, wagons lie, arched with hoops and designed to rumble behind oxen on vast wheels of solid wood: evidence that rich chiefs could carry out ambitious building projects despite a herding life that required constant mobility. Few other societies were rich enough to bury objects of such size and value. Central Eurasia became a birthplace for transportation technologies: the earliest recognizable chariot dates from early in the third millennium BCE in the southern Urals.

Even more mysterious structures adorn an extensive area to the south, stretching from the Zagros Mountains eastward to Baluchistan. People at Susa, for instance, built a terraced mound of mud bricks more than 75 m square and 10 m high, nearly 1,000 years before the earliest Mesopotamian ziggurats. From a slightly later date, the same excavations have yielded cylinders of colourful stone, carved with the façades of many-windowed buildings.

Meanwhile, monumental building projects, on a scale only agriculture could sustain and only a state could organize, were underway in the Mediterranean. The remains of the first known large stone dwellings are on Malta. Here, in the fourth and third millennia BCE, at least half a dozen limestone temples arose around spacious courts shaped like clover leaves. Inside one building, so-called sleeping beauties, made of clay, attended a colossal, big-hipped goddess. There were altars and wall carvings—some in spirals, some with deer and bulls—and thousands of bodies piled in communal graves.

On Europe's Atlantic edge at about the same time or soon afterwards luxury objects found markets, and monumental buildings arose. Beside aristocrats' bones, buried

ONE OF THE WORLD'S OLDEST SURVIVING STONE EDIFICES: a temple at Tarxien in Malta.

THE CARVED 'SLEEPING BEAUTIES' OF TARXIEN attended this well-dressed, big-hipped sleeper.

possessions defined high status and still evoke a way of life—weapons of war and drinking cups that once held liquor or poured offerings to gods. Chiefs lay under enormous standing stones, near stone circles probably designed to resemble the forest glades that preceded them as places of worship. In the Orkneys, for instance, an elaborate tomb at Maes Howe is close to a temple building, filled with light on midsummer's day. Nearby stone rings hint at attempts to monitor the sun and, perhaps, control nature by magic. A stone-built village to the west has hearths and fitted furniture still in place. It is tempting to imagine a far-flung colonial station here, preserving the styles and habits of a distant home in southwest Britain and northwest France, where similar but bigger tombs and stone circles are found.

In the world of increasing diversification, four river valley areas stand out: the middle and lower Nile in Egypt; the so-called Harappan region of the Indus and the now dried-up Saraswati; Mesopotamia, between and around the Tigris and Euphrates in what is now Iraq; and China's Yellow River. In these areas, people exploited more land and changed at a faster pace than elsewhere; they modified the landscape with fields and irrigation works, and smothered it with monumental buildings. Their ruins and relics still inspire advertisers, artists, Hollywood screenwriters, toy makers, and computer game designers, and they shape our ideas of what civilizations ought to be. When we hear the word 'civilization', we picture Egyptian pyramids, sphinxes, and mummies; Chinese bronzes, jades, and clays; Mesopotamian ziggurats and writing tablets scarred with cuneiform; or we conjure the windblown wrecks of almost-vanished cities in landscapes turning to desert. We call them seminal civilizations, as if they were seed plots from which civilized achievements spread around the world, or great civilizations, and we begin our conventional histories of civilization by describing them. If we consider them together we can see how relentless divergence opened cultural chasms inside a common ecological framework of gradually warming, drying climate; relatively dry soils; and a reliance on seasonally flooding rivers and, therefore, on irrigation.

The populations surely numbered growing millions, crowding the heartlands. In Egypt people spread fairly uniformly throughout the narrow floodplain of the Nile but in the early third millennium BCE lower Mesopotamia was already a land of cities, each home to its own deity and king. Ur had royal tombs of staggering wealth and towering ziggurats, so impressive that centuries later, people venerated the biggest of them as a work of gods. In any Harappan city of the same era, a citizen would have felt as at home as in any other, for streetscapes and dwellings were everywhere much the same. Every brick was uniform. Mohenjodaro was big enough to house perhaps 50,000 or 60,000 people and Harappa, over 30,000. No other settlements were anything like as big, but there were plenty of them—at least 1,500 known to archaeologists. Parts of China, too, gradually acquired an urban look. In the second millennium BCE frontier towns—modest places like Panlongcheng in Hubei, with a governor's house surrounded by a colonnade of 43 pillars—charted the spread of civilization and the growth of states.

The common environment suited tyranny, or, at least, strong states exercising minute control over subjects' lives. On the banks of silt-bearing, flood-prone rivers security of life demanded collective action to manage the floods. The mace head of an Egyptian king of the fourth millennium BCE shows him digging a canal. Proverbially, a just judge was 'a dam for the sufferer, guarding lest he drown', a corrupt one 'a flowing lake'. From Larsa in Mesopotamia, the archive of an irrigation contractor named Lu-igisa has survived from around 2000 BCE He surveyed land for canal building, organized pay and provisions, and supervised digging and the dredging. Procuring workers was the key task—5,400 to dig a canal and 1,800 on one occasion for emergency repairs. Lu-igisa had the potentially profitable job of controlling the opening and closing of the locks that released or shut off the water supplies. He was bound by oaths enforced by threat of loss. 'What is my sin,' he complained to a higher official when he lost control of a canal, 'that the king took my canal from me and gave it to Etellum?'

It is tempting to attribute loss of freedom to the rise of a strong leader, but the one does not necessarily have to follow from the other. In ancient Egypt, the most common image of the state was of a flock the king tended like a herdsman. The comparison probably reflects political ideas of earlier herder communities: farming involves more competition for space than herding does. Disputes and wars over land strengthen rulership. Increased war and wealth would also shift patriarchs and elders out of supreme office in favour of stronger and wiser leaders.

Women, perhaps, suffered most. A shift from matrilineal to patrilineal descent accompanied rapidly rising birth rates, which tied women to child rearing. To judge from surviving Mesopotamian law codes and Chinese texts, women's talents became increasingly focused on the family. Yet outside the home, urban life created new opportunities for specialized female labour. Women and children, for instance, were the textile workers in Ashur in northern Mesopotamia and probably wove cotton in Harappan cities. Art, meanwhile, depicted them in servile roles, like those of Harappa's pouting, languid bronze dancing girls—or are they temple prostitutes? Women, however, could exercise power as rulers, prophetesses, and priestesses. Domestic life gave them informal opportunities. Surviving texts demonstrate their rights to initiate divorce, to recover property, and, sometimes, to win additional compensation from former husbands. A wife, says the Egyptian *Book of Instructions*, 'is a profitable field. Do not contend with her at law and keep her from gaining control'.

The need to warehouse and guard food also empowered rulers. In societies that rely on a narrow range of crops, food shortages are a routine hazard, especially in the unproductive season before the harvest. The biblical story of Joseph, an Israelite who became a pharaoh's chief official and saved Egypt from starvation, recalls 'seven lean years'. Such bad spells were part of folk memories, as were times when 'every man ate his children'. Defying nature meant stockpiling against disaster. A tomb scene in Amarna shows a storehouse with only six rows of stacked victuals, including grain sacks and heaps of dried fish, laid on shelves supported on brick pillars. The temple

DANCING GIRLS—FORERUNNERS, perhaps, of the temple prostitutes of later Indian tradition—are among the few sculptures of human subjects to survive from the Harappan civilization that vanished in the third millennium BCE.

built to house the corpse of Rameses II, who probably ruled around 1300 BCE (no dates in ancient Egyptian chronology are certain), had storehouses big enough to feed 20,000 people for a year. The taxation yields proudly painted on the walls of a high official's tomb are an illustrated menu for feeding an empire: sacks of barley, piles of cakes and nuts, hundreds of head of livestock. The state as stockpiler existed, it seems, not to redistribute goods but for famine relief.

To legitimize royal power, theorists appealed to deities. In Egypt they spoke of the king as a god. In the diplomatic correspondence known as the Amarna letters, the ruler of a city in Palestine around 1350 BCE wrote, 'To the king my lord and my Sun-god, I am Lab'ayu thy servant and the dirt whereon thou dost tread.' Some 400 years earlier, a father, Sehetep-ib-Re, wrote advice to his children—'a counsel of eternity and a manner of living rightly'. The king 'illumines Egypt more than the sun; he makes the land greener than does the Nile.' What did Egyptians mean when they said their king was a god? They made images and shrines as places where the gods could manifest themselves: the image 'was' the god only when the god inhabited it. The pharaoh's person could provide a similar opportunity for a god to take up residence.

In Egypt law remained in the mouth of the divine pharaoh. The need to put it in writing was never strong. Instead, religion defined a moral code that the state could not easily modify or subvert. Around 2000 BCE, a new idea of afterlife emerged. Earlier tombs were antechambers to a life for which the world was practical training. Those built later, where wall paintings show the gods weighing the souls of the dead, were places of interrogation after a moral preparation for the next life. Typically, the deceased's heart lay in one scale, balanced in the other by a feather symbolizing truth. Anubis, jackal-headed god of the underworld, supervised the scales. Examined souls renounced long lists of sins, typically of sacrilege, sexual perversion, and the abuse of power against the weak. Good deeds replied: obedience to human laws and divine will, acts of mercy, offerings to the gods and the spirits of ancestors, bread to the hungry, clothing to the naked, 'and a ferry for him who was marooned'. The reward of the good was a new life in the company of Osiris, the sometime ruler of the universe. For those who failed the test, the punishment was extinction.

In Mesopotamia, kings were not gods, which is probably why the earliest known law codes come from there. The codes of Ur from the third millennium BCE are fragmentary—essentially, lists of fines. But that of King Lipit-Ishtar of Sumer and Akkad, around 2000 BCE, explained that the laws were ordained 'in accordance with the word of Enlil', the supreme god, to make 'children support the father and the father children, . . . abolish enmity and rebellion, cast out weeping and lamentation, . . . bring righteousness and truth and give well-being'. Hammurabi, ruler of Babylon in the first half of the 1700s BCE, gets undue credit because his code survived intact, having been carried off as a war trophy to Persia. Engraved in stone, it shows the king receiving the text from the hands of a god. It substituted for the physical presence and words of the ruler. 'Let any oppressed man who has a cause come into the presence of the statue of me, the king of justice, and then read carefully my inscribed stone, and give heed to my precious words. May my stone make his case clear to him.' These were not laws as we know them, handed down by tradition or enacted to restrain the ruler's power. Rather, they were means to perpetuate royal commands. Obedience was severely enforced in Mesopotamia—to the vizier in the fields, the father in the household, the king in everything. 'The king's word,' says a representative text, 'like a god's, cannot be changed.' Even if we had no written evidence to confirm it, royal power would gleam from luxurious artefacts that filled rulers' tombs: a gilded harp carved in the form of a ram; dice and gaming boards of inlaid shell and polished stone; lively animals sculpted in gold and silver with eyes of shell and lapis lazuli; tapering vessels of gold, and golden cups modelled on ostrich eggs. In Mesopotamian carvings, the king is commonly the biggest figure in any scene that includes him. He drinks. He receives supplicants who petition for help and citizens and ambassadors who pay tribute. He presides over armies and processions of chariots drawn by asses. He carries bricks to build cities and temples, purifying them with fire and consecrating them with oil. To form

A SUMERIAN LAW CODE OF THE
LATE THIRD MILLENNIUM BCE,
inscribed on a clay cylinder.

the first brick from mud was the king's exclusive right. Bricks from the state kilns were stamped with royal names. Royal seals make plain why this was the case. They show gods building the world out of mud, which they mix, carry up ladders, and fling to the men who set bricks, layer by layer. The transformation of mud into city was royal magic.

Oracles—means of supposed access to knowing the future—told kings what to do. Augurs were the hereditary interpreters of oracles. They read the will of the gods in the livers of sacrificed sheep, in the drift of incense, and, above all, in the movements of heavenly bodies. Their predictions of royal victory, danger, anger, and recovery from sickness fill surviving records. Religion, however, did not necessarily limit royal power. Normally, kings controlled oracles. Sometimes they slept in temples to induce prophetic dreams, especially during a crisis, such as the failure of the Nile floods. Of course, the predictions they reported may have merely legitimated the policies they had already decided to follow.

Yet these rulers were there to serve the people: to mediate with the gods on behalf of the whole society, to organize the collective effort of tillage and irrigation, to warehouse food against hard times, and to redistribute it for the common good. A comic dialogue from Akkad illustrates the delicate politics and economics of control of the food supply in the second millennium BCE. 'Servant, obey me,' the master begins.

> I shall give food to our country.
> Give it, my lord, give it. The man who gives food to his country keeps his
>   own barley and gets rich on the interest other people pay him.
> No, my servant, I shall not give food to my country.
> Do not give, my lord, do not give. Giving is like loving . . . or like having a son. . . .
>   They will curse you. They will eat your barley and destroy you.

The most famous relic of ancient Mesopotamian literature, the epic of *Gilgamesh*, sheds further light on the nature of leadership, or at least of heroism, on which leadership is modelled. In the surviving versions, written down perhaps about 1800 BCE, the natural forces that moulded the Mesopotamian environment shaped the story. When Gilgamesh, hero of the poem, confronts a monster who breathes fire and plague, the gods blind the creature with a scorching wind. When he explores the Ocean of Death to find the secret of immortality, Gilgamesh encounters the only family to have survived a primeval flood. The disaster, wrought by divine whim, had destroyed the rest of the human race and even left the gods themselves 'cowering like dogs crouched against a wall'.

The poets' Gilgamesh is an invention, embroidered onto the stuff of legends. But there was a real Gilgamesh, too, or at least a king of that name in historical sources. The poem quotes a proverbial saying about the historical Gilgamesh: 'Who has ever ruled with power like his?' He was the fifth king recorded in the city of Uruk around 2700 BCE (according to the most widely favoured chronology). Some of the genuine wonders of the city appear during his reign—its walls, its gardens, the pillared hall where the deity dwelt at the heart of the city.

The earliest recorded kingship traditions of China resemble those of Egypt and Mesopotamia. They show the same connection between royal status and the management of water resources and the distribution of food. The legendary engineer—Emperor Yu the Great—was praised for having 'mastered the waters and caused them to flow in great channels'. Early folk poetry describes a period of city building after his time, so fast 'that the drums could not keep pace'. The legendary ruler Tan-fu

> 'made them build houses,'
> Their plumb-lines were straight.
> They lashed the boards and erected the frames.

The earliest China we know of was a unitary state. The dynasty known as Shang dominated the Yellow River valley for most of the second millennium, evoked in inscriptions on animal bones and turtle shells, which professional diviners heated to breaking point before reading the gods' answers to kings' questions along the lines of the cracks. The king, as the readings reveal, was most often engaged in war and sometimes in diplomacy. Marriage was part of it; later emperors called it 'extending my favour'. To their soldiers, 'our prince's own concerns' rolled them 'from misery to misery' and gave them homes 'like tigers and buffaloes . . . in desolate wilds'. Above all, the king was a mediator with the gods, performing sacrifices, reading oracles, breaking the soil, praying for rain, and founding towns. He spent half his

ANCIENT CHINESE 'ORACLE BONES' OR TURTLE shells were heated in fire until they cracked. The pattern of the fissures was the diviners' clue to the future.

time hunting—presumably as a way to entertain counsellors and ambassadors, train horsemen, and add meat to his diet. Scholars claim to detect an increasingly businesslike tone in the oracles. References to dreams and sickness diminish as time goes on, the style becomes terser and the tone more optimistic. Sometimes the bones reveal revolutions in the conduct of rites from reign to reign, evidence that kings fought tradition and tried to give the world a stamp of their own. Tsu Jia, for instance, a king of the late second millennium BCE, discontinued sacrifices to mythical ancestors, mountains, and rivers and increased those to historical figures. Beyond reasonable doubt, he was modifying the practices of the longest-lived and most renowned of his dynasty, Wu Ding.

The chronology is uncertain, but Wu Ding must have ruled about 1400 BCE He was remembered 1,000 years later as a conqueror who ruled his empire as easily 'as rolling it on his palm'. One of his 64 consorts was buried in the richest known tomb of the period, with her human servants, dogs, horses, hundreds of bronzes and jades, and thousands of cowrie shells, which were used as money. Although there is room for confusion because of the court habit of calling different people by the same name, court records probably identify her correctly. Wu Ding repeatedly consulted the oracles about her childbeds and sickbeds. She was one of his three principal wives, and not only wife and mother, but an active participant in politics. She had a domain of her own, including a walled town, and could mobilize 3,000 warriors on command.

By taking over the divination of bones and turtle shells, the king transferred the most important political functions of magic and religion—foretelling the future and interpreting the will of the spirits—to the state. No longer in the hands of diviners, recording and preserving the results of divination became a secular—or nonreligious—function. The king became the guardian of a secular bureaucracy—a slowly developing corps of court historians, who could acquire experience on which predictions could be based more reliably than on the shamans' supposed insights.

At this stage, the Chinese viewed kingship in practical terms—how well the ruler looked after his subjects. Shang rulers claimed to have come to power as executors of divine justice against an earlier—doubtless mythical—dynasty, the Xia, whose last representative had forfeited his right to rule by 'neglecting husbandry': failing, that is, in his duty to look after the realm as a farmer cares for his fields. The earliest scholars' texts that describe the emergence of China probably reflect traditional propaganda fairly accurately. They depict kind, generous rulers who fostered the arts of peace. The Yellow Emperor, a mythical figure, was credited with inventing the carriage, the boat, the bronze mirror, the cooking pot, the crossbow, 'and a kind of football'. Poems and popular legends, however, reveal more of the bloody business of kingship, which inherited ancient clan leaders' rights of life and death. An axe engraved with the emblems of the executioner—hungry smiles and devouring teeth—signified the original term for rulership. 'Bring your tongues under the rule of law', says a late Shang ruler in an approving poet's lines, 'lest punishment come upon you when repentance will be of no avail.' Wealth and warfare were inseparable essentials of kingship. The tombs of Shang rulers around 1500 BCE display the nature of their power: thousands of strings of cowrie shells, bronze axes and chariots, lacquer ware, and hundreds of intricately carved treasures of jade and bone. The greatest treasures were bronzes of unparalleled quality, cast in ceramic moulds. Bronze making was the supreme art of Shang China, and its products were a privilege of rank. Thousands of human sacrifices, buried with kings to serve them in the next world or to sanctify their tombs, were—to those who buried them—among the cheapest sacrifices.

In the Indus Valley, in present-day Pakistan and western India, the Harappan world exhibited extraordinary consistency in urban layout and building design did not necessarily arise from political unity. Hierarchically ordered dwelling spaces hint at a class or even a more rigid caste structure. In a class system, individuals can rise or fall through the ranks of society. In a caste system they are stuck with the status with which they are born. In Harappan cities, the extensive communal quarters must have had something to do with the organization of manpower—soldiers, perhaps, or slaves or scholars. Huge warehouses suggest a system to distribute food. The waste-disposal system looks like a masterpiece of urban planning, with clay pipes laid under the streets. The uniform bricks must have come from state kilns and pans. The imposing citadels or fortresses enclosed spaces that might have had an elite function, like the spacious bathing tank at Mohenjodaro. Harappan sites, however, have no rich graves, and the absence of kingly quarters or regal furnishings tempts us to imagine Harappan societies as republics or theocracies, god-centred governments run by priests.

For a society like Harappa's, whose writings we cannot read, we would hope to learn something from works of art. But no pictorial art has survived, and Harappan artists seem to have produced little sculpture, except on a small scale in clay and sometimes bronze. One extraordinary figure from Mohenjodaro, of great seriousness, with almond eyes and rigidly fluted beard, wears a headband with what looks like the setting for a gem. He has a rich garment slung over one shoulder and extends what is left of his arm in what must surely have been a symbolic or ritual gesture. He has been called a priest-king or a philosopher-king, but these romantic terms are valueless. Although just about everything in Harappan politics remains mysterious, the reach of the culture seems so vast it is hard to imagine how it can have spread so far, into a range of different environments, except by force of arms. A sense of what the Harappan frontier was like—expanding and violent—grips you when you see the garrisons that reached toward the interior of Asia, in unirrigable deserts and siltless hills. In what is now northern Afghanistan, lapis lazuli and copper were traded at oasis settlements that reached westward toward the Caspian Sea. Mundigak, a fortified trading centre, was equipped to house entire caravans. Today, behind formidable walls with square bastions, the wreck of a great citadel lunges over the landscape, baring rows of deep, round columns at its flank, like the ribs of a huge, squat beast crouched to guard the routes of commerce.

ALMOND-EYED, WITH HIS DIADEM, SASH, AND COMBED BEARD, this rare survivor among the sculptures of Mohenjo Daro recalls—presumably— what the Harappan elite looked like.

In Egypt, Mesopotamia, and China, the sources are ample enough to reveal how states grew by conquest. In Egypt, the Nile was the spine that supported a unitary state. Pharaohs took the river route for inspection tours of the kingdom. Conveyance by river was one of the features this world had in common with heaven. To accompany the immortals as they were ferried across the sky, the pharaoh Cheops was provided with transport. In one pit adjoining his pyramid lies the barge that carried his body to the burial place. Egyptologists are currently excavating an adjoining pit, where his celestial boat is buried. In this sailing vessel, he would navigate the darkness, joining the fleet that bore the Sun back to life every night.

In retrospect, the unity of Egypt seems 'natural'—river shaped. Mesopotamia was not so easy to unify. Inscriptions addressed to their cities' patron gods are full of victories against rivals, each one's propaganda bewilderingly contradicting the others. Around 2000 BCE, the most boastful author of inscriptions, Lugal Zagesi, king of the city of Umma in Sumer, claimed more. The supreme god, Enlil, 'put all the lands at his feet and from east to west made them subject to him', from the Persian Gulf to the Mediterranean. This was almost certainly just a boast. Left to themselves, the warring Sumerian city-states could never have united for long. Around 2500 BCE, however, invaders from northern Mesopotamia forced political change. The conquering king,

Sargon of Akkad, was one of the great empire builders of antiquity. His armies poured downriver and made him King of Sumer and Akkad. 'Mighty mountains with axes of bronze I conquered', he declared in a surviving chronicle fragment, and dared kings who came after him to do the same. His armies were said to have reached Syria and Iran.

Such a vast empire could not last. After a century or two, native Sumerian forces expelled Sargon's successors. Nevertheless, Sargon's achievement set a new pattern—an imperial direction—for the political history of the region. City-states sought to expand by conquering each other. For a time, Lagash, a northern neighbour of Ur, dominated Sumer. One of its kings was the subject of 27 surviving images. We have no better index of any ruler's power. But around 2100 BCE, Ur displaced Lagash. The new capital began to acquire the look for which it is renowned, with showy ziggurats and daunting walls. A 4,000-year-old box—the soundbox of a harp, perhaps—gorgeously depicts the cycle of royal life in imperial Ur—victory, tribute-gathering, and celebration. Thereafter, leadership in the region shifted among rival centres, but it always remained in the south.

In China, itineraries for royal travel dating around 1500 BCE reveal a different political geography. Kings rattled up and down the great vertical artery of the realm, the eastern arm of the Yellow River, and frenziedly did the round of towns and estates to the south, as far as the river Huai. Occasionally, they touched the northernmost reach of the Yangtze River. This was a telltale sign. Shang civilization was expanding south from its heartlands on the middle Yellow River, growing into a regionally dominant super-state. Gradually, the worlds of Chinese culture and politics absorbed the Yangtze valley. The result was a unique state containing complementary environments: the

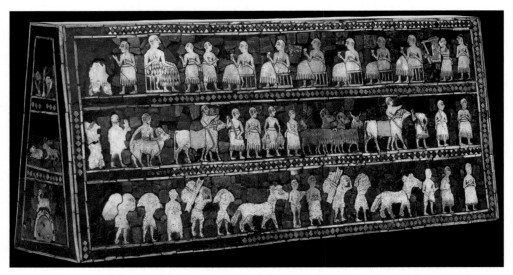

PAINTED ON WHAT MAY HAVE BEEN THE SOUNDBOX OF A HARP, palace life in ancient Ur is captured in scenes of rulers and courtiers drinking while receiving tribute.

millet-growing lands of the Yellow River and the rice fields of the Yangtze. The new ecology of China helped protect it against ecological disaster in either zone. It also formed the basis of the astonishingly resilient and productive state seen in subsequent Chinese history. The consequences will be apparent throughout the remainder of this book. For most of the rest of our story, China wields disproportionate power and influence.

Moreover, the broadening of China's frontiers stimulated rulers' ambitions. They became boundless. Religion and philosophy conspired. The sky was a compelling deity: vast and pregnant with gifts—of light and warmth and rain—and bristling with threats of storm and fire and flood. A state that touched its limits would fulfil a kind of 'manifest destiny'—a reflection of divine order. The Chinese came to see imperial rule over the world as divinely ordained. Emperors treated the whole world as rightfully or potentially subject to them.

The concept spread to neighbouring peoples. On the Eurasian steppes, the immense flatlands and vast skies encouraged similar thinking. We have no documentation for the ambitions of the steppe dynasties until much later. But, as we shall see, steppe-landers with conquest in mind repeatedly challenged empires around the edges of Eurasia in the first millennium BCE. It is probably fair to say that for hundreds, perhaps thousands, of years, the concept of a right to rule the world drove imperialism in Eurasia.

Despite the similarities among them, the great river valleys help us identify at least two reasons for the cultural divergence of the era. First, divergence was environmentally conditioned: the greater or more diverse the resource base, the bigger and more durable the society it feeds. Environmental diversity gave the river valley peoples extra resources, compared with less privileged regions. Egypt had the Nile delta at hand. In the Yellow River and Yangtze valleys, China had two complementary ecological systems. Mesopotamia had a hinterland of pastures, and Mesopotamia and Harappa had access to each other by sea. Secondly, interactions matter, as societies learn from each other, compete, and exchange culture. Egypt was in touch with Mesopotamia and Mesopotamia with Harappa. China's relative isolation—like the extreme isolation of many New World civilizations—may help to explain its late start in some of the common processes of change that these societies all experienced.

Crises of the late second millennium BCE

The grandeur of the great river valley civilizations raises questions about their sustainability. Their wealth and productivity excited envy from outsiders and invited attack. Continued population growth demanded ever more intensive exploitation of the environment. The vast collective efforts required for irrigation, storage, and monumental building left huge classes of people oppressed and resentful of elites. As a result of these and other stresses, beginning around 1500 BCE, transformation or collapse threatened.

Meanwhile, peoples in less easily exploitable environments found the will and means to reproduce, challenge, or exceed the achievements of the great valleys. In central Anatolia, for instance, between about 1800 and 1500 BCE, the people who called themselves children of Hatti—Hittites—drew millions of people into a single network of production and distribution, under a common allegiance. The state, which we can fairly call an empire, had palace complexes, storehouses, towns, and—to take the example that the Hittites themselves would probably put at the top of the list—vast armies. All were comparable in scale with those of the river valley peoples. Egyptian pharaohs treated Hittite kings as equals. When one pharaoh died without heirs, his widow sent to the king of Hatti for 'one of your sons to be my husband, for I will never take a servant of mine and make him my husband'.

We can picture the Hittites with the help of images they have left us: hook-nosed, short-headed, and—more often than not—arrayed for war. But how did their empire happen in such a hostile environment?

The strength of the Hittite kingdom was that it brought farmers and herders into a single state and economic system. This was how to make the most of the rugged Anatolian environment, with its small concentrations of cultivatable soil surrounded by marginal grazing land. The wool production of specialized herders combined with the food production of small farmers—not bonded or enslaved workers or wage earners. Livestock produce fertilizer, and milk-rich diets can provide the calories and nutrients that improve human fertility. Overall, the consequences are positive: more opportunity for economic specialization, urbanization, and the mobilization of manpower for war.

The surviving inventory of the estate of a typical Hittite peasant, Tiwapatara, lists one house for his family of five, three dozen head of livestock, one acre of pasture, and three and a half acres of vineyard, with 42 pomegranate trees and 40 apple trees. The pasture must have been for his eight precious oxen. His goats, hardier animals, presumably foraged where they could. Farmers like Tiwapatara were the manpower that, for a time, made Hatti invincible. Children such as his worked the farms during military campaigns, which usually coincided with sowing and harvest. He and his kind were willing, presumably, to support the state, which in turn protected them, for Hittite law laid down harsh penalties for theft or trespassing on private property. We do not know the total productivity of the economy, but a silo excavated in the major city, Hattusa, held enough grain for 32,000 people for a year.

The king was the sun god's earthly deputy. Subjects called him 'My sun', as modern monarchs are called 'Your Majesty'. His responsibilities were war, justice, and relations with the gods. Hardly any case at law was too trivial to be referred to the king, although, in practice, professional clerks dealt with most of them on his behalf. A vast household surrounded him: 'the Palace servants, the Bodyguard, the Men of the Golden Spear, the Cupbearers, the Table-men, the Cooks, the Heralds, the Stable boys, the Captains of the Thousand.' It was a bureaucratic court, where writing perpetuated the king's commands and conveyed them to subordinates, commanders, viceroys, and subject kings. Royal concubines were rivets of the kingdom. The size and origins of the ruler's harem reflected his political reach. In turn, he had to engender many daughters to contribute to the harems of allies and tributaries.

To judge from surviving law codes, Hittites observed many apparently arbitrary sexual taboos. Intercourse with pigs or sheep was punishable by death, but not cases involving horses or mules. Hittites evidently measured the civilization of other societies by the severity of their incest laws. Their own code forbade intercourse between siblings or cousins. Any sexual act, however, was polluting in some degree and had to be cleansed by bathing before prayer. If we knew more about Hittite religion, we might understand their morality better. Strong sexual taboos are usually found in 'dualist' religions, alongside belief in the eternal struggle of forces of good and evil or spirit and matter. Hittite attitudes toward sex contrast with those in Mesopotamia, where—in what seems to have been a more typical pattern—sex was in some sense sacred, and temples employed prostitutes.

In some ways, Hatti was a man's world, with the masculine attitudes and values typical of a war state. To break the oath taken by army officers would turn 'soldiers into women, and let them dress in the fashion of women and cover their heads with a length of cloth! Let them break the bows, arrows and clubs in their hands and let them take up instead the distaff and the looking-glass!' Women, however, exercised power. Old women acted as diviners at court. Others, lower down the social scale, were curers, waving sacrificial piglets over the victims of curses, with the cry, 'Just as this pig shall not see the sky nor the other piglets again, so let the curse not see the sacrificers!'

The Hittite state was formidable in war. It had to be. Its domestic economy was fragile and its homeland poor in key resources. It needed to grow. Conquests were, in extreme circumstances, the only way to guarantee supplies of food for an increasing population and of tin to make bronze weapons. But even successful conflicts can weaken a state by overextending its power and disrupting its trade. In other words, growth is paradoxical. For many states, it is both a means of survival and an obstacle to survival. It butts against immovable limits. In Hatti's case, those limits were the frontiers of Egypt and Mesopotamia.

The Hittite kingdom suffered from other weaknesses. As with all communities that made the transition to agriculture, it was vulnerable to famine and disease. Around 1300 BCE, King Mursili II reproached the gods for a plague: 'Now no one reaps or sows your fields, for all are dead! The mill-women who used to make the bread of the gods are dead!' A couple of generations later, there was reputedly 'no grain in Hatti', when Puduhepa—a formidable royal spouse—wrote to Egypt demanding some as part of the dowry of her daughter. For one of the last Hittite kings, Tudhaliya IV, an order not to detain a grain ship bound for his country was 'a matter of life and death'. Nomadic prowlers from the hinterlands were another common hazard. People the Hittites called *Kaska* invaded repeatedly to grab booty or extort protection. On at least one of their raids, they robbed the royal court.

In the late 1300s BCE, the Hittite state was in obvious decline. Hatti lost southern provinces and (by Tudhaliya's own admission in a letter scolding a negligent subordinate) at least one major battle to an expanding kingdom in Upper Mesopotamia. The oaths the king demanded from his subordinates have an air of desperation:

> If nobody is left to yoke the horses, . . . you must show even more support. . . . If . . . the chariot-driver jumps from the chariot, and the valet flees the chamber, and not even a dog is left, and if I do not even find an arrow to shoot against the enemy, your support for your king must be all the greater.

Among the last documents the court issued are complaints that formerly subject kings were neglecting tribute or diplomatic courtesies. After 1210 BCE, the Hittite kingdom simply disappeared from the record.

The Hittite story sums up the problems of the time. It demonstrates how agrarian communities consolidated as states, expanded as empires, and—typically—failed to survive past 1000 BCE.

The civilization scholars call Minoan or Cretan, for instance, took shape in the second millennium on the large Mediterranean island of Crete, which lies between what are now Greece and Turkey. Nearby in the southern Peloponnese, the peninsula that forms the southern part of Greece, the civilization we call Mycenean emerged. Both have inspired Western imaginations. Europeans and Americans view Crete and Mycenae as part of their history, assuming that they can trace the civilization of classical Greece—and therefore of the Western world—to these glamorous, spendthrift cultures of 3,500 years ago. That now seems a doubtful assumption. By the time Plato and Aristotle formulated classical Greek philosophy in the fourth century BCE, the last cities of Mycenae had been ruins for 1,000 years. Crete and Mycenae were subjects of myth—civilizations almost as mysterious to the Greeks as they are to us, and almost as remote. Still, they are worth studying for their own sake and the light they cast on their times.

Crete is 3,200 square miles, big enough to be self-sustaining, but mountains cover two-thirds of it, leaving little land to cultivate. To modern mainland Greeks, it is an impossible island, a land of devastating droughts and earthquakes. But to anyone looking today at the wall paintings from around 2000 BCE, when the first palace-storehouses arose there, ancient Crete seems a paradise of plenty. Fields of grain and vines; orchards of olives, almonds, and quince; forests of honey and venison surround gardens of lilies and iris, gladioli and crocuses. The seas teem with dolphin and octopus, under skies where partridges and brightly coloured birds fly.

This lavish world was painfully carved from a tough environment, harsh soil, and dangerous seas. And it depended on two despotic methods to control an unpredictable food supply: organized agriculture, embracing, as in Hatti, both farming and herding, and state-regulated trade. The function of the palace as storehouse was a vital part of how the system worked. The greatest palace complex on the island, Knossos, covers more than 40,000 square feet. When it lay in ruins, visitors from Greece who saw its galleries and corridors imagined an enormous maze, built to house a monster who fed on human sacrifices. In fact, the labyrinth was an immense storage area for clay jars,

DOLPHINS—MUCH PRIZED FOR THEIR MEAT AT THE TIME—dance in palace wall paintings from ancient Crete.

12 feet high, filled with wine, cooking oil, and grain, some still in place. The wool of 80,000 sheep was collected here. Stone chests, lined with lead to protect the foodstuffs they contained, were like strongboxes in a central bank waiting to be distributed or traded. The Cretans were such skilled sailors that the Greeks said Cretan ships knew their own way through the water. Trade brought exotic luxuries to the elites. Ivory tusks and ostrich eggs can still be found at another palace complex at Zakros. Palace walls depict blue baboons from Egypt. Craft workshops inside the palaces added value to imports by spinning and weaving fine garments, delicately painting stone jars, and hammering gold and bronze into jewels and chariots. Palace records suggest a staff of 4,300 people.

Yet Knossos and buildings like it were also genuine palaces—dwellings of an elite who lived in luxury. Majestic stairwells rose to the noble floors, supported on squat columns with tops like fat pumpkins. These pillars, and those supporting the principal chambers, were lacquered red, and the wall paintings glowed with a wonderful sky blue—scenes of feasting, gossiping, playing, and bull leaping. At Zakros, a site that was never plundered, you can see marble-veined chalices, stone storage jars, and a box of cosmetic ointment with an elegant little handle in the form of a reclining greyhound. To judge from the frequency with which women occur in the wall paintings, they were active all over the palace complexes, as priestesses, scribes, artisans, and revellers in the dangerous, demanding game of bull-leaping, somersaulting between the horns of fighting bulls.

Lesser dwellings, grouped in towns, were tiny imitations of the palace. Many had columns, balconies, and upper-storey galleries. In the houses of more prosperous inhabitants, colourful pottery that was as thin as porcelain, elaborate stone vases ground into seductively sinuous shapes, and elaborately painted groundstone baths survive in large numbers. Yet at lower levels of society there was little surplus for luxury or time for leisure. Few people lived beyond their early 40s. If the purpose of the state was to recycle food, its efficiency was limited. Skeletons show that the common people lived near the edge of malnutrition. Earthquakes exacerbated the potentially destructive environment. On the nearby island of Thera, which a volcanic eruption blew apart around 1500 BCE, ash and rock buried the lavish city of Akrotiri. Knossos and similar palaces along the coasts of Crete were all rebuilt once or twice on an increasingly generous scale, after unknown causes, possibly earthquakes, destroyed them.

The way the palaces were reconstructed suggests there was another hazard—internal warfare. Fortifications began to appear. Some of the elite from the eastern and southern ends of the island apparently moved to villas near Knossos about the time the palaces were rebuilt. There may have been a political takeover. At the time of the last rebuilding of Knossos, generally dated around 1400 BCE, a major change in culture occurred. The archives began to be written in an early form of Greek. As a result, we can now read them. The language previously in use is unknown, and its records are undecipherable. By this time, the fate of Crete seems to have become closely entangled with another Aegean civilization—the Mycenean.

The fortified cities and gold-rich royal tombs of the Mycenean civilization began to appear in the 1500s BCE. States in the region already had kings who made war and

RECORDS OF THE ACTIVITIES OF THE PALACE BUREAUCRATS OF ANCIENT PYLOS— warehousing goods, itemizing valuables, gathering taxes—were inscribed on clay tablets.

hunted lions, shortly before these creatures became extinct in Europe. The kings' courts were centred in palace-storehouses like those of Crete. At Pylos, one of the largest Mycenean palaces, clay tablets list the vital and tiresome routines of numerous palace officials: levying taxes, checking that the landowner class observed its social obligations, mobilizing resources for public works, and gathering raw materials for manufacture and trade. In the palace of Pylos, workshops turned out bronzeware and perfumed oils for export to Egypt and the Hittite empire. More than for luxury, however, bureaucrats' main function was to provide for war. As well as fighting each other, the kingdoms felt the threat of the barbarian hinterland, which may, in the end, have overwhelmed them. Paintings on the walls of Pylos show warriors, in the boar's-head helmets also worn on Crete and Thera, in battle with skin-clad savages.

Stunned by earthquakes, strained by wars, Mycenean cities followed those of Crete into abandonment by 1100 BCE What is surprising is not, perhaps, that they should ultimately have perished, but that their fragile economies, sustained by elaborate and expensive methods of collecting, storing, and redistributing food, should have managed to feed the cities and support the elite culture for so long.

Although we could explain the extinction of Crete, Mycenae, and Hatti in terms of local political failures or ecological disasters, it is tempting to try to relate them to a general crisis in the eastern Mediterranean. For not only was the grandeur of the Aegean civilizations blotted out and the Hittite empire of Anatolia overwhelmed, but nearby states also reported fatal or near-fatal convulsions. The Egyptians almost succumbed to unidentified invaders, who exterminated many states and cities in the region. The descent of the 'Sea Peoples', as Egyptians called them, in about 1190 BCE, is well documented because the pharaoh who defeated them, Ramses III, devoted a long inscription to his achievement. It is glaring propaganda, a celebration of the pharaoh's power and preparation: 'Barbarians,' it says vaguely, 'conspired in their islands. . . . No land could withstand their arms.' A list of victims follows, including Hatti and a string of cities in southern Anatolia and along the eastern Mediterranean, while an anguished king in Upper Mesopotamia prayed to the city's god, 'Darkness without sunshine awaits the evildoers who stretch out threatening hands.' They were heading for Egypt, Ramses' narrative continues, 'while we prepared flame before them. . . . They laid their hands on the land as far as the edges of the Earth, their hearts confident and trusting'. The Nile delta, however, 'made like a strong wall with warships. . . . I was the valiant war-god. . . . The full flame was in front of them at the river mouths, while a stockade of lances surrounded them on the shore. They were dragged in, enclosed, and prostrated on the beach, killed and made into heaps.' After unpicking the propaganda, we can be confident that the pharaoh's boasts reflected real events. For example, when the city of Ugarit in Syria fell, probably early in the twelfth century BCE, never to be reoccupied, messages begging for seaborne reinforcements were left unfinished. The reply from the governor of Carchemish, an inland trading centre on the way to Hatti and Mesopotamia, was typical—too little, too late: 'as for what you have written me, "Ships of the enemy have been seen at sea." Well, you must remain firm. . . . Surround your towns with ramparts. Have your troops and chariots enter there, and await the enemy with great resolution.'

The image of a general crisis brought about by barbarian invasions has had an almost irresistible romantic appeal for Western historians influenced by a familiar episode of their own past: the decline and fall of the Roman Empire. A general crisis also fits with a popular conception of the past as a battlefield of barbarism versus civilization. However, such an idea is, at best, a gross oversimplification because both barbarism and civilization are relative, subjective terms. We can best understand the violent arrival of the Sea Peoples as a symptom of a broader phenomenon of the period: the widespread instability of populations driven by hunger and land shortages. Egyptian carvings show desperate migrations, would-be invaders with ox carts full of women and children. From Mesopotamia and Anatolia comes evidence of savage marauders in the late thirteenth century BCE. But migrants probably did not cause the decline of the states they ravaged. Rather, they were among the consequences of that decline. Environmental and economic historians have scoured the evidence for some sign of a deeper trauma, such as earthquakes or droughts or commercial failures that might explain grain shortages and disrupted trade. But they have found nothing of the sort at the time of the migrants' invasions.

The causes of the crisis lay in the common structural problems of the states that faltered or failed, namely, their ecological fragility and unstable, competitive politics. In this respect, the crisis was even more general, not just confined to the civilizations around the eastern Mediterranean where the Sea Peoples roamed. If we turn to trace the fate of communities elsewhere in Asia, and even to some examples in the New World, we can detect similar strains and comparable effects.

In the Indus valley, for instance, city life and intensive agriculture were in danger of collapse even when they were at their most productive. Many sites were occupied only for a few centuries. Some sites were abandoned as early as about 1800 BCE, and by 1000 BCE, all had dwindled to ruins. Meanwhile, in Turkmenia, on the northern flank of the Iranian plateau, relatively young but flourishing fortified settlements on the Oxus River, such as Namazga and Altin, shrank to the size of villages. We know little about these places, and what brought about their end has provoked furious debate among scholars. Some believe in a sudden and violent invasion, but the more likely explanation speaks of a gradual decline—a climacteric, a point at which Harappan civilization collapsed, and its cities were abandoned.

The climate was getting drier in the Indus valley, and earthquakes may have shifted riverbeds. Unlike the crisis in the eastern Mediterranean, events in the Indus valley seem to fit with the chronology of environmental disaster. The Saraswati River, along which settlements were once densely clustered, disappeared into the advancing Thar Desert. Yet not even the loss of a river adequately explains the abandonment of the cities. The Indus River is still disgorging its wonderful silt, year by year, over vast, shining fields, which would have been sufficient to maintain the urban populations. Presumably, something happened to the food supply that was connected with the drying climate or human mismanagement of environmental resources—the cattle and other products that supplemented the wheat and barley of the fields.

In addition—or instead—the inhabitants apparently fled from some plague deadlier than the malaria that anthropologists have detected in buried bones. In an environment where irrigation demands standing water, mosquitos can breed. Malaria is inevitable. The people left, 'expelled by the fire-god', as the *Rig Veda* says, and 'migrated to a new land'. This is probably an exaggeration. People stayed on or squatted in the decaying cities, inhabiting the ruins for generations. But the fall of Harappan civilization remains the most dramatic case of large-scale failure in the second millennium BCE. In broad terms, Harappa suffered essentially the same fate as the Hittite and eastern Mediterranean civilizations: the food distribution system outran the resource base. And when networks of power began to break down, invaders broke in.

China experienced no large-scale population loss, no wholesale abandonment of regions, or wreck of cities. Nonetheless, what the Chinese of the period experienced was in some ways similar to other peoples in what looks increasingly like a global pattern. The basis of the Shang state had always been shaky. War, rituals, and oracles are all gamblers' means of power, vulnerable to the lurches of luck. Manipulating the weather, the rains, the harvests, for instance, was a big part of the king's job, but in reality, of course, it was not one he could accomplish. Failure was built into his job description. It was a common problem for monarchs of the time, exposing pharaohs to blame for natural disasters, driving Hittite kings to depend on soothsayers.

The late Shang state was shrinking. Beginning about 1100 BCE, the names of subject, tribute-paying, and allied states gradually vanish from the oracle bones. The king's hunting grounds grew smaller. The king took on greater personal responsibility, becoming the sole diviner and army general, as the numbers of courtiers and commanders at his disposal fell. Former allies became enemies.

Meanwhile, just as Mesopotamian culture had been exported to Anatolia and Cretan ways of life to Mycenae, so Shang culture was exported beyond the Shang state, and its effects were becoming obvious. For one, new chiefdoms were developing in less favourable environments under the influence of trade. As far away as northern Vietnam and Thailand, bronze-making techniques similar to those of China, appeared at the courts of chiefs who delighted in personal ornaments, spittoons, and, in Vietnam, heavily decorated drums. More ominously and closer to home, right on the Shang border, a state arose in imitation and, increasingly, in rivalry: Zhou. The earliest Zhou sites—of the 1100s BCE—are burials in the Liang Mountains above the Wei River in western China. This was probably not the Zhou heartland, but the area they had migrated to from grazing country farther to the north. Their own legends recalled time spent 'living among the barbarians'. The Zhou were highland herders, an upland, upriver menace to the Shang just as Akkad was to Sumer in Mesopotamia.

Except for the material culture visible in their graves, we know nothing of the Zhou before they attacked and conquered the Shang—not their origin, or their economic or political systems, or even their language. We know them after they had fallen under the

AS FAR AWAY AS NORTHERN VIETNAM AND THAILAND, bronze-making techniques similar to those of China, appeared at the courts of chiefs, who delighted in personal ornaments, spittoons, and, in Vietnam, heavily decorated drums.

Shang's spell, imitating Shang culture and, presumably, envying its wealth. They had also learned the Shang's most accomplished art: bronze casting.

According to the chronicles, Shang-style turtle-shell oracles had inspired the Zhou to conquest, and later Zhou rulers upheld that tradition. Chronicles composed in the third century BCE tell the same story as texts hundreds of years older. If they can be believed, the Zhou 'captured'—as they put it—the Shang state in a single battle in 1045 BCE. They annexed it as a kind of colony and established garrisons all along the lower Yellow River to the coast. Archaeological evidence shows that they shifted the centre of the empire north, to the hilly Shaanxi region, west of where the Yellow River turns toward the sea.

Once the Zhou conquered the Shang, they did not continue all Shang traditions. Indeed, despite pious declarations, they gradually abandoned the most sacred Shang rite: divination by bone oracles. Although the Zhou extended China's cultural frontiers before their own state dissolved in its turn in the eighth century BCE, their leaders were not universal emperors in the mould of the Shang, ruling all the world that mattered to them. Rival states multiplied around them, and their own power tended to erode and fragment. But they originated the ideology of the mandate of heaven, which 'raised up our little land of Zhou'. All subsequent Chinese states inherited the same notion that the emperor was divinely chosen. Furthermore, all subsequent changes in rule appealed to the same claim that heaven transferred power from a decayed dynasty to one of greater virtue. The Zhou created an effective myth of the unity and continuity of China that dominated the way the Chinese came to think of themselves. This myth has been passed on and is now the standard Western view of China, too, as a monolithic state—massive, with a uniform culture of exceptional durability, and a tendency to claim dominion over all the world.

Continuity is not easy to achieve. By 1000 BCE, failed states of the previous millennium littered the landscapes of Eurasia. Some of the world's most spectacular empires broke up, and mysterious catastrophes cut short the histories of many of its most complex cultures. Food distribution centres controlled from palace labyrinths shut down. Trade was disrupted. Settlements and monuments were abandoned. The Harappan civilization vanished, as did the Cretan and Mycenean. Hatti was obliterated. In Mesopotamia, Akkadian armies spread their own language along the length of the Tigris and Euphrates. Sumerian speech slowly dwindled from everyday use to become—like Latin in the Western world today—a purely ceremonial language. The cities of Sumer crumbled. Their memory was preserved chiefly in the titles that invaders from uplands and deserts used to dignify the rule of their own kings. Ur declined to a cult centre and tourist resort.

Something similar occurred in China, which succumbed to the Zhou. Aspects of the civilization survived, but its centre of gravity was shunted upriver. Society and everyday life remained essentially intact. This was a pattern often repeated in Chinese history. In the New World, meanwhile, Mesoamerica and the Andean region undertook environmentally ambitious initiatives, but none of them showed much staying power.

Though there were more losers than winners after the climacteric of the second millennium BCE, the outstanding case of endurance was Egypt. Invasions in the late second millennium failed, and the basic productivity of the Egyptian agrarian system remained intact. But even Egypt was reined in. Nubia—the region upriver of the cataracts, what is now Sudan—disappeared from Egyptian records by 1000 BCE. This was a major reversal because extending its empire along the Nile had been one of Egypt's most constant objectives. The abundant ivory, the mercenaries that Nubia supplied, and the river trade that made gold in Egypt 'as plentiful as the sand of the sea' had long drawn Egypt southward. Egypt originally became interested in Central Africa when the explorer Harkhuf made three expeditions around 2500 BCE. He brought back 'incense, ebony, scented oil, tusks, arms, and all fine produce'. Harkhuf's captive pygmy, 'who dances divine dances from the land of the spirits', fascinated the boy pharaoh Pepi. Writing to the explorer, the pharaoh commanded the utmost care in guarding him: 'inspect him ten times a night. For my Majesty wishes to see this pygmy more than all the products of Sinai and Punt.'

Contact and commerce led to the formation of a Nubian state in imitation of Egypt, beyond the second cataract. From about 2000 BCE, Egypt tried to influence or control this state, sometimes by erecting fortifications, sometimes by invasion, sometimes by pushing its own frontier south to beyond the third cataract. Pharoahs' inscriptions piled curses on the Nubians as the latter became more powerful and more difficult to handle. Eventually, around 1500 BCE, Pharoah Tut-mose I launched a campaign beyond the fourth cataract, conquering the kingdom of Kush and making Nubia a colonial territory. Egypt studded Nubia with forts and temples. The last temple, to Ramses II, at Abu Simbel, was the most crushingly monumental that Egyptians had built for 2,000 years. It has remained a symbol of power ever since. But during the reigns of his immediate successors, disastrously little flooding of the Nile, on which the success of Egyptian agriculture depended, was recorded. This was the era, toward the end of the thirteenth century BCE, when Egypt came close to destruction. To abandon Nubia in the late second millennium BCE, after investing so much effort and emotion, shows how severe Egypt's need for retrenchment must have been.

The causes of instability in the four great river valleys and the smaller states that arose later were much more general than any general crisis theory suggests. If Harappan society was unsustainable in the silt-rich Indus valley, how realistic were the Hittite or Olmec or Cretan or Andean ambitions in much less favourable environments?

Paradox racked the most ambitious states of the era. They were committed to population growth, which imposed unsustainable goals of expansion as conquered territory became farther and farther away from the centre. They were founded on intensified methods of production, which drove them to overexploit the environment. They concentrated large populations, making them more vulnerable to famine and disease. Enemies surrounded them, jealous of their wealth and resentful of their power. They created more enemies for themselves by inspiring rivals and imitators in their hinterlands. When their food distribution programs failed, disruptive migrations resulted. Their rulers condemned themselves to failure and rebellion because they lived a lie, manipulating unreliable oracles, negotiating with heedless gods, bargaining with hostile nature. In some cases, the traditions that failed or faltered during the great climacteric simply got displaced, to reemerge elsewhere. In others, dark ages of varying duration—periods of diminished achievement, about which we have little evidence—followed the climacteric.

PART 3

The Oscillations of Empires

―――――

From the 'Dark Age' of the Early First Millennium BCE
to the Mid-Fourteenth Century CE

CHAPTER 5

Material Life
Bronze Age Crisis to the Black Death

JOHN BROOKE

A LITTLE more than two millennia separated the crisis of the Late Bronze Age civilizations from the advent of the Black Death. Erupting out of Central Asia with the first tremors of the Little Ice Age, the bubonic plague of the mid-fourteenth century would fracture societies across Eurasia and Northern Africa, killing as much as one half of the population. Its devastating impact would drive a revolutionary reordering of societies and economies and set the stage for the launch of modernity in the Renaissance. Much the same can be said of the Bronze Age crisis that started around 1200 BCE. The ensuing Iron Age forged new technologies and social formations that reshaped the circumstances of humanity. This specific rupture brought a dynamic of change on a scale that can be compared—if distantly—to the industrial revolution.

If so, this was relative to what came both before and after. Relative to its past, the change in the first millennium BCE was dramatic, although it pales in comparison with what was to come after 1350. Despite this difference, it is important that we look carefully at the earlier epoch on its own terms. In a pre-scientific intellectual world that severely curtailed technological change, with a pre-democratic political sensibility that limited human potential, human societies remained locked in an organic economy, driven by solar power, and constrained by the same broad natural forces that had prevailed since the first emergence of civilization out of early agricultural societies. But within these limits, recovery after the Bronze Age set important changes in motion—a new order of things.

Broad global geographies and broad global climatic regimes each exerted critical forces. In Eurasia, the critical geography was a powerfully connected one of dry continental steppe, semi-arid middle latitudes, and well-watered oceanic and tropical equatorial peripheries, all intimately linked with an African geography of deep desert, savannah, and equatorial rainforest. The New World's formative geography was a more segmented mosaic of Pacific-facing western mountain cordillera and great continental drainages to the east.

Coherent global Late Holocene climate regimes had roughly simultaneous—if different—manifestations throughout the world. Patterned, if irregular, cycles of solar intensity and more erratic clusters of volcanic eruptions operated upon the great systems of atmospheric circulation: the equatorial monsoon domain and the mid-latitude westerlies operating just beyond the polar vortex. The result was an oscillating wave in the human condition of two long climatic 'Optimums' which allowed population expansion and growing stability, even prosperity, to rise and fall between three eras of crisis and decline. In sequence, these were the Bronze Age Crisis, the Iron Age recovery, the Classical Optimum, the so-called Dark Ages (or Late Antiquity), the Medieval Optimum, and then the Little Ice Age. This chapter follows the global story from the aftershocks of the Bronze Age crisis around 1000 BCE to the onset of the Little Ice Age crisis in the decades leading to 1350.

Climatic context from the Bronze Age to the Iron Age: the Hallstatt solar minimum, 1200–700 BCE

Whatever the limitations of the earliest civilizations, they had encouraged population growth. At the end of the Ice Ages around 9500 BCE, one estimate shows the global population at about seven million, and over the next six millennia numbers grew to perhaps 40 million when the first early states emerged around 3000 BCE. Over the next two thousand years, our ancestors' numbers reached about 100 million by the time of the Bronze Age crisis; at least half of this population was concentrated in the mid-latitude locations of Bronze Age empires and state: Egypt and greater Mesopotamia, China, and India. Similar, smaller concentrations were emerging in the South American Andes and Mesoamerica, where dense corn-growing villages began to grow more complex around 1500 BCE. This comprised a fundamental divergence, as state regimes, however imperfect, fostered a ballooning of agrarian population around the southern rim of Eurasia and along the American cordillera.

As noted, the human condition experienced grand cycles of 'optimum' and crisis at the end of the long Bronze Age Optimum, which began around 3000 BCE. All these societies would suffer in the global crisis around 1200 BCE, the overarching factor rooted in the energy output of the sun, which changes from 'maxima' to 'minima' relatively regularly. These changes can go from an eleven-year cycle to cycles of larger periodicities of hundreds and thousands of years. Often enhanced by volcanic activity, solar minima periods also entail disturbed weather conditions around the world that are shaped by a cooling of the northern hemisphere. The largest of these, the grand minimum of the 2000 year 'Hallstatt' solar cycle, one of which began at the end of the second millennium BCE, was last seen in the fourth millennium BCE and which would return at the onset of the Little Ice Age. Such was the background driver of the oscillation of 'optimum' and crisis in human affairs. Starting around 1200 BCE, declining solar input cooled the northern hemisphere and sent icebergs into the North Atlantic and frigid blasts of cold dry winter winds—the Siberian High—south across

Eurasia and into North America. Around the great Indian-Pacific circuit, the Asian summer monsoons declined, while El Niño rains increased in the Americas. While the Americas suffered—and sometimes benefited—from rising precipitation, southern Eurasia suffered rising frequency and intensity of drought. Around the eastern Mediterranean the shift toward drought was—it seems—compounded by a wave of earthquakes estimated to have struck between 1225 and 1175 BCE.

As discussed in Chapter 4, the result around Eurasia, from China to Egypt, was a great jostling of peoples—and the fall of great kingdoms. Around the eastern Mediterranean, the great Bronze Age states—Mycenae, Crete, the Egyptian New Kingdom, the Hittite empire, the Mittani kingdom to the southeast, and the Kassite regime in Babylonia—all collapsed by 1050 BCE. Whether by earthquake, rebellion, or invasion, cities were burned and palaces were looted and destroyed. In China, the 700-year-old Shang kingdom was overturned in 1046 BCE by the Zhou people from the edge of the western desert. Defeating the Shang lords during a period of harsh dry winters and decreasing monsoon activity, the Zhou were the first dynasty to invoke the Mandate of Heaven, the doctrine that China could be governed by only one virtuous ruler who ruled with divine blessings. But a dynasty—like the Shang—could lose their mandate if the monsoons (and their virtues) failed, as would happen time and again over the next 2600 years.

Across the Pacific, the play of El Niño rains worked differently from region to region. Along the Andes the rains brought devastating flooding to narrow river valleys, peaking between 1000 and 700 BCE, undermining the perpetuation of complex culture. In Mesoamerica, on the other hand, rising rainfall as early as 1500 BCE encouraged the growth and consolidation of small chiefdoms that united clusters of villages—the first step toward state formation. In eastern North America, the effects of the cold north and the El Niño regime after 1200 BCE brought an end to the conditions that had supported large foraging populations.

Epidemics and the Eurasian steppes

Old World evidence suggests at the harsh conditions of these crisis centuries, and that epidemic disease must have struck with the Bronze Age crisis. Reports survive from the Hittites in the fourteenth century, the siege of Troy, and the Israelites in the twelfth century. It appears that the plague, once thought to be unique to late Middle Ages, has much deeper roots. The earliest genetic evidence comes from a mass grave in the Altai in Central Asia dating to roughly 2800 BCE, which shows that the plague, in some form, was endemic in the steppe throughout the Bronze Age and closely associated with nomadic Indo-European peoples drifting west into Europe. It may well have made its way into the channels of commerce and war that closely connected the peoples of eastern Mediterranean during the Late Bronze Age.

Of course, the collapse of great civilizations might have had some health benefits, despite the stresses of the harsh conditions of the early first millennium. These stresses were real, but local. On Crete, where late Bronze Age settlements had been situated on the coast and the houses open to the sea breezes, the survivors now huddled in fortified hilltop villages, closed tightly against the now-harsh winters. We can image the skies filled with winter hearth-smoke, and the huddled villagers increasingly burdened with respiratory ailments, which probably included tuberculosis. Chemical assays of human bone suggest that few individuals ventured out onto the now-dangerous seas to fish. Skeletons from burials across Western Eurasia dating down into the Iron Age suggest generally poorer health and shorter stature than those of the Late Bronze Age. On the other hand, there may have been a trade-off. The declines of commerce and the marches of large armies isolated the smaller, stressed communities of the Iron Age, and insulated them from the wide reach of epidemic disease.

Nonetheless, the association of the plague with the rise and spread of horse-riding nomadic steppe peoples had established key elements of a geopolitical structure that would endure down into the early modern era and shape Eurasia for almost four millennia. The earliest plague appears around 2800 BCE in Early Bronze Age proto-Indo-European graves from the Altai and the Baltic; it next appears around 2200 BCE in the graves of the Sintashata people in the steppe north of the Caspian Sea.

Sometime after 2000 BCE, the Sintashata transformed the heavy, four-wheeled wagon into a light two-wheeled war chariot. Chariot warriors, chariot warfare, or Indo-European speakers began to spread in all directions. Chariot warriors arrived in the eastern Mediterranean around 1600 BCE and shaped the warfare of the Late Bronze Age; chariots, if not Indo-European warriors, arrived in China and were adopted by the Shang, and then their successors, the Zhou. The connection between the steppe and the imperial lowlands was solidified by the trade in horses, who pulled the chariots, as well as other important commodities. Among these warriors and traders were Old Indic speakers, some of whom also migrated west to Anatolia, south into Iran, and southeast to the Punjab, where the great Harappan city states had faded away by 2000 BCE. Seven hundred years later, a branch of these Old Indic peoples was well established in the northern tributaries of the Indus River, had committed the Rig Veda to written text, and was poised to begin a long migration east into the forests of the Ganges Valley.

As the Bronze Age ended however, two important shifts occurred on the steppe: steppe warriors shifted from the horse-drawn chariot to the mounted horse, and the plague increased in virulence, while its means of transmission multiplied. Starting around 800 BCE, a new warrior culture, the Scythians, emerged on the steppe north of the Black Sea, perhaps with deeper connections to Central Asia. They carried the short, compound bow, which, unlike the older long bow, could be used on horseback. The Scythians were the first of a host of warrior cultures to emerge on the steppe across Eurasia; they would be followed by the Huns, the Turks, and the Mongols. Century after century, mounted nomads would emerge to raid and conquer the old primary civilizations on the southern rim of Eurasia. Starting with the Scythians during a solar decline around 800 BCE (known as the Homeric minimum), these warrior societies—or more precisely their horses—would thrive during periods of cooler climate, which

ASSYRIAN CAVALRY RELIEF FROM SENNACHERIB'S PALACE AT NINVEH *c.* 700 BCE. Steppe warriors first utilized the horse for chariot warfare around 2000 BCE, and developed riding skills by 800 BCE. The spread of horse-powered warfare may have tracked the diffusion of the plague from the steppe to the Eurasian rimlands.

brought moist westerly winds and winter snow to the steppes and deserts from the Black Sea to Mongolia. These conditions enabled marmot and great gerbil colonies to flourish and expand: these rodents were essential hosts of the fleas harbouring the plague bacillus *Yersinia pestis*. Strikingly, genetic study indicates that, sometime between 1700 and 950 BCE, the bacillus mutated in two ways: it developed genes that allowed transmission by fleas, and it developed into full-virulence bubonic form. Thus, from the rise of the Scythians to the eradication of steppe-warrior societies and the containment of the plague in the eighteenth century, the steppe—a great inland sea of grass and scrub—stood as a threat to the great populations around the southern edge of greater Eurasia, from China and India to the Middle East and Europe. The warriors of the steppe and the rulers and peasants of the monsoonal rimlands together comprised an interacting world system.

Into the Iron Age and Steel Age

Such conditions were obviously not conducive to rapid recovery. Nor were the continuing, if erratic, forces of the Halstatt solar grand minimum, which may have ended around 700 BCE, but produced further cold conditions between 400 and 300 BCE.

For the next 600–700 years, most of the world had a relatively favourable climate, with a warmer northern hemisphere, strong Asian monsoons, and preponderantly La Niña conditions. During these centuries Inner Asia—and perhaps North America—must have suffered droughts, but otherwise, conditions were set for a grand expansion.

Worldwide human population must have lost ground in the crisis centuries from a high of perhaps 100 million around 1200 BCE, but by 300 BCE it had rebounded to about 185 million. Of these, 130 million were located in the three primary Eurasian civilization regions of China, India, and Southwest Asia/Egypt, and comprised over 70 per cent of the world's population. If we add Europe's 22 million to the count, this Old World core population encompassed more than 80 per cent of the world's total. This was a peak that persisted to about 300 CE, when the global tally crested at about 250 million. Of the rest of the world's population, about 15 per cent was located in three large regions: greater Russia and Inner Asia, sub-Saharan Africa, and Mesoamerica and the Andes. Across all these regions, trajectories of change and expansion developed across the first millennium CE, slowly at first, but accelerating toward a synchronous florescence into a global classical antiquity.

This slow but accelerating process followed a similar trajectory in both the Old World and the New, but our focus is on the interconnected worlds of Eurasia and Africa, particularly the core populations between China and Egypt. Across this grand arc, the crisis and collapse of rigidly hierarchical Late Bronze Age polities opened new possibilities.

In a host of domains, both new local autonomy and the press of circumstance opened paths toward innovation. With the collapse of the palaces went the scribes and their ancient pictographic writing systems, which were gradually replaced by new alphabetical writing systems that were potentially more accessible to ordinary people. Historians of ideas often see these centuries as what Karl Jaspers called an 'Axial Age' which spanned Eurasia, where parallel developments occurred within cultures that had no direct cultural contact. Clerics and scholar-priests, freed from the imperative of legitimating the heavenly mandates of the Bronze Age monarchs, developed monotheistic world-religious traditions, framed by remarkably homogeneous ethical and philosophical traditions.

In technology, metallurgical innovation was critical. Over the first millennium BCE iron replaced bronze as the dominant metal across the entire Old World. Bronze, as discussed in Chapter 3, was an amalgam of soft copper and the hardening agent of tin. Tin was difficult to find, and in ancient times was mined in Anatolia, Iran, Afghanistan, Central Asia, northern Europe, northern China, and Southeast Asia. Finding sources of tin required trade connections. As deposits were played out, the networks stretched further and further into Eurasia. Palace authorities, who controlled the trade, also oversaw the production of the bronze. When the great glittering Late Bronze Age palace regimes collapsed, to earthquake, rebellion, or violent raids, so too did the trading networks, at least for a time. With the interruption of trade, metal workers may have lost their access to tin.

Bronze did not disappear, but it became rarer and more difficult to make. In its place, iron emerged slowly as the essential metal. Iron production involved more complex chemistry, but once the secrets became widely known, it was a far superior, far more accessible metal. The process started as with copper or tin—crushed, roasted ores smelted in a charcoal furnace until liquid; the secrets involved getting air into the furnace, and using a calcium flux, either crushed limestone or seashells, to separate the free iron from the slag of charcoal remnants and impurities. The result, until the development of the blast furnace, was a 'bloom'—a spongy mass of iron extracted from the furnace and pounded on an anvil to produce wrought iron.

The secrets of the flux and the bloom opened to door to the wide availability of metal throughout ancient societies. Bronze had been expensive to produce, and it was only for elite individuals; common farming households continued to use flaked stone tools for all their cutting needs. But iron was 'a democratic metal'. Iron deposits were widely distributed, and its production involved only wood and calcium, equally

WORKERS OPERATING A BLOOMERY
FURNACE IN A WOODCUT PRINTED
IN BASLE IN 1566.

available to common people, rather than distant and expensive copper and tin ores. Operating a bloomery furnace, once the secrets of the air flow and flux was mastered, was a relatively simple thing. Bloomeries might be a shallow pit or a stack of bricks sealed with a layer of clay, equipped with ceramic tubes to allow air into the furnace bed; some might have a leather bellows to force in air; most were situated to exploit prevailing winds to force a natural draft. The result was a malleable material, softer perhaps than well-forged bronze. But iron could be transformed into grades of steel by tempering and carbonization—repeated heating over charcoal and cooling in air—or quenching in water and carburization by further heating. It may be that it was the easy production of steel, rather than a critical lack of tin, that tipped over the technological revolution. The result was a massive expansion of weapons production, but a far more important production of tools for farming, for woodworking, and for more iron work. Cutting, digging, sawing, pounding: human torque on the natural, material world was ratcheted up dramatically.

Iron artefacts appeared occasionally as rare ornaments throughout the Bronze Age, as coppersmiths fell upon a rare combination in their work. But widespread production apparently first began on the island of Cyprus, where there is evidence of a proliferation of autonomous iron production after 1200 BCE. Iron ornaments and weapons, and perhaps tools, circulated from Cyprus, and evidence suggests minor production spreading, but it was not until the ninth century BCE that iron production became wide spread in the eastern Mediterranean; the oldest bloomery so far discovered on the mainland dates to 800–700 BCE.

Iron production required not only iron ore, but also huge harvests of timber, to be reduced to charcoal. The combination of iron mines and hardwood forests became a determinant of economic survival. Iron use came later to Egypt, around 500 BCE, and here—and perhaps in southern Mesopotamia—the lack of both mines and forests in these now-ancient regions shaped their decline. Egypt never really recovered from the collapse of the New Kingdom around 1100 BCE, and for several centuries power shifted upriver to the Nubian Kushite Kingdoms, which ruled Egypt from the south, until the invasion of the Assyrians in 760 BCE. Retreating south, by the sixth millennium BCE the Nubians established the Kingdom of Meroe, famous for centuries for its ironworking, fed by ore and timber at the confluence of the Upper Nile and the Atbara River. Ironworking developed elsewhere along the northern forest boundary with the Sahel across Africa, in the Great Lakes region of the Rift Valley by 600 BCE, and to the west on the Niger River in the Nok culture by 500 BCE. From there, it spread south into the forest among the Bantu peoples in Cameroon, who would carry the bloomery production system with them on their epic migrations east and south. Iron production was probably independently developed in India; after 1000 BCE it developed in the Ganges Valley with the eastward spread of Indo-Aryan peoples, devouring the great primeval forests, and independently in the forested south. At roughly the same time across Inner Eurasia, the steppe nomad tribes seem to have carried iron production east and west. In the east, Scythians and other nomads are credited with

WU BLACKSMITHS WITH A CAST-IRON BLAST FURNACE.

bringing iron to Zinjiang, and bloomery production was underway in China by the eighth century BCE, roughly when horse-riding nomad raiders sacked the Zhou capital, displacing the Zhou to the east, and fatally weakening their hegemony. During the subsequent Warring State period, around 500 BCE, blacksmiths in the small state of Wu developed the first cast-iron blast furnace technology, probably from Chinese bronze casting techniques. Essentially, the earlier blast furnaces were taller bloomeries with a more careful arrangement of ore and charcoal and a constant flow of forced air, blown by a bellows. The blast furnace, which dramatically increased the quantity and quality of iron production, would not spread to Europe for almost 2000 years.

Far to the west, steppe nomad influences, if not direct migrations, in what is known as the Thraco-Cimmerian culture, spread bloomery iron production—and the horse-mounted steppe warrior culture—deep into continental Europe by the seventh century BCE, forging the archaeological culture known as the Hallstatt (not to be confused with the 2000-year solar pattern). Suggestively, these nomadic impacts at either end of the continent occurred during the Homeric solar minimum, when cooler temperatures brought more rainfall to Central Asia. More rain supported more horses—and more marmots. It is entirely possible that the eighth and seventh centuries BCE brought not only nomadic warriors and iron, but also the plague, out to the edges of the continent.

Commerce and empire

As pervasively as iron production, the collapse of the Bronze Age palaces gradually led to a proliferation of relatively autonomous trade and commerce. Rather than the hegemonic imperatives of the palace command economy, trade now followed its own logic, and perhaps in this age the market was born. Certainly, merchants moved goods on their own terms, and to their own ends. Such trade would have to be carried on carefully due to the threats of enemies and pirates. Local short-distance ventures recorded in the movement of pottery and metal goods suggest a commodities trade filling the needs of less-than-elite households. Some of this rising early Iron Age trade crisscrossed the Near East in growing camel caravans; additionally, much of it was seaborne. It spawned the rise of small autonomous polities, some quasi-republican merchant city-states, others mini-kingdoms: on the Levant coast and hills, for instance, the Phoenician and Philistine city-states, and the Kingdoms of Israel, Judah, Edom, Moab, and Ammon. Sitting astride the routes linking Egypt, the Aegean, Mesopotamia, and Arabia, all these were, to some degree, centres of trade; Edom controlled the valuable trade in incense that flowed north through Arabia from Yemen. The Phoenicians and the emerging city-states of Greece and the Aegean dominated the trade across the Mediterranean. Distant seaborne trade stimulated colonizations: around the Mediterranean by the eighth century BCE Phoenician and Greek settlements, as much local hybrids as they were colonies, were sprinkled along the North African coast to Carthage in what is now Tunisia, and to southern Italy, Sicily, and Sardinia. The Etruscans of northern Italy had their origins in a migration from the Anatolian coast. Trade moved from these coastal enclaves among distant interior peoples. Prestige goods flowed north from Greece and Italy to the warrior cultures of continental Europe in exchange for salt, copper, iron, and horses; Phoenicians at Carthage traded south across the Sahara for salt and slaves.

Eventually these trade routes would connect most of the Old World into what is known as a world system, already inchoately discernible in the Late Bronze Age in trade between the Persian Gulf and the cities of the Indus valley. The same axis featured in the early Iron Age in the incense trade running north overland from Arabia to the Levant. The rise of the trade drove the predatory reemergence of empire; small trading states were forced into the tribute orbit of rising powers with growing armies who carried new weapons of iron and steel, and compound bows on horses traded from the steppe. In east and west, both the Zhou from 1046 BCE and a neo-Assyria from 934 BCE took the form of loosely organized tribute empires, with local rulers paying protection money to the new powers. By the late 700s BCE, Assyria had conquered a vast swathe of territory running from Egypt through central Anatolia to the Persian Gulf, only to collapse under the assault of bands of Cimmerian steppe nomads, allied with recently subjected Medes and Babylonians. Ultimately, Assyria's vast domain was overtaken by the Achaemenid Persians, who, by the 480s BCE, ruled from the Black Sea to the Indus and across Arabia to Egypt.

With the Persians, imperial domains began to reach enormous dimensions. The Neo-Assyrians had controlled territories on a scale with Egypt and the Shang, the Late Bronze giants. The Achaemenid Persians at their peak in the 480s BCE claimed five time as much territory, and a number of the great empires of the next few centuries— the Seleucids, the Bactria and Parthia, the Mauryan empire in India, the nomad Xiongnu in Mongolia—claimed domains twice the scale of their Late Bronze Age counterparts. The greatest and most stable empires of the age, of course, were the new empires in east and west rising at the end of the millennium: the Qin and then the Han Empires in China, and the Roman Empire around the greater Mediterranean. Such geographies, after brutal conquest, were ruled effectively for centuries, requiring something more than simple systems of tribute. These great classical empires began to develop the rudiments of a bureaucratic governance in which a hierarchy of officials coordinated a system of imperial peace with local governors.

In the Americas, the lack of the horse and of smelted metals made circumstances very different. But in the Andes and in Mesoamerica, it is not difficult to discern a roughly parallel sequence of development leading from the stressed early first millennium BCE to a Global Classical Age. Here, the press of El Niño floods and droughts made conditions for wider integration difficult, but between 1200 and 800 BCE, peoples in the Andes, Mesoamerica, and eastern North America all developed what are called 'interaction spheres'—repertoires of ritual and iconography shared across vast terrains that suggest a common system of exchange at many levels.

Peoples along the South American coasts, and increasingly into the interior valleys, were stressed by the erratic play of precipitation and drought brought by an extreme El Niño regime among American Pacific Cordillera. These impacts seem to have peaked between 1000 and 700 BCE, when massive beach ridges were formed by mega-El Niños— compounded by highland reglaciation and even a tsunami—that shattered the remaining coastal settlements and provoked general depopulation. Andean recovery came in what is known as the 'Early Horizon' of 800 to 200 BCE, with growing populations now protected by large fortifications. In this Early Horizon context of competing chiefdom societies, a wider integration was forged in the great common ritual culture known as the 'Chavín,' involving a cult of a supernatural jaguar. In manner broadly analogous to Copper Age interaction spheres of fifth and fourth millennium BCE Mesopotamia, these societies managed complex irrigation systems in an arid climate, moved goods on herds of pack animals—llamas rather than donkeys—and crafted an elaborate ornamental metallurgy from copper, silver, and gold. It also might well be appropriate to compare Chavín to the Axial Age world religions that were emerging in the Old World Iron Age societies. The Chavín sphere reached its peak of influence in a period of intense drought between 400 and 200 BCE, providing, as did later Andean empires, a system of geographical connection across regions beset by unpredictable droughts and floods.

In Mesoamerica, a mild version of the global climatic decline had important impacts, and the sequence of cultures was again strikingly similar. The rising scale of

El Niño-Southern Oscillation (ENSO) activity seems to have reached the region around 1500 BCE, bringing shifting patterns of rainfall that benefited a few important regions. Horticulture based on corn/maize began in the Early Formative around 1500 BCE to support growing villages and populations, especially in the central highlands and on the Gulf coast. By 1200 BCE, in a rough parallel to the Chavín, the great Olmec pilgrimage sites in the Gulf coast began to provide a religious integration of large reaches of Mesoamerica. In North America, the impact of the Hallstatt minimum was more obvious, with decline of the relatively sizeable Late Archaic societies between 1200 and 800 BCE. When what is known as the 'Early Woodland' proto-agricultural period stabilized, it too developed an extremely wide-ranging interaction sphere, first in the Adena and then the Hopewell cultures, which both managed burial cults and a widespread trade throughout eastern North America.

As the El Niño climate effect faded around 200 BCE, new local powers emerged in the Andes—expansive militarized states including the Moche, Nasca, and Tiwanaku. In Mesoamerica, the Olmec civilization went into decline by 600 BCE and, as in the Andes, China, and Rome, emerging militarized city states—most importantly in the valley of Teotihuacan—came to dominate Mexico by 300 BCE. The Maya emerged as a series of ritual states at about the same time in the Guatemalan Petén lowlands.

Thus, the improved and stable climate conditions (a climatic optimum) running at least from 200 BCE to 200 CE saw the global consolidation of relatively large and stable militarized states. The Mesoamerican and Andean states broadly echo, on a smaller scale, the rise of Old World powers: the Han in China, the Maurya and Gupta empires in India, the Persians and the short-lived empire of the Alexander the Great, and the Romans.

The classical empires rested on a great paradox: overwhelming military force on frontier societies was followed by stable, perhaps improving, economic conditions for the ruling governments and subject peoples. Imperial rule created the conditions for a certain predictability and security, which drove population growth, and indeed concentration. Of a global population at roughly 100 CE, more than 80 per cent were located in the greater Eurasian core: 65 million in China, 45 million in India, 60 million in Southwest Asia and North Africa, and 30 million in Europe. In the Americas and sub-Saharan Africa, the numbers would have been smaller. Perhaps two-thirds of the roughly 15 million population of the Americas lay within the orbit of the Andean and Mesoamerican polities. Of the thirteen million people of sub-Saharan Africa, about a third or more might have been in the Horn of Africa, the Sudan and wider Sahel, the domain of the Aksum Kingdom, successor to Meroe, and in the region about to consolidate at the Ghana Empire.

Rotary mechanics

If we give credit to copper and bronze as the conceptually revolutionary transition in technology, like the conceptual revolution of earliest domestication, the development and spread of iron was analogous to the Late Neolithic revolution in secondary products. Here, animals and plants—sheep, cattle, and fruit trees in particular—were managed not simply to eat, but to harvest wool, milk, and fruit, the secondary products. Just as the Late Neolithic saw the full realization of agriculture, the Iron Age saw the full realization of metals: these were the truly consolidating epochs for these early economies. And the spread of iron—and certainly steel for special purposes—in the first millennium BCE contributed to an industrial revolution of its own time.

As long as human or animal muscles were providing the direct striking action—cutting, chopping, threshing, pulling—that transformed nature into nutrition, there were real and absolute limits to the improvement of the human material condition. Metal—bronze and iron—both improved the efficiency of muscle action in these direct striking actions. But the mechanics of rotary action—a fundamental principle of all modern technologies—further multiplies the efficiency of direct muscle action.

If its earliest use was the wheel, rotary power did not spread beyond transport until the first millennium. The earliest continuous development of rotary power in the eastern Mediterranean was a late Iron Age innovation. Before it can be baked into bread, grain must be ground into flour, and since the Neolithic, this process had involved grinding grain between two stones, the upper stone pushed by hand in a

A HAND-POWERED ROTARY QUERN, A MILL OF TWO STONES for grinding grain. Replacing the reciprocal back and forth motion required for flat, horizontal grinding stones in use for thousands of years, the rotary quern reducing the physical effort involved in grinding grain.

TO CULVERT

OVERSHOT WATERWHEELS are conjectured to have driven the 16 mills at Barbegal.

reciprocating, back and forth motion. Starting in the fifth century BCE, various rotary mills began to be developed across the Mediterranean for grinding grain and crushing olives: some were small hand-turned devices—rotary querns—and some were larger ones operating like a capstan, with grindstones in a tight box attached to a spoked shaft, which could be turned by one or more men, or a donkey. The rotary quern was gradually converted into a water-powered grinding mill via the development of geared irrigation devices, such as the saqiya around 240 BCE by Hellenistic intellectuals at work in Alexandria. Before the first century BCE, the vertical water mill was common-place in western Anatolia, and from there it spread around the Roman world over the next several centuries. The city of Rome would have massive grinding mills operating by the third century CE. Similarly, water-powered ore-crushing trip hammers were in use by the beginning of the first millennium CE to support Roman mining in Spain.

The trip hammer was an invention rooted in foot-powered tilt hammers for grinding grain and the Greek reciprocating cam.

It seems that water-powered mills did not develop in China until the fifth century CE, possibly through exposure to the Mediterranean mill at the Hellenistic Central Asian empire of Bactria. Nonetheless, the Han period (206 BCE–220 CE) brought innovations that radically increased agricultural productivity. Settled, rather than slash-and-burn, agriculture had been established after 600 BCE, and fallowing and manuring patterns developed over the next several hundred years. The Han developed the curved, cast-iron mouldboard ploughshare (cast in new state-controlled foundries) and the horse-drawn seed drill, which were put to a new rationalized ploughing and planting regime on the royal lands in the dry wheat and millet farming north, and spread from there to the large-landed ruling classes. A rotary winnowing fan, a hand-cranked machine separating grain from chaff, was invented in the wheat/millet north around the same time, and later spread to the rice-growing south. And new and more efficient breast band and collar harnesses allowed for more horse traction to be converted into useful energy. These developments all contributed to the rising productivity of Chinese agriculture.

At the other end of the continent, Roman agriculture did not so much improve as it spread, south into the old Carthaginian domain in Tunisia, and by appropriation, the great breadbasket of the Nile, and north across Gaul into southern England. Here, the key innovations involved the landscape and architecture of empire. The Romans constructed a far-flung, meticulously designed road system that facilitated fast communications across their empire. They also constructed impressive aqueducts to move reasonably clean water into growing cities dominated by grand imperial buildings: the Parthenon, the Coliseum, the Forum. The construction of bridges, aqueducts, and great imperial buildings all featured key Roman innovations: the serial segmental arch and concrete, which has allowed examples to survive for the past two millennia. This architecture would have been impossible without the steel saws and cutting tools pioneered in the Iron Age, and without the mathematics appropriated from Greek intellectuals. Here, impatient Romans, purportedly Julius Caesar himself, abandoned ancient record-keeping methods, discarding the scroll for the codex—the bound book—to allow rapid access to information.

Iron, steel, and rotary mechanics in the longer Iron Age all should be seen as components of a critical energy revolution, contributing to new innovations, and enhancing the circumstances of favoured populations. Of course, the ballooning populations of these societies may well have overwhelmed the economic advantages of the new technologies. The people of the empires may simply have been marching in place, rather than getting ahead, and the evidence emerging from ancient skeletons suggests as much: palaeobiologists are unearthing a story of unhealthy conditions. Generally, agricultural peoples had higher fertility than hunter-gatherer peoples, but unhealthier lives, and the stresses of both climatic reversals and class inequality in state societies seem to have added to the burden. From the Neolithic, the trauma to bones suggests rising rates of tooth decay, anemia, and episodic nutritional stress.

COBBLED SURFACE, ENGINEERED FOR DRAINAGE: a characteristic Roman road, still usable after about 2,000 years, at Blackstone Edge in Lancashire, England.

Circumstances might have improved generally with the advent of the climatic optimum as early as 500 BCE, but the adult heights of Italians, for example, were shorter during the Roman era than they had been in the Iron Age or would be in the post-imperial centuries, and they were very much shorter than the barbarians in northern Europe, who were better fed in less dense populations. Nonetheless, the political security of the empires meant that there were relatively few outright famines, as food supplies could, and did, circulate in protected imperial space, offsetting local stress.

Epidemics and climate reversal: into the 'Dark Ages'

In the Roman world, the circulation of food centred on great fleets bringing grain north from the Nile to Italy. Augustus's conquest of Egypt in 30 BCE led to a new oceanic trade in high-value goods moving from India. Egyptians had been trading in the Red Sea since the Bronze Age, when a loose maritime network linked the Indus with Arabia. Cut off by the collapse of the high civilizations, trade between India and the Mediterranean was restored by 700 BCE through the overland incense route through Arabia. This in turn was slowly undermined by Greek and Roman shipping down the Arabian coast. The rising Roman demand for eastern goods established the basis for the Aksumite

THE PONT DU GARD, THE HIGHEST OF SURVIVING ROMAN AQUEDUCTS, bearing water for the Roman colony now known as Nîmes.

Kingdom, which was established on the Eritrea/Ethiopia coast as the Kingdom of Kush on the Nile went into decline. The Aksumites, with merchants on the south Arabian coast and in the ports of the 'Land of Punt' on the Somali coast, controlled the valuable trade in cinnamon and other spices coming from India, Ceylon, and even China.

But if food and luxury goods could circulate in imperial space, so, too, could disease. While epidemic disease was a constant in the Roman world, three epidemics stand out as particularly intense, with impacts perhaps rivalling that of the Black Death of the 1350s. The first of these, the Antonine Plague, circulating up the Red Sea trade routes, struck a reasonably stable empire in 165. Generally thought to have been smallpox, the Antonine Plague lasted for fifteen years, and ended after it may have killed Marcus Aurelius, the last of a line of five so-called 'Good Emperors' who had ruled since 96 CE. Epidemics then struck various parts of the empire every twenty-five to thirty years: in Nubia in 200, in the armies on the Euphrates in 232, and then another fifteen-year long epidemic, 'Cyprian's Plague'—probably haemorrhagic fever—apparently emerged from Ethiopia in 251. Localized epidemics are recorded over the fourth and fifth centuries CE and are often associated with warfare, but the eruption of Justinian's Plague in 542 would change the face of western Eurasia. Justinian's Plague flared, ebbed, and flared again for centuries, before it finally faded in the 800s. Justinian's Plague also seems to have come up the Red Sea trade, but it now clear that it was bubonic plague, and was carried by a vector of the silk trade through India or Iran from its genetic origin in the east-central Asian steppe.

The impact of these plagues was catastrophic. The Antonine Plague seems be the best explanation for why circumstances in the Roman Empire seemed to shift in the second century CE. Annual lists of taxpayers in rural Egypt suggest certain districts lost as much as 70–90 per cent of their population between the late 150s and the late 160s, which must have shattered agricultural productivity. Series of dated documents and artefacts indicate a steep if temporary decline in Roman economic activity, building construction, marble production, and even coinage in the late 160s and 170s CE. Roman silver mining in Spain collapsed in these years, though raids by North African warriors apparently had a role as well. The numbers of animal bones in Roman sites dropped precipitously, suggesting a poorer diet, and the number of recovered wrecks fell, suggesting a slowing of trade. Population began to decline in Italy, Spain, and France from peaks in the late second century CE, which never really recovered until medieval times. Archaeological analysis of the distribution of African Red Slip Ware, the most widely used form of pottery in the empire—and so a useful diagnostic marker— suggests a massive collapse in production at 250, the beginning of Cyprian's Plague, and a long 'third-century crisis'. Population around the Mediterranean might have fallen by a third between 165 and 400.

Climate did not become a critical factor across the globe until the sixth century CE, generally maintaining through 400 CE warm northern hemispheric temperatures, a strong Asian summer monsoon, and a moderate El Niño regime across the Pacific. The Han dynasty briefly was overthrown during a short sharp monsoon reversal in 9 CE, but quickly regained the mandate of heaven and governed China until another more enduring reversal led to a its final collapse in 220, launching a four-century era of war and disunity. Northern hemisphere temperatures did begin to decline slightly around 200, but the global system did not decisively shift toward a 'Dark Age' climatic regime—now called the "Late Antique Little Ice Age"—until after 400, punctuated by a massive volcanic mega-eruption in 536, and major solar minimum—the Vandal minimum—around 650–700. This colder global regime was marked by advancing sea ice in the North Atlantic, winter rains increasing through the Mediterranean and probably into Central Asia, and the ENSO system shifting toward a stronger El Niño pattern, weakening the summer monsoons from East Africa to India and China, and bringing more rain—and erratic sharp droughts—to the Americas. If the 'Late Antique' global system became cooler, in a pattern enduring for almost 500 years, the Siberian High did not go into its extreme mode as it had at the end of the Bronze Age and would again in the early modern Little Ice Age. It was thus a 'mild' half-cycle climatic decline, separating the Ancient Optimum ending at roughly 400 from a Medieval Optimum beginning after 900.

With the general transition toward more stressful global climates, the ecology and peoples of the Asian steppe once again became a critical part of Eurasian history. During the warm northern climates of the Classical Optimum, the steppe had not impinged decisively upon the rimland societies of Eurasia. In China, the Qin dynasty, ruling briefly between the Han epochs, held off the northern Xiongnu and ordered the massive expansion of the Great Wall. But in subsequent centuries these efforts failed, and nomadic tribes invading from the north brought war, famine, and epidemics. They also drove huge numbers of Han Chinese out of the north, into the Yangzi Valley, where they had to shift from traditional wheat and millet agriculture to rice grown in wet paddies. Similarly, at the other end of the continent in the fourth century CE, barbarian tribes from beyond the frontier began to press in upon the Roman Empire, and within a century controlled much of its domain in western Europe. Here a devastating steppe drought from 350–370 CE played a role in these incursions. But so did the Huns, who emerged out of the steppe in the fourth century CE, and under Attila claimed a domain stretching from the Caspian Sea to Germany. The Avars, ejected from a splintering nomad Rouran empire in Mongolia, arrived in the 560s and established a khaganate between eastern Europe and Anatolia; various Turkish-speaking peoples were intermingled with this movement, and established a khaganate east of the Caspian by 650.

From the sixth century these movements may well have been facilitated by cooler northern climates and greater precipitation on the steppe, which provided grass for their horses. Such higher levels of moisture in the Central Asian steppe might well explain the reemergence of the plague, which struck the Mediterranean in 542, and may well have been impacting China for several hundred years. In the Mediterranean, Justinian's Plague resulted in a collapse of population around the Eurasian rimlands. China's population was cut in half by 400, India by perhaps a third, and Southwest Asia, Egypt, and Europe by a half by 700. Between 200 and 500, this Old World Core dropped from 211 to 147 million total people, or from 82 per cent of the world's population to 71 per cent.

This global climatic stress also hit the societies of the great American cordillera. As the Asian monsoons faded, precipitation shifted east across Pacific, where all the evidence suggests a sequence of wild extremes of precipitation between 400 and 1000. The onset of this dark El Niño epoch drove the collapse of two Early Intermediate Peruvian cultures, the Moche and the Nasca, which had emerged around 200 BCE and collapsed with in a burst of mega El Niño flooding and a severe drought in the late 500s; at roughly the same time, the great city-state of Teotihuacan collapsed as droughts hit the Mexican Highlands. As the Moche and Nasca faded, new cultures of the 'Middle Horizon' emerged, deploying new strategies of settlement and subsistence to withstand the challenges of an epoch of erratic El Niño impacts. The Huari, in the southern highlands, invested in extensive irrigation systems that drew from high altitude water sources; Tiwanaku, around high-altitude Lake Titicaca, grew crops on unique raised beds in the lake; both states lasted several hundred years as coherent urban-centred empires. In the Yucatán peninsula, pre-Classic Mayan culture developed during the relatively stable conditions of the Classical Optimum over several centuries leading up to 200, when a series of sharp droughts coincided with a period of abandonment. Classical Mayan culture developed for more than three hundred years more before another abandonment in the 580s, known as the Mayan hiatus, coincided with the droughts that undermined Teotihuacan in Mexico and the Moche and the Nasca in Peru.

Around the Mediterranean, the collapse of the Ancient World had profound environmental impacts, as depopulation by epidemic was preceded by the intensification of severe winter rainfall. During Roman times the growing population had spread in marginal regions, cultivating hillside terraces with careful labour. As Justinian's Plague sliced through the population, the hillside terracing collapsed under the weight of torrential winter rains, destroying the agricultural improvements of the previous several centuries and setting off a wave of soil erosion. As the hillside fields collapsed, the survivors retreated. In Roman Italy, the farming population had been densely spread across lowlands and uplands; with the onslaught of rampant warfare in late Antiquity the people abandoned the towns and villas in the lowlands and huddled, as in Early Iron Age times, in walled mountain villages.

Paradoxically, many of these survivors fared better than their forebears in the classical age. Smaller populations meant more resources for fewer people, and the collapse of imperial trade minimized the circulation of the diseases that had killed so many. If adult stature is any measure, depopulation was reasonably good for routine health. We do not have global data, but the European evidence for stature is quite striking. Those people who survived the onslaught of plague, and made the adjustment to both the advance of colder climates and the erosion of imperial structures, were larger than their ancestors. The results of a variety of studies suggest that Europeans living in the sixth century CE were roughly 2–2.5 cm taller than those of the age of empire. While these heights declined somewhat in the next few centuries, they remained taller than the Roman era average, and generally climbed in the first two centuries of the Medieval Optimum, the eleventh and twelfth centuries CE. British skeletons indicate that post-Roman peoples were not only taller but moderately healthier, as measured by tooth loss, Harris lines (physical marks of childhood starvation), and caries (dental decay). Strikingly, stature declined in Viking Denmark, where population growth, internal stratification, and long-range raiding and trade may have taken a toll. But the prevailing story is plain: once freed of the density, inequality, and exposure to disease of imperial times, European health improved.

Transformation, contest, and crisis in the Dark Ages, 400–950 CE

The end of the Ancient World, or what we now called a wider Late Antiquity, saw the rise of powerful new religions. Christianity, a radical sect in Rome's high imperial centuries, spread with the onset of the plagues; the new religion's emphasis on brotherhood and charity may well have been a vehicle of survival and conversion. It was adopted as the imperial religion in 380, two years after the Goth barbarians had defeated a Roman army at the battle of Adrianople. Islam was founded in Arabia as the wider cold Late Antique regime set in two hundred years later. The wider authority of the empire crumbled even more dramatically in the late sixth century CE, in the wake of the climate disturbances following the possible volcanic winter in 536, and the onslaught of Justinian's Plague in 542. Born around 570, the Prophet Muhammad received his divine revelations around 610, and fled to Medina in 622. From thence arose a new world religion.

Within 50 years, the Islamic domain had spread from Arabia east through Mesopotamia and Persia, north into Anatolia, and west to Egypt and along the North African coast. By 750 it reached from Spain to the Sind, and to the arid southern steppe. The Late Antique climate pattern seems to have contributed to the rise and spread of Islam. The catastrophic flooding of the sixth and seventh centuries, coupled with the ongoing impacts of the Justinian Plague, certainly weakened the resistance of the Byzantine heirs of Roman imperium. On the other hand, Southwest Asia, the North African coast, and Persia continued to benefit from stronger southerly flow of the Atlantic winter westerlies and to receive relatively high precipitation throughout the period. This pattern may well have enhanced the agricultural base for the great cities that rose across the Arab-Islamic domain. It may also have shaped the fortunes of the Kingdom of Ghana in the west African Sahel, which saw the rise and fall of moderately strong precipitation from around 450 to 1050–1100, when Ghana was finally overwhelmed by Islamic raiders.

Newly Christian Europe suffered during this golden age of Islam. An age of invasions had begun long before, with arrival of the Goths, Alans, and Huns from the eastern steppe, and when the Muslim warriors of the Umayyad Caliphate began to sweep across Spain in 711, they captured cities commanded by Gothic kings. Stopped by the Franks at the battle of Tours in 732, the continuing threat of Islamic invasion was compounded by the rise of the Vikings, who began raiding the northern European coast in 793, which continued for over two hundred years. During these centuries, the Carolingian Franks claimed to have briefly restored the authority of the Roman Empire: Charles Martel had led the forces at Tours in 732; his grandson Charlemagne was crowned by the Pope in 800. Carolingian legal reform and support for the Catholic church would provide a basis of important developments in the centuries to come, but it did so under the pressure of a final intensification of the Late Antique climate regime.

These stresses were manifested in Europe between the 760s and 940s in a series of harsh winters and extremely rainy summers that seem to have been directly caused by a string of severe volcanic eruptions. This harsh weather assaulted man and beast, causing a series of famines and shortfalls, most strikingly in the ninth century CE, between 820 and 845, and 867 and 874, as the Carolingian dynasty was collapsing. These famines were bracketed by two great cattle epidemics, in the 560s and the 980s, apparently rinderpest. The explosion of disease among European cattle in these years seems to have spread to humans as well, followed by the emergence of measles around 1000 in a recognizably modern form.

These late Dark Age European events had their analogues on both sides of the Pacific. The final transformation of the Maya around 900 was one symptom of this wider global event. Reestablished in the 600s, the Mayan hierarchy contended with dry Dark Age conditions by constructing their primate temple cities as elaborate water-management systems, building temples on high points, and collecting rainy season runoff in adjacent quarries and lagoons. While Mayan agricultural practice and population growth might well have been unsustainable in the long run, when crisis came it was driven by exogenous climatic conditions. After a recovery and two hundred years of further expansion, Mayan cities faced a series of sharp droughts beginning in 760; about 150 years later, the great lowland cities had utterly collapsed. This advancing drought was linked with a rising volatility of El Niño flooding and droughts in the Andes: here, the Huari empire splintered after 800, and the Tiwanaku around 1100. The Maya may not have collapsed, precisely; rather, the main centres of urban civilization continued in the uplands or, within the Yucatán, shifted to a more trade-oriented economy in coastal regions.

A similar and simultaneous trajectory unfolded across the Pacific in China. With the collapse of the Han, competing polities struggled in a cold and unstable era of 'Disunity' running from 220 to 589, when China was finally reunited under the Sui, and then more decisively the Tang dynasty in 618. The summer monsoon records suggest that the entire period of Disunity was one of moderate summer monsoons, but increasing around 550. The brief but significant span of the Sui dynasty from 589 to 617, which reunified China for the first time since the Han, coincided with the end of this period of strong monsoons, and its final years saw a series of floods, setting off the rebellions that brought down the dynasty. The Tang dynasty dates from 617 to 907, which is almost the exact chronology of the Late Classic Maya, and coincided with the height of Huari and Tiwanaku Peru. Successfully ruling a united and expanding China in its first century CE, early in the eighth century CE the Tang regime was stressed by recurring onslaughts of flood, drought, and locusts from roughly 710 to 730. Simultaneously it became embroiled with frontier struggles in the west, during which a severe 'pestilence' broke out among the steppe tribes. These frontier wars set off the punishing An Lu-Shan Rebellion of 755–763 that sapped the resources and legitimacy of the Tang. In its closing years, bubonic plague—probably introduced from the nomad steppe via the rebel armies—devastated broad regions of coastal southern China, cutting Chinese populations drastically. Weakened by rebellion, the collapse of central authority, and the impact of plague, the Tang court struggled on for another century or so, before finally it collapsed in 907 as the droughts, floods, locusts, and famine caused by fifty years of harsh winter monsoons and weak summer monsoons, and thirty years of plunging summer temperatures, launched waves of brigandage and rebellion.

Warming global climate: into the Middle Ages, 950–1260 CE

Around 950 the climatic conditions shaping the Dark Age began to recede. Northern hemispheric temperatures rose sharply, with a fifty-year solar maximum and the end of the Dark Age eruptions. These temperatures peaked for over a century and a half—the highest since the Classical maximum, and the highest until the twentieth century. The entire global climate system shifted with these temperatures: ice rafting retreated from the North Atlantic as the winter westerlies intensified and shifted from south to northern Europe; the summer monsoons watering India and China recovered.

Similarly, the southern hemisphere westerlies shifted toward the pole, allowing moist air to flow in off the Indian Ocean to coastal east and southern Africa. All of these shifts would underwrite the great prosperity in northern Europe, India, and China, and in Southeast Asia as well. But other parts of the world did not do as well. Across the Pacific, the Americas were gripped by intense La Niña drought, reaching mega-drought conditions from California to the Mississippi Valley between 1100 and 1250. Additionally, drought struck across parts of the African Sahel: in Egypt the Nile flood failed in a series of historic low floods starting around 930, and as the winter westerlies shifted north, much of the Mediterranean got much drier, as did Central Asia, which saw a deep drought that did not break until the early 14th century CE. Thus, this period, once called the Medieval Warming, is now known by the more neutral term 'the Medieval Climate Anomaly'.

Hard times struck where the rains failed. In Mesoamerica, power was dispersed among a variety of regional polities, perhaps united by what is known as the feathered serpent cult from the spread of a common stone-carved iconography. Along the Andes, as the drought intensified, the reach of larger polities faded except for an emerging coastal group, the Chimú, known for their ocean-going trading along the Pacific coast. Advancing drought in North America shaped a tightly compressed period of proto-state formation. In both the plateau regions of the Southwest and in the middle reaches of the Mississippi Valley, extensive village-based populations had emerged with the onset of warm dry conditions around 900, now fed by corn/maize agriculture; east of the Mississippi, these were the Late Woodland peoples. Powerful, coercive social hierarchies rapidly emerged in what is known as the Mississippian culture. Chaco Canyon, in the southwest, and the city-state of Cahokia, at the confluence of the Ohio and the Mississippi, were important centres for large areas. Both regions and their respective centres went into significant decline at the middle of the thirteenth century CE, during the peak of the dry medieval La Niña. In the southwest, a first phase of megadrought between 1120 and 1150 forced the abandonment of the ritual centre at Chaco; around 1250, under continuing impact of drought, the ancient Pueblo congregated at Mesa Verde in great cliff-towns built for defence, before suddenly abandoning the plateau for the Rio Grande Valley around 1300. In the Mississippi valley the droughts hit in a series of progressively deep swings between 1100 and 1245, as a result of which the population of Cahokia progressively declined from a peak at 1075–1100. The first truly severe drought struck around 1140, forcing the abandonment of prairie farming communities in Illinois that had supported the Cahokia population. The 1140–55 drought and three successive droughts through 1245 each coincided exactly with four constructions of palisade fortifications, suggesting periods of recurring warfare and perhaps predatory refugee bands; Cahokia was essentially abandoned by 1350. Similarly, drought seems to have played a role in the various abandonments of smaller Mississippian mound building polities to the south between 1250 and 1375.

Across the Middle East, the great Islamic centres were severely affected by the changing climate. The suppression of the Nile flow and the northward shift of the winter westerlies brought devastation to societies around the eastern Mediterranean and to the east, with intense droughts starting around 950 but particularly focused between 1020 and 1070, precisely the period when Europe was emerging from a cold Late Antiquity. Harvests failures in Egypt were followed by cold droughts from southern Italy to Iraq, and then by agricultural and political collapses in Iran and Baghdad, the weakening of cities, the abandonment of lands, and the rise of nomadic incursions on all sides. During the droughts, Egypt suffered catastrophic famines, often compounded by earthquakes and epidemics, in the 960s, the 1020s, and around 1200.

Elsewhere, however, the Middle Ages were times of recovery, prosperity, and expansion. The effects of the variable medieval climate regime on humanity are perhaps best sketched in terms of population. As of 700, when global population may have reached a low Dark Ages point of about 200 million, the ancient Eurasian core of China, India, Middle East, and North Africa plus Europe—though much reduced—still accounted for the largest populations, and about 75 per cent of the world's people. By 1000, sub-Saharan Africa had joined these largest populations, but over the next two hundred years, the opening of the Medieval climate regime, the Middle East and North Africa lost population, while China, India, Europe, sub-Saharan Africa, and now Southeast Asia had recovered or suddenly doubled, and accounted for almost 80 per cent of the world's 400 million people.

These numbers followed the benefits of the new climate regime. In India, which grew perhaps more drastically in the century after 1200, the strengthened monsoons increased the longevity of the Hindu and Buddhist kingdoms of the Classical Age, particularly across south India, where stronger monsoons underwrote an expansion of agriculture in the dry interior. By 1000, merchants in these South India kingdoms were engaged in a vigorous trade with newly emerged complex societies across the Bay of Bengal. Here in Southeast Asia, the strong Medieval monsoons shaped a parallel florescence, contributing to the region's first development of state polities: the Pagan in Burma, the Khymer in Cambodia, the Champa on the central coast of Vietnam, and the Ly and Than dynasties in the Red River valley in northern Vietnam. The flow of moist tropical easterlies brought similar summer rainfall to east coastal and southern Africa, benefiting the emerging city-states on the Swahili coast engaged in the Indian Ocean trade, and the cattle-herding, ironworking Bantu peoples moving through the interior, founding proto-states like that preserved at the Great Zimbabwe. In Western Africa, the Mali empire, focused on the Gambia and Senegal Rivers, west of the centre of the collapsed Ghana empire, controlled the trade in gold moving north from the forest region across the desert to Morocco and the wider Mediterranean.

The largest expansions came in China and Europe. Where the Islamic world had been the dynamic force in western Eurasia from 700 to 1000, the initiative fed by warm temperatures and regular rains now moved toward Europe. While Europe doubled its population from 36 to 79 million between 1000 and 1300, the Middle Eastern and North African population dropped from 42 to 29 million. Europe's growth rested on a burgeoning trade, and in improvements in agriculture. The origins of Europe's revival

THE ANGKOR WAT TEMPLE COMPLEX IN CAMBODIA, the biggest temple in the world when King Suryavaram II built it in the twelfth century.

went back to the ninth century CE as a growing trade with the Islamic Mediterranean began to develop. By the eleventh century CE this trade had both internal and external dynamics, with the emergence of towns and cities, and a merchant class operating from within their walls, protected by new legal codes defining property relations. As agriculture expanded it moved from the dry uplands into the rich wet river valley soils, as the ancient light scratch plough was replaced with a new heavy wheeled mouldboard plough, drawn first by teams of oxen and increasingly by faster, stronger horses. The adoption of the yoke harness, first developed in China, allowed horses much greater efficiency over the ancient and Roman breast band harness, which choked the horse as it leaned into the load. If Europe was divided into a series of competing kingdoms, the Catholic Church provided an integrating institutional structure, with Latin as a common elite language driving a massive expansion of manuscript book production and the rise of universities throughout Europe. The common intellectual and institutional structure of the church was reinforced by doctrine, and a 'Pax Christiana' shaped a common peace that allowed the flourishing of great medieval commercial fairs, operating on a cycle over vast distances, on a corridor linking Flanders, France, and Italy. The church was also an economic actor in its own right, financing the construction of great stone-built cathedrals, abbeys, monasteries, and universities. Given the demand for iron and steel in construction, the church also played a role in metallurgy; the Cistercian order in particular was known for metalworking. But despite wider European advances, ironworking still involved the bloomeries of the early Iron Age, and the blast furnace would not make its general appearance in Europe until the end of the fifteenth century CE, and indeed milling technology remained essentially where the Romans had left it.

China under the Song Dynasty, running from 960 to 1279, was an even more dramatic story. Between 1000 and 1200, Chinese populations more than doubled from 56 to 128 million. Urban populations reached into the millions. Behind this explosive growth lay two centuries of warm temperatures and strong summer monsoons—and a short-lived economic revolution. Song governance supported innovation and commercialization. The government opened seven new ports to trade with Japan and Southeast Asia, and massively expanded its coinage to support commerce. Rice paddy agriculture was transformed into an advanced cycle of two and three crops per year with new tools and methods, new seeds, and massive investments in irrigation. Iron production for commerce and war was revolutionized, increasing twelvefold. The expansion of iron production contributed to a wood supply crisis in north China;

A PLOUGH PULLED BY YOKED OXEN ILLUSTRATES AN OFTEN MISTRANSLATED TEXT OF PSALM 93: 'Shalt thou cleave to the throne of iniquity, thou who feignest work in thy speech?'.

THE CATHEDRAL AT CHARTRES; CATHEDRALS MULTIPLIED in the twelfth and thirteenth centuries, and forests—the sacred groves of paganism—were felled and their trees appropriated for the rafters and scaffolding of the huge engineering works the church sponsored.

coal had been in use in small quantities since the fourth century, but between 1050 and 1126 it became the primary source of domestic and industrial fuel in North China. Key innovations elsewhere in the Song economy included paper making, printing, gunpowder, and the first mechanical processing of textiles. Sending shipping out into the China Sea—and trading caravans overland—the Song dominated an emerging medieval world system running east through Central Asia and India. The historian William McNeill has argued that China's economic revolution during the Song 'tipped a critical balance in world history' toward the rise of the modern market economy and its power and reach.

Into the Little Ice Age, and the Black Death, 1260–1350: the Hallstatt solar minimum returns

Once again, the now-ancient oscillation took its toll. The climate regime that broadly defined the global Middle Ages started to reverse itself in the thirteenth century CE, in the first stages of the Little Ice Age that would run down to the opening of the eighteenth century. The nearly coincidental mega-eruption of El Chichón in 1258 and the sharp onset of the sixty-year Wolf solar minimum in the 1260s seem to have acted as a trigger leading to a new climatic regime. The Wolf was the first of three major solar minima that together composed a Hallstatt grand minimum, which had not been seen since the Bronze Age crisis. At its height, the Little Ice Age would see advancing ice rafts in the North Atlantic, the fading of Asian Monsoons, and the return to a strong El Niño pattern bringing rains to the American coast. The northern winter westerlies shifted south, bringing strong rains again to the Mediterranean—and moisture to the dry Eurasian steppes. As the winter Siberian High strengthened, northern temperatures would fall dramatically, reaching their lowest point between the 1560s and 1690s. In the short term, the opening phases of the Little Ice Age brought erratic wet summers to Europe from the 1270s to the 1350s.

Once again, the effects on societies of these shifting patterns varied. The Hindu kingdoms in south India, and the new states across South East Asia, all suffered with the decline of the South Asian monsoon. In the Americas, the increased El Niño precipitation may have contributed to the rise of two great empires: the Aztecs in Mexico and the Inca in the Andes. In Europe, the explosive rise of population was already pressing on the limits of the organic economy, as illustrated in worsening diets and health of the poor. The wet summers at the end of the thirteenth century CE set off miseries last seen in Carolingian times: starting in the 1280s, sheep were afflicted with scabies, liver flukes, and murrain, and harvests began to fail. Excessive rains drove a continent-wide famine from 1315 to 1321, immediately followed by a rinderpest plague that killed half of the cattle in Europe.

China's crisis was even more catastrophic, and its onset involved both climate and the ancient threat of the nomadic peoples of the steppe. China's Medieval crisis came in three stages. First the Northern Song domains fell to the Manchurian Jurchen tribal nomads in a sudden onslaught in the late 1120s. Ninety years later, in 1214–15, the Mongols led by Genghis Khan invaded north China. After continuing economic development in the southern Song regions, the Mongols finally conquered the Song in 1279. Violent conquest in a time of cold brought mass death. The Mongol conquest of north China was insanely destructive: peasants were massacred or forced into human wave attacks, food production was disrupted, and presumably epidemics took their toll. Population in the north dropped from 50 million in 1195 to 8.5 million in 1235. Overall, China's population fell from a peak of 128 million in 1200 to 70 million in 1400. The invasions of the Jurgen and the Mongols both appear to have occurred in special climatic junctures, when cold dry winters in China coincided with brief periods of summer warmth and rainfall on the northern steppe.

Genghis Khan and his sons forged a powerful, tightly organized military machine, and these qualities may well explain why the Mongols were able to move west through a still very arid central Asia with such speed and force. By the time of his death in 1227,

'LET US BUILD OURSELVES A CITY AND A TOWER' (Genesis, 11:1). The Tower of Babel symbolized human arrogance but also represented a response to ecological disaster: according to the Bible story at Babylon, its builders had found a spot to settle after the flood.

they had reached the Caspian Sea, and by 1241 they had destroyed much of Russian Kiev, and were on the edge of Central Europe. In 1258, they captured and sacked Baghdad, the seat of the Islamic Abbasid Caliphate. By the 1280s, four great khanates controlled Eurasia from the Black Sea to the Persian to South China. The steppe had once again consumed most of two of the great primary hearths of Old World civilization.

The unification of Eurasia by the Mongols would have devastating impacts across the Old World starting in the 1340s. But it was already intersecting with the contest of Europe and Islam. During the High Middle Ages, Europe of Pax Christiana had turned its sights on the Levant. Asked to defend Byzantium from the Turks in 1096, Crusader armies had fought their way to Jerusalem and established a series of mini-states from southern Anatolia through the Holy Land. From here, European merchants, led by the Venetians and Genoese, carried on a lucrative and addictive trade reaching east to the Indian coast, the source of spices and silks. As fortunes turned, the last of these states was destroyed by the Mamluks in 1291. Three decades before, increasingly cut off from the maritime routes to the east, these traders moved to the northern Black Sea coast, on the edge of the Kipchak Khanate of the Golden Horde, to intercept a rising trade moving west overland from the east.

The onset of plague across the Old World was intimately connected to the climatic conditions on the steppe. Rain fed grass for the horses that carried the nomad armies, and it also fed the biota supporting the *Yersinia pestis* bacillus. After a parched Middle Ages, the winter rains began to return to the steppe, ever so slightly and intermittently from the 1220s to the 1270s, and then more decidedly, if with some sharp oscillations, in the 1330s and 1340s, as the Little Ice Age pattern set in. Plague may have hit China in 1331, and it may have hit the town of Issyk-Kul in Kyrgyzstan in 1338–9. Genetic research now indicates that it emerged in a focus on the eastern end of the Silk Road network, in the high Qinghai-Tibetan plateau roughly halfway between Kyrgyzstan and the Yellow Sea. In 1346, after a petty quarrel, the Golden Horde besieged Genoese traders in the town of Kaffa on the Crimean coast of the Black Sea. By 1347–8, ships fleeing Kaffa had brought the bubonic plague to ports around the eastern Mediterranean. Within two years, as much as a third of the population of Europe and the Middle East had died, and the epidemic was making its way across the Sahara to the west African coast.

The onset of the Little Ice Age and the march of the Black Death marked the final and catastrophic downturn in a cycle that ran back two millennia to the close of the Bronze Age, and before. This oscillating pattern took its global shape and coherence from the great repeating pattern in global climate history: the 2200-year Hallstatt solar cycle manifested in the Bronze Age-Iron Age crisis and the Little Ice Age, with warmer Ancient and Medieval regimes separated by the half-cycle Dark Ages. In the Old World, particularly greater Eurasia, the impact of these warmer and colder epochs was intensified by the drier and wetter conditions that resulted in the great interior steppe.

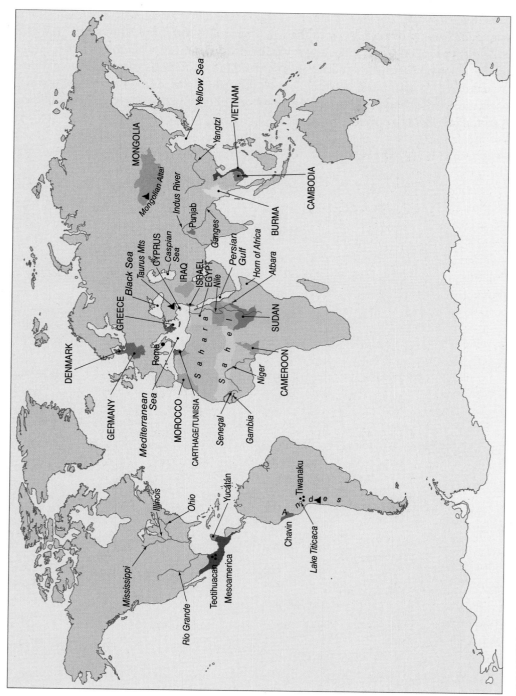

LOCATIONS AROUND THE ANCIENT AND MEDIEVAL WORLD DISCUSSED IN THIS CHAPTER.

Against the wider forces of nature, humanity could mobilize limited resources. Their skeletons tell a sobering story. Throughout these two millennia human health was poor, people did not grow to their potential, and their lives were short. The Old World shift to iron-based metallurgy was the most significant technological departure of the entire era. Fundamental changes in the life conditions of the great majority would have to await the scientific revolution. But with each turn of the natural oscillation, culture and institutional practice, generation upon generation was building a cumulative foundation for the future.

CHAPTER 6

Intellectual Traditions

Philosophy, Science, Religion, and the Arts, 500 BCE–1350 CE

DAVID NORTHRUP

HUMANS have always explored their world, attempting to make sense of what they see and speculating about things that are too distant to examine or that cannot be seen at all. Archaeologist Brian Fagan suggests that by 10,000 years ago, people around the world had concluded that human life was governed by the cycle of the seasons, by the movements of heavenly bodies, and by invisible spirits. They believed that communication with spirits was possible at certain special natural places, such as caves, tall mountains, and sacred springs, as well as in man-made pyramids, towers, and shrines, and temples. People held that departed ancestors also mediated such communication, as did certain living individuals through dreams, visions, or other forms of altered consciousness. Though such beliefs were widespread, each society had its own ancestral spirits, deities, sacred places, and mediums. Therefore, the ideas and practices of one society were as foreign to its neighbours as were the mutually unintelligible languages each society spoke.

Beginning some 2,600 years ago, seminal thinkers created new intellectual systems that succeeded in crossing cultural boundaries and endured into present times. These included the ways of thinking, now called philosophy, that originated in South and East Asia and the Hellenic world, early mathematics and scientific inquiry, and two new religions founded in the Near East by Jesus and Muhammad. Although it is convenient to describe philosophy, science, and religion as distinct entities, during most of this era the lines between them were fluid. Logical systems of ethics referenced supernatural beings; believers in supernatural revelations sought to reconcile them with rational thought; and those conducting scientific investigations did not exclude explanations that were magical or mystical. Thus, alchemy was the mother of chemistry and astrology underpinned efforts to trace the movements of heavenly bodies.

This chapter's exploration of such intellectual traditions is confined to Asia, Europe, and parts of Africa for two reasons. First, the traditions that arose in these lands left considerable evidence of their existence, not only stone buildings and art, but also

THE TEMPLE OF CONCORD, AGRIGENTO, SICILY, *c.* 430 BCE, became a Christian church about a thousand years after it was built. This well-preserved Doric temple in the Greek colony of Sicily, incorporates Classical Greek design with 13 columns at each side.

abundant written evidence that documents the development and spread of their intellectual traditions. Although monumental architecture, art, and writing also existed elsewhere in this period, such as among the Maya of Central America, it is not yet possible to write a coherent and factual account of *intellectual* history elsewhere. The second reason for privileging Eurasia is more speculative: the fact that these lands had dense populations, bustling urban centres, and cross-cultural interaction due to trade may have increased the likelihood of seminal thinkers emerging there. Put another way, even though great thinkers may have existed in other parts of the world, there is too little evidence to prove their existence and reason to doubt that their teachings could have survived and spread without a means to record them.

An 'Axial Age'?

After World War II, a prolific German existential philosopher named Karl Jaspers popularized the notion of a unique 'Axial Age' in late antiquity, during which fundamental categories of thinking were born—including religions and philosophies—that continued down to his time. Jaspers argued that this period was a turning point in world history, which separated earlier civilizations from a new age. The idea has been widely discussed and disputed. Even if not everything Jaspers proposed is accepted by historians today, there is no denying that this era saw the rise of Hinduism and Buddhism in India, Confucius and Laozi in China, Zarathustra (somewhat earlier) in Persia, the Jewish prophets in ancient Israel, Plato and Aristotle in Greece, and many other traditions. Nor is there any denying that these traditions spread outside the areas of their origins and have long endured.

What gave rise to the seminal thinkers of this era? Even though each intellectual tradition had its own distinct origin, some scholars have argued they shared similar philosophical principles or religious insights. Others have noted that such great sages arose at a time when literacy, empires, and coinage were also spreading. Although empires, coins, writing, and intellectual traditions were not directly connected, it seems probable that common material conditions promoted them all. Expanding commerce and empires promoted networks of interaction through which ideas as well as goods could move; and socio-economic hierarchies in densely populated societies gave some people the leisure to pursue speculative ideas, whether as teachers or as students. The exceptionally talented individuals of the Axial Age deserve credit for their intellectual and spiritual insights, but a key reason their teachings endured was because they were written down. Written texts could be hidden to survive persecutions, could be carried to distant places, and could be rediscovered centuries after their penning. Yet it is a curious fact that none of the founders of the philosophical and religious traditions examined in this chapter wrote anything themselves; rather, it was their followers who recorded their words.

Traditions might claim to be the product of reason, divine revelation, or some mixture of the two, but history shows that their founders and early followers also incorporated the beliefs, customs, and trends of their times. Just as styles of art and architecture were codified and modified over time and space, later generations of followers both solidified and elaborated the beliefs and practices of these intellectual traditions and reinterpreted them for the societies to which they spread. For these and other reasons, the more successful traditions fragmented into different sects or schools.

All sources agree that Siddhartha Gautama was the founder of Buddhism, though he may have lived earlier than the period from about 563 to about 483 BCE that is often given for his lifespan. Reconstructing the Buddha's original teachings is also challenging because the oldest texts were written centuries after his death, by which time competing Buddhist schools had produced quite different teachings. Even so, scholars believe certain facts are likely. Gautama grew up in a wealthy family living in the southern foothills of the Himalayas. His search for understanding led him to denounce material comforts and take up rigorous fasting and meditation, a path common among Indian holy men of his day. After six years he reached the conclusion that the ascetic life brought him no closer to spiritual insight than his earlier comforts had. Gautama opted for a 'middle path' between the two. At the age of 35 he succeeded in his spiritual quest, becoming the Buddha, i.e. the enlightened one.

The Buddha's insights are summarized as the Four Noble Truths: 1) life is suffering; 2) suffering arises from cravings and attachments; 3) the solution to suffering lies in curbing desire; and 4) desire can be curbed if one follows the Buddhist path. In a nutshell, this Eightfold Path consists of correct views, thought, speech, conduct, livelihood, effort, attention, and concentration. This very compressed list can be subdivided into three different and slightly overlapping categories (or pillars). The first pillar concerns wisdom, i.e. the renunciation of material values and the embrace of benevolent and non-violent attitudes. The ethical second pillar counsels avoiding violence, lies, theft, and sexual misconduct. The third pillar calls for meditation techniques that give one wisdom and insight and ultimately lead beyond perceptions and feelings. This latter state is called *nirvana*, a word meaning 'blown out' (like a candle flame). Although Siddhartha shared the common Indian belief of his day that humans were spirits forced to reincarnate again and again until they somehow escaped material existence, he believed nirvana was less a heavenly state of spiritual bliss than it was a sort of nothingness, an extinction of existence. Insofar as can be known, the Buddha's original philosophy did not include belief in a creator or other deities.

During his lifetime the Buddha attracted a community of followers, male and female, both lay and monastic. They undertook the first large-scale missionary movement in world history, initially throughout India and in later centuries across the face of Asia. The conquests of Alexander the Great as far as the Indus valley may have opened communication all the way to the Mediterranean, where ancient sources mention early visits by Buddhist monks. Following the disintegration of Alexander's empire after his death in 323 BCE, the rise of the Maurya Empire in the Punjab provided favourable conditions for the spread of Buddhism. With the strong backing of Emperor Asoka (r. 269–232 BCE) Buddhism spread within his vast empire that came to include most of India. Asoka's support gave Buddhism an advantage over other Indian religious traditions and set it on its way to becoming a major religion. Asoka's son is said to have led missionaries south to Sri Lanka and there are other reports of monks taking the Buddha's teachings to Burma, Thailand, and Sumatra. By the first century CE there is evidence of Buddhist monks living in caves in a high mountain pass in Afghanistan, continuing an association of Buddhism with that area that may date back to Gautama's lifetime.

In China, the teacher Kong Fuzi (c. 551–479 BCE), known as Confucius in the West, may have been a near contemporary of the Buddha. Distressed by warfare and the venality of rulers, Confucius revived the belief that rulers were governed by the 'mandate of heaven' that required them use to use their power fairly and justly. Confucius also echoed the traditional Chinese belief in the central importance of the family. He encouraged children to respect their parents and revere departed ancestors, family members to be loyal to each other, and wives to obey their husbands. Although Confucius believed in ancestral spirits, gods, and the power of heavenly bodies, what he taught was not a new religion as much as a philosophy of how to live ethically and honourably.

In a key departure from the aristocratic notion of inherited nobility, Confucius taught that true nobility (or gentility) was a product of education and conduct. In the

NANJING CONFUCIAN TEMPLE, ELEVENTH CENTURY, but repeatedly reconstructed, demonstrates the durability of Confucianism in China.

book known as the *Analects,* which his disciples later compiled, Confucius offers these insights: the gentleman concerns himself with the true way (*dao*) rather than luxury, gluttony, and material success; he should be diligent in work, cautious in speech, and revere the mandate of heaven, and the words of the sages. The *Analects* and other texts that deal with Confucius' homeland, divination, history, and poetry are revered as the Wu Ching (the Five Classics).

A later follower, Mengzi (327–269 BCE), known as Mencius in the West, greatly increased Confucianism's appeal through clever stories, sayings, and parables that expressed Confucian values. At the same time, he defended the great inequality in China by arguing that those who worked with their heads were more important than those who worked with their hands. He defended the mandate of heaven but also reminded rulers of the basic duty to see to the welfare of their people. As Confucianism gained popularity its followers began to revere the founder as a sort of god and added other religious features, so that by the first century CE, it resembled a religion.

Around the time of Confucius, another influential Chinese philosophy came into existence: the School of the Dao (or Daoism). Their meaning of *dao* (way or path) was alignment with nature. Early Daoism emphasized right living and freeing oneself from desire through mystical contemplation but differed from Confucians in advocating minimal government interference. Daoism gradually took on the features of a religion, with many deities (including its supposed founder Laozi), temples, monasteries, and rituals. As discussed later in this chapter, Daoism's further development was strongly influenced by interactions with Buddhism.

At about the same time, a complex of teachings was emerging in ancient Greece, known as Hellenism. An early teacher named Socrates (469–399 BCE) taught ethical views similar to those of Confucius and the Buddha and was adept in pursuing propositions to their logical conclusions. Socrates called his method 'philosophy', from the Greek meaning 'love of wisdom', a term that the Greek thinker Pythagoras of Samos may have coined a century earlier. His questioning of prevailing ideas was so forceful that Socrates' enemies accused him of religious heresies and of corrupting the youth. Although he denied the charges, he was convicted and forced to commit suicide. His star pupil Plato (*c.* 427–*c.* 347 BCE) wrote down what we know of the Socratic method. Plato sought to avoid public criticism and may have held back some of his master's more advanced views. He founded a school called the Academy in Athens to teach mathematics and philosophy. The heart of Platonism is the theory that there exist ideal forms, such as Beauty, Truth, and Good, with reference to which individuals can recognize real, but imperfect, examples of things that are beautiful, true, or good. The pure forms exist outside the material world and outside the human mind. Like Socrates, Plato believed that the search for knowledge was needed for virtue and happiness and that proper understanding was formed from a process known as the dialectic, in which all assumptions are questioned and particulars are compared to ideals. In the various dialogues Plato wrote, Socrates and other philosophers debate the logic of certain propositions, often without reaching a final conclusion. A different approach is found in the *Republic*, where Plato argued that the philosopher would be the best ruler, with others, such as warriors or labourers, performing the tasks best suited to them.

Aristotle (384–322) was for many years a pupil of Plato's at the Academy, but in later life he moved away from Plato's deductive reasoning to a more empirical and analytical approach to understanding. Like Plato, he prized the rational search for truth, but he rejected his master's belief that the form and matter of something were separable. For Aristotle, the shape of a ball was intrinsic to its propensity to roll. More profoundly, he held that the natural makeup of a living thing determined how it acted and that, because human nature includes great reasoning capacity, humans should live in a moral, rational way. Aristotle wrote on a vast number of subjects, including many aspects of the natural world, including biology, geology, physics, and psychology, as well as on logic and metaphysics, ethics, politics, and rhetoric. He was also the tutor of Alexander the Great, whose conquests in Egypt and east to the Indus River helped spread Greek thinking and aesthetics over a vast area.

The foundations of science

Besides exploring the best ways to live and reason, the thinkers of the Axial Age undertook important investigations of the natural world that built on the practical and theoretical achievements of earlier people around the world, who had devised calendars, purified metals and made alloys, domesticated plants and animals, and learned the secrets of herbal medicines. The new scientific contributions are particularly important because they were written down, copied, and studied by succeeding generations.

A key area of investigation was mathematics. During the millennium after 500 BCE, Indian specialists had devised a clever system of numerals (including zero) with place-value, and symbols for unknowns and mathematical operations both elementary (addition, subtraction, etc.) and advanced (algorithms, quadratic equations, square roots, and calculus). Later, Islamic scholars borrowed the Indian mathematical systems and symbols, which spread to Jewish scholars in Muslim Spain in the 1200s, and eventually to the Latin West. In early China, mathematicians also employed place-value in writing numbers, leaving a blank space for a null quantity and also recording decimal places. In Europe one of the best remembered ancient mathematicians was Pythagoras of Samos (c. 570–c. 495 BCE), although it is not certain that he personally had a role in formulating the famous theorem that bears his name. Even earlier, the mathematical relationship of the sides and angles of a right-angled triangle were known to Babylonians and Indians, so it is possible he learned the theorem on his travels. Another Greek mathematician, Euclid of Alexandria (c. 323–283 BCE), summarized and systematized the fundamentals of geometry in his famous *Elements of Geometry*, which remained the beginning point for subsequent generations.

Mathematicians interested in astronomy helped reform solar calendars, identify the causes of eclipses, and predict their occurrences. Pythagoras, for example, worked out that the Earth might be round. Working independently a millennium later, the great Indian mathematician-astronomer Aryabhata (476–550) not only predicted eclipses of the sun and moon, but also speculated that the earth was round and rotated on its axis. Euclid also worked in spherical astronomy. Chinese astronomers made the first recorded planetary grouping in the fifth century BCE and the first recorded mention of comets a century later. Sassanid Persia (226–652 CE) also became centre of mathematics and scientific research.

Medicine, biology, and physics saw advances as well. An Indian is said to have devised a primitive form of surgery to remove cataracts in the eye, and Chinese healers devised the system of acupuncture still in use today. In Greece, Aristotle wrote the earliest surviving texts on empirical biology, based on his own careful research. By direct observation he identified 500 animal species, and devised a classification system that echoes modern ones. To describe the development of sea creatures in accurate detail, he broke open fertilized eggs at regular intervals to observe the embryos' development. In physics, Chinese scholars were making contributions in optics, acoustics, and magnetism.

Natural philosophers cautioned against unnecessarily comingling explanations that were natural with those that were supernatural. For example, in the late seventh century BCE the Chinese sage Shen Xu suggested that people who saw ghosts were projecting their own fears and guilt. This is echoed in Confucius' suggesting one should not think 'about the dead until you know the living'. Around the same time, Thales, the father of Greek science, was arguing that lightning and earthquakes had natural causes rather than being displays of the power and wrath of the gods. Only in much later times did astronomy cease to be about fortune telling and omens. Other parts of the natural world that were closer at hand were less mysterious. Successful building required accurate measurements and calculations of angles, although a small offering to the gods might be made to ensure success as well.

Keeping rational and supernatural causes separate was not easy, even for would-be scientists. In many cultures the sun, moon, and stars were seen as the home of supernatural beings—or they were gods themselves. Serious illness was often attributed to spirit possession or evil magical spells. The investigation of chemical reactions was dominated by alchemistic pursuits, more magical than scientific. Astronomy might exist as a separate field of study, but in most places, it was the hand servant of astrology, the study of how the heavenly bodies control human fate.

Other limitations of ancient science were compounded by the limits of human observation. For example, the Greeks imagined that the heavens must be made of insubstantial materials so light that they could float above the earth. Much in ancient science seems based on overgeneralization. The widespread idea that the physical world was composed of four elements—earth, water, fire, and air—was a poor basis for research. A fifth element, ether, said to compose the heavens, set up a false dichotomy that long endured. Almost equally durable was the idea that the human body consisted of four humours—black bile, yellow bile, phlegm, and blood—which, when a person was healthy, were in balance.

World religions: Christianity and Islam

The phrase 'world religions' has various meanings. Some use it to include any faith tradition that has achieved some degree of global distribution, counting faiths such as Judaism or Shinto that today have followers in many lands, even though their adherents are largely confined to people of Jewish and Japanese ancestry, respectively. Others limit the phrase to universal religions, i.e. those that from early in their history sought to reach beyond the particular ethnicities where they originated to include all humans. This chapter uses the second definition and, for reasons of space, emphasizes the three largest and most dispersed universal religions during the first thirteen centuries of the common era: Christianity, Islam, and Buddhism.

Because Christianity and Islam developed from Judaism, it is useful to start by explaining why the Jewish tradition did not become a world religion. After early Israelites formed a kingdom, they developed a national religion based on the god Yahweh. Later Jewish theologians came to hold that Yahweh was not just their god and not just more powerful than the gods of neighbouring peoples, but was the only God. Jews explained their special relationship with Yahweh by saying He had chosen them above all other peoples. The divide this raised between Jews and Gentiles (a name

Jews used for non-Jews) was bridged by the belief that Yahweh meant Israel to be a beacon to the world through whom His plan for universal redemption would be achieved at some later date. Early Christians and Muslims shared the Jews' devotion to monotheism and their sense of a divine plan, but both religions managed to take the difficult step of opening their faith to all people.

Christianity arose from the teachings of the Jesus of Nazareth, a Jew in Roman Palestine. As with the other intellectual traditions already considered, the message of the founder is known through the writings and elaborations subsequently made by his followers. The Christian scriptures known as the New Testament mix historical events with theological arguments. The four Gospels present Jesus's message, which encourages humility, repentance, kindness to those less fortunate, and peacemaking, along with the details of how the opposition of some Jewish leaders led to his execution by crucifixion. In addition to these plain historical facts there are events of a more mystical nature. Like other holy men, Jesus is credited with healing and exorcism; other assertions are more extraordinary: his mother was a virgin; he arose from the dead and ascended into Heaven. In whatever way these natural and supernatural events may be connected, it is clear that Christians in the late first century believed them all. The community of believers held that Jesus was the Son of God and the Messiah foretold by the Jewish scriptures. The book of Acts recounts the activities of early Christians and describes how Jews rejected Jesus and how his apostles carried his message from the holy city of Jerusalem to Rome, the capital of the Gentile world. In his Epistle to the Romans, the Apostle Paul spelled out the universalism of Christ's message, arguing that converts did not need to become Jews through male circumcision in order to then become Christians.

Christianity was fortunate to emerge within the political boundaries of the Roman Empire and within the cultural boundaries of the Hellenistic world that had developed in the wake of Alexander the Great's conquests. Jesus spoke Aramaic, but all of the books of the New Testament were written in Greek. When St Paul wrote to the fledgling Christian community in Rome, he wrote in Greek, and Christians there remained Greek-speaking until the mid-third century. The Greek in question was Koine, or Alexandrian Greek, the supra-regional language that later became the liturgical language of the Greek Orthodox Church and is the ancestor of Modern Greek. Even the Hebrew Bible (the Old Testament) had been translated into Koine by the mid-third century BCE. Because the Greek word used for Messiah was *Christos*, the anointed one, members of the new religion called themselves Christians. By 100 CE Christian communities had sprung up in Syria, Asia Minor (Anatolia), Greece, and Italy, as well as at Alexandria (Egypt) and Tripoli (Libya). It soon spread across Roman 'Africa', the western part of North Africa. Most early Christians were poor and urban.

Although political and cultural unity made it easier for their faith to spread, early Christians also faced three serious challenges: Roman persecution, the challenge of Hellenic philosophy, and controversies about theology. The early Roman persecutions were aimed at compelling Christians to conform to rituals that recognized the Roman

Emperors as deities, which had the effect of driving the Christians into hiding. Though not very effective, these persecutions gave rise to martyrs whose steadfastness inspired others to believe. However, Emperor Diocletian (r. 284–305) launched a more severe persecution after he became convinced that the poor performance of the Roman legions against northern invaders was due to the Roman gods' displeasure with the Christian legionnaires being allowed to make the sign of the cross instead of offering the traditional sacrifices. In 303 Diocletian purged Christians from the legions and then began a ferocious persecution of other Christians, which included the destruction of churches and large-scale torture and execution of those who refused to offer sacrifices to the established gods.

More enduring than the persecutions was the intellectual challenge Hellenism posed. More educated and sophisticated people often found Christianity's beliefs lacking in logic or overly mystical. Christian leaders had varied responses to this. The great Christian apologist Tertullian (c. 155–220) of Carthage, for example, asked what Athens (classical learning) and Jerusalem (Judeo-Christian revelation) had to offer each other. He answered that 'the first article of our faith is that there is nothing beyond it which we are to believe'. More intellectual Christian leaders of the day took a different tack, employing Hellenic philosophy to defend their beliefs against the criticism of non-believers as well as to gain deeper insights into their religion. Clement of Alexandria (150–215), an Athenian by birth and the first Christian of high learning, cautiously proposed that philosophy might be capable of providing a third Testament consistent with Christian beliefs and even supporting them. The School of Alexandria's brilliant, if eccentric, thinker Origen (182–254) went further. Growing up in Egypt during an early persecution that had killed his father and friends, he recognized the need to be able to counter Christianity's critics. He studied Greek philosophy with such diligence and tenacity that the ardent opponent of the Christians, Porphyry of Tyre, praised him: 'Origen lived as a Christian, but he thought as a Greek.'

Augustine of Hippo (354–430) produced the greatest synthesis of faith and philosophy in the early church. The son of a Christian North African mother and a non-Christian Roman father, the young Augustine struggled with religion and the temptations of the flesh. While reading St Paul's Epistle to the Romans in the summer of 386, Augustine felt his conflicts evaporate. He accepted Christian baptism the next year and dedicated himself to an ascetic life that led to his ordination as a priest in 391. Five years later he was made bishop of Hippo. Augustine wrote extensively in defence of Christian orthodoxy and against various heretical sects (including the Donatists, whose refusal to readmit Christians who had handed over their Scriptures during Diocletian's persecution had split the North African church). Using Platonist ideal types to frame a theology that dominated the Latin Church for a millennium, he wrote that the human being was a marriage of soul and body and the church was the city of God. Augustine died of natural causes as the Vandals were besieging Hippo.

The third challenge to early church came from tensions within Christian beliefs. How could the humanity of Jesus be reconciled with his divinity? How could the belief that Jesus was the Son of God be reconciled with monotheism? To resolve these and other dilemmas, church leaders called councils to work out common professions of beliefs called 'creeds' from 'credo', the Latin word for 'I believe', with which the statements opened. Subtle nuances that the Greek language had gained from philosophical discourse aided finding the right wording for these theological creeds. Such terminology seemed intelligible when translated into Latin, but the fine distinctions could seem nonsensical to those less familiar with Greek. This, it has been suggested, is the reason many Egyptian, Syrian, and Ethiopian Christians did not accept the neo-Platonic formulation approved at the Council of Chalcedon in 451 that Jesus was a single 'person' in whom two 'natures' (one divine, one human) were perfectly united. Of course, it would be simplistic to expect that any dispute was due just to a single cause. Language cannot explain why the Greek Patriarch Nestorius also refused to accept this formulation, giving rise to a Christian sect known as the Nestorians. Personalities, rivalries, and ethnic and regional identities also played roles in theological conflicts.

The Christians' struggles with the Roman Empire, Hellenism, and theological disputes entered a new phase after Emperor Diocletian fell ill and the Roman legions in York proclaimed Constantine the new emperor. The story that Constantine gained victory over his rivals after displaying a Christian banner emblazoned with a Christian cross with the slogan 'in this sign conquer' cannot be taken literally, but the new emperor certainly moved to make Christianity a tolerated religion in 313. He also moved to resolve conflicts among Christians, using force to suppress the Donatists in Roman Africa and calling the Council of Nicaea in 325, which approved a major Creed. By the year 400 Christianity had become the only legal religion in the empire, and by 430, Christians were the majority of its population, though converts who embraced Christianity to curry favour with authorities lacked the fervour of earlier and harder times. If scholars debate how deeply the Christianization of the empire went, there is no doubt that the Church became thoroughly Romanized. Church law and titles derive from their Roman counterparts. The clothing fashions of well-off Romans survive as liturgical vestments. For some time, church buildings reflected Roman architectural models.

Imperial patronage also helped shape the divisions between Eastern and Western Christians. On the one hand, it encouraged the Patriarch of Rome to claim an authority well beyond the Latin West. On the other hand, Constantine's decision to establish a second administrative capital in the East at Constantinople (now Istanbul) strengthened the Greek Patriarch's notion of ecclesiastical autonomy. After several centuries of sparring, the split became permanent in 1054 when each patriarch excommunicated the other. Finally, when the Western Roman Empire imploded and Germanic and other invaders overran most of its former territory, the institutions of the Latin Church became the means of preserving and eventually rebuilding Roman law, culture, and civilization. Before that process could advance very far, another invasion out of Arabia beginning in the seventh century would conquer North Africa, and most of Iberia and the Middle East, and over time, those once-Christian lands became Muslim.

DOME OF HAGIA SOPHIA, BASILICA, CONSTANTINOPLE (ISTANBUL). The current structure was built by order of Emperor Justinian in the 530s on the site of earlier church buildings dating back to the fourth century. It is surmounted by a gigantic dome. Original decorations were destroyed by Christian iconoclasts in the eighth and ninth centuries, and looted and desecrated by Latin Christian Crusaders in the fourth Crusade.

Starting in the year 609, an Arab merchant named Muhammad from the city of Mecca reported receiving revelations from God through the Archangel Gabriel. Muhammad was not literate, but his companions wrote down what he recited. These writings were compiled (and lightly edited to remove small inconsistencies) in a book known as the *Quran*. The revelations read like a more mystical version of the *Analects* of Confucius and are thus not easily summarized. Put simply, the contents of the *Quran* emphasize monotheism, eschatology, and prophecy. All humans are under the rule of a single God (*Allah* in Arabic); the world will soon end, leading to God's final judgement (a belief also common in early Christianity); Muhammad is the last of the line of messengers, including the Jewish prophets and Jesus, through whom God has communicated. The *Quran* also specifies legal prescriptions and punishments, encourages charity to the less fortunate, and calls for submission to God's will. The name of the new religion, Islam, means submission, and its followers are Muslims, those who submit.

Although Muhammad's teachings drew opposition from traditionalists of his native Mecca, the prophet's eventual personal success and the triumph of Islam among the Arabs stood in contrast to Jesus's execution and the general rejection of his teachings by his fellow Jews. Rallying support in the rival city of Medina, Muhammad made peace with Meccan authorities, and consolidated power there. By his death in 632 his

DOME OF THE ROCK, MUSLIM SHRINE, JERUSALEM, 885–891, on the site of earlier Jewish temples. Its design may reflect earlier Byzantine churches in Jerusalem.

teachings had gained wide acceptance in the Arabian Peninsula, uniting the Arab tribes for the first time. Within a century of his death Muslim Arab conquerors had created an empire that extended north to the Caspian Sea, west to the Atlantic, and east to the Indus River.

Early Islam was influenced by the monotheism of Jewish and Christian communities in Arabia. Muslim places of worship borrowed from Christian and classical designs, evident in the architecture and mosaic decoration of the oldest surviving mosque, the Dome of the Rock on Temple Mount in Jerusalem, completed in 691. Most of all, early Islam drew on Arab culture. Only the Arabic language was thought to convey the fullness of the revelations in the Quran. The Ka'ba, a great stone in Mecca that had long been revered for associations with many gods, became a destination for Muslim pilgrims. First the site was cleansed of its many idols, and Islam imposed a strict prohibition of representations of humans and animals in religious precincts, lest such forms become objects of worship. Islam also continued the Arab custom of male circumcision and the possibility of plural marriage, though with the number of wives newly limited to four.

The predominance of Arab culture and power eroded only slowly within their empire, but assimilation was a two-way street. Where Arabs were numerous, especially around garrisons, many local people converted to Islam and the Arab language spread even faster. Over a few generations, the line between Arab and non-Arab became harder to draw, as Arab men married local women and raised Muslim families that were effectively bicultural. In Iran, Arabs by and large came to speak Persian and dressed like Persians. Outside of the empire Arabization was less pronounced among Muslims. In India, Southeast Asia, and sub-Saharan Africa, Muslims retained their local languages and were more selective in adopting Arab customs. The blurring of the distinction between Arab and non-Arab facilitated Islam becoming a multicultural world religion.

Yet the Islamic world remained a very diverse place religiously for many centuries. Initially most of the inhabitants of the Arab Empire were Christians, who were welcome to join Islam but, if they did not, were normally accorded toleration and protection. Muslims recognized Christians and Jews as fellow 'People of the Book', who shared in the long tradition of revelation. Thus, in Iraq Nestorian Christians regained much of the autonomy they had lost under Byzantine rule and were freer to operate their own courts, churches, and schools. In Egypt, Muslim leaders defended Coptic Christians, who were widely employed in administration. African Christians in Nubia and Ethiopia to the south of Egypt remained politically independent and religiously vigorous. The vibrancy of Ethiopian Christianity in the twelfth and early thirteenth centuries is evident from the splendid churches hewn from living rock associated with

THE CHURCH OF ST GEORGE AT LALIBELA, ETHIOPIA, BUILT *c.* 1200. After the volcanic tuff was excavated to a depth of forty feet, the cruciform structure was painstakingly hollowed out for use as a church. It is thought to be the last of eleven monolithic churches constructed at Lalibela.

King Lalibela. If the Western belief that Christians were compelled to become Muslims is thus exaggerated, it is also true that Islamic rule could be a heavy burden, since building or repairing of Christian churches was usually prohibited, people who converted to Islam were not allowed to change their minds, and toleration sometimes lapsed. (For examples see the next section of this chapter.)

Theologically, Islam escaped the kinds of controversies that divided Christianity. Muhammad never claimed to be more than God's messenger, nor did his followers claim a higher status for him after his death. In contrast to the lengthy, complex, and controversial creeds of the Christians, Muslims had a simple statement of faith: there is no god but God; Muhammad is His messenger. In general, Islam stressed orthopraxy (correct practice) more than orthodoxy (correct belief). A good Muslim heeded God's instructions to pray at specified intervals, give alms, observe the fast during the holy month of Ramadan, abstain from alcohol, dress modestly, and, if possible, make the pilgrimage to Mecca.

Yet Islam became divided by a bitter long-term dispute that was political at root but included personal, religious, and regional issues below the surface. A succession dispute in the mid-seventh century over who would be the next caliph or ruler of the Arab Empire split the Shi'a Muslims, who supported the continuation of hereditary succession within Muhammad's lineage, and the Sunni Muslims, who supported the election of caliphs. The Sunni gained the upper hand, but the dispute became permanent.

While Christianity and Islam were spreading in the West, branches of these and other world religions were expanding in Asia. By the first century CE Confucianism had taken on features of a religion: followers worshipped Confucius as a deity and sacrificial offerings were made to him at shrines. Confucianism spread to Korea, Japan, and Southeast Asia, and while it became important regionally, it did not make the leap to becoming a world religion. Around the first century CE the first statues of the Buddha were erected, perhaps owing to Greek influences. Later Buddhists in China developed a distinctive art style.

The transformations in Buddhist belief may be represented by the Mahayana school, which became paramount first in India and then in China. Two new beliefs emerged. The first was that the Buddha ceased to be regarded as merely a human being who became exceptionally enlightened; rather he was revered as an omnipresent truth present in all things. Extending this doctrine were the stories of the Buddha's multiple reincarnations in different places and times. Closely allied with this view of the Buddha was the concept of bodhisattvas, those spiritual saviours who chose to live in the service of others, rather than escaping through nirvana. These new concepts enabled Buddhism to augment the abstract philosophical system and meditation of early Buddhism with an appeal to the Indian masses, who were devoted to numerous deities and magical possibilities.

Besides this populist appeal, Mahayana Buddhism in India promoted intellectual pursuits, of which the most prominent example was the community of scholars and students at Nalanda. Seventh-century Chinese pilgrims described the monastery as

SEATED BUDDHA, GAL VIHARAYA, POLONNAWURA, SRI LANKA, TWELFTH CENTURY. Despite checks in India, Buddhism proved, in the long run, almost as adaptable as Christianity and Islam to a variety of cultural environments, and therefore capable of becoming a 'world religion'.

consisting of several three-storey buildings, in which thousands of students followed serious academic debates among scholars from the various schools of Buddhism. Indian rulers continued to promote the spread of Buddhism up to the mid-seventh century. However, after that time, reports of abandoned monasteries and shrines suggest Buddhism was beginning to decline, in part because of the growing strength of Hinduism, which competed with Buddhism for followers and political supporters. The final blow to Buddhism was delivered by the Muslim conquest of north India that destroyed monasteries, libraries, and, in 1197, the monastic school at Nalanda. Monks were persecuted, killed, or driven out. Buddhism largely disappeared from the country of its birth.

Long before its destruction in India, Buddhism had spread elsewhere in Asia. Buddhism reached China from Central Asia, where it had been established by the first century BCE. From China Buddhism spread to Korea before 400 CE, and from there it spread to Japan, the eastern end of the Silk Road, in the sixth century. By the end of the ninth century, Buddhism became an enduring presence in Tibet. The success of Buddhism in becoming the principal religion in China is particularly important because of that land's huge population and cultural prestige.

Religious conversion strategies

As the world religions expanded considerably during the millennium before 1350, each followed its own trajectory, but all employed similar strategies. One strategy made use of the merchant networks that were also spreading over land and sea at this time. A second strategy was to form alliances with powerful political authorities, in some cases involving military conquests. Missionary work was a third way of gaining converts, and relied on extraordinary individuals, often members of disciplined religious orders, to win converts by the example of their holiness or by direct proselytizing. The examples that follow show how these strategies often overlapped. All of them involved adapting religious concepts and practices to accommodate the cultures of would-be converts, often as part of a long-term strategy of bringing local cultures into line with the core value of the particular religion.

All three religions spread along the Silk Road, a complex of overland routes that extended across central Eurasia to the Far East. Nestorians were the first Christians to expand along this route, but Buddhists achieved greater successes, especially in East Asia, as Muslims did later in Central Asia.

Among the oldest and most spectacular examples of a Buddhist presence along the Silk Road are the network of caves associated with a near-by monastery at Kizil in far western China. Generations of artists decorated the walls of the caves with brilliant murals painted in many different styles. A painting in one cave of the Buddha lighting the way for a merchant is powerful reminder of the close ties between religion and commerce. By the year 500, Chinese records indicate Buddhism had a powerful presence, with 77,000 monks and hundreds of thousands of monasteries in the north of China and another 83,000 monks in the south. By that date Buddhism had already spread into Korea and during the sixth century it spread to Japan, the easternmost end of the Silk Road.

Muslims were more inclined to engage in trade than Buddhists, and Baghdad was an important trading centre on the Silk Road, as well as a Muslim political stronghold. In the vast area between Persia and China, many local merchants adopted the religion of the Muslim merchants passing through, since a common faith promoted trust among merchants of different backgrounds. Some local rulers also embraced Islam to profit from hosting merchants and to escape military attacks by Muslim rulers further west. Although these motives may seem calculating, most conversions were sincere, and Central Asian Muslims subsequently had a powerful political and cultural impact in the Middle East. Following the spread of Islam among the Turkic peoples of Central Asia, the Seljuk Turks established hegemony over Baghdad in 1055. The Seljuk caliph became a champion of Sunni Islam and the promotion of the Turkization of his realm. In Western China foreign Muslim merchants who settled along the trade routes gradually increased the size of their community by marrying local women and by adopting unwanted children, whom they raised as Muslims. Following the Mongol conquest across the breadth of Asia, the *pax mongolica* of the thirteenth century greatly increased the volume of trade along the Silk Route, as well as the number of Muslims.

GODDESS AND CELESTIAL MUSICIAN. Buddhist Cave Painting in Kizil, western China. Seventh century. Height: 2.03 m. Lighter in theme and more vibrant in design than religious art from other medieval traditions, this painting is one of hundreds in the cave complex along the Silk Road, where merchant patrons endowed monasteries and spread Buddhism and Nestorianism.

The Mongol conquests also opened a Roman Catholic mission to China. As a result of a brief correspondence between the Mongols in Persia and the Papacy, a Franciscan named John of Montecorvino (1247–1328) was an emissary to Kublai Khan. Father John reached the Mongol capital Khanbalik (Beijing) in 1294, where the elderly Kublai Khan helped him get established but declined to become a Christian. During the next decade, the Franciscan (later joined by others) built a church with a belfry, baptized some 6,000 people, translated the New Testament and the Psalms into the Mongol language, and bought 150 poor boys, who were baptized, taught Latin and Greek, and trained as a church choir. In 1307 Father John was appointed the first Catholic archbishop of Beijing. If any of the new Chinese Catholics remained in 1369, they would have been affected (along with the Nestorians) by the Ming order to expel all Christians.

Maritime routes in the Indian Ocean also facilitated the spread of the world religions. By the third century (if not earlier) Christians had reached South India, giving rise the St Thomas Christian community, which John of Montecorvino visited on his way to China. Islam spread even more widely along the merchant routes of the Indian Ocean with Muslim communities present in nearly every port. About the ninth century, Arab and Persian merchants settled in the city-states of the 3,000 kilometre-long stretch of the East African coast known as the Swahili Coast and mingled with indigenous Africans who gradually adopted Islam. The Moroccan scholar Ibn Battuta wrote with great admiration of the hospitality, well-built mosques, and prosperity of the Swahili towns he visited in 1331.

Islam also spread to the African people south of Sahara through merchant contacts, where local merchants were the earliest converts, followed by the rulers of trading states there. The Muslim geographer al-Bakri recorded how a North African merchant mediated the conversion of a West African king in the eleventh century by suggesting that the terrible drought afflicting his land could be cured by reciting Quranic prayers. The two prayed all night, with the African king adding 'amen' to the trader's Arabic prayers. The king's belief in the power of Islam was confirmed when torrential rain fell at dawn. Though this tale may not be completely historical, it illustrates the larger reality that pious merchants were instrumental in spreading Islam through the markets and courts of the lands below the Sahara.

As al-Bakri's story suggests, conversion to Islam could be a simple process on the surface. The convert needed to know only a few words of Arabic, often no more than the simple creed, 'there is no god but God, Muhammad is his messenger'. A new Muslim needed to observe the basic practices of Islam: prayer, almsgiving, fasting during the lunar month of Ramadan, and, if possible, the pilgrimage (*hajj*) to the holy city of Mecca. Other customs and beliefs could be picked up gradually, often in schools where boys memorized the Quran, but the process of full conversion might take place over several generations. Damascus-born chronicler al-'Umari tells of the pilgrimage of Mansa Musa, the famous sultan of the West African empire of Mali. Sultan Musa was no new convert, as al-'Umari describes him as 'pious and assiduous in prayer', but he learned for the first time in Cairo in 1324 that Islam did not accept the Malian custom of taking the daughters of free subjects as concubines. 'Not even for kings?' the sultan asked in amazement, and then vowed to amend his ways.

The conversion of rulers was a common strategy in other religions. After the collapse of the Western Roman Empire Christian missionaries sought to win over rulers among the so-called 'pagan' peoples of Europe. In the early fifth century St Patrick concentrated on local chieftains in his early efforts to convert the Irish. The baptism of Clovis, king of the Franks, at the end of that century was hugely important, for it ensured that the powerful successor dynasties of Merovingians and Carolingians would be great allies of the Roman pope. A century later St Augustine of Canterbury persuaded the king of Kent to become a Christian.

Further east, rulers and Christian proselytizers also found common ground. The most famous early missionaries were the Greek brothers Constantine (later called Cyril) and Methodius, who went on from a successful mission among the Slavs in the Balkans to work in the 860s with King Ratislav of Moravia (now part of the Czech Republic) in converting his people. The greatest Byzantine success was the conversion of King Vladimir I of Kiev, ruler of the Rus from 980 to 1015. Vladimir seems to have been encouraged to put aside old beliefs by the example of neighbouring rulers who had adopted Christianity or Islam. After listening to pitches from Muslims and Jews (whose customs of circumcision and not eating pork repelled him), Vladimir chose Christianity, preferring the Eastern tradition because of the magnificence of the Greek liturgy and because his grandmother Olga had been baptized into that tradition by the Byzantine emperor in 957. Despite this Greek connection, from the beginning, the Russian church adopted the Slavonic liturgy created by the sainted Cyril and Methodius. Vladimir's decision had enormous future implications since the kingdom of the Rus grew into the Russian Empire, whose adherence to Orthodox Christianity was an important addition the Eastern Church after the split between the Greek and Roman patriarchs.

Beginning with support from northern invaders after the fall of the Han Dynasty in 220, Buddhists in China also gained from political patronage. In fourth century China the invading rulers of the Northern Wei Dynasty adopted Buddhism because it offered access to high culture and a sophisticated religion, a move which gave the Buddhists the patronage and protection of the of the largest and strongest government in early fifth-century China. As patrons, the Wei and many private individuals supported a massive undertaking in the late fifth century that decorated the walls of 53 caves in Yungang (in today's Shanxi province) with over 50,000 Buddhist carvings. Soon after the Wei moved their capital south, another monumental set of cave sculptures were begun at Longmen, a project that continued for four centuries. Unfortunately, rulers could be persecutors as well as patrons. The most destructive of these came in the ninth century when the wealth and influence of Buddhists in China provoked criticism of the religion as alien and contrary to Confucian family values. Tang Emperor Wuzong launched a furious attack in 845 that supposedly destroyed 4,600 monasteries, 40,000 shrines and temples, and killed 400,000 monks and nuns. Although Chinese Buddhism never fully recovered, there were reported to be over 450,000 Chinese Buddhists by

1021 and the tradition again found patronage under the Yuan (Mongol) Dynasty (1279–1368), only to again come under attack again after that dynasty ended.

Religious orders were another major instrument for spreading world religions. Even those who lived in remote monasteries might provide edifying examples of piety. Highly mobile missionary orders could be even more effective in spreading their message. Some Christian and Muslim orders used military might to spread their faith.

As already mentioned, Buddhist monasteries and convents became a major presence in China—and a peaceful one. As places of prayer, contemplation, and scholarship, monasteries were instrumental in overcoming the cultural and linguistic divide between India to China. Under the supervision of the linguistically adept half-Indian monk Kumarajiva (344–413) hundreds of monks translated thousands of manuscripts into Chinese at a temple in the capital city of Chang'an (today's Xian). This pioneering effort was repeated in the seventh century by a Chinese Buddhist named Xuanzang, who had journeyed to India in 628 and studied at the famous centre of Buddhist learning at Nalanda. Returning to China in 643, Xuanzang brought hundreds of Buddhist manuscripts and many religious objects and established a new translation bureau. The translations from Sanskrit to Mandarin showed as much concern for cultural acceptance as for literal accuracy. Thus, the familiar Mandarin term *dao* (the way) was used to translate *dharma* (teaching), enlightenment (*bodhi*), as well as *yoga*. That appeal to Daoists was balanced by an appeal to Confucianism: a Chinese word meaning filial piety was used for the Sanskrit word for morality.

Members of Christian orders likewise played critical roles in spreading their religion. The pioneering missionary to the Germans, St Boniface, was a monk as well as a bishop. Monasteries were the centres of the early Irish church. A very influential new order begun in sixth-century Italy was the Order of St Benedict, whose monasteries had spread across Western Europe by the ninth century. The Benedictines' piety and learning impressed local people, as did their works of charity and healing. In the early thirteenth century, two important new orders were founded: the Franciscans and Dominicans, both noted for interacting with common people as well as for their learning. The Franciscans begged for charity and the Dominicans were preachers.

The Latin Church also had military religious orders whose members sought to conquer new lands for the faith or reconquer old ones. These orders grew out of the religious fervour surrounding the First Crusade between 1096–99, which successfully freed the Holy Land from Muslim rule for the better part of a century. The Crusade reshaped the medieval knights' code of chivalry, placing new emphasis on defending Christianity and fighting fearlessly against infidels. Along with other military orders the new Knights Templar participated in the ongoing reconquest of Iberia from Muslim rule. By the mid-thirteenth century, only the southernmost part of Iberia was still in Muslim hands. A German order, popularly known as the Teutonic Knights, participated in military campaigns to spread Christianity in the Eastern Baltic, whose high point in the mid-1300s was the decision of the powerful king of Lithuania to become a Roman Catholic. Using conventional military forces, the Byzantine Empire also reclaimed possessions from the Muslims by 1000, first in Crete and Cyprus in the Mediterranean and later in Armenia and Syria. Monks in the Greek Church were more likely to be hermits, living ascetic lives in remote places, but even so, some had powerful influences. For example, the tomb of the tenth-century ascetic St Luke of Steiris in Crete became a place of pilgrimage that was famous for miraculous cures.

Some Muslim communities similar to Christian religious orders promoted proselytization and others organized religiously motivated conquests. The branch of the Shia known as Ismailis undertook some of the purest forms of missionary activity. The sect was intensely mystical and militant, believing that a messiah (*mahdi*) would come to reveal the ultimate truth and establish justice. Fired by a sense of urgency, the Ismailis became fervent proselytizers in the ninth century, spreading their message among the peasant peoples of Arabia, Syria, Iraq, and North Africa, as well as among the inhabitants of Persian cities. The revolutionary fervour of their message of equality, justice, and reform also sparked many rebellions against the Abbasid caliphs.

In Sunni Islam, religious movements known as Sufi performed similar roles. Like religious orders in Europe, Sufi groups took the names of their founders, who were commonly venerated as saints. Wishing to do more than conform to the laws and duties of Islam, Sufis sought to align their inner wills with God's will. Such religious devotion naturally affected many of those around them, who converted to Islam, or became better Muslims. A century after the establishment of the Delhi Sultanate in northern India in 1206, a famous Sufi saint called Baba Farid fled from the capital city to seek solitude in the plains of what is now Pakistan. His asceticism and otherworldliness gradually attracted the respect of local people, who sought his advice or healing power. Baba Farid's reputation as a holy man also attracted powerful people from among the landowners, chiefs, and merchants. Small gifts given by the grateful eventually allowed him to open a hospice. Inspired by his example, many Indians converted to Islam. Many low-caste Hindus also joined the Muslims, who welcomed them as equals.

Besides the Muslim conquerors of India, there were other fervent conquerors whose exploits echoed those of the early Arab Muslims. For example, in the eleventh century the Almoravids (from the Arabic 'al-Murabitun') imposed their rule on the Maghreb (western North Africa), Spain, and attacked south of the Sahara. In the twelfth century another militant group, the Almohads conquered the Maghreb, displacing the Almoravids and added Islamic Spain to their empire after being invited to help halt the advances of Christian Crusaders there. New conquerors were often less tolerant than those they displaced. The Almohads, for example, offered the surviving Christians in the Maghreb the choice of conversion to Islam or death, a policy that led to the extinction of Christianity there.

A different sort of intolerant Muslim conquest took place south of Egypt in Nubia. The ancient Christian community there, vibrant enough in the eleventh century to erect new churches and a cathedral, was weakened after the collapse of the Fatimid Dynasty in 1171, which opened the way for the entry of nomadic Arab bands on a large scale. In the early fourteenth century, a Muslim replaced the last Christian ruler in

Nubia. Churches became mosques, and Christianity was forcibly extinguished. Such exceptionally intolerant Muslim actions, of course, had their counterparts in the lands conquered by Christian Crusaders where Muslims fled and mosques became churches. In Jerusalem, for example, the Dome of the Rock mosque was reconsecrated as a church, and in Iberia, after the Christian reconquest of the thirteenth century, the splendid Great Mosque of Córdoba was converted into a cathedral.

Before turning to the intellectual efflorescence among Muslim and Christian literati, it is important to discuss the depth of religious belief among more ordinary folks. As seen earlier, rulers usually received careful instruction in the faith, but the conversion of the masses could be a rough and ready process, as there was little time (and sometimes no common language) for careful individual instruction. The deeper process of Christianization thus played out over generations. Just as sprinkling 'pagans' with Holy Water could absolve them of their sins, a few drops also served to transform 'pagan' holy sites into places for Christian worship. Poor discipline among the parish clergy led Pope Gregory VII (1073–1085) to make this strong outburst: 'I can hardly open my eyes for rage against the wolfish heretics and asinine Catholics who [continue to frequent services conducted by]...priests condemned by fornication.' Anyone reading Gregory of Tours' *History of the Franks* (c. 500), Venerable Bede's *Ecclesiastical History of the English People* (c. 720), or *Beowulf* from a century later might well conclude that the 'wolfish' behaviour deplored by the pope was the norm among the Christians high and low. Though detailed records are few, the situation among new converts to Islam and Buddhism is likely to have been similar. Indeed, the frequency of reform movements in all three religions suggests that syncretism remained a persistent issue.

Intellectual renaissances

Ibn Sina (980–1037) was born into a Persian administrative family and educated by Ismaili teachers in Bukhara, Uzbekistan, a thousand miles east of Baghdad on the caravan route to China. In addition to mastering Islamic doctrine and law, he studied Aristotelian logic, Euclid's geometry, and the astronomical treatise (later known by its Arabic name *Almagest*) of Claudius Ptolemy, a Greco-Egyptian also known for his geography. Ibn Sina also studied natural science, medicine, and metaphysics. When only sixteen the brilliant lad was given the run of the royal library as a reward for curing the king of an illness. Soon Ibn Sina began writing his own books, eventually completing 50 (or perhaps twice that number) covering philosophy, medicine, poetry, astronomy, and mathematics. After his death Ibn Sina's books became celebrated among Muslim and Jewish thinkers as far away as Spain. Latin translations appearing by 1200 called him Avicenna, trusting that a Latin sounding name would make the Muslim's identity less problematic for Christians.

Ibn Sina was a prime example of the intellectual flowering set in motion by the Abbasid Caliph al-Mansur (r. 754–775), who founded a translation school that produced the first Arabic versions of Aristotle, Ptolemy, Euclid, ancient Indian animal fables, and

THE PUBLIC LIBRARY OF HULWAN, BAGHDAD FROM A SCENE IN MAQAMAT AL-HARIRI. The Persian author of this scene lived from 1054 to 1122. The leather-bound books were stacked into niches cut into the wall. The last line in the Arabic text above is a common proverb still in use: 'During an exam, a person is either honoured or disgraced.'

other works, along with translations of astronomical tables from Sanskrit. To supply the Muslim demand for secular literature, Byzantine scribes made copies of classical Greek manuscripts from which Syriac Christians in Baghdad prepared Arabic translations. By the tenth century, cheap hand-made paper copies of thousands of manuscripts of classical and post-classical Greek authors were widespread in the Islamic world. Ibn Sina in Bukhara was one beneficiary. Another was Ibn Rushd (1126–98), known as Averroes in the Latin West, born in Muslim Spain, who was famous for his commentaries on Aristotle.

In time this Muslim revival of learning spread from Islamic Spain to the Latin West, which was slowly recovering from the 'dark age' caused by the collapse of Roman rule, urban life, and learning. The recovery of classical learning in the Latin West came in stages. In the ninth century there was the modest Carolingian Renaissance. The next three centuries saw the growth of formal education, first in cathedral schools and then in universities. The earliest universities in Italy focused on medicine and law. The more substantial twelfth-century renaissance was associated with greater depth of learning, new classical texts, and the development of scholasticism, essentially the marriage of reason and religion. In the thirteenth century, Latin translations of works from the Abbasid renaissance prepared by Jews in Spain found a ready market in the new universities in Western Europe, where philosophical, theological, and scientific learning was flourishing. The University of Paris became preeminent in philosophy and theology, while Oxford and Cambridge were stronger in science. At all three universities, members of the clergy held most teaching positions.

In 1257 the pope appointed two outstanding but very different individuals to the school of theology in Paris. The Franciscan chair went to Bonaventure (1221–74), who became the champion of the Christian Neo-Platonist tradition that went back through several generations to St Augustine of Hippo. The Dominican chair went to Thomas Aquinas (1225–4), who would devise a daring and controversial synthesis of Christian theology and Aristotelianism. Aquinas believed that faith and reason were complementary, maintaining that reason could help inform faith and extend knowledge, but it could never trump faith. In 1277, shortly after Aquinas's death, the bishop of Paris issued a detailed and stinging condemnation of the rising tide of Christian Aristotelianism in the university. Although aimed primarily at the more radical and secular school of philosophy that had come under the influence of Averroes, the condemnation cast a distinct shadow over the new scholastic theology for a time. However, a half-century later, Pope John XXII proclaimed Thomas Aquinas a saint, an honour not bestowed on the Franciscan Bonaventure for another 150 years. The Catholic Church formally recognized the respectability of St Thomas' synthesis in 1568 by naming him to the theologically elite group of Doctors of the Church. St Bonaventure gained the same honour twenty years later.

At the same time in China, traditional philosophy was also undergoing a revival. After several centuries in decline, Confucianism underwent rehabilitation and reinterpretation during the Song Dynasty (960–1279). In contrast to the more mystical and unworldly approach of Buddhism and Daoism, the revived Confucianism stressed

INTERIOR OF AACHEN CATHEDRAL, COMPLETED 813 CE. The burial place of the Emperor Charlemagne. An architectural triumph of the Carolingian Renaissance, the octagonal chapel is surmounted by a dome whose height would not be exceeded in Northern Europe for two centuries.

ALHAMBRA GAZELLE, POTTERY OF NASRID TIMES, PROBABLY OF THE EARLY FOURTEENTH
CENTURY.

reality and reason. A second similarity with the Latin West was that the Song also
revived the Imperial Academy for the study of Confucian texts and reformed the exam
system for recruitment of imperial administrators. In contrast to the clerical domination of the Latin universities, this Confucian revival was secular and political. Confucian scholarship continued during the Yuan (Mongol) Dynasty (1260–1368).

During both dynasties, Chinese scholars also increased their global leadership in
science and math. As had long been true, Chinese science emphasized practical appli-
cations, whether for warfare, healing, navigation and shipbuilding, printing, or metallurgy. One example of the achievements of this period is the Astronomical Clock Tower
of the polymath Su Song (1020–1101) in Kaifeng. His construction used a water wheel to
turn a mechanical clock system with an escapement mechanism, figures to announce
the hour, bells and gongs, and a rotating celestial globe. The clock tower reflects Chinese
astronomical skill as well as the incorporation of Indian and West Asian influences.
Though spectacular, other Song achievements were more far-reaching than the tower:
by the late eleventh century China was the greatest producer of iron and steel weapons,
and in the next century the Song experimented with gunpowder, flaming arrows, and
exploding shells. To meet the needs of students in the examination schools, books were
mass-produced by printing with moveable metal type.

New thinking about science also appeared in the Latin West after the edict of 1277,
which specifically condemned Aristotle's proposition that there could be only one
world and that that world (Earth) lay at the centre of a set of heavenly spheres.

Although compelled to believe that God could create other worlds, no medieval thinker seriously endorsed the proposition that God had done so. But it did open discussion about whether the known world was surrounded by a vacuum, in which God might exercise His right to create another world. The brilliant Oxford mathematician Thomas Bradwardine (c. 1290–1349) saw that the door was open to an infinite and boundless universe, but, since he was also Archbishop of Canterbury, he was disinclined to make the heavens a physical place. Rather he proposed that the infinite universe and God might be one and the same. Like St Thomas, medieval European natural philosophers were constrained by their need to reconcile faith and reason. They also lacked instruments to extend their observation beyond the human senses and had not developed a useful concept of scientific progress.

Conclusion

The long centuries surveyed in this chapter saw both disruption and continuity. The violent rise and fall of political institutions detailed in Chapter 7 make the disruption obvious, so the continuing vibrancy of the classical traditions consolidated at the beginning of our period is remarkable. Greco-Roman ideas and values survived the collapse of the Roman Empire; Chinese traditions continued despite violent changes of dynasties, and in India, Hindu traditions endured the Muslim conquest of northern India, even if Buddhism did not. Equally remarkable are the ways Buddhism, Confucianism, Christianity, and Islam spread and survived calamitous changes. Part of the continuity reflects the strength their followers found in these traditions. At the same time, these traditions often needed to evolve in order to survive, a circumstance that is most obvious in religious traditions' intellectual and cultural adaptations as they spread. Even as it lost ground in its South Asian homeland, Buddhism acquired new strength in East Asia, in part through selective adoption of local traditions. As they spread, Christianity and Islam similarly made accommodations to local customs, and both blended Hellenistic and other intellectual traditions with their core beliefs. Borrowing was a part of non-violent change. Muslims aided the spread of Indian numerals to Europe; Muslim astronomers worked for Kublai Khan's Astronomical Bureau; and Mongol expansion in the thirteenth century helped the spread of gunpowder, the magnetic compass, and printing.

However, in spite of the transformations that took place in religious allegiance, this era was strongly conservative. Christians copied the architecture of Greco-Roman buildings, sometimes converting temples into churches. The statues of the old gods might be tossed out, but often enough their altars were transferred to saints with similar appeals. In other places Christian churches or Hindu temples became mosques, and the depictions of human forms were effaced or plastered over. Recycling and recapturing the glories of the classical past also featured in the several 'renaissances' occurring across the period discussed. As Bernard of Chartres observed in the twelfth century, scholars of his day might see a bit farther because they were 'like dwarfs

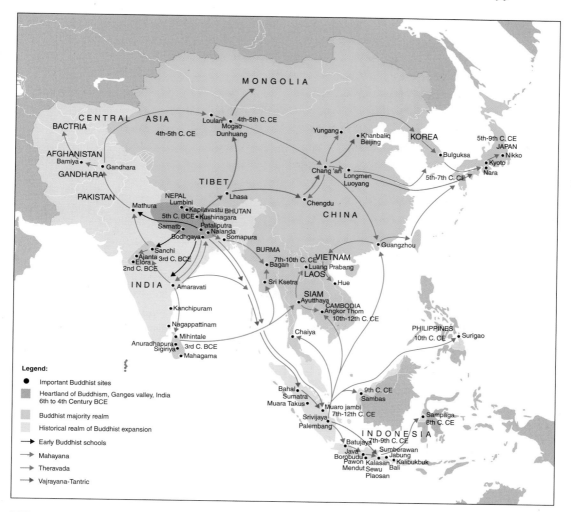

BUDDHIST EXPANSION TO ABOUT 1300 CE.

standing on the shoulders of giants', i.e. the ancient scholars. Others noted that the ability of the dwarfs to see farther did not make them wiser or smarter than the giants of old. Followers of the world religions also revered the teachings attributed to their founders and early disciples.

Tradition was a source of strength, but it could also be an impediment to innovation. At the university of Paris in the thirteenth century, St Bonaventure spoke humbly but truthfully when he said his goal in teaching was to transmit the insights of his teacher, Alexander of Hales, and other masters, adding 'I do not...wish to combat new opinions, but to develop old ones'. Such a point of view would not have been out of place in a Muslim law school or a Buddhist university.

SCROLL PAINING, 'RELOCATING,' by the court painter Wang Meng, one of the 'four masters' of his day from fourteenth-century China, records the journey of a Taoist sage to the sacred Mount Luofu to practise alchemy and esoteric medicine.

Such devotion to intellectual continuity could be stultifying, but it did not have to be. Many thinkers and artists found space for innovation under the mantle of tradition. The fourteenth-century Chinese master landscape painter Wang Meng turned away from the very spare style of his contemporaries, using an older, cruder form that piled up brushstrokes to create depth and intensity. He was later heralded the father of modern Chinese landscape painting. Even St Thomas Aquinas's celebrated blend of Aristotelian philosophy and Christian theology was meant to prove that the two could be made compatible.

Other visions departed from tradition more dramatically, perhaps none so much as the new Gothic cathedrals of Western Europe. Instead of the Romanesque style, whose rounded (Roman) arches and barrel vaults required heavy masonry walls for support, some master builders in France adopted a pointed arch, used earlier in some structures in the Islamic Middle East. The change greatly altered the form of the rest of the structure, giving rise to external 'flying' buttresses absorbing the lateral thrust of the structure and permitting side walls to glow with giant windows of coloured glass.

CHOIR OF ST DENIS BASILICA, FRANCE, COMPLETED 1144. Considered the first Gothic church, St Denis exhibits the high vaulting, pointed arches, and stained-glass clearstorey celebrated in later Gothic cathedrals in France.

The style also spread to England, where it became a feature of cathedrals and the new university buildings of Oxford and Cambridge. Those universities, along with others on the European mainland, were a special feature of the Latin West. They played a special role in promoting the discovery, discussion, and dissemination of philosophical inquiry, in metaphysics as well as the study of the natural world. Nevertheless, the Islamic world was still in the forefront of scientific knowledge in the late Middle Ages, and the Chinese of the Song Dynasty were most advanced in astronomy, even recording two supernovas. While Western scholars had more limited scientific knowledge and lagged in direct observation, their universities had taken rigorous inquiry in natural philosophy to new heights. Some historians believe that this method explains how the West later gained scientific leadership.

CHAPTER 7

Growth

Social and Political Organizations, 1000 BCE–1350 CE

IAN MORRIS

The story

HUMANS, like all animals, need to cooperate to get things done, and this chapter tells the story of how people organized cooperation between 1000 BCE and 1350 CE.

Through most of history, kinship had been the main basis for cooperation, and families, clans, and tribes remained important institutions throughout the period discussed in this chapter. However, kin-based organizations have their limitations (try building a Roman road if only your brothers and cousins show up), and people began forming non-kin groups well before 1000 BCE. Many social scientists would say that the state, an organization claiming to monopolize the right to use or authorize violence, is the most important of these, and the first states had been created around 3500 BCE in the Middle East. In this chapter, 'social and political organizations' mean primarily families, clans, tribes, cities, states and empires, although I touch on other kinds of organizations as well, particularly churches and businesses, because it is hard to separate social and political organizations from religious and economic ones.

Thanks to the work of generations of historians and archaeologists, we can tell the story of social and political organizations between 1000 BC and 1350 CE in rich and fascinating detail. However, the point of the short chapters on large subjects in this volume is not to cram in as many facts as possible; rather, it is to step back from the details to see the wood rather than the trees. When we do so, we see that the story of these 2,350 years can be summed up in one word: growth.

Humans learned to cooperate on larger and larger scales, as small organizations were swallowed up by larger ones, and large organizations became larger still. 'Cooperation', however, is an antiseptic word that covers a multitude of sins. Much of the time it was obtained through violence or threats and its fruits were very unevenly distributed. But despite their brutality, the social and political organizations created between 1000 BCE and 1350 CE left a remarkable legacy. Not for nothing do most people in the world today hark back to this period as a classical age, and without these twenty-four centuries of growth, the revolutionary changes which fill Parts 4 and 5 of this book would not have been possible.

Bigger, wider, stronger, deeper

The facts of growth are easy enough to demonstrate. At its most basic level, growth was human. In 1000 BCE, there were about 120 million people in the world. By the midpoint of our story, in 175 CE, the population had roughly doubled to 250 million. It kept growing until the early fourteenth century, but only by another 50 per cent, to close to 400 million, before falling back—for reasons we will return to—to about 350 million in 1350.

The social and political organizations that these more numerous people created grew even faster. In 1000 BCE, the world's largest cities—probably Qi in China and Susa in Iran—had around 30,000 residents, but by 175 CE, Rome was over thirty times bigger, at about a million people. Seventh-century Chang'an and eleventh-century Kaifeng (both in China) probably matched this, but the biggest city in 1350, Hangzhou (again in China), had about 750,000 souls.

The size of states followed a similar pattern. Space and demography are the two obvious ways to measure this. Spatially, the biggest state in 1000 BCE was probably Egypt, at about 400,000 square kilometres, but by 175 CE, Rome and Han China were

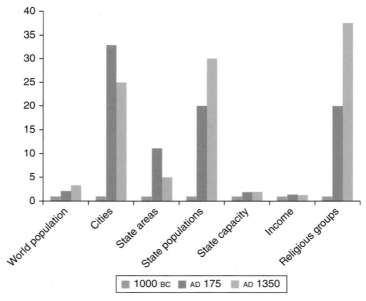

SOME DIMENSIONS OF ORGANIZATIONAL GROWTH, 1000 BCE to 1350 CE. For each category of analysis, the blue column represents 1000 BCE as 1.0 on the vertical axis and the red and green columns shows the equivalent scores for 175 CE and 1350 CE. World population almost quadrupled across this period, but the biggest changes were in the scale of the largest organizations. Wealth, inequality, and development grew more slowly.

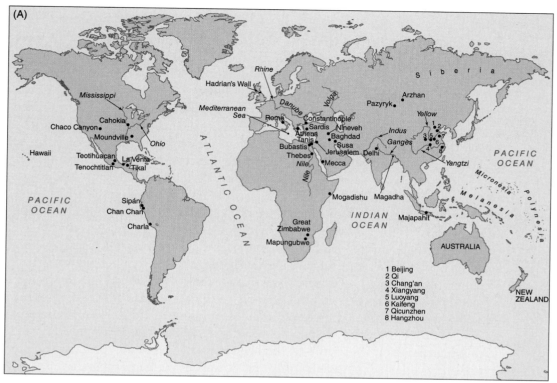

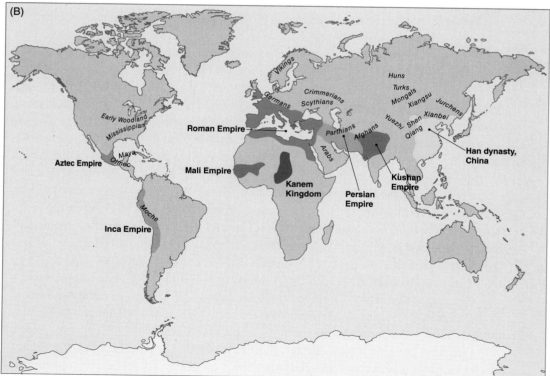

(A) AND (B) PLACES NAMED IN THE CHAPTER.

more than ten times bigger, each ruling about 4.5 million square kilometres. It is more difficult to reach a figure for 1350 because there is more than one way to count. Conventional agrarian empires, like the Sultanate of Delhi and the Mamluk sultans of Egypt, each ruled about 2 million square kilometres. However, the Mongol Yuan dynasty, which had conquered China, ruled 10 million square kilometres, and the Golden Horde, another Mongol empire, controlled a further 5 million. However, historians often hesitate to put the empires of steppe nomads in the same category as conventional agricultural empires, because most of the nomads' territory had no one living in it.

If we count heads, the pattern is somewhat similar. The most populous state in 1000 BCE was again Egypt, with around 2.5 million subjects. In 175 CE, both Rome and Han China were twenty times as big, with roughly 50 million members. Growth then continued, but more slowly, with China reaching the 75 million to 100 million range in 1350.

Measuring states' capacities to get things done is trickier, and sociologists have been designing metrics for a century. I have previously suggested yet another method, which is a numerical index of social development that measures societies' abilities to organize and get things done, on a scale running from 1 to 1,000 points. Criteria used in this index includes use of urban engineering, examples of infrastructure in place, economic standards relating to commerce and tax collection, highly organized public arts and education facilities, etc. In 1000 BCE, the highest-scoring region by this method was Egypt, with a little over 22 points; in 175 CE, it was the Roman Empire, at just over 43 points; in 1350 it was China, with a little over 40 points.

The histories of families and states can be difficult to separate from those of firms or churches, partly because one of the major ways they overlap is that bigger states provided bigger stages for economic and religious cooperation to play out. Trade networks, for instance, regularly extend beyond political frontiers, but when political frontiers are enlarged, supply chains often grow with them. In 1000 BCE, Egypt's trade routes in the Mediterranean barely reached as far as Greece, and the *Story of Wenamun*, set around 1076 BCE, vividly describes the difficulties pharaohs encountered as close to home as Phoenicia, where the ruler of Byblos imposed tough terms for the export of timber. By the second century CE, however, connections had grown so much that a Roman embassy made it all the way to Chang'an and, as his DNA shows, a recent immigrant from East Asia was buried in Italy. The archaeologist Barry Cunliffe nicely observes that 'a member of the Korean elite could admire a glass vessel made in the Roman world, while soldiers stationed on Hadrian's Wall could spice their meals with Indian black pepper'. In the 70s CE the Roman geographer Pliny the Elder worried that rich Roman women were buying so much silk from China that they were depleting their empire's stocks of silver. But this was just the beginning: by 1350, dense overland and seaborne routes linked China to Southeast Asia, India, Europe, and the Arab world. In the 1420s, sailors from Nanjing even walked the streets of Mogadishu and Mecca, and Ming dynasty porcelain was common on the coast of Kenya.

As markets grew wider and deeper, standards of living rose, although compared to modern times growth remained glacially slow. Converting ancient consumption into

A GLASS VESSEL MADE IN THE
ROMAN WORLD, which could
be admired by someone as far away
as Korea.

modern currency is fraught with obvious problems, but one of the better studies, made by the economist Angus Maddison, suggests that the incomes of preindustrial peasants were typically equivalent to figures around USD1.50–2.20 per person per day. In Egypt, the richest part of the world in 1000 BCE, incomes lay towards the lower end of that range. In the extraordinary Greek cities of the fourth century BCE, they sometimes surged up to USD3–4 per person per day, but even across large parts of the Roman Empire in 175 CE they were not much over USD2 per day. Incomes in great Chinese cities such as Kaifeng were probably also at the top end of Maddison's range in 1100, although they were probably declining by 1350. Using the World Bank's definitions, we can say that at the beginning of this period, almost everyone in the world lived in 'extreme poverty', but in the second half, most people had clawed their way up to mere 'poverty'.

That said, some always lived well above the poverty line, and on the whole, inequality grew alongside income. Economists typically measure inequality with the Gini coefficient, which scores groups on a scale from 0 (everyone has exactly the same amount of the good in question) to 1 (everything belongs to just one person). Gini scores for income inequality in preindustrial peasant societies mostly range between about 0.30 and 0.60, with a mean around 0.48. We have no good figures for Egypt in 1000 BCE, but the archaeological evidence implies that scores were in the lower half of this range. For Rome, the data are better, and its Gini score in 175 CE was around 0.44. For China in 1350, trustworthy data are lacking, but a score even higher than Rome's seems likely. Across 2,350 years, the poor became slightly less poor, while the rich became a lot richer.

Religious organizations also grew in numbers and in influence. Polytheistic communities usually have blurry boundaries (where, for instance, do we put a first-century BCE worshipper rejoicing in the solidly Greek name of Heliodorus? He set up an inscription honouring the Hindu god Vishnu.). On the whole, though, in the first half of our period, the main mechanism of religious expansion was for conquering empires to spread their gods, or something like them, as they went. Probably a couple of million people worshipped Amun and Re in 1000 BCE and some 40 million acknowledged Jupiter, Zeus, or a close cognate in 175 CE. In the first millennium CE, however, religious organizations increasingly operated independently—beyond or alongside states—and vastly increased their proselytizing power. By 1350 more than half the world's

DETAIL OF INSCRIPTION IN HONOUR OF Vishnu and celebrating the erection of the Heliodorus Pillar at Vidisha. Note the sunburst devices that presumably allude to the patron's remarkably Greek-sounding name.

population followed Jesus, Muhammad, or the Buddha (about 75 million, 60 million, and 50 million people, respectively).

The big story, then, is of growth, although—as is usually the case—on closer inspection there turn out to be several ways to tell it. No two of the traits described so far followed exactly the same path; and even within any single trait, there is normally more going on than initially meets the eye. The example of state capacity (the ability to get things done) has been quantified in greatest detail. At the global level, this follows a double-hump pattern, with rapid growth in the first millennium BCE, decline in the first half of the first millennium CE, recovery in the second half, and then further decline in the thirteenth and fourteenth centuries CE.

However, even this oversimplifies the story: first because it shows us only the biggest organizations on the planet, and second, because the global-scale picture conflates two distinct regional patterns. First, I want to disaggregate the data shown in the previous image into Western and Eastern Eurasian curves—because between 1000 BCE and 1350 CE, the world's highest development scores always came either from societies lying between Iraq and Italy or from societies in China. In the next two figures the double hump disappears, but in different ways.

The figure that shows Western development would have made sense to many educated Europeans between the fifteenth century and the mid-twentieth. By then historians tended to depict a glorious Greco-Roman antiquity succeeded by a depressed (and depressing) Middle Ages and finally a late medieval revival. Since the 1970s, revisionists have rebelled against such 'decline and fall' models, seeing them as blind to the cultural accomplishments of medieval Christendom and Islam. But despite all the

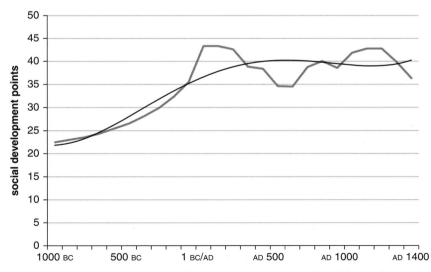

RISE AND FALL: cycles of growth and collapse in state capacity at the global scale, 1000 BCE to 1350 CE. The graph shows the highest scores in the world, measured century by century, and fitted with a fourth-order polynomial trend line.

revisions, the figure on Western economic development suggests that scholars from Petrarch to A. H. M. Jones were less misguided than many moderns seem to think. The end of the Roman Empire really was, as Edward Gibbon said in 1776, an 'awful revolution . . . which will ever be remembered, and is still felt by the nations of the earth'.

By contrast, the East Asian story was very different. There were ups and downs, which to some extent coincide with the rise and fall of specific Chinese dynasties, but

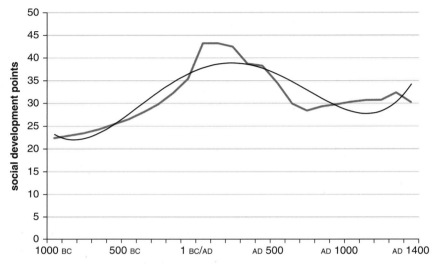

GIBBON WAS RIGHT: Western social development scores fitted with a fourth-order polynomial trend line.

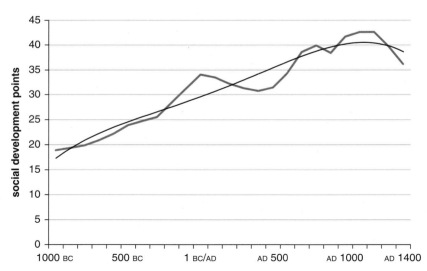

THE CONTINUITY OF CHINESE CIVILIZATION? Eastern social development scores fitted with a fourth-order polynomial trend line.

broadly speaking Eastern social and political organizations grew steadily for over two millennia before taking a downswing after 1200.

The figures showing cycles of growth and collapse conflate the scores on the left-hand side of the figure showing Western social development scores and those on the right-hand side of the figure showing Eastern social development scores, meaning that, while it gives a fair overview of trends averaged out at the global level, it gives a poor sense of what happened in any specific place. To get a sense of how the planet's parts fit together and to see how the story of the biggest social and political organizations compares to that of smaller units, we need to switch from graphs to maps.

The following three world map images show the distribution of forms of social and political organization around the world in 1000 BCE, 175 CE, and 1350 respectively, divided into six crude categories: foraging families, pastoral tribes, pastoral empires, agricultural villages, 'low-end' agricultural states, and 'high-end' agricultural states (these terms will be defined more carefully later in this chapter).

The maps fill in some of what is missing from the graphs. Basically, the area occupied by foraging families shrank steadily between 1000 BCE and 1350 CE, as farmers expelled foragers from their homelands, pushing them back into ecological

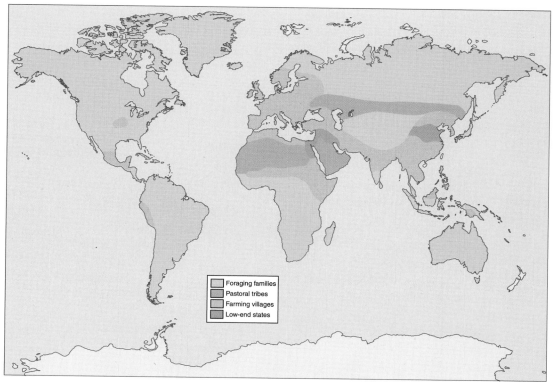

THE GLOBAL DISTRIBUTION OF SOCIAL AND POLITICAL ORGANIZATIONS IN 1000 BCE, divided into the four crude categories of foraging families, pastoral tribes, farming villages, and low-end states.

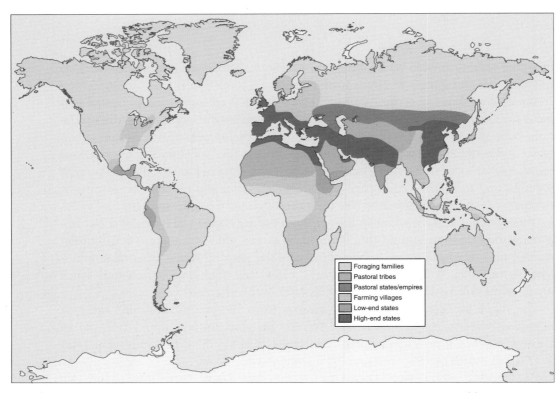

THE GLOBAL DISTRIBUTION OF SOCIAL AND POLITICAL ORGANIZATIONS IN 175 CE, adding two new categories of pastoral states/empires and high-end states.

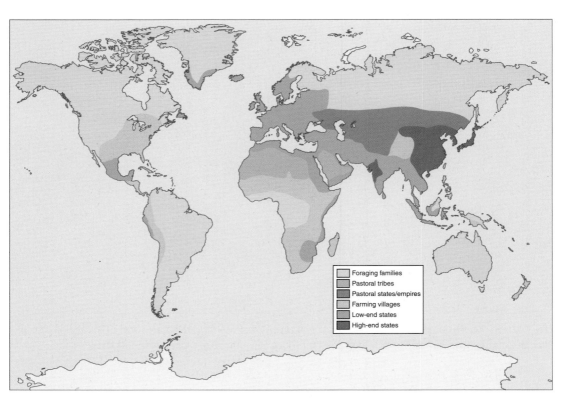

THE GLOBAL DISTRIBUTION OF SOCIAL AND POLITICAL ORGANIZATIONS IN 1350.

niches that the farmers did not want (such as Siberia) or had not yet reached (such as coastal Australia). The area occupied by pastoral tribes also shrank as huge areas of the steppes came under the control of pastoral empires. The area occupied by agricultural villages increased at the expense of foraging families between 1000 BCE and 175 CE (especially in Africa), but then shrank as villages were brought under the control of states faster than farmers dispossessed foragers. The area occupied by agricultural states grew massively across the whole period, mostly at the expense of farming villages, but the balance between low-end and high-end states varied significantly. In 1000 BCE, there were no high-end states, but between then and 175 CE, two separate patterns unfolded. In the Americas and Africa, low-end states grew at the expense of agricultural villages, but in Eurasia low-end states were largely wiped out by high-end states. After 175 CE, this was partly reversed, as low-end states replaced high-end ones in western Eurasia. In South and East Asia, high-end states took over some of the area where there had once been low-end states, while in Southeast and Northeast Asia and the Americas, low-end states expanded dramatically.

Behind the long-term, large-scale story of growth, then, lie more complicated shorter-term, smaller-scale stories. This chapter cannot address them all, but it at least raises five interesting questions. First, why did social and political organizations grow in scale, wealth, hierarchy, complexity, and effectiveness between 1000 BCE and 1350 CE? Second, why did growth differ so much before and after 175 CE? Third, why did growth so often turn into collapse? Fourth, why did the forms of organizations vary so much from one place to another at any given point in time? And fifth, why did Eastern Eurasia displace Western as the heartland of the world's biggest, most powerful states after 175 CE?

I suggest that the answers to these questions point us towards a big conclusion: that between 1000 BCE and 1350 CE social and political organizations reached the limits of what was possible under purely agrarian conditions. The Roman Empire was the first to reach this ceiling, two thousand years ago, and Song dynasty China repeated the feat a millennium later. In each case, however, growth then turned into stagnation and collapse. Not until the eighteenth century did a society—Britain—shatter the old order by unlocking the energy trapped in fossil fuels. After that, as the chapters in Parts 4 and 5 show, nothing would ever be the same.

Homo superans

To some extent, the answer to all these questions is simply that what happened between 1000 BCE and 1350 CE was pretty much continuous from the end of the main phase of the Ice Age around 12,700 BCE. These 2,350 years are simply one chapter in a much longer story of growth.

To explain, let us make a quick jump back into prehistory. There were approximately 4 million people on earth in 12,700 BCE, none of them living in communities of more than a few score members, whereas today there are 7 billion, of whom one in twenty lives in 'mega-cities' of ten million-plus residents. The average nation has 34 million citizens, and China and India each have well over a billion. In 12,700 BCE, by Maddison's estimates, the average standard of living was equivalent to something like USD1.10 per day; now it is USD25 per day. Fifteen thousand years ago, the typical hunter-gatherer band had a Gini score for income inequality around 0.25; now most nations score higher, around 0.30–0.35 (although this is a substantial decline from typical scores of 0.40–0.50 in 1350; what economists call the 'great compression' in incomes between 1920 and 1970 was a remarkable break with long-term trends, which seem now to have resumed). And the power of states has surged; on my index measuring capacity to get things done (discussed earlier), scores leap from under 5 points in 12,700 BCE to 906 points in 2000 CE. Organizational growth has exploded since 1800 CE, but it has been a big part of life for fifteen millennia.

And yet, growing social and political organizations were not *always* a big part of life. Two conditions were required for growth: first, the exceptionally productive brains that *Homo sapiens* evolved roughly 100,000 years ago, and second, the warm and wet climate—what the archaeologist Brian Fagan calls 'the long summer'—that has prevailed since the end of the Ice Age. There were several long summers before 100,000 BCE, but no *Homo sapiens* to respond to them by creating bigger organizations; and between 100,000 and 15,000 BCE there was *Homo sapiens*, but no long summers. Only in the last 15,000 years have both conditions been present, and these turned *Homo sapiens*, 'Knowing man', into *Homo superans*, 'Growing man'.

In the warm, wet, post-glacial world, plants converted a bonanza of solar energy into more of themselves, and animals ate the abundant plants (and each other) and multiplied, too. Every species, including *Homo sapiens*, reproduced until it outran the resources available, whereupon its population crashed. *Homo sapiens*, however, had brains so fast and flexible that we could potentially react to shortage (and, for that matter, to abundance) by innovating, and changing how we gathered plants and hunted animals. No one knew what the results would be, but by applying new selective pressures to food sources, humans created the world's first genetically modified organisms. Some plants and animals evolved into new, domesticated forms, which provided far more food for humans than their wild precursors.

Domestication brought both costs and benefits. There was more food, which gave more people a better chance to live, but also more work; and people had to reorganize their societies to manage increasing scale. Reorganization typically meant more permanent villages, stronger property rights, and greater political, economic, and gender inequality, but it also brought increasing knowledge, labour specialization, and sophistication. People had free will, and could (and did) choose to resist some or all of these trends, but across thousands of years, groups that moved towards 'growth-friendly' institutions and values—including patriarchy, hierarchy, and slavery, as well as literacy and high culture—replaced those that did not.

Village life appeared in the Middle East by 12,500 BCE, domestication by 9500 BCE, and full-blown agriculture over the following two millennia, but none was a one-off event. Farmers kept learning—to rotate cereals and pulses so as not to exhaust the soil;

to terrace hillsides; to harness animals to ploughs and carts and to use their manure to increase yields; to redirect rivers to irrigate crops; to desalinate the ground as irrigation deposited salt in it; to use metal tools to dig their fields—and so on. Innovations raised output, supporting more people and requiring bigger social and political organizations; but to support these innovations and hold together these groups, people had to keep revolutionizing their institutions and worldviews. Each solution created new problems, but over the very long run, one of most consistently adopted strategies has been to increase the scale of social and political organizations.

A single formula explains many of the statistics at the beginning of this chapter: *Homo superans* + long summer = growth. However, it clearly does not explain everything in the images shown thus far. Some *homines* were more *superantes* than others, and we need to know why.

The power of place

The maps that appear earlier show that the world's biggest social and political organizations normally clustered in what I call the 'lucky latitudes', where environment and history combined to enrich economies, stimulate innovation, and accelerate change: a band stretching from China to the Mediterranean in the Old World, and from Peru to Mexico in the New World. The evolutionist and geographer Jared Diamond explained why in his classic book *Guns, Germs, and Steel*, but historians have not always appreciated the implications of his arguments for the period from 1000 BCE to 1350 CE. We cannot make sense of these centuries without knowing a few facts about prehistoric geography.

The hard truth, Diamond points out, is that potentially domesticable plants and animals were very unevenly distributed at the end of the Ice Age. The vast majority had evolved in the lucky latitudes; which, given that human beings are much the same everywhere, meant that it was overwhelmingly likely that people there would domesticate plants and animals earlier than people in other places. The job was simply easier in the lucky latitudes.

Further, Diamond observes, even within the lucky latitudes, resources were distributed unevenly. The most richly endowed part of Eurasia was what we now call the Middle East, followed by East and South Asia, and then Mexico and Peru. Consequently, signs of domestication come first in the Middle East (around 9500 BCE), followed by Pakistan and China (about 7500 BCE), and then Mexico and Peru (about 6250 BCE). Outside the lucky latitudes, where resources were scarcer, moves towards domestication began in eastern North America by around 4500 BCE, in the Sahel and southern Africa before around 3000 BCE, and—in a fascinating outlier, to which I will return—in New Guinea at least as early as 6000 BCE.

On the whole, each part of the world followed a roughly similar timetable once it started down the path of growth. It normally took two to four millennia to go from the first intervention in other species' genomes to permanent farming villages with hundreds of residents. It then took another two to four millennia for agricultural villages to grow into what I call 'low-end' states with monarchs, priests, aristocrats, and (usually) writing, and a further 1,500–2,500 years for these to turn into 'high-end' empires with tens of millions of subjects and extremely sophisticated elite cultures.

The details of the timing depended on local resources, the peculiarities of each culture, and the specific decisions its members made. In the New World, perhaps because there were so few domesticable large mammals, people generally took twice as long (four rather than two millennia) to get from simple to advanced farming as those in the Eurasian lucky latitudes; while New Guineans, despite having enough domesticable plants to be able to begin farming almost as early as people in Mexico and Peru, lacked the resources to generate the kind of surplus that fed the first states within the lucky latitudes. The unsuitability of the main local crops—taro and bananas—to long-term storage (compared, say, to rice, wheat and barley, all of which store well) was probably also important.

Each region was unique, yet it is broadly true that the earlier an area started down the path of sociopolitical growth, the bigger its organizations were in 1000 BCE. Thus, the largest, richest, most unequal, and most complex social and political organizations clustered toward the western end of Eurasia (particularly in a triangle with points in what are now Egypt, Turkey, and western Iran), followed by northern China and India, and then Mexico and Peru.

Some parts of the world, such as Australia and Siberia, were so short of domesticable plants and animals that they had barely started down this path by 1350 CE, while others found different paths of growth. On the steppes, the arid grasslands running across the Old World from Manchuria to Hungary, almost nothing grows that humans can eat; but cattle, sheep, and horses thrive on its grass, and humans eat animals. By about 5000 BCE, farmers had migrated into the western steppes from the Balkans and turned into herders, and before 4000 BCE herders in what is now Kazakhstan had domesticated wild horses. Between 1000 BCE and 1350 CE, steppe horsemen created distinct kinds of pastoral states and empires that fought and even overthrew the agrarian societies of the lucky latitudes.

Much of this chapter's story, then, was simply the playing out of trends that had been at work since about 13,000 BCE. Humans kept finding that bigger social and political organizations were good solutions to their problems, and so these organizations grew almost everywhere; and organizations inside the lucky latitudes, which had been the world's biggest since the end of the Ice Age, remained bigger, richer, and more sophisticated than those outside them.

However, the maps in the images also show that this is not the whole story. Although in 175 CE the world's biggest organizations were in western Eurasia, and had been for more than ten thousand years, by 1350 East Asia had taken the lead and the Mediterranean and Middle East had seen their biggest states shrink (but neither their biggest religious organizations, and in certain senses, nor their biggest economic organizations). This was one of the biggest shifts in wealth and power in history, but to date there is little agreement on its causes.

Biology and geography, we should conclude, do much to answer the five questions posed earlier in this chapter, but they do not answer everything. It is time to look at other causes by taking three snapshots of the world at the beginning, middle, and end of our period.

The world in 1000 BCE

By 1000 BCE, farmers had already spread over much of the world's arable land, and by 1350 CE almost all of it was under hoe or plough. Archaeologists still dispute the details, but a great Bantu migration, which carried farming, herding, and ironworking from west and central Africa to the continent's eastern and southern regions, probably began soon after 1000 BCE. Metal-using rice farmers were colonizing Sri Lanka from India by 600 BCE and southern Japan from Korea by 500 BCE, and by then other East Asian farmers had taken to their canoes to settle the westernmost islands of Oceania. These islands were normally uninhabited until the farmers arrived, but in most places the advance of agriculture meant the retreat of hunting and gathering.

Probably less than one per cent of world's population still lived in egalitarian foraging bands in 1000 BCE. Most of these groups were highly mobile and family-based, often of fewer than a dozen people. Their hierarchy was normally very limited

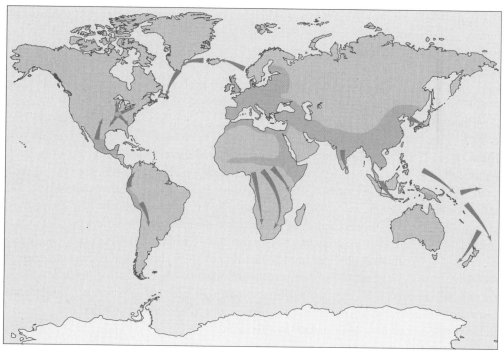

MAJOR AGRICULTURAL EXPANSIONS, 1000 BCE to 1350 CE. The shaded area represents the world's farming zones in 1000 BCE.

and based mainly on age and sex. Multiple bands would periodically gather at festivals for activities which required larger groups and—equally important—to provide a viable gene pool for exchanging marriage partners, and temporary chiefs might take charge of these meetings.

That said, foraging societies were highly varied, and where resources were very abundant or it was possible to store gathered foods, larger, more permanent and hierarchical groups grew up. The most famous of these 'affluent foragers' lived in the Pacific Northwest, where the invention of plank canoes around 800 CE allowed foragers to catch huge hauls of wild salmon.

Another small percentage of the world's population in 1000 BCE lived as herders, mostly on the steppe and desert fringes of the Eurasian lucky latitudes or the African savannahs (the Americas and Australia had few large mammals to herd). They typically lived in kin-based groups a few dozen or hundred strong. Within these groups ('clans' and 'tribes' are common labels) some families might be much richer than others, although because wealth was embodied largely in livestock, a family's fortunes could fluctuate wildly.

These pastoral groups became much more mobile after 1000 BCE, thanks to the domestication of the Arabian camel and the breeding on the steppes of horses big and strong enough to be ridden for long distances. Mobility massively multiplied nomads' military power, which created incentives for chiefs to form larger alliances that could field thousands of riders to plunder the borderlands of agrarian states or to extort protection money from agrarian rulers. Assyrian letters say that Cimmerian horsemen defeated the king of Urartu as early as 707 BCE. Assyria fought back, hiring steppe cavalry as mercenaries, and in 677 BCE defeated the Cimmerians and slew their king; but in 652 BCE the nomads returned, sacking Sardis and killing Lydia's King Gyges. In 612 BCE, the nomad Scythians played a large part in destroying the Assyrian Empire itself.

More than 95 per cent of humanity, however, were farmers, the great majority of them in relatively simple groups lacking centralized governments that monopolized legitimate use of violence. As with foragers, organizations varied widely. At one extreme were small-scale, quite egalitarian villages such as those of the Early Woodland cultures of the American Midwest (c. 1000–300 BCE), which rarely had more than about fifty residents, combined simple agriculture with foraging, and practised communal rituals. At the other were places like the Olmec town of La Venta, which, by 750 BCE, had several thousand residents busily erecting massive earth platforms, a hundred-foot-tall pyramid, and monumental basalt heads. Olmec leaders clearly mobilized labour on a large scale, perhaps through feasting and mutual obligations between kin groups; most archaeologists doubt that Olmec leaders commanded permanent, coercion-wielding state institutions.

Almost without exception, these non-state farming societies were illiterate because they lacked organizations large enough to make writing a requirement. The main exceptions were in the East Mediterranean, where a band of states with literate bureaucracies had stretched from Elam to Egypt and Greece before the great collapse around 1200 BCE. In places where some state institutions survived, such as Egypt, so did writing, but in those where the state vanished altogether, such as Greece, writing vanished, too. However, Greeks remained in contact with the still-literate societies and around 800 BCE adapted the Phoenician alphabet for their own purposes. As a result, in Greece and also in Israel, early-first-millennium BCE literature gives vivid glimpses into the internal workings of stateless farming societies, graphically describing unstable political organizations going though painful and often violent processes of state formation.

Just 10 million to 20 million of the world's 120 million people lived in states in 1000 BCE, all them in the Eurasian lucky latitudes. Government had survived the 1200 BCE collapse in a scatter of places between Egypt and Elam, but in South Asia, a millennium would pass between the Indus Valley collapse around 1900 BCE and the formation of new city-states in the Ganges Valley after 900 BCE. In East Asia, the first states only formed around 1900 BCE, but by 1000 BCE their descendants ruled much of northern China. In the New World, however, the Olmecs mentioned previously and the Chavín civilization in Peru were, at best, borderline examples of states.

The diagram (on p. 220) drawn by the anthropologist-cum-philosopher Ernest Gellner is an abstract but helpful summary of how these few early states worked. Gellner called this ideal-type early state 'Agraria', and suggested that in this mythical but typical community, 'the ruling class forms a small minority of the population, rigidly separate from the great majority of direct agricultural producers, or peasants.' A double line in Gellner's diagram marks this rigid mass-elite division, while single lines mark the ruling class's internal divisions, between specialists in military, administrative, clerical, and other tasks, with their own hierarchical ranking and legally defined boundaries.

'Below the horizontally stratified minority at the top,' Gellner explained, 'there is another world, that of the laterally insulated petty communities of the lay members of society'—that is, peasant villages. Gellner called these 'laterally insulated' because peasants do not get out much; through most of history, most farmers probably stayed within walking distance of their birthplace. In Agraria, peasants in each district tend to have their own dialects, rituals, and traditions—living, says Gellner, 'inward-turned lives'. The broken vertical lines in the diagram symbolize the fragmentation of the peasant world, in sharp contrast to the bigger world in which its rulers live. 'The state,' Gellner observes, 'is interested in extracting taxes, maintaining the peace, and not much else.'

Only a few societies looked much like Agraria in 1000 BCE, and by the standards of what would come later, even they were decidedly ramshackle; I therefore call them 'low-end' states. Egypt was probably the biggest and strongest, but had lost its Levantine and Nubian empire by 1100 BCE. By the 1060s BCE, the Nile Valley had fragmented, too. One dynasty ruled from Tanis in the delta, while the high priests of the god Amun acted as kings in their own right at Thebes. By the 940s BCE, a Libyan dynasty of 'Great Chiefs of Ma' was also ruling from Bubastis, and in the ninth century BCE, things fell apart even more. These mini-states coexisted reasonably peacefully

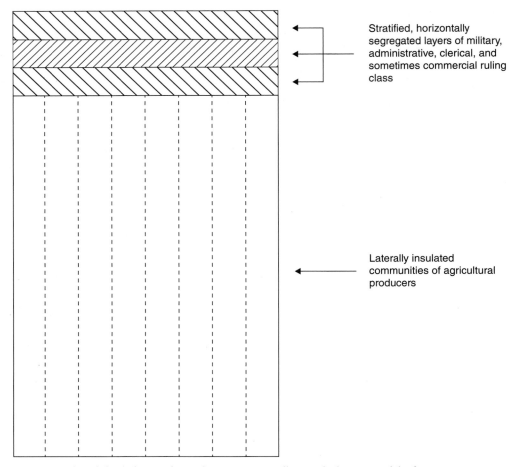

AGRARIA: the philosopher-anthropologist Ernest Gellner's ideal-type model of agrarian states.

('As for pharaoh,' asks a letter dated to 1072 BCE, 'whose superior is he anyway?'), if only because none seems to have been capable of doing very much. Their administrations produced few texts, raised few taxes, and launched few expeditions, and when rulers did build monuments they normally cannibalized architecture from older structures. Already in the 1150s BCE, Ramses III's government had apparently lost the ability to enforce law and order. Royal workers were constantly striking because there was no money to pay them.

Other contemporary states were just as shaky. In 1046 BCE, for instance, when a group called the Zhou overthrew the Shang who ruled China's Yellow River Valley, they realized that they lacked the capacity to garrison and govern the conquered territories and did not even try. Instead, the Duke of Zhou encouraged members of his family to found new cities in the former Shang lands. Each new lord would be his own master, enriching himself as he saw fit. This saved the Duke from having to pay them to govern for him; all he asked was that when he went to war, the 'Many Lords' would join him, bringing contingents from their own cities. The Duke would then share the plunder with his chiefs.

Everyone in the upper reaches of society won. This low-end state did not bring in much revenue for Zhou rulers, but it did not cost much either, because the Duke and his successors paid no wages and kept part of the plunder for themselves. So long as the receipts were bigger than the expenditures, Zhou rulers stayed solvent. They could not afford to do much beyond building palaces, sacrificing to their ancestors, throwing enormous parties (which lowered the costs of ensuring elite compliance by persuading

A GIANT BRONZE VESSEL PROBABLY OF THE TENTH OR ELEVENTH CENTURY BCE, buried with its owner in an elite Western Zhou tomb to perpetuate after death the prestige it conferred in life. Caption informations: Prof. Dame Jessica Rawson of the Institute of Archaeology, University of Oxford.

the Many Lords that the Zhou dynasty had a mandate from heaven and was therefore the sole human source of authority), and waging war, but they did not need to do much more than this.

It is less clear whether people in the lower reaches of society also won. The state's weakness meant that peasants paid the government little or no tax, but rather than leaving the poor better off, this might just have meant that peasants had more property for the Many Lords to extract as rent. It is hard to know which outcome predominated, since few ordinary villages and towns have been excavated. On the one hand, later literary traditions remembered the first century of Zhou rule as a golden age of fairness and justice, but on the other, the gigantic bronze vessels and entire chariot teams found in elite tombs suggest spiralling aristocratic competition and perhaps also oppression of the peasantry, at least until about 850 BCE, when a degree of restraint set in.

This low-end model was reinvented multiple times. In Assyria, for instance, government broke down so profoundly in the twelfth century BCE that no surviving texts whatsoever date between 1076 and 934 BCE. In one of the first post-934 BCE documents, King Ashur-dan II even claims that 'I brought back the exhausted peoples of Assyria who had abandoned their cities and houses in the face of want, hunger and famine, and had gone up to other lands. I settled them in cities and houses'. The inscriptions set up by Ashur-dan and his successors insist that their main jobs were to restore the lands that Assyria had lost and to compel everyone to recognize that Ashur, Assyria's chief god, was the greatest of all gods. To these ends, they needed to raise armies and turn the region into 'Ashur's hunting ground'.

Assyrian kings did this by surrounding themselves with great men (often kinsmen) whom they called *mar banûti*, or 'Sons of Heaven', who functioned very like the Zhou 'Many Lords'. Kings granted the Sons of Heaven vast estates, asking in return that the Sons bring their retinues to fight in the king's wars. At the end of a successful war the king and the Sons would share the plunder between them. Once again, relatively little came in to the royal treasury but relatively little went out either, and although states lacked the capacity to do much apart from fight, feast, and hold festivals, that pretty much covered rulers' requirements.

One state stands out as a possible exception to these generalizations: the United Monarchy of Israel. According to the Hebrew Bible, by 950 BCE King Solomon ruled everything from Sinai to Syria, presiding over a huge bureaucracy which mobilized taxes and manpower for great buildings, trade, and war. He is said to have faced opposition from both elites and commoners, and the kingdom split in two around 930 BCE over resistance to taxes; but if the biblical account is true, Solomonic Israel was the most centralized state on earth.

However, there are difficulties with this account, not least the poor fit between the Biblical story and the archaeological details, particularly at Jerusalem. Controversy swirls around every detail, but many scholars suspect that the Bible's authors, writing hundreds of years after the events, projected the conditions of the ninth and eighth centuries BCE back onto the tenth, exaggerating the Israelite state's capacity. A few even suggest that the United Monarchy was a complete fiction, which may be going too far, but on present evidence, we should probably conclude that in 1000 BCE, all states were small, low-end organizations and very weak compared to what would come later.

Their greatest weakness was that they ran on a diet of military victory. Only success could confirm that the king had the mandate of heaven (or of Ashur, or whoever the local equivalent was) and provide plunder to share with his lords; so, when the war machine failed, everything failed. In 957 BCE, for instance, things went horribly wrong for the Zhou when King Zhao attacked a neighbouring state. 'The heavens were dark and stormy', says the chronicle. 'Pheasants and hares were terrified. The king's six armies perished in the River Han. The king died.'

The Zhou state never recovered. Around 950 BCE, inscriptions from the eastern end of the Yellow River valley stopped mentioning the king. By 900 BCE, 'barbarian enemies' outside the realm and lords within it were rebelling. In 885 BCE, King Yih was deposed, and the final blow came in 771 BCE, when the Many Lords refused to come to King You's aid when Shen barbarians attacked his capital.

By then, it probably makes sense to think of both northern China and Egypt as clusters of separate city-states rather than rickety but unified Agrarias. In the early first millennium BCE, similar small units (typically with populations under ten thousand, organized around a fortified town) dominated the Levant from the Philistines in the south to the Neo-Hittites in the north. As population grew in the eighth century BCE, Greeks and Italians adopted and adapted similar forms of organization, and throughout the first millennium BCE, city-states flourished in the oases of central Asia. Their commercial elites often enjoyed more freedom and power than those in Agrarias, their hierarchies were often less rigid, and some enjoyed astonishing cultural creativity.

Over the long run, groups of city-states tended to coalesce into larger Agrarias, either because one city-state conquered its peers or because all were conquered from outside; but on the other hand, when an Agraria broke apart (as happened in Egypt and China) it might decompose into dozens of city-states. This cycling back and forth was an important dynamic in the first millennium BCE, but, as we shall see, the long-term trend was very much towards large states absorbing small ones. The Indian epic the *Mahabharata* called this 'the law of the fishes': in times of drought, the big fish swallow the little ones.

The world in 175 CE

Much had changed by 175 CE, our period's midpoint. Most obviously, the world's population had roughly doubled (from 120 million to 250 million people) while the numbers living in states had leaped tenfold (from under 20 million to 200 million).

Foraging had continued to contract as farmers colonized more of the world's arable land. By the second century CE, the farms and ranches of what archaeologists call the Chifumbaze Complex were firmly established in southern Africa, the best land in Melanesia and Micronesia had been dug up for sweet potatoes, and farmers of the Hopewell Culture were expanding along the Ohio and Mississippi Valleys in North America.

Herders on the Eurasian steppes saw astonishing institutional growth in the first millennium BCE. When the Greek historian Herodotus described the Scythian horse nomads in the fifth century BCE, they lived under kings who sometimes forged large federations to plunder agrarian societies. In 209 BCE, however, a chief named Maodun created such a huge alliance among the Xiongnu in what is now Mongolia that it seems reasonable to call it a nomadic state, or even an empire.

The growth of pastoral social and political organizations on the steppes went hand in hand with that of agrarian empires in the lucky latitudes, with men like Maodun building their followings by extorting wealth from settled societies using it to buy tribal chiefs' loyalty. The contrast between tombs 1 and 2 at Arzhan in southern Siberia—the richest steppe burials of the eighth and seventh centuries BCE—and tomb 2 at Pazyryk—the richest of the third century BCE—is instructive: while the former featured huge tumuli and piles of gold ornaments and sacrificed horses, the latter was also heaped with Persian, Indian, and Chinese treasures.

FROM EARLY IN THE FIRST MILLENNIUM BCE HUGE TUMULI at Tuva in Arzhan contained burials adorned with an abundance of gold objects, like this bowl decorated with a serpent biting its tail.

Agrarian states were hard-pressed to hold off these highly mobile nomads, who had the advantage of surprise on the offence and the option of fleeing into the steppes in defence. Agrarian kings who were willing to spend enough on logistics could sometimes kill so many nomads that the survivors were afraid to raid for generations, as Darius I of Persia did against the 'Pointy-Hatted Scythians' in 519 BCE, and Wudi of Han China did against the Xiongnu after 134 BCE. More often, though, farming societies were reduced to bribing nomads not to raid (even though nomads regularly took bribes then raided anyway). When there were no rich empires to rob or extort, nomads sometimes even took control of parts of the lucky latitudes and looted them more thoroughly.

Nevertheless, in two main ways, agrarian states grew even more than those on the steppes: geographically, as Agraria spread into regions where it had previously not been known, and organizationally, as low-end states turned into high-end ones and deepened their capacity to intervene in their subjects' lives.

THE IMAGE ON A FELT CARPET (perhaps brought from Persia, though no carpets of comparable antiquity have survived there) from a fourth- or fifth-century BCE tomb at Pazyryk captures the splendour of the way of life of the nomad chief buried there.

There were two main mechanisms of growth, which we might call primary and secondary state formation. Primary state formation meant the creation of governments without borrowing ideas and methods from pre-existing states, while secondary state formation involved groups responding to neighbouring states by adopting and adapting their forms of government. In practice, of course, the two mechanisms can be difficult to separate. In the Mediterranean, for instance, a wave of state formation rolled from east to west between 800 and 100 BCE, but scholars rarely agree on the relative importance of indigenous developments, the influence of Phoenician and Greek colonists, or the impact of Roman conquerors.

In the Americas, by contrast, we can be certain we are often dealing with primary state formation. The lavish tombs at Sipán and the enormous Pyramid of the Sun surely mean that by 175 CE, the Moche people in the Andes had found their own route to Agraria. In contemporary Mesoamerica, Maya city-states were taking shape at Tikal and elsewhere, while Teotihuacan, with its spectacular monuments and population of 150,000, was clearly the capital of a state.

Because the New and Old Worlds had so little contact, they offer a 'natural experiment,' allowing us to test the notion of *Homo superans* by comparing two independent cases. In some ways, the New and Old Worlds followed rather similar paths. In both, organizational capacity deepened as population grew, following more or less the same timetables. In Mexico and the Andes, just as in the Middle East, India,

THE PYRAMID OF THE SUN, TWO HUNDRED FEET TALL, BUILT AROUND 200 CE, dominates the ruins of the vast metropolis of Teotihuacan, which covered about eight square miles at its height.

and China, roughly six thousand years passed between the beginnings of cultivation of plants and animals and the rise of the first states. We might also note that the rulers of the earliest states all relied heavily on religion to legitimate their power and regularly advertised their godlike qualities with pyramidal monuments.

However, there are also striking differences. In the Old World, state formation, metallurgy, and writing usually came together as a package, but in the New World, only the Maya made much use of writing and although the elite had copper and gold ornaments, people were still living largely in the Stone Age when Columbus arrived. Explaining these similarities and differences should be a high priority for historians.

Having begun down the path of agriculture and organizational growth roughly two millennia earlier than New World societies, by 175 CE the Old World boasted vastly bigger and stronger states. Well before 175, in fact, the biggest Old World states had reached a threshold beyond which low-end institutions simply did not work very well. Low-end institutions were fine for states with populations of just a few millions, but not for societies of tens of millions, and across the first millennium BCE the biggest Old World states either reinvented themselves or fell apart under the stresses of clinging to outdated ways of operating.

The Middle East had had the world's biggest sociopolitical organizations ever since the end of the Ice Age, and not surprisingly it was the first place to reach this threshold. In the 780s BCE, the Assyrian Empire had lurched into crisis as its kings lost control of the aristocracy, and a bloody coup launched in 744 BCE by a general named Pulu initially seemed to be one more step in the downward spiral. However, by the time Pulu (better known by his throne name, Tiglath-Pileser III) died in 727 BCE, he had transformed Assyrian state power.

The sources do not tell us exactly what he did, but Tiglath-Pileser somehow bypassed the old Sons of Heaven. Instead of asking them for troops and then sharing his spoils with them, Tiglath-Pileser created a bureaucracy to raise taxes with which he hired his own troops, keeping all the plunder for the state. The king continued to trust senior aristocrats with high administrative office, but now they were employees working for and paid by him, rather than free agents who could withdraw their support at will. This 'high-end' state cost much more to run than the old low-end organizations but it also brought in much more profit and proved much more scalable. The biggest low-end states so far, fourteenth-century BCE Egypt and ninth-century BCE Assyria, had each controlled 1 million square kilometres and 3 million to 4 million people, but by 175 CE Rome and China each ruled more than 5 million square kilometres and 50 million people.

Assyria's passage from the low to the high end in the 730s BCE must have been painful, but the consequences were dramatic. Within fifty years it had become the biggest and richest empire yet seen. Its growth forced its neighbours to choose between being absorbed into it or emulating its methods and fighting back. Enough chose the latter that in 612 BCE a grand coalition (including, as mentioned earlier, Scythians from the steppes) destroyed Nineveh, but the cycle of growth could not be broken. The high-end genie was out of the bottle.

By 490 BCE Persia had conquered an even bigger empire, stretching from the Balkans to India and ruling some 35 million people, and in the 510s BCE, King Darius I had given it modern, high-end institutions able to mobilize enormous revenues and armies. In the 330s BCE, Alexander of Macedon overthrew its rulers, however, and after 301 BCE, his successors broke the empire into smaller units and set to fighting one another. Starting around 245 BCE, Parthian nomads infiltrated into Iran from the steppes and by 135 BCE they had reunited it and Mesopotamia under their own rule.

By then, giant new empires had also emerged further east. Persia and Macedon, both of which conquered the Indus Valley, must have influenced developments in India, but consolidation also began independently at the east end of the Ganges Valley. Progressively larger kingdoms formed around the city-state of Magadha in the sixth and fifth centuries BCE, and around 321 BCE Chandragupta created the much larger Mauryan Empire. Historians dispute how high-end this was, although the *Arthashastra*, a handbook on governing written by Chandragupta's chief advisor Kautilya, certainly makes it sound very strong. In the 260s BCE, King Asoka claimed to have so much authority that he could renounce violence altogether.

The empire unravelled after a military coup in 185 BCE, with a smaller Shunga kingdom forming around Magadha along with several clusters of city-states and areas conquered by outsiders. Descendants of Alexander's Macedonians carved out Greco-Indian kingdoms in the northwest and Scythians created two new Shaka kingdoms, but the most successful conquest state was the Kushan Empire. Yuezhi nomads built this on the ruins of the Greek and Shaka lands in the mid-first century CE, and a century later, its King Kanishka ruled most of the Ganges plain.

China went through its own process of consolidation and growth. War whittled the 148 city-states documented around 700 BCE down to just 14 Agrarias by 450 BCE, and a single empire in 221 BCE. After an abrupt breakdown and civil war from 209 to 206 BCE, the Han dynasty created a flexible and stable system, although a second round of civil war in the 20s CE led them to cede much power back to the landed aristocracy. By 175 CE, the dynasty was struggling to contain elite feuding, internal revolts, and pressure on the frontiers.

The grandest empire of all was at the western end of Eurasia, which had had the biggest social and political organizations since the end of the Ice Age. Here, the city-state of Rome violently united the entire Mediterranean basin in the last three centuries BCE, swallowing up the Greek city-states along the way. These had been the most successful city-state system on record, with hundreds of statelets scattered from Spain to Crimea. These *poleis* supported a population of six million, enjoyed remarkable economic growth, and created an extraordinarily seductive culture, but could not compete with Roman military power. Rome even pushed its boundaries beyond the lucky latitudes, seizing northwest and parts of central Europe.

By the first century BCE, Rome's republican, city-state institutions had proved inadequate to the task of running the world's greatest empire, and they disintegrated in terrible civil wars. When peace was restored after 31 BCE, Octavian—the last warlord standing—renamed himself Augustus, decreed that he was really no different from anyone else (just a lot richer), proclaimed that the Republic had been restored, and quietly began a half millennium of autocracy at Rome.

To different degrees, all these Eurasian empires moved toward a high-end model, distinguished by strong central institutions that effectively sidelined aristocrats and established direct links between the government and the peasants. The further a state moved in this direction (Rome and China went furthest, the Parthians and Kushans least far), the more it began dissolving the line separating its elites from the mass of peasants, reaching across it to grant farmers legal ownership of their land (rather than holding it as tenants of great lords), in return for which farmers paid taxes to the kings and accepted conscription into their armies. Rich, educated men still served as administrators and generals, and the richest were much richer in 175 CE than in 1000 BCE, but aristocrats' power now typically depended on the king's favour, rather than the reverse. In a high-end state, tax took precedence over rent; the minute the formula was reversed, as happened in China in the first century CE, the state started sliding back toward the low end.

Ultimately, kings needed tax revenues to create mass, iron-armed armies, usually dominated by infantry, with which they could deter or fight rival kings while also intimidating their own noblemen and peasants. Taxes, the army, and professionalized elites turned together in a tight circle, and once someone like Tiglath-Pileser dragged one state towards the high end, the only way its neighbours could survive was by following it.

High-end states remade organizations of every kind. Big empires required big cities, where services of every kind were concentrated. There were probably 100,000 people at Nineveh by 700 BCE and a million at Rome in 100 CE. To fill so many empty stomachs, the Roman Empire turned the whole Mediterranean into a marketing system to funnel food into the always-hungry capital. Agricultural output had to rise (as early as the fourth century BCE, Greeks were manuring and multicropping their fields, and population reached densities that would not be matched again until 1900 CE). Roads, ships, and harbours had to be improved so people could move the food around. New media of exchange were needed, and so coinage was independently invented in the East Mediterranean and China. Greeks and Romans invented increasingly complex instruments of credit and banking. More people had to be able to read and write, so education expanded. In the Mediterranean simple alphabets replaced tricky syllabaries, although even in Athens and Rome probably no more than one man in ten (and far fewer women) ever learned them. Abundant cheap tools and weapons were required, so iron replaced bronze. Necessity drove innovation and growth.

Last, but by no means least, rulers had to reinvent themselves. One of the low-end king's chief tools for getting people to do what he said had been to claim that he was the only point of contact between this world and the divine sphere, meaning that anyone arguing with him was going against the will of the gods. In the first millennium BCE, however, one king after another found that his high-end state worked better if he recast himself as

IN FRONT OF THE SOMETIME SITE OF A TEMPLE dedicated to the Emperor Augustus, an inscription in Latin and Punic celebrates the repaving of the Old Forum by Emperor Claudius in 53 BCE at Leptis Magna in Libya.

something more like a CEO, working with a bureaucracy rather than interpreting the will of the gods on behalf of mere mortals. Of course, plenty of people after 1000 BCE kept on seeing kings as gods, just as plenty before 1000 BCE had known that their rulers were all too human (even in Egypt, where pharaohs were technically gods incarnate, scribes happily described them as being too hung over to speak and getting excited watching teams of naked oarswomen rowing on the Nile). But by 175 CE, rulers almost everywhere were making fewer claims to godlike status than in earlier centuries.

The 'Axial' revolution in Eurasian thought (see Chapter 6 this volume) was in part an intellectual response to this development, offering meaning in a world in which kingship was losing its power as a cosmic principle. Each in its own way, Confucianism, Buddhism, Judaism, and Platonism (and later Stoicism, Christianity, and Islam) showed individuals how to transcend this sullied world and find truth within themselves now that they could no longer rely on kings to do the job for them.

Axial thought typically began as a countercultural movement challenging norms and speaking truth to power. Its founding fathers mostly came from the margins, belonging to the lower rungs of the elite and preaching their good news not in the great imperial capitals, but in provincial backwaters or independent city-states. Rulers and bureaucrats regularly persecuted its prophets, but eventually learned that co-opting its best and brightest worked better than killing them. Whether Confucian, Christian, or something in between, Axial intellectuals found comfortable berths in the

IN WAYS PARALLELED IN OTHER CIVILIZATIONS, Chinese painters continually looked back to monarchs and sages of the 'Axial' era. In this image, Yang Jian, the Emperor Wen, who founded the Sui dynasty in 581 CE, is depicted in ways familiar from renderings of emperors of a thousand years earlier.
Caption informations: Mr Stephen Bradley.

service of the state, diluting their messages to make faiths in which everyone could believe. All over the Eurasian lucky latitudes, the intellectual movements of the first millennium BCE became 'the classics', timeless wisdom which continues today to give meaning to the lives of billions of people.

Eurasia's classical empires were extraordinary organizational achievements, dwarfing everything that had gone before and everything in other parts of the world. In fact, the Roman Empire might well have reached the upper limit of what was possible in a purely agricultural world. A thousand years would pass before another society—Song dynasty China—came near matching second-century Rome's level of development, and no one surpassed it until eighteenth-century Britain stood at the brink of its industrial revolution.

The world in 1350 CE

Population kept growing after 175 CE, but more slowly than before. The 250 million people at our period's midpoint had increased to 350 million by its end, albeit after peaking around 400 million soon after 1300. But while total population grew by about 40 per cent, the share living in states jumped by 60 per cent, from about 200 million to roughly 325 million.

Foragers kept retreating as farmers advanced, particularly in Africa and North America, and where there were no foragers to displace, as in most of Oceania, farming spread even faster. Melanesians colonized New Zealand by 1200, and a few intrepid Argonauts of the Pacific even paddled all the way to the America and back (there is no other explanation for how American sweet potatoes made their way to Polynesia around this time). Many islands saw booming population, and on some, such as Hawaii, great warriors brought villages together to form larger and stronger organizations. By the time Captain Cook arrived in 1778, Hawaiian chiefs could almost be called kings.

Similar processes were also under way in mainland North America, although here there were few empty landscapes to expand into. Mexican immigrants probably carried the triad of maize, squash, and beans to Chaco Canyon around 500, Vikings temporarily brought European crops to Newfoundland around 1000, and the maize-based agricultural complex that archaeologists call the Mississippian Culture spread widely in the Midwest and Southeast after 1000. Its farming communities created organizations even bigger than Hawaii's; by 1150 perhaps ten thousand people were living around the ceremonial centre of Cahokia, and although the site was in decline by 1350, a major new settlement was thriving at Moundville. Some archaeologists think we should speak of Mississippian cities and low-end states, although most suspect that despite mobilizing so much labour, Mississippian leaders—like the Olmecs two millennia earlier—did not monopolize the legitimate use of violence.

The older state systems in Mesoamerica and the Andes remained grander than these new North American proto-states, although in 1350 none had yet regained the scale and complexity which Teotihuacan had boasted before its fiery destruction around 750, or the Classic Maya city-states before their ninth-century breakdown. The biggest city in the Americas in 1350 was Chan Chan, the capital of the Chimù Empire in the old Moche territory in the Andes, which probably had thirty thousand residents. Not till the early sixteenth century did any city—the Aztec capital Tenochtitlan—rival Teotihuacan at its height.

Primary and secondary state formation both remained important. In Africa, the inroads of Muslim merchants provided incentives for the formation of numerous small, mercantile city-states down the east coast and in the oases of the Sahara. Some of these, such as the Kanem Kingdom around what is now Chad and the Mali Empire in the Niger River Valley, coalesced into larger organizations which might almost be called low-end states. Further south, however, the low-end states of Mapungubwe and Great Zimbabwe were entirely indigenous.

In Eurasia, secondary state formation mattered more than primary, with merchants and missionaries from older states often playing major roles. In the tenth century, low-end states formed in Southeast Asia just as Chinese merchants became common, which might mean that local chiefs leveraged new economic opportunities to turn themselves into kings. Some of these states achieved remarkable things: according to the *Nagarakretagama*, a eulogy composed in 1365, King Hayan Wuruk of Majapahit on Java controlled 98 tributary cities. He was very much a godlike king, according to his eulogy, managing to be not only 'Buddha in the body' but also 'Shiva incarnate'.

Northern and Eastern Europe went similar ways, and as the vast area between the Rhine, Danube, and Volga Rivers—which had been virtually stateless in 175 CE—filled up with low-end states, self-aggrandizing chiefs learned that turning Christian was a good way to get people to do what they said. Christian rulers could invite clerics into their kingdoms to share administrative know-how, and marrying into established Christian royal families or even putting themselves under the protection of bigger Christian states could make all the difference in local power struggles.

Christianization, state formation, assassination, and civil war often went together, as in tenth-century Bohemia, where the Christian Duke Wenceslaus—the 'Good King Wenceslas' of Christmas carol fame—saw his equally pro-Christian grandmother strangled (perhaps with her own veil) and was then himself murdered by his pro-pagan brother, who subsequently made peace with Christianity anyway. And where locals failed to see Jesus' appeal, conquest and colonization might convince them. 'These pagans are the worst of men but their land is the best', a recruiting drive for a crusade into what is now Poland announced in 1108. 'Here you will be able both to save your souls and, if you will, to acquire very good land to settle.' Plenty of Franks and Germans agreed, and by 1350 almost all of Europe was at least nominally ruled by Christian kings.

Comparable mechanisms of secondary state formation were working everywhere from Germany to Japan, turning village societies into bigger organizations. But from England to Iran, low-end states were also created by the breakdown of older, high-end empires. The great ancient empires were already in crisis by 175 CE, and over the next half-millennium all of them shattered into smaller units.

Why this happened is one of the biggest questions in ancient history. The sheer scale of the phenomenon suggests that the answers cannot lie at the local level; we must surely look for systemic causes, and the most important among them might be that growth of the first millennium BCE had self-undermining effects: the bigger the empires and commercial networks of Eurasia's lucky latitudes grew, the more they became entangled in hostility with each other, and the more emulous and predatory the societies on the steppes became.

Steppe tribes had grown into empires in the first millennium BCE by acting as parasites on the agrarian empires in the lucky latitudes, but in the first millennium CE, the parasites started killing their hosts. In part this was because the nomads were unleashing more violence than before. Their migrations and raids disrupted other peoples around the edges of the steppes, knocking over dominos and setting huge numbers of people in motion. At the eastern end of Eurasia, Qiang farmers along China's western frontier formed their own states in the second century CE to fight back against Xiongnu and Yuezhi raids, but then used their newfound strength to push into the Han Empire to escape the nomads. At the western end of Eurasia, Germanic farmers did much the same thing to fight against and/or escape from the Sarmatians, Alans, and eventually, the Huns.

As if this were not bad enough, the nomads got better at fighting. Cimmerians and Scythians had generally stayed away from walled cities, but when Attila the Hun invaded the Balkans in 442 his engineers—often ex-Roman military man—were unstoppable. Archaeologists trace his advance through the shells of burned-out cities.

The nomads' deadliest weapons, though, were too small to see. Their rapid movements across vast distances had merged eastern and western disease pools that, before the first millennium BCE, had largely evolved in isolation. This unleashed new microbes onto populations that were completely unfamiliar with them. It cannot be a coincidence that terrible new plagues broke out on both Rome's Syrian frontier and China's northwest frontier in 161 CE. Scientists have not yet pinpointed the pathogens responsible, but eyewitness accounts make both diseases sound a lot like smallpox. He Gong, a fourth-century Chinese doctor, recorded that 'epidemic sores…attack the head, face and trunk. In a short time, these sores spread all over the body. They have the appearance of hot boils containing some white matter. While some of these pustules are drying up a fresh crop appears. If not treated early the patients usually die. Those who recover are disfigured by purplish scars.'

By 200 CE, the disease had killed one Egyptian in four and uncounted but vast numbers across the rest of the Roman and the Han Empires. Nor did it end there; the plague kept coming back, roughly once per generation, for a century and a half. Around 250, we are told, five thousand people died from it every day in the city of Rome. In China, the worst years were between 310 and 322.

The Han, Kushan, Persian, and Roman Empires all collapsed between 200 and 700, mostly being replaced by clusters of low-end Agrarias. Sometimes the decline in scale is astonishing; in Britain, few if any social or political organizations could project capabilities more than fifty miles in the year 550. In this chaos, religious institutions regularly stepped in to fill the void left by state failure, organizing defence and food supply as well as offering people explanations for why the world they had known was ending.

This at least partly explains how Christianity and Mahayana Buddhism each won tens of millions of adherents between the first and fifth centuries CE, but the other great religious success story, Islam, was rather different. It began in the seventh century CE as a provincial variant on Judaism and Christianity, but was then carried across much of the old Roman Empire and the whole of the Persian by invaders. As conquerors, the highly mobile Arabs had a certain amount in common with the steppe nomads, but were far less destructive and much better at inserting themselves into the tottering structures of the agrarian empires.

Between 750 and 800, the Abbasid caliphs, based in Baghdad, appeared to be forging a vast empire stretching from Iberia to the Indus, but by 850 they had clearly failed. Arab caliphs, like the khans and kings of so many steppe societies, found it almost impossible to convert tribal organizations into imperial ones, and the job was made harder still in their case by the influence and unruliness of Muslim holy men. The caliph al-Ma'mun (reigned 813–833) probably came closer than anyone to creating a high-end Arab Empire, but his efforts to play religious factions against each other and to bully religious experts eventually shattered his government's authority, while his final solution—bringing Turkic nomads into the heart of Iraq to force everyone to obey him—went even more badly wrong. By 860, the caliphs were hostages of their own mercenaries; in 945, the caliphate decomposed into a dozen independent emirates; and by 1000, pastoral nomads had driven long-established farmers off much of the best soil in the Middle East. Although Egypt escaped the worst of the breakdown, Turkic horsemen seized control there, and Iran remained politically splintered until 1500.

What makes this messy story so important is the contrast between Western and Eastern Eurasia. A string of efforts to reunite the West, including Justinian's attempt from Constantinople to reconquer the Roman Empire in the sixth century CE and Charlemagne's to create a new version based in France around 800 failed just as badly as al-Ma'mun's. In China, however, the Xianbei nomads who had overrun much of the North went through an extraordinary modernizing revolution in the sixth century CE. After creating a high-end state in the Yellow River Valley and rebranding themselves as the Sui dynasty, their Emperor Wendi built a fleet and raised an army of 500,000 men in 589 (at which point no Western ruler could raise even 50,000) and united the whole country after a lightning campaign down the Yangzi River.

Why Wendi succeeded where Justinian, Charlemagne, and al-Ma'mun failed remains debated, but the consequence of his success is clear: the world's organizational centre of gravity moved from Western to Eastern Eurasia. By 700, a million people were living at Chang'an and another half million at Luoyang. A Grand Canal had been dug to move rice from the expanding paddies south of the Yangzi to the booming cities of the north (much as the Mediterranean had once allowed traders to ship grain from North Africa to the booming city of Rome). Through battlefield victories and clever diplomacy Tang emperors (who replaced the Sui in 618) had won control of the eastern steppes and even intervened in India. A cultural and commercial efflorescence began. The eighth century CE became the golden age of Chinese poetry. In the ninth, firms whose business stretched from Sichuan to Korea invented paper money, which the state began issuing in 1024. By 1078, Chinese foundries were smelting 125,000 tons of iron ore—almost as much as the whole of Europe would be producing in 1700, on the eve of the industrial revolution.

Eleventh-century CE China's social and political organizations were as big and complex as Rome's had been a thousand years earlier and were going from strength to strength, while those of Europe, the Middle East, and India were all heading the opposite way, crumbling before attacks from Vikings, Turks, and Afghans. Some historians even suggest that Song dynasty China stood at the verge of an industrial revolution of its own in 1100. In its biggest cities, coal was replacing wood as the main fuel (twenty new coal markets opened in Kaifeng alone between 1102 and 1106, and a well-documented iron foundry at Qicunzhen was burning 42,000 tons of it every year), and textile manufacturers were using water-powered spinning machines strikingly like those that Europeans would reinvent in the eighteenth century.

Why the Chinese economic takeoff faltered is yet another great unknown, but I suspect that the answer lies largely in the continuing entanglement of the lucky latitudes and steppes. No agrarian empire really mastered the nomads until effective guns came on the scene in the seventeenth century. The oldest known gun, found in Manchuria, probably dates to 1288, and a carving from Sichuan around 1150 probably shows an even earlier gun, but such crude weapons could not fire fast enough to stop cavalry. So long as that remained true, so did the old formula that the more than an agrarian empire grew, the more likely it was to attract the devastating attentions of nomads.

In 1127, Jurchens from Manchuria sacked Kaifeng and overran northern China. This dislocated the Song Empire's economy, separating the main cities and coalfields (in the north) from the main source of rice (in the south). Worse still, China's combination of wealth and military weakness made the nomads even more aggressive, and in 1206 Genghis Khan combined the tribes of Mongolia into the most terrible of all pastoral empires. In 1215, he sacked ninety Chinese cities (the ruins of Beijing burned for a month) and considered depopulating the entire Yellow River plain to use as winter pasture for his herds. Wiser counsel prevailed, but in the 1260s his grandson Kublai Khan returned. It took the Mongols six years to capture Xiangyang, the strongest fortress in the world, but a dozen years later all of China was in Kublai's hands.

Even then, China's organizations remained the wonder of the world. 'I can tell you in all truthfulness,' Marco Polo wrote in the 1290s, 'that the business [conducted in Hangzhou] is on such a stupendous scale that no one who hears tell of it without seeing it for himself can possibly credit it.' But what Marco did not know was that Chinese organizations were now contracting. China in 1300 no longer looked like a society on the verge of an industrial revolution, and over the next forty years the Mongol Yuan dynasty lost control of the country. Bandits, warlords, and famine stalked the land; and in 1345 the greatest blow of all—the Black Death—fell.

As in the second century CE, the creation of larger organizations on the steppes probably had much to do with the scale of this epidemic. As the dust settled after the thirteenth-century wars, something of a 'Pax Mongolica' had emerged, making it much easier for migrants, missionaries, and merchants (such as Marco Polo) to move back and forth across Eurasia, but also making it easier to mix disease pools into toxic new brews. Between 1340 and 1360 the populations of Europe, the Middle East, and China probably fell by one-third. 'Civilization both in East and West was visited by a destructive plague which devastated nations and caused populations to vanish', the Arab traveller and philosopher Ibn Khaldûn wrote in 1377. 'It swallowed up many of the good things of civilization and wiped them out.'

Ibn Khaldûn famously saw history as a series of cycles, and this should perhaps not surprise us. The events of his own era were part a repeated pattern in which social and political organizations grew until their interconnections set loose contrary forces that undermined them, at which point they collapsed in the face of migration and disease. There was no sign in the fourteenth century that the future would be any different, and the larger shape of history seemed to be clear.

Conclusion

But that, obviously, was not the case. Over the next quarter of a millennium, world history headed off in a very new direction. Asians closed down the steppe highway, ending the parasitical relationship between nomadic and agrarian empires. Europeans, meanwhile, colonized the Americas, built an unprecedented Atlantic economy on the back of intercontinental trade and slavery, and launched a scientific revolution. Another quarter-millennium after that, Britain had industrialized its economy and bestrode the world like a colossus.

So enormous is the difference between the world of 1350 and that of 1850 that scholars often assume that the pre-1350 period is simply not very important to the larger story. According to the geographer Al Crosby, 'Between that era [when the horse was domesticated] and the time of development of the societies that sent Columbus and other voyagers across the oceans, roughly 4,000 years passed, during which little of importance happened, *relative to what had gone before*' (emphasis in original). Domestication was important; globalization was important; but the 2,350 years reviewed in this chapter were not.

But this view is mistaken. The scale of cities, states, religious groups, and trade grew by an order of magnitude between 1000 BCE and 1350 CE. Without this, the steppes could not have been closed, the oceans could not have been opened, and the modern world could not have been born. In these centuries, the world's biggest social and political organizations reached the limits of what was possible in a purely agrarian context and the world's organizational centre of gravity shifted—for the first time ever—from West to East. And while these great events were unfolding in Eurasia, farming and low-end states spread across most of the planet. In 1000 BCE, only about one human in ten lived under a government; by 1350 CE, at least nine in ten did so, and the stage was set for the creation of the social and political organizations which we still live with today.

PART 4

The Climatic Reversal

—

Expansion and Innovation amid Plague and Cold from the Mid-Fourteenth to the Early Nineteenth Centuries CE

CHAPTER 8

A Converging World
Economic and Ecological Encounters, 1350–1815

DAVID NORTHRUP

THE world grew smaller in the centuries after 1350, as maritime trade routes tightened connections among people and increased the movement of goods. For the first time, ships sailed regularly between the Atlantic and the Indian Ocean, across the Atlantic, and across the Pacific. Along with goods and people, microbes, plants, and animals spread to the far corners of the planet. Diseases spread to new lands, causing the deaths of millions of people. Plants from one region, such as maize, potatoes, tea, and coffee, found new consumers in distant places. New World tobacco became a drug of choice in Europe, Africa, and parts of Asia. Cattle, sheep, and horses from the Old World fostered the development of new ways of life in the Americas. Spices and textiles from Asia found markets in the Atlantic continents, and plantations in the Americas made sugar a common food in Europe. The largest and most brutal intercontinental movement of people in history, the transatlantic slave trade, supported economic development in the Americas. In short, after 1350, forces for global convergence that had been quite contained became commonplace with consequences, whether good or bad, that by 1815 appeared unstoppable.

Historical evidence is unevenly distributed, but a greater reason for the geographical emphases of this chapter is the uneven distribution of people. Over 80 per cent of humans dwelt in the great Eurasian landmass in 1400, and Eurasia's share rose to nearly 90 per cent by 1800. Population was densest in three regions: China, India, and Europe. At the beginning of our period, one in four people lived in China proper; at the end it was more than one in three. The Indian subcontinent's population doubled during this period, although its share of the total slipped a bit. Europe, with one-sixth of the world's people in 1400, increased its share to one-fifth by 1800. The dense populations of these areas justify giving them greater attention.

Although human numbers overall rose during these centuries, the period saw three massive population calamities. In the second half of the 1400s, the worst pandemic ever recorded struck the Old World continents. During the 1500s and later, newly introduced diseases devastated the native peoples of the Americas. Meanwhile, the planet was experiencing the most prolonged era of below normal temperatures since the Pleistocene Ice Age ended about 12,000 years before. That human population could still increase overall is testimony to the positive effects of the resettlement of new lands, the cultivation of more productive plants, and changing economic circumstances that set the stage for the far more dramatic changes in the next 200 years.

Environment, economics, and expansion from the East

China was the source of two major westward movements in the century after the mid-1300s, one accidental, the other very deliberate. The first was the bubonic plague, known in the West as the Black Death. It is not known precisely what set this pandemic in motion, but modern research suggests that the plague had been present in Yunnan Province of southwest China for centuries. Increased contacts during Mongol rule helped spread the disease to other parts of China and eastward in Central Asia. Although it is not known whether the plague spread overland through Central Asia or along maritime routes, in 1347 an outbreak of the disease occurred among the residents of the port city of Kaffa on the Crimean Peninsula of the Black Sea. Soon Greece and islands in the northern Mediterranean mainland were suffering from the plague. According to observers, the next year a Genoese ship carried the disease from

THE BURIAL OF THE VICTIMS OF THE PLAGUE IN TOURNAI. Detail of a miniature from 'The Chronicles of Gilles Li Muisis' (1272–1352), abbot of the monastery of St Martin of the Righteous.

Kaffa to Italy, from where it spread rapidly across much of southern and western Europe and around the southern Mediterranean. Recently epidemiologists have suggested that the carriers of transmission were complex, depending more on rodents than human carriers. By 1349, in any case, the plague was causing unprecedented mortality across the face of Europe. Some places were spared; others seem to have lost up to two-thirds of their population. The gross symptoms and the speed with which death came added to the horrors. Most victims suffered severe pain, fever, vomiting and diarrhoea and exhibited black splotches on their skin and swellings the size of eggs in their groins and armpits. These swellings of the lymph nodes are known as buboes, from which the popular name of bubonic plague is derived. However, it is suspected that many other diseases, ranging from typhoid and smallpox to anthrax were spreading at the same time, complicating the symptoms victims displayed.

Studies of medieval graveyards in France, Britain, and the Netherlands have clarified some facts. From ancient DNA extracted from victims' remains it has been possible to reconstruct the entire genome of the principal plague organism, *Yersinia pestis*, and confirm it as the main culprit. Being able to assign the proper scientific name to their affliction, however, would have been of no consolation to those who were its victims. At the time it was commoner to blame evil spirits, witches, and Jews. The Muslim historian Ibn Khaldun summed up the consequences for a converging and interacting world:

> Civilization both in the East and the West was visited by a destructive plague which devastated nations and caused populations to vanish. It swallowed up many of the good things of civilization and wiped them out.[. . .] Cities and buildings were laid waste, roads and way signs were obliterated, settlements and mansions became empty, dynasties and tribes grew weak. The entire inhabited world changed.

Everywhere the demographic and psychological impacts of the bubonic pandemic were calamitous. People died by the millions. Survivors were haunted by grief, fright, and a sense of doom. By a conservative estimate the population of Europe fell from a peak of about 80 million on the eve of the pandemic to perhaps 60 million in 1400. Historians think that North Africa also lost a quarter of its population. Yet societies can be very resilient. By 1500 Europe's population was back where it had been, and China's had rebounded from some 75 million in 1400 to 100 million in 1500. Elsewhere, the evidence is too fragmentary to cite with any confidence.

In Europe the population loss from the Black Death caused a labour shortage, which had some positive effects. Serfdom nearly disappeared because rural labourers held in such bondage could easily run away. Skilled rural workers (smiths, millers, carpenters) were able to push for higher wages. If those in authority resisted these changes, revolt and rebellion might occur. Given the dispersal of the rural peasants and the difficulties of organizing any sustained resistance, most uprisings were local and of brief duration. However, in England the Peasants' Revolt of 1381 led by Wat Tyler was the largest popular uprising in Europe before the eighteenth century. Spreading across the eastern third of England and into London, the rebels demanded an end to serfdom and duties owed to the lords of the manors. Their anger led to murders, including the Archbishop of Canterbury, and other violence. Those in power used violence even more freely in suppressing the revolt. Some peasants gained access to land and rose in status, but many others gained little or nothing. In parts of Eastern Europe where the effects of the plague were less severe, landowners used the opportunity to reduce free peasants to servitude.

The second Chinese movement to the west was a spectacular set of maritime ventures between 1405 and 1433. The motives of emperor of the Ming Dynasty who commissioned these seven expeditions into Southeast Asia, India, and on to East Africa was not discovery, for these seas had long been the maritime crossroads of the world. Although the expeditions may have updated information about China's long-standing trading partners and led to some enhancement of trade, their primary purpose appears to have been to impress the outside world with China's wealth and importance. Having succeeded in ending a century and a third of foreign rule by the Mongols in 1368 and consolidating power at home, the Ming were 'showing the flag' overseas.

The fleets would have inspired awe anywhere in the world. The first consisted of 62 large junks, described as 'treasure ships' and about a hundred smaller junks. The 'treasure ships' were loaded with rich Chinese manufactures (including silk, precious metal goods, and porcelain) to be given to rulers and other dignitaries along the way. The ships also carried enough humans to populate a small city. Allegedly, one fleet carried over 27,000 individuals, including infantry soldiers and cavalry troops and their horses.

Admiral Zheng He (1371–1435), who commanded the fleets, was a suitable ambassador as well as an experienced mariner. He had some ancestors from the Persian Gulf and was a Muslim. Other Arabic-speaking Chinese came along to interpret. One of the interpreters, Ma Huan, kept a diary that has survived, in which he described the customs, dress, and beliefs of the different places. After returning to China he went on a speaking tour telling of these exotic peoples and their amazement at the majesty of the fleets and gifts.

The rulers who received lavish gifts from the Chinese reciprocated with their own exotic presents. The Swahili city-state of Malindi, for example, sent the Ming emperor a giraffe, an animal exotic enough to impress the normally staid court officials; a drawing of it has survived in the margin of a Chinese manuscript. Three more fleets sailed to the Swahili coast and these contacts seem to have stimulated African demand for Chinese porcelain and silks. Other places the fleets called at also seem to have increased trade with China. Yet, because promoting commercial exchanges was not the purpose of these expeditions, imperial officials questioned whether increased contacts with people the Chinese considered inferiors justified their high cost. The fleets were suspended for several years, and, after a final expedition in 1432–1433, the practice was halted. Apparently to prevent a revival of interest the vessels most records of them were destroyed.

ON 20 SEPTEMBER 1414, BENGALI envoys presented a tribute giraffe in the name of King Saif Al-Din Hamzah Shah of Bengal (r. 1410–1412) to the Yongle Emperor of Ming China (r. 1402–1424), who commissioned Shen Du (1357–1434) to paint it. The Yongle Emperor commissioned Shen Du to paint this giraffe. This file depicts the original painting by Shen Du 沈度 (1357–1434).

Zheng He's voyages were quite different from those typical of the Indian Ocean. Rather than royal patrons seeking diplomatic ends, merchants sponsored most voyages between independent port cities for commercial purposes. Each region of the Indian Ocean had its own merchants' leagues, and the richest ports were those at the boundaries of two regions. United by a common desire, port officials and merchant leagues aimed to profit from moving goods from where they were abundant to where

JAPANESE EXPORT POTTERY WITH
VOC SYMBOL. See p. 251

they were scarce and would command a higher price. So much Chinese porcelain found its way to East Africa that modern archaeologists are able to date sites from the style of the broken shards they find. By the seventeenth century the fine porcelain dishes reaching England were known simply as 'china,' a term employed earlier in Persia and India. Luxury goods of this type had been the original mainstay of the networks, but in the period from 1350 to 1500, shipments of bulk commodities (such as grain) were also becoming important.

Indian Ocean trading benefited from the predictable wind system known as *monsoon*, from the Arabic word for season. From December to March the winds propelled trading ships west and south from India to Arabia and East Africa, with the merchants confident that they could return home with the moist northeast monsoons at their backs from April to August. Merchants also relied on two versatile ship designs. In the Arabian Sea the characteristic ship was the dhow, whose timbers were sewn together with heavy cord. East of India the junk was the most common vessel, originally a Chinese design built with heavy spruce or fir planks held in place with large nails. A large junk had watertight bulkheads, a dozen bamboo sails, cabins for scores of passengers, and space for a thousand tons of cargo, but many were much smaller. By the fifteenth century, junks made in China were supplemented by others from shipyards in Bengal, Southeast Asia, and elsewhere.

Regional trading networks

In order to comprehend the decentralized nature of Indian Ocean trade, it is important to consider some regional trading networks. The first was centred in the Middle East and dominated by merchants of different Muslim traditions, though non-Muslims also participated. Arab and Persian merchants had pioneered maritime connections across the Arabian Sea to India and south to East Africa. Strategically located ports served as transfer points. Hormuz and other ports at the mouth of the Persian Gulf handled trade to and from India, while Aden and other ports in South Arabia dominated connections to the Red Sea. A string of coastal towns along the Swahili Coast blended African, Arab, and Persian elements. The name Swahili came from the Arabic *sawahil* meaning 'coast.' The port of Mombasa in the centre of the coast was the largest of the Swahili city-states, but the finely built island town of Kilwa to the south was crucially important because of its inland connections to the gold mines, which were controlled by a powerful empire south of the Zambezi River. Its capital, Great Zimbabwe, was the most impressive inland city south of Egypt, containing large stone structures spread out over 78 hectares and perhaps 18,000 inhabitants.

At the western edge of the Middle East, traders in Cairo and Beirut managed connections with Christian counterparts in the Mediterranean. The rival city-states of Venice and Genoa had long prospered from these links, finding mutual profit more important than religious rivalries. The northern Italians, in turn, had developed trade routes across the Alps and on to the Low Countries along the North Atlantic, where the merchant communities of Bruges, Ghent, and Antwerp plied sea routes across Northern Europe. After the fall of Constantinople to the Ottomans, Venice increased its wealth from its strategic connections by water and overland. The famous Rialto market along the Grand Canal in the mid-1400s was the commercial heart of Venice. Every merchant worth his name had a shop there with a secure storeroom and a simple dormitory for sleeping. The best families strove to outdo each other by the splendour of their palatial residences along the Grand Canal. Genoese and Florentine merchants had simple shops and, eventually, elegant homes.

In the centre of the ocean the merchant communities of the Indian subcontinent handled exchanges westward to the Middle East as well as eastward to Southeast and East Asia. The merchants of Gujarat in west-central India had long been important in trade to the Middle East, which prized their fine leather goods and beautiful cotton and silk carpets. After regaining independence from the Delhi Sultanate by 1390, the rulers of Gujarat expanded control over adjacent Hindu states, which gave its merchants better access to valuable trade goods, such as cotton textiles and indigo dyes, and enabled them to rebuild their connections west to the Middle East and East Africa. South India was a second centre of similar commercial activity between places east and west. On the Malabar Coast of the southwest, the rulers of Cochin, Calicut, and other ports presided over a loose network of inland suppliers and diverse communities of merchants. Muslims from Arabia and Persia formed the largest community, but there had long been Jewish communities there as well, with connections to the Middle East and Africa. On the Coromandel Coast of the southeast, other ports were even more involved in the trade across the eastern Indian Ocean and had connections that extended all the way to China.

The natural passage from the eastern Indian Ocean to the South China Sea was the Strait of Malacca between the Malay Peninsula and the island of Sumatra. In 1407, on the return leg of his first expedition Zheng He's fleet destroyed a nest of Chinese pirates based in Sumatra that was hindering trade. In the power vacuum that followed, the new port of Malacca (Melaka) on the Malay side of the Strait rose to prominence. Offering security and low taxes, the port soon attracted merchants from Southeast Asia, China, and India, whose presence made Malacca the preferred place to trade spices from the Moluccas (Spice Islands), rubies, musk and tin from Burma, gold from Sumatra, as well as all sorts of Chinese and Indian goods. According to a visitor just after 1500, the merchant communities there spoke 84 different languages. Four Malaccan officials maintained order among the babel of languages: one for the numerous Gujarati merchants, one for the rest of India and Burma, a third for the Southeast Asians, and the fourth for Chinese and Japanese traders.

Environment, economics, and expansion from the West

In the century following the plague pandemic and the Ming voyages, Europeans set in motion a series of maritime expeditions, smaller in size than those of the Ming but of more lasting importance in expanding global connections. Additionally, Europeans caused the unintended spread of contagious diseases that wiped out much of the native population of the Americas, which is discussed in the next section. While superficially similar, these two sets of parallel events from East and West were inherently different in their motives, circumstances, and consequences.

The Christian West had a long history of indirect connections to the riches of the East. As discussed, Venice and Genoa had pioneered trading connections to the Indian Ocean through Muslim merchants in North Africa and the Middle East. Northern Italian merchants had also extended trading connections across the Alps to the Netherlands, and the Hanseatic League had extended ties to German and Russian areas. The pandemic of the mid-fourteenth century and the conquests of Ottoman expansion in the fifteenth century had frayed these connections, but the commercial networks were rebuilt after the crisis eased. As a result, most Venetian and Genoese merchants had no interest in discovering new sea routes. Even if they had, the galley ships of the Mediterranean were ill suited to the stormier challenges of the Atlantic.

Instead, the impulse to seek new maritime routes came from the Iberian kingdoms of southwestern Europe whose commercial connections to the East were weaker than the Italians'. Equally important was the fact that Iberian Christians' long struggles to free themselves from Muslim domination made them disinclined to make alliances with Muslims. Rather, the crusades to recapture lands had ingrained an abiding anti-Islamic mentality. For Queen Isabella of Castile and King Ferdinand of Aragon, married in 1469, crusading in Iberia lasted until 1492 when Grenada, the last Muslim-ruled state, fell to their troops. After completing their own re-conquest in 1250, the Portuguese had extended their crusading to Islamic North Africa. When the Muslim kingdom of Morocco was weak, a Portuguese force was able to seize the rich port of Ceuta in 1415.

The leader of the attack on Ceuta, Prince Henry (1394–1460), the third son of the king of Portugal, must have learned that the port's wealth was due to the gold that came to it from across the Sahara. His patronage of subsequent explorations down the coast of Africa, which earned him the title of Henry the Navigator, seem also to have had non-commercial motives. Contemporary accounts assign high-minded motives to these efforts, echoing the Ming motives behind the voyages of Zheng He. Writing shortly after Henry's death in 1460, his official biographer listed first among Prince Henry's motives intellectual curiosity about what lay beyond North Africa, followed by personal ambitions, and a series of religiously informed reasons: establishing contact with existing African Christians and making new African converts, both of whom might be valuable allies in continuing the campaigns against Muslim hegemony.

To finance this colonization scheme, Prince Henry was able to draw on the resources of the military Order of Christ, of which he had been named the administrator general in 1420. Rewarded with huge tracts of land for their part in driving the Muslims out of Portugal, the order retained the role of promoting Christianity in any new lands the Portuguese found. The red Crusaders' cross of the Order of Christ that the Portuguese emblazoned on the sails of their well-armed ships suggests a mixture of motives for exploration. Whether part of a long-term plan or not, the colonization of Madeira and other uninhabited islands off the African coast provided additional income in Henry's lifetime, as well as strategic bases for later voyages of exploration down the African coast.

Portugal's challenges in exploring the unknown Atlantic were greater than those Zheng He faced in following well-known trading routes of the Indian Ocean. With a population equalling less than two per cent of China's, Portugal's resources were proportionally smaller as well. Even so, the Portuguese made advances in navigation techniques and geographical knowledge. On their early and relatively short voyages they made use of the very manoeuvrable vessel known as a caravel, equipped with a triangular lateen sail. By the time of Henry's death, the Portuguese had explored the coast south of Morocco as far as Sierra Leone. As subsequent explorers crossed the equator they learned how to plot their latitude by using a device called the astrolabe to measure the height of the noonday sun instead of using the familiar stars of the northern sky. In 1488 an expedition led by Bartolomeu Dias rounded the southern tip of Africa, proving that a sea connection to the Indian Ocean was possible, though difficult. After careful preparations a new expedition led by Vasco da Gama set sail in 1497, making a broad arc through the South Atlantic and eventually reaching India the next year.

Although da Gama's fleet had only four modest-sized ships (compared to the 62 reputedly in Zheng He's first expedition), they were carefully built to survive the long voyage to India and back. Their hulls were strengthened to withstand both rough seas and the weight of the cannon on their decks, and each ship carried two spare sets of sails and plenty of extra rigging. The ships' supplies of water and other provisions for the mariners were stored in extra-strong barrels. Additional supplies of water and fresh meat were acquired at the southern tip of Africa. Even so, by 25 December 1497, when the fleet reached the Indian Ocean coast (still called Natal—'Christmas' in Portuguese), drinking water was again in short supply and many of the men were ill with scurvy, a disease caused by too little vitamin C. Purchases of water, vegetables, and citrus rich in vitamin C obtained from friendly Africans over the next two months relieved the problems. However, as the fleet moved up the Swahili Coast, local Muslim rulers were very suspicious of ships whose sails bore Crusader crosses. First encounters were also awkward because while the Portuguese could offer only coarse cloth and rough clothes as gifts, Swahili rulers in contrast presented delectable foods and spices as welcoming gifts. By luck, da Gama was able to hire a Gujarati pilot to guide them across the Arabian Sea to Calicut on the Malabar Coast, where the fleet anchored for the night on 20 May 1498, some ten months after they had left Lisbon.

In Calicut, the Portuguese were as out of their depth culturally and economically as they had been on the Swahili Coast. One well-travelled Muslim merchant there greeted (or rather cursed) the Portuguese in Castilian. Later another spoke to them in Venetian. For his part, da Gama mistook the Hindu ruler for a Christian and made other cultural errors. Perhaps worse of all was the Portuguese all-too-vivid display of mundane trade goods. When the chief official in Calicut sneered at the twelve striped cloths, four scarlet hoods, and six wash basins that da Gama asked him to present the ruler, the explorer tried to defend himself by claiming he was just an explorer, not a rich merchant. The official asked what he came expecting to discover: stones or people?

After opposition and delays, da Gama managed to return to Lisbon with a partial cargo of Indian goods on his two surviving ships, arriving on 10 July 1499, two years after they had originally set off, and with half of the original crew. Though the cargo of 'sample' goods and spices from India was small, it confirmed that the riches of the East were real and could be accessed via the route around Africa. The Portuguese homeland might be poor and their cross-cultural sophistication limited, but they did possess two distinct advantages: the military superiority of their ship-mounted cannon and the cargo capacity of their fleets. And they were sufficiently ruthless in spreading their power and faith. The scale of the Portuguese investment in securing dominance over the main trade routes and ports suggests that they expected the profits would be considerable. In 1505 an armada of eighty new ships and seven thousand men bombarded the coastal towns of East Africa into ruin or submission. Subsequent incursions established Portuguese control of the major ports of the India Ocean world: Goa (1510), Malacca (1511), and Hormuz (1515) at the mouth of the Persian Gulf. Control of the termini enabled the Portuguese to impose a system of 'passes' on merchant shipping along some trade routes. From the new capital in the Indian port of Goa, the grandly named Viceroy of India sent out well-armed ships that dealt ruthlessly with merchant vessels that lacked the proper papers. Enough Asian and Arab merchants paid the fee to cover the costs of the patrols. Most Portuguese commerce, however, remained in private hands and relied on the tolerance or protection of local rulers and collaboration of indigenous merchants.

State-sponsored commerce remained in the market-based trading systems of the Mediterranean and Indian Ocean. In the seventeenth century, the Dutch and English pioneered an approach that stood between these two systems. The English East India Company (EIC) began in 1600; the better capitalized Netherlands' East India Company (Verenigde Oostindische Compagnie, or VOC) dated from 1602. To fund their operations both companies were able to raise capital by selling shares on the stock exchanges in Amsterdam and London that entitled investors to a share of future profits. The new trading companies also had government charters giving them exclusive rights to trade overseas for their nations and to make war, treaties, and alliances. France founded its own Company of the Indies, but, lacking funds and facing stiff opposition, it had smaller operations and fewer trading outposts, as did the Spanish and Portuguese ventures modelled on the English and Dutch companies.

MARKET IN BATAVIA (NOW JAKARTA) IN THE 1600s, when Java was a Dutch colony.

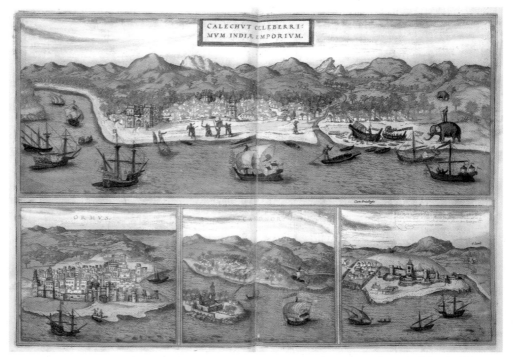

A VIEW OF SIXTEENTH-CENTURY CALICUT (KOZHIKODE), the principal port of the Malabar Coast, known as the 'City of Spices'. Indian and European ships as well as tame elephants are shown. From Georg Braun and Franz Hogenberg, *Civitates orbis terrarum*, Vol. 1 (Cologne, 1572), after an unidentified Portuguese drawing.

The VOC and EIC sought to establish strongholds by force, but could not escape the need to cultivate local trading partners. Initially, each established a headquarters east of the Portuguese base at Goa. The VOC gained a commercial advantage by using fixed winds and currents to create a fast route to their base at Batavia (now Jakarta). In addition to attacking their European rivals, they used force to establish strategic bases in the Moluccas (the Spice Islands). From there they moved to wrest both the spice trade and strategic ports from the Portuguese, gaining control over Malacca and Ceylon by mid-century. It was a big operation for the time: in 1690 the VOC was sending two hundred ships a year to trade in the East and employed 30,000 men. For its part the EIC established a base at Madras (now Chennai) in southeast India in 1639 and three decades later at Bombay (now Mumbai) on the west coast south of Gujarat, both outside the Mughal Empire. After several misadventures, the EIC was finally able to establish a fort at Calcutta (now Kolkata) in Mughal-ruled Bengal in 1690. The EIC and VOC cooperated at times to gain advantages over the Portuguese, but their commercial rivalry also led to armed conflict. Four hard-fought Anglo-Dutch Wars between 1652 and 1784 eventually gave the EIC the upper hand, and the Seven Years War (1756–63) limited any expansion by the French Company.

Traditionally, historians have focused on the Europeans' role in promoting trans-oceanic trade that linked maritime Asia directly with European and American markets. But in volume and value, intra-Asian business far exceeded intercontinental exchanges in this period. Patterns of prices within Asia gave Europeans their main opportunities to profit. Silver and copper were relatively cheap in Japan but more valued in China, while Indians valued gold highly. Shipping charges and profits from other commodities could be invested in specie so as to take advantage of the differentials. The VOC's biggest coup occurred in 1639, when Japan banned other Europeans, leaving the Dutch with privileged access to Japanese silver. To an extent specie from the Americas, especially from Spanish mining ventures in Mexico and Peru, helped Europeans fund operations in China and India.

Initially, the Europeans sought spices, specifically pepper from India and 'fine spices' such as cloves, nutmeg, and mace from the Moluccas, partly for export to Europe but chiefly for the huge Chinese market. The exotic spices had a higher profit margin, but popular demand for Asian pepper in Europe became enormous, some 3.4 million kg a year in the first third of the eighteenth century. Unexpectedly, other goods became even more important. During the seventeenth century the value of Indian cotton-textile exports to the Atlantic came to surpass the spice trade. By the 1670s over a million pieces of cotton cloth reached Europe each year, enough for Britain to enact laws to protect domestic production. At that point, pepper amounted to a fifth of EIC exports, but textiles were three times as important. There was also a valuable trade in

RELIEF PANEL OF AN INDIAN OCEAN SHIP at the ninth-century Buddhist temple at Borobudur, Java.

INDONESIAN SPICE MARKET. An assortment of spices of the Indian Ocean such as have been traded for centuries.

the more luxurious silk textiles, primarily from China. By the middle of the eighteenth century, coffee beans from south Arabia and Java, and especially tea from China, had become very hot exports to Europe. Tea became twice as valuable as pepper or fine spices, and coffee was almost as profitable. The custom of drinking tea became established in the West, along with the Chinese names for the infusion (tea, chai).

Even though the new sea routes reduced the price of Asian goods and greatly increased their flow into the Atlantic, it would be misleading to assume that Europeans were in total control. From the mid-1600s the VOC gradually gained sway over a considerable part of what is now Indonesia, and a century later the EIC was expanding direct control in parts of India, but the key holdings were tiny outposts with docks, warehouses, and a European quarter. European merchants were participants in a much larger economic system that no one controlled. Long-term alliances and cooperation with local and regional merchants and manufacturer were far more important to the Europeans than the short-term advantages they sometimes gained by violence. The Europeans deserve credit for their initiative, but focusing attention on the roles of their Asian and African partners and opponents makes the story more complex and more realistic. Non-European growers, manufacturers, traders, and statesmen each deserve attention.

'A VIEW OF THE EAST INDIA DOCKS', by William Daniell, 1808. The view is taken looking south to the Greenwich peninsula, with the sweep of the river around the Isle of Dogs at the right.

Layers of skilled farmers, artisans, and local traders lay behind the trades in spices, textiles, and other products. Growers in India and elsewhere, for example, were indispensable to the steady trade in pepper from 1500 onward. Similarly, other Asian farmers were the source of fine spices, and the labours of Chinese peasants were the basis of the immense tea trade. Spinners and weavers in Bengal and South India produced the high-quality cotton textiles that became the most sought after manufactured good in the world. Silk making had been dominated by Chinese artisans since the days of the ancient Silk Road. The twelfth-century Venetian merchant Marco Polo had reported that every day of the year, a thousand cartloads of silk thread entered the single giant market outside Kublai Khan's capital. The Portuguese bought vast quantities of silk at Macao, and Chinese traders brought even more to markets in Manila and Malacca that were frequented by the European trading companies and by traders of many other nationalities.

Indian Ocean port cities had to decide whether to ally with the Europeans or oppose them, a decision often influenced by religion. For example, two rival ports dominated the centre of the Swahili Coast. As previously mentioned, Mombasa shunned the arrival of da Gama's fleet, but the Muslim rulers of smaller port of Malindi provided a guide across the sea to the Malabar Coast. The favour was returned seven years later when a strongly armed Portuguese armada sailed up the Swahili Coast bombarding Mombasa, but sparing Malindi. Similarly, at the premier port of Calicut, mutual antipathy between the militant Portuguese and the Muslim trading community there convinced its Hindu ruler not to trust the Portuguese. Subsequently, in a series of

ASIAN AND EUROPEAN SHIPS AT BATAVIA, 1649. This painting from 1649 shows Asian and Dutch ships anchored off Batavia and a Dutch East Indiaman being loaded with goods that are being brought down the Ciliwung River. On the left side of the river is the former Kasteel Batavia, which protected the city from attack, and on the right are the Western Warehouses (Westzijdsche Pakhuizen).

conflicts Calicut suffered devastating damage, while its smaller neighbour and rival, Cochin, went on to become more important by allying with the Portuguese. Elsewhere, European conquests of strategic ports often led Asian trading communities to move their operations to another port in the same area.

Another strategy involved blending cooperation and evasion. The large Gujarati Indian community, deeply invested in the trade to the Middle East, skilfully defended their best interests. The Gujarati paid the Portuguese protection money to ensure their safety on sea routes that the Portuguese patrolled heavily but evaded the fees on routes where the risk was less. Such self-interest is also evident among the trading communities that formed the majority of the population in the main European ports. In 1600, Gujarati Hindus, Jains, and Muslims were the largest segment of the population of the port of Hormuz at the mouth of the Persian Gulf; the nominal 'rulers', the Portuguese, were just 17 per cent of the inhabitants. In the Spanish headquarters of Manila in the Philippines, Chinese residents in 1600 outnumbered Spanish and Mexicans by 8:1; similar proportions prevailed elsewhere. Moreover, most of the Europeans were single men, who acquired girlfriends and wives from the local populations. The Portuguese favoured Asian Christians as mates; the Dutch often chose half-Portuguese Catholics. This new intermediate community, biologically and culturally linked both to the

AGED VASCO DA GAMA as Viceroy of India from Livro de Lisuarte de Abreu, *c.* 1565.

Europeans and to the local people were linguistically fluent and cross-culturally adept, and they were powerful intermediaries.

By 1350, the merchant community of the southern coastal city of Guangzhou (Canton) dominated China's foreign trade. Shortly thereafter, the first Ming emperor restricted foreign trade there to tributary missions and prohibited Chinese merchants from travelling abroad. As a result, the Hokkien (or Fujian) merchants tended to settle abroad. Two early communities formed on the northern coast of Java and on Sumatra. As China's official restrictions proved unenforceable, large Chinese merchant communities emerged in Manila and Batavia, as well as at Nagasaki, Japan, from about 1600. The Hokkien merchants often took on cultural characteristics of their surroundings, those on Sumatra being described as Muslims, while a sizeable minority at Manila identified as Catholics. After the expulsion of the Portuguese from Japan in 1639, the Hokkien, like the Dutch, became restricted to their own special quarter in Nagasaki. The Hokkien were important to all their Asian and European hosts, each side benefiting from the connections of the other—excepting, of course, the periodic massacres of Chinese in Manila and in 1740 in Batavia.

THE GREAT PAGODA, KEW GARDENS, UK, erected in 1762 by Sir William Chambers, who had made three voyages to China in the 1740s, where he studied the architecture. In imitation of a Chinese design, it rises to a height of 50 metres.

The common assumption among traditional Western historians that large Asian and African states tended to disregard trade because they derived revenues mostly from land taxes is not completely true. The importance of trade to Egypt explains why Mamluk rulers sent out two fleets against the Portuguese, the first suffering a humiliating defeat off Gujarat, and the second being diverted to conquering the rich trading ports of Yemen, perhaps to close off Portuguese access to the Red Sea. The attack on Yemen seems to have been instrumental in spurring the Ottoman conquest of Egypt in 1517, which produced a more nuanced Ottoman understanding of the importance of the Indian Ocean trade and of the new routes in the Atlantic. The Ottomans assured merchants in Egypt of protection, while promising Venetians and other European merchants that the spice trade in Cairo would continue reliably. Then they moved to secure the Red Sea from Portuguese attack by taking control of most of Yemen in 1527, and next secured control over the mouth of the Persian Gulf in 1534. Subsequent battles between Ottoman and Portuguese throughout the Indian Ocean culminated in the decisive battle for Mombasa on the Swahili Coast in 1589. The Ottomans lost, but Portugal's power soon waned, owing to the impending challenge of the Dutch and English companies.

Half a century later, the Sultanate of Oman—an Arab maritime state with imperial ambitions of its own—expelled the Portuguese from the Persian Gulf and attacked their outposts on the Swahili Coast, capturing the large island of Zanzibar in the 1650s, eventually taking Mombasa in 1696. For a time, Oman ran a profitable trade in Indian textiles and African ivory and slaves. At the beginning of the 1800s a new Sultan rebuilt Oman's East African empire and made Zanzibar the world's greatest producer of cloves.

Politics and commerce played out differently in India, where the Mughal rulers largely left challenging the Europeans to merchants. The emperor had some interest in English art and skills but little in trade and treaties. Mughal officials allowed the early EIC trading rights at the busy port of Surat in Gujarat, where they were operated as simply one more trading unit in the very large Gujarati system. Outside the Mughal control on the Coromandel Coast of southeast India, local authorities also allowed the EIC and French Company to open trading posts bases, notably the EIC's fortified factory at Madras. Local rulers near the mouth of the Ganges allowed EIC traders from Madras access to Bengali markets, and eventually the EIC opened another fort in Calcutta in 1696. When the Company became too obstreperous a few years earlier, the Mughals closed its factory at Surat, blockaded its post in Calcutta, and thus forced the EIC to accept Moghul peace terms. However, as the empire's power ebbed and was challenged by other Indian states, the Mughal rulers were more inclined to welcome the Company as a powerful ally. By the early 1800s the EIC ruled all of eastern India, nominally in the name of the Mughal emperor, who was in reality the Company dependant.

The Chinese emperors' relations with Europe remained quite the opposite of the Mughals', as two European diplomatic missions illustrate. In 1519 the first Portuguese emissary, Tomé Pires, made a poor impression on the Chinese in Guangzhou. He was unfamiliar with the protocols the Chinese expected and surprised to be kept waiting for many months—an imperial custom. When the emperor finally permitted Pires to enter Beijing in February 1521, he was in no mood to be cordial, having heard of Portugal's seizure of Malacca, which he considered under his protection. Pires and his men were condemned as sea pirates, clapped in prison, and later executed. Guangzhou authorities did let the Portuguese establish a base at Macao in mid-1550s, but the Ming and later the Qing emperors took little interest in foreign traders. Lacking direct access to China, the EIC and the VOC relied on the Hokkien traders to bring Chinese goods to them at ports in the East Indies. At the end of the eighteenth century, with the VOC on its last legs and the tea trade of growing importance, Britain made a major effort to improve the trading situation with China. In 1792 the British government sent George Macartney to negotiate a treaty to open trade. Better informed than Pires, Macartney was supplied with £15,000 in 'tribute' by the EIC. His delegation escaped ill-treatment, but the Qianlong emperor refused to open new ports of trade or sign a treaty. The emperor later wrote to King George III praising Macartney's 'respectful humility' but insisting that China had no need to expand trade, or allow a permanent envoy from Britain. 'I set no value on objects strange or ingenious', the emperor famously wrote, 'and have no use for your country's manufactures'. This aloof response is misleading since many Chinese were eager for Western technology, knowledge, and goods, but for a few more decades mercantile Europe and imperial China would remain worlds apart.

Population, plants, and plantations in the Atlantic world

World historians have challenged the Eurocentric assumptions that the causes of Western economic and social advances after 1800 lay within Europe. Historians like Kenneth Pomeranz have countered that rural Chinese and rural Europeans had much in common, including struggling to eke out an existence and survive ecological crises both natural (like the Little Ice Age) and human-made (like deforestation). Pomeranz suggests that the principal source of Europe's subsequent divergence lay not at home, but rather overseas. Partly, as this chapter has recounted, Europeans profited from the commercial operations in Asia, despite the outflow of silver in return. Even more, he argues, the divergence of the West resulted from the bonus effect of the Americas, which opened a giant territory for exploitation and, in time, created an Atlantic economy that grew to be even more important than the Asian trade. Not only did the Americas supply the silver for the Asian trade and sugar to sweeten Westerners' Chinese tea, but also provided valuable new crops from the humble potato to tobacco, as well as wheat and timber to relieve Europe's shortages. Even if this reinterpretation is not yet conclusively proven, it provides a useful framework in which to explore some important global topics.

After 1400, densely populated areas of northern Eurasia faced three overlapping events: a period of cooling continued and worsened, new foods crops from the Americas took the edge off of hunger among the poorest of the populations, and new systems of production and distribution greatly increased food supplies. Despite destructive wars, Europe's population tripled between 1400 and 1800; China's more than quadrupled. Population growth is not necessarily a sign of prosperity, for it may mask social inequalities and environmental strains, but it is a more hopeful indicator than population decline.

Temperature began to fall globally in about 1200 and continued to do so, plunging to new lows in the seventeenth century. In 1600, northern Eurasia experienced the coldest summer in two centuries, in part because Huaynaputina's massive volcanic eruption in the Andes had blown so much ash into the upper atmosphere that a grey shadow blocked sunlight in much of the world. Other volcanic eruptions helped trigger four more major cold spells during the century. Severely diminished sunspot activity added to the cooling. Glaciers from New Zealand to the Alps grew larger. Growing seasons started later and ended weeks earlier, causing unripe grain to die in the fields. As summers shortened, winters grew longer and colder. Rivers and canals that usually remained navigable for most of the year were frozen for weeks, hampering the movement of grain by barge. In Estonia and other places around the Baltic and the North Sea, a quarter to a third of the population may have starved as the result of a cold spell in the mid-1690s. Famines also occurred in China, although it is not clear if they were due to climate change or other causes.

This Little Ice Age was a serious threat because agricultural output was already stressed. Agricultural productivity was low due to limited use of animal power and machinery, unimproved seeds, and depletion of soil fertility. Europeans had long sought to restore exhausted fields by letting land lie fallow every second or third year, although that further reduced productivity. Another problem was that many landowners found it more profitable to grow crops for distant markets rather than for local consumption. In sixteenth-century Spain, for example, landowners chose to raise sheep (for their wool) rather than growing grain, shipping the wool to the Netherlands for processing into cloth, further impoverishing the underemployed local rural poor. The twice-yearly movement of the sheep between summer and winter pastures trampled the crops of small peasants along the way and caused erosion. In the plains of the eastern Baltic Sea another type of change around rural land and labour was taking place in the seventeenth century. Faced with a shrinking population due to devastating wars, estate owners imposed restrictions that turned the rural poor into serfs who were forbidden to leave the estates where they were born. Ironically this took place in lands where serfdom had rarely existed in earlier times. The serfs were employed growing wheat that was shipped to Western Europe. While this helped relieve food shortages in the Netherlands, it further impoverished the eastern Baltic as well as Russia, where an analogous system of serfdom was spreading. In China agriculture was generally more efficient, but farm plots were typically smaller than in Europe.

Under these circumstances, the arrival of new plants from the Americas provided some protection against hunger. Poor people in central Europe and Ireland began to consume potatoes instead of grain. In Italy, maize meal (*polenta*) became the food of the rural poor. China already produced high-yielding rice in great quantities, so potatoes were adopted there only at altitudes where rice could not grow. Some Chinese also began to grow sweet potatoes and maize introduced from the Americas.

'HUNTERS IN THE SNOW', 1565, BY PIETER BREUGEL. This is the most famous of several winter landscape paintings by Pieter Breugel the Elder, which are all thought to have been painted in 1565, after an unusually severe winter, during the Little Ice Age.

A second set of favourable trends involved redistributing labour, reclaiming land, and improving productivity. In the seventeenth and eighteenth centuries, Chinese governments resettled at least ten million peasants from overpopulated regions to parts of the empire that were underpopulated or had been depopulated by warfare. No such resettlement took place in Europe, but engineers in the Netherlands undertook the opposite strategy: reclaiming new land within or adjacent to their densely populated country. Between 1540 and 1715 the construction of dykes and pumping out the seawater reclaimed nearly 1,500 square kilometres of land from the sea and draining lakes freed up another 1,850 square kilometres. In the eighteenth century, some wealthy English landowners hired Dutch engineers to drain wetlands for farming. Later (mostly after 1815), they improved crop yields with better farming methods, which included fencing off common land for their own use.

Rising population numbers in eighteenth-century Europe and China put a strain on forests as well as land. Part of the strain was due to households' demand for cooking and heating fuel, but high demand for firewood to smelt iron and for timber to build ships caused greater deforestation. By the end of the century, no more than ten per cent of Britain was forested, leading smelters there to turn to coke (from coal) rather than charcoal to make iron. The situation was better in France, but by 1800, a wood shortage was evident even in Sweden and Russia. Overall deforestation was less serious in China, where iron smelters had turned to coke much earlier than in England, and where peasants made more efficient use of wood in cooking and heating than did Europeans. Even so, the destruction of forests in heavily populated parts of China led to serious flooding and the silting up of the Grand Canal that linked northern and southern China.

In comparison with northern Eurasia, transformations in agriculture and ecology in the Americas were far more revolutionary. Early in the 1490s, Portuguese probes into the Indian Ocean prompted the Spanish monarchs to attempt to open a rival route to maritime Asia by sailing west across the Atlantic. Although the Genoa-born Christopher Columbus's idea that this would be a shorter route to the East was based on a woefully mistaken sense of the size of the Earth, by accident he bumped into the West Indies in 1492. The consequences would be horrific and momentous. Columbus brought back some promise of riches, but almost immediately diseases began to decimate the native people of the islands, and then those on the mainland. It is impossible to say how many people died, but the deaths came quickly and in very large numbers. As indigenous communities declined, the 'widowed lands' were repopulated through an overseas movement of people that had no prior historical precedent. Part of this was a colossal slave-based plantation system. The investors in these population movements and land development reaped the profits from the burgeoning transatlantic trade.

The tragic demographic collapse of indigenous peoples in the Caribbean, Mexico, and Peru that occurred in the first fifty years of contact was phase one of a longer process. For another century, microbial diseases continued to carry off 50 to 90 per cent of Amerindian communities, as infectious diseases brought from Europe, including smallpox, measles, and influenza, were joined by malaria and yellow fever introduced from Africa. Once Amerindian populations acquired resistance to the infections, their numbers began to increase, most successfully in Mexico and Peru, where densities had been highest earlier. The cost of introducing new populations from across the Atlantic and the reluctance of people to leave home meant that Amerindians remained the overall majority until the mid-eighteenth century. Well into the 1800s, European immigration to the Americas was smaller than the forced immigration of enslaved Africans.

Human demographic change was just one part of what has been called the 'Columbian Exchange'. Also introduced into the Americas were four-legged animals large and small: horses, cattle, pigs, sheep, and goats, which often escaped into the wild and, with abundant food and few predators, multiplied rapidly. Re-domesticated, the larger beasts could be ridden or made to pull wheeled vehicles; the smaller provided food and skins. Their presence led to new ways of life for some Amerindians, most dramatically the horse-riding Plains Indians of North America. New plants also crossed

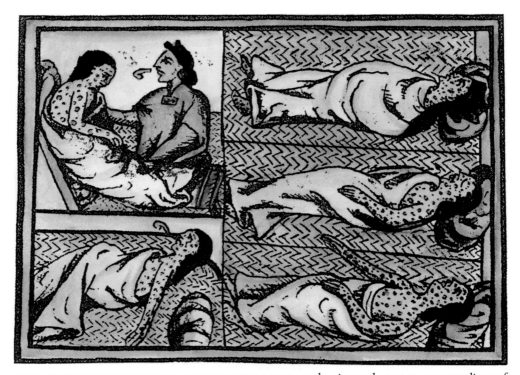

AN ILLUSTRATED PANEL FROM THE *FLORENTINE CODEX*, the sixteenth-century compendium of materials and information on Aztec and Nahua history collected by Fray Bernardino de Sahagún, shows Nahuas infected with smallpox disease. The accompanying Nahuatl text says, '. . . [The disease] brought great desolation: a great many died of it. They could no longer walk about, but lay in their dwellings and sleeping places, ... And when they made a motion, they called out loudly. The pustules that covered people caused great desolation . . . starvation reigned, and no one took care of others any longer.' English translation from Lockhart J., *We People Here: Nahuatl Accounts of the Conquest of Mexico* (Berkeley: University of California Press, 1993), 181–5.

the Atlantic in both directions. The spread of the American cultigens, such as maize potatoes, tomatoes, sweet potatoes, manioc, squashes, and beans, had great impacts in some parts of Europe, Asia, and Africa. Crops introduced from Africa (bananas, some grains, okra, and black-eyed peas) had a smaller impact in the Americas during the period covered by this chapter. Wheat, grapes, and olives introduced by the Spanish also took a very long time to produce major changes. However, the spread of sugar caused momentous transformations in the Americas and around the Atlantic before 1800.

Despite the economic distress at home, relatively few Europeans emigrated to the Americas before the nineteenth century. Government regulations impeded emigration, as did the perils and costs of transportation. For those who did move, European cities were more attractive and, for those who ventured abroad, opportunities in Asia and Africa were often more alluring than those in the Americas. By 1760 the Americas had received some 1.2 million immigrants from the Iberian kingdoms, along with 30,000 Dutch, but only about 54,000 from populous France (males predominated among all of these). Religious motivations created some exceptions. Persecution drove Jews from Iberian kingdoms to Africa and the Americas, as well as to other parts of Europe. Calvinist Protestants, both male and female, also sought new homes. French Huguenots went to Cape Town, Charleston (South Carolina), as well as London. English Pilgrims and Puritans went to Plymouth and Boston. Emigration from Britain became proportionately larger than from other parts of Western Europe during the 1700s and had a more balanced sex ratio. Still, even the so-called 'Great Migration' to New England in the 1630s probably did not exceed 30,000 people. Overall perhaps half a million left the British Isles in the seventeenth century, most defraying the costs by signing contracts of indenture that granted them free passage in exchange for four or five years of servitude to an earlier settler. This explains why some 200,000 went to the British West Indies and 120,000 went to the Chesapeake colonies, which were developing early plantation systems, whereas only about 80,000 went to New England and Mid-Atlantic colonies. Yet the 2.5 million Europeans who went to the Americas by 1815 were few compared to the immense size of the American continents.

The number of enslaved Africans reaching the Americas was four times that from Europe during these centuries. African immigrants already constituted over 60 per cent of new arrivals during the period from 1580 to 1700, and their share rose to over 80 per cent from 1701 to 1820. Large-scale deployment of African labour had not been the first solution to the labour problem. The Spanish had used enslaved Amerindians who were accustomed to high altitudes to mine the silver in the Andes. The Portuguese had also initially used enslaved Amerindians to grow sugar cane and the English had used indentured Englishmen to grow tobacco in the West Indies. Only when labour demands exceeded supplies was there recourse to importing slaves and then only for tasks profitable enough to bear the costs. Before 1600 the Spanish had bought African slaves to replace or supplement native labour in cartage to and from the Potosí mines. High mortality among enslaved Indians in Brazil forced the Portuguese to turn to African labour for their expanding sugar plantations. Similarly, when it became hard to get enough indentured servants, the English West Indian colonies turned to Africans, who cost twice as much, and switched to growing the more profitable sugar cane crop. Others followed suit. To serve these and other operations, the volume of the slave trade rose from 275,000 between 1601–25 (11,000 a year) to 1,750,000 between 1790–1815 (70,000 a year). The transport of millions of Africans across the Atlantic was the largest migration in history up to that time.

As already suggested, the massive use of African slaves was not due to their cheapness. Slaves were expensive to purchase in Africa and expensive to transport. As the plantation system spread, the price of slaves went up, partly because of the high demand in the colonies and partly because the cost of buying slaves in Africa was also rising. In Jamaica, for example, the price of a slave rose from £25 in 1700 to £35 at mid-century—four times the annual salary of a British soldier and over five times the

SLAVES HARVESTING SUGAR CANE IN ANTIGUA. 'Cutting the Sugar Cane on Delap's Estate.' Men and women in first gang, black driver supervising; white manager/overseer on horseback. Little is known of William Clark, although he was probably a manager or overseer of plantations in Antigua. The ten prints in the collection are based on his drawings, converted into prints by professional printmakers. From William Clark, *Ten Views in the Island of Antigua*, London, 1823.

yearly wage of a female servant in a good house in England. At the end of the eighteenth century the price of a new slave in the West Indies reached £50. Nor did the hereditary nature of slavery give much of a bonus to sugar plantation owners in the West Indies and Brazil. For example, the Jamaican planter Edward Long recorded nearly twice as many deaths as births among his slaves during the period from 1779 to 1785. To sustain his work force Long needed to spend large sums buying new slaves. Because of this high mortality, most slaves in the West Indies were African-born throughout the eighteenth century. Only in the more temperate and healthier parts of North America did the American-born slaves predominate. Fortunately for the planters, the rising price of sugar offset the high cost of slave labour.

Although enslaved Africans were an expensive necessity, there was a long historical precedent for their use on sugar plantations. The first sugar plantations using enslaved African labour were on Mediterranean islands under Arab control. In the fifteenth century, the Portuguese had introduced this plantation complex to the islands they discovered along the Atlantic coast of Africa: the Canaries, the Cape Verdes, and then the island of São Tomé on the equator, which became Europe's greatest source of sugar for a time in the early 1500s. Eventually, the Portuguese introduced African slavery and sugar plantations to Brazil, which became the world's greatest source of sugar after 1600. Dutch ships dominated the transport of Brazilian sugar to Europe and some Dutch invested in Brazilian sugar plantations. The dynastic inheritances that placed both the Netherlands and Portugal under the Spanish crown in the early 1600s set in motion new movements of the plantation complex. In the course of their struggle to escape from onerous Spanish rule, the Netherlands chartered a West India Company, which had a monopoly over Dutch trade in the West Indies and West Africa as well as founding the colony of New Netherland along the Hudson River. The company also successfully seized the Portuguese sugar plantations in Brazil. Expelled after Portugal regained its independence from Spain in 1640, the Dutch planters introduced the sugar plantation complex to the West Indies, where it became extremely successful. Sugar made the Caribbean the second greatest market for slaves after Brazil, and the richest economy in the Americas.

Sugar cultivation rapidly transformed the economies of the West Indies. Between 1640 and 1680 the British colony of Barbados shifted from a population that was primarily European tobacco growers to one that was predominantly African sugar growers, in the process becoming the wealthiest and most populous of Britain's colonies in the Americas. Sugar consumption in Britain in the 1700s went from four pounds to 18 pounds per capita, much of which went into sweetening China tea. Because the small island lacked enough land to satisfy the rising demand for sugar, the British wrested the large island of Jamaica from Spain in 1655. By 1700, massive investments in land, machinery, and slaves propelled Jamaica ahead of Barbados. Then the French colony of Saint Domingue, seized earlier from Spain, took the lead in sugar production until the massive slave revolt of 1791–1804 destroyed the plantation complex.

After its introduction by the Dutch, tobacco became Brazil's second most important export (after sugar). The growing demand for tobacco in Europe and elsewhere was also supplied from the British colony of Virginia from 1612. Indigo and rice were other tropical export crops. The French, Dutch, and British colonies of North America became substantial suppliers of furs and timber to Europe. The New England colonies also traded food and timber to the British West Indies.

All these exports from the Americas were matched by imports. European manufactures were of major importance in the Americas, unlike in the Indian Ocean and China trades. Dutch products were dominant in the 1600s, but French and British goods and shipping expanded rapidly after 1670, with Britain taking a commanding lead after 1750. In 1815 the West Indies were the most important market in the empire for British exports, along with Asian textiles and ceramics. It is notable that British India then was a slightly smaller market than Canada.

The role of Africa in the Atlantic economy went well beyond being a source of slave labour. Africa's overall engagement with international trade resembled Asia's experience much more than the Americas'. Like Asians, Africans had long participated in market-driven exchanges with the outside world (largely through Muslim intermediaries) and they interacted with new European visitors from a position of strength. Unlike the Americas, Africa shared the same diseases as Europe and Asia, so new contacts brought no demographic collapse. There were few colonial conquests in Africa in this period.

Sub-Saharan Africans engaged with the Atlantic for much the same reasons they had long traded across the Atlantic and Indian Ocean: to obtain goods they desired at prices they found attractive. Because of the Europeans' far-flung commercial networks, they could supply Africans with a variety of goods, including Asian and European textiles, Brazilian tobacco, and rum made from West Indian sugar. The strongest demand in Africa was for textiles of greatly varied designs and materials. For example, the Dutch alone sold some 30 million yards of linen on the Gold Coast between 1593 and 1607, along with many other textiles. Metals were also in high demand by Africans, including items of copper and brass, as well as iron bars and various manufactured metal items. As European traders came to know all too well, Africans bargained hard and were very choosy about the quality and variety of goods they bought.

Gold was prominent in the earliest Atlantic trade of West Africa, just as it had been in the trans-Saharan and Indian Ocean trades. To promote the trade, coastal Africans agreed in 1482 to allow the Portuguese to build a small fort. Though the Portuguese called it St George of the Mine (later called Elmina), the actual gold mines lay well inland. The gold trade also attracted English traders to this 'Gold Coast' from 1553 as well as the Dutch, who seized Elmina from the Portuguese in 1637. West Africa became a major source of gold for Western Europe, with exports rising from an annual average of 20,000–25,000 ounces in the second half of the sixteenth century to 32,000 ounces during the next half-century. Mining, smelting, and trading in gold were closely guarded African monopolies.

West Africans also supplied forest products for sale, ranging from a red dyewood known as camwood and civet oil (from the musk glands of the civet cat) to elephant tusks, animal skins, and beeswax. The kingdom of Benin in the Niger Delta sold the early Portuguese a pungent black pepper they grew and manufactured goods, including cotton textiles and stone beads, both of which were highly valued on along the Gold Coast. Before 1650, slaves were a minor part of West African exports, unlike the case in Angola and other parts of West-Central Africa where the slave trade to Brazil grew to 13,000 a year in the first half of the seventeenth century. In part this was because that region had no gold or other products that the Europeans wanted, yet the people there were also eager to receive the goods brought in European ships. After 1650, the importance of slaves from Africa grew rapidly to satisfy the rising demand in the Americas. Of the 12.5 million Africans who entered the Atlantic slave trade, over three-quarters made the journey between 1651 and 1815. For comparison, the Arab slave trade across the Sahara had been about 6,300 a year from 1350 to 1600 (much higher than the Atlantic slave trade of that era) and reached approximately 8,000 a year from 1601 to 1800 (much less than in the Atlantic). Much more difficult to describe with certainty are the effects of the trade on those enslaved, and on the African societies they left behind.

The experience of becoming a slave and being transported overseas was brutal and wrenching. On the basis of the limited number of first person narratives and from other sources, it seems that most were captured in a war or in a raid. The captors were other Africans, but a common African identity was as rare as common Asian or European identities. The captors were seizing people belonging to enemy communities, or at least communities not their own. Many were captured as part of family groups, but were then traumatically separated from spouses, siblings, or children. African captors might incorporate captured women and young children into their own societies, but always sold away grown men, who typically were resold several times on the way to a coastal port. Along the way captives suffered greatly from alienation from their relatives and homeland, sometimes becoming despondent and losing the will to resist or even to go on living. Once at the port, the captives were given food and sufficient care to make them sellable, since the European slave traders usually employed a doctor to examine the captives for physical defects that might make them less useful or illness that might threaten not only their own lives, but those of fellow passengers. Once selected and loaded on a ship with hundreds of others, the captives were sorted by age and sex. Grown men were considered the most dangerous and were confined below decks, often chained in pairs. Because the women were less inclined to fight their new captors, they were generally confined separately and not chained. Babies and other children stayed with their mothers or other women, while children able to take care of themselves were given similar freedom. The slave quarters were very cramped, so having enough room to stretch out to sleep was rare. Slaves were fed twice a day from food like beans and corn meal brought from Europe, supplemented with flavourings purchased in Africa. Ships usually took on fresh water in Africa in quantities sufficient to last the ocean crossing, but rations sometimes had to be cut if supplies ran low. The captives had to relieve themselves in tubs placed in the open. These were emptied periodically but rough seas might delay the emptying of them or spill their contents. The insanitary mess was commonly made worse by vomiting due to seasickness or by diarrhoea caused by illness. On a well-run ship, the slave quarters were cleaned regularly with seawater and perhaps vinegar to control odours. Even so, sicknesses could spread rapidly in the confined and unsanitary quarters.

The men who worked on a slave ship became inured to the miseries they encountered daily, but they were probably, on the whole, no more cruel than other people. Their treatment of slaves was governed by two larger factors. First, the fear of a slave revolt was very real, even though few were successful. The crew naturally sought to protect themselves and to punish any captives attempting to take over the ship. Revolts were most common when the shore was still in sight. On open sea, revolts were rarer, but another risk was captives choosing to escape their cruel fates. Slave traders erected netting designed to prevent suicides. The second and even more critical consideration governing the treatment of the captives was the desire to make money.

A slave who died of ill treatment or illness was a total loss. One maimed might be unsellable. Ministrations of the ship's doctor and efforts at minimal hygiene and adequate feeding were not kindness but simply efforts to deliver as many captives alive as possible. Depression was another problem among the enslaved. To raise the captives' mood music was played and they were forced to dance. Those who refused to eat were forcibly fed. On average, survival rates improved over the centuries, suggesting such efforts were successful. On the other hand, an average mortality rate of 11 per cent in the latter 1700s was still frighteningly high. The underlying problem for the shippers was that contagious diseases, such as smallpox and dysentery, could carry off large numbers. Averages were not norms. Profits were not certain for the owners and investors. Death was too often the fate of the enslaved.

It is hard to measure the effects within African of the slave departures and the attendant losses in the conflicts that ensnared them. Abolitionist-minded Europeans were of the opinion that much of the continent must be depopulated and reduced to savagery, but when explorers first went inland behind slave ports in the nineteenth century they were surprised to find orderly, prosperous, and well-populated communities. Several conditions are thought to have mitigated the demographic effects of the slave trade: slaves came primarily from regions that were fairly densely populated; rather than coming continuously from the same places, the slaves tended to derive from further and further inland as the trade grew; the disproportionate number of males exported (about two-thirds of the total) had a smaller effect on the birth rate than if the opposite had been true. In addition, research has shown that plants from the New World, particularly the hardy tuber manioc (or cassava), mitigated periodic famines the region of West-Central Africa that was the largest supplier of captives. The best estimate is that, at the peak of the Atlantic slave trade, the growth rate of sub-Saharan Africa's population stagnated or fell into negative territory. When the Atlantic slave trade fell in the 1800s, Africa's population rose again.

Other once-common beliefs about social and economic damage in Africa also turn out to be misguided, such as the idea that the firearms that arrived in exchange for slaves was destructive, ignored the fact that firearms were as useful for defence as offence, warfare was less likely to have been caused by the availability of such weapons, and the quantity of weapons exported to Africa was not particularly large per capita. The argument that the imported goods undermined African livelihood also appears to be exaggerated. For the most part, textile imports supplemented, rather than displaced, local cloth making. Iron imports probably did undermine African iron smelting to some extent, but the iron bars gave more work to local blacksmiths, who turned them into useful objects. Although there is no exaggerating the sufferings of those shipped away, the harm slave trade caused in Africa was less enduring than was once thought.

In the eighteenth century, the volume and value of Europe's trade in the Atlantic became as important as its trade in Asia. The slave-based economies of Brazil supplied sugar, tobacco and gold, and the West Indies sugar and coffee. North America furnished fish, furs, timber, rice, and indigo. These goods were balanced by exports from Europe as well as a steadily increasing supply of slaves from Africa. Asian goods grew in importance for Atlantic markets. Indian cotton cloth was essential for the African market and important in the Americas. Britain's Atlantic trade expanded sixfold. Ships grew larger, and marine insurance reduced the risk of loss. The cost of shipping commodities across the Atlantic dropped, as merchants learned to cut time in port from an average of 100 days at the beginning of the century to 50 days at the end. As a result, the cost of a round-trip voyage fell, making it possible for a ship to complete two round trips a year instead of one.

Conclusion

How much had the world changed between 1350 and 1815? Rather more than in the previous era perhaps, but less than would come in the next two centuries. Global contacts and exchanges had grown more frequent and intense. It is true that the world economy had grown roughly threefold since 1350, but the per capita distribution of wealth was about the same because, despite the plague and demographic collapse of Amerindians, world population had grown by a similar magnitude. Of course, some people were much better off, but the number of slaves around the world had also increased substantially. Food supply and distribution improved, but larger populations placed additional pressures on the environment and resources.

Some things were clearly cyclical. By 1815, the chartered trading companies founded in the seventeenth century were gone or transformed. The French and Dutch companies had ceased operations in the 1790s, and by 1815 the EIC had moved away from trading and was focused on administering its Indian territories. Yet the supporting institutions—stock markets, insurance companies, banks—continued to thrive. By 1815, the Dutch, the British, and the new United States had all outlawed the Atlantic slave trade, although their slave plantations continued for some decades.

The economic balance between East and West had not budged much. Asians were still the greatest producers of goods, whose distribution had expanded into the Atlantic. Economic leadership in Europe had moved north from Iberia and the Mediterranean to the Netherlands, France, and especially Britain. Africans below the Sahara were more closely linked to the world economy, but were still in control of their continent, except for a few European and Arab enclaves. The greatest economic and demographic changes had come in the Americas. Europeans had called their colonies there by names that suggested they were new Europes: New Spain, New Netherland, and New England. However, demographically and culturally, large regions of the Americas in 1815 remained Amerindian, or had become New Africas.

CHAPTER 9

Renaissances, Reformations, and Mental Revolutions
Intellect and Arts in the Early Modern World

MANUEL LUCENA GIRALDO

'PREVIOUSLY, we were on the edge of the world. Now we are at the centre.' That was the justification the engineer and humanist Hernán Pérez de Oliva offered the city patricians of Córdoba in 1524 when he proposed an urgent project for making the Guadalquivir River navigable. 'Such a change of fortune,' he continued, 'has never been seen before.' Western Europeans, indeed, after long enduring anxieties about their own global marginalization, now suddenly, unforeseeably, found themselves entangled in the middle of a sort of world-wide web of inescapably dynamic interconnections. Nor was their experience unique: people in other continents underwent the same mutation. New, often violent encounters on Atlantic coasts and islands, where European explorers, slavers, and missionaries first experienced the shock of meeting previously undocumented and unreported peoples in the fourteenth century, launched a process of mutual adjustment and discovery in which increasingly peoples took part, and which led most of them to the conclusion that 'humankind is one'.

Before the industrializing era, Europe had no dominant role in the process. From the Renaissance to the Enlightenment, globalization occurred in slow, multidirectional phases, as different cultures became gradually acquainted and fitfully communicative. First, mutually strange people initiated imperfect conversations, mixing gesture, grimace, and voice. Translators and interpreters mediated every exchange, sometimes with adverse effects when they aggravated misunderstandings or, by luck or judgement, engineered conflicts. Take the example of Columbus's first transatlantic crossing, in the company of Luis de Torres, a polyglot who knew Hebrew, Arabic, and perhaps Aramaic, among other languages. We can imagine the astonishment with which, for instance, he might have beheld the natives as they smoked tobacco, while he tried to interrogate them bootlessly in European and Asian tongues. First contacts often ended, with the abandonment of attempts at reciprocal understanding, in a spell of violence and mortality. The systematic strategy—flight or self-concealment—that we associate with peoples we now call 'uncontacted' was not yet widely practised. From the survivors' point of view, adjustment to the inevitable was usually the best option. The newcomers from afar were there to stay and there was no prospect of their return home. The possibility the Aztecs, for instance, envisaged—an exchange of gifts, after which the foreigners, duly impressed, would depart—proved unworkable. Displays of wealth and power attracted, rather than deterred, European invaders, whom dreams influenced more than realities, and imagined triumphs more than actual achievements. A fictional model of heroism, derived from the chivalric literature of seafaring, bound adventurers together. Portugal's national poet, Luis de Camoens, captured its spirit when he adapted a classical trope in his *Lusiads* of 1572, shortly after his own return from a voyage to Asia: 'Set sail. That's essential. Survival? That's supererogatory.'

The traditional narrative of wars by sea and 'land to conquer and control' does not encode what we might call the DNA of globalization. Rather, it can be traced through the routines of cultural relations, slowly, sometimes painfully, but usually peacefully forged, between arriving outsiders and established indigenes, in the context of a long period of convergence, in which widely separated cultures exchanged features and grew, in some respects, ever more alike. The process, though irreversible—or at least not yet reversed—was, nonetheless, of trial and error, disrupted at intervals by lurches and contingencies.

It was part of an even bigger process of global environmental change. Microbes, animals, and plants, exchanged between formerly sundered continents, changed existing landscapes and lives forever. From the sixteenth century onwards, nothing could convincingly seem perfectly 'pure' or 'primordial', nothing discretely 'human' or merely 'natural' again, except to minds committed to dogma. The web of worldwide links has 'corrupted' every people and place it has touched. Just about all of us are where we are because we or our ancestors came from somewhere else.

Fascination with the exotic, moreover, generated new or newly extended habits of desire, consumption, and addiction from Beijing, say, to consumers as far afield as, for example, imitators of porcelain in Mexico, tea-partiers in Boston, and cultivators of rhubarb (formerly a secret of Chinese pharmacopoeia) in Amsterdam. The limitations of language intervened. How could you explain what a pineapple is to an interlocutor who had never seen one? Once chocolate, coffee, or tea became part of the rites of sociability—or the technologies of pleasure, or the courtship practices, or, later, cheap sustenance for workers—in any given community, could there be any going back?

In any case, the worldwide mental revolutions of the early modern period happened only because of the emergence of vast frameworks of common understanding—at least at some level—and accepted codes of translation, in huge new spaces or arenas of communication, where ideas and institutions could incubate, reproduce, and deploy. Global empires supplied these prerequisites not so much by fomenting conflict as by forging community. Eventually, in varying degrees, they usually found ways of linking their subject peoples in common interests, collaborative ventures, networks of interdependence, foci of allegiance, marriage alliances, opportunities for material enrichment, and even shared emotions, beliefs, and ideologies.

The oldest form of globalization is cultural. It made all other forms possible—economic, technological, scientific, and ecological. We need to bear these facts in mind as we try to transcend the limitations of formerly favoured narratives of global history—providential, linear, and progressive—as a process of projection of Europe onto the rest of the word, as if what happened from the fourteenth century to the nineteenth was an evolutionary episode in the teleological triumph of a superior civilization, equipped for fitness, over barbarism, or of selective 'humanity'—or the only part of it that counts—over supposed savagery. In reality, at the time, 'centres' where people defined themselves as civilized were widely scattered around the globe, as were the 'peripheries' they saw as inferior and available for conquest or exploitation.

The outcomes of their encounters were not always as the conquerors or colonialists expected. Supposedly inferior cultures demonstrated human resilience by surviving. Creole communities emerged. Whites went native. African settlements and cities, projecting ways of life from Guinea or Angola, took shape in the Americas. Chinese quarters throve in Manila and Mexico. Native American or Asian chiefs and paramounts appeared in Europe to demand their rights. North America welcomed Hindu merchants and Chinese Muslims, and bred Americans of mixed race. All these and other human novelties reflected or created intermediate forms of society, culture, and life.

In consequence, geopolitics took on a new aspect, as metropolitan centres multiplied, nurturing unprecedentedly mixed populations and creating new peripheries. The new centres typically had their own encomiasts, who wrote them up as places propitious for the cultivation of virtue and excellence, designated by God and elevated by the presence or relics of 'pilgrims,' saints, or heroes. What we might call competitive polycentrism was among the effects of cultural convergence, in an age when, if you travelled far enough—and at some times in some places it did not necessarily have to be very far—you could meet indigenous Catholic priests, mulatto anchorites, mestizo illuminati, holy 'half-breeds', charismatic Protestant pastors, and Buddhist and Muslim proselytizers. In a different way, political mélanges co-existed in, say, Europe's 'composite monarchies', which combined disparate realms and lordships in allegiance to a common dynasty, or, despite the rulers' policy of excluding influence from most of the rest of the world, in China, which became bigger and more diverse than ever under the Manchu, or in Tokugawa Japan, where provincial lordships developed remarkable levels of autonomy and, in some cases, developed, over time, along distinctive lines.

Christendom

Global events challenged thinkers to respond to huge new questions. In Europe, Christendom fragmented in the sixteenth century. The Council of Trent (1545–63) turned the Catholic Reformation into a Counter-Reformation that made the Protestants' secession from the Church irreversible except by force. Meanwhile, schism divided Protestants among ever multiplying sects. Rival charisms and spiritualities proliferated, while the discovery of vast, previously undetected pagan worlds far afield ignited long and complicated debates among theologians and disclosed puzzling novelties for philosophers. In 1577, Philip II's government in Spain sent questionnaires to officials in the New World with the aim of compiling systematic data, known as 'Relaciones Geográficas'. The questions covered natives' 'understanding, inclinations, and ways of life, whether they have different languages or some common tongue, what they were like in the time of their paganism, their devotions, rites, and customs both good and bad'. To the astonishment of the officials who received the replies, there were pagans who had no notion of authority or of divinity. For some peoples, the past, it seemed, did not exist, and there was nothing real beyond what was immediately present to the senses. Other communities—equally strangely, from the Spanish point of view—had no concept of property or were unaware of the natural laws against cannibalism and incest.

FOLDING SCREENS PAINTED WITH SCENES of the conquest of the Aztecs were popular decorative items, always showing—as here—the influence of Filipino and Japanese artworks, in seventeenth-century Mexico. Absorption into the Spanish monarchy vastly extended the range of trade open to inhabitants of the New World.

Caption informations: Prof. Amara Solari and Prof. Matthew Restall of the Pennsylvania State University.

Christendom changed, even as European explorers and missionaries evangelized the world. Europe served as a laboratory of methods of catechesis and experiments in communal life transferable to other regions. Many observers put American natives and Castilian peasants in the same category—simple, rustic creatures, of limited intellect, and therefore imperfectly responsible, in law, for their actions. To save them from grave errors of judgement or errant behaviour, they all needed the tutelage of guardians or moral guides. Overseas expansion, in this light, appears as a vast exercise in legal intervention and comparative moral ethnography. It made scrutineers seek or devise similarities or common elements in different societies, so as to render alien ways intelligible. Explorers were always asking, 'What does this or that structure or tribe or custom resemble, strange as it may seem?' In one of his famous 'Cartas de relación', Hernán Cortés, the conqueror of Mexico, mentioned that the great temple of Tenochtitlan had towers and looked like a mosque.

In a similar way, the inhabitants of newly discovered lands had to work at understanding the newcomers, if only to stave off attack. Some Maya, for instance, seem to have docketed Spaniards as yet another bunch from the long-standing reservoir of invaders in central Mexico. In Bungo, Japan, Japanese merchants and missionaries

'DESIMA' BY C. W. MIELING, AFTER J.M. VAN LIJNDEN. A painting of the Dutch trading post on an artificial island in the Bay of Nagasaki, the only place where Japan allowed direct trade and with the West during the Edo period.

found themselves apostrophized as 'men from India'. Perhaps the best way of responding to the new arrivals was to adapt to and manage their impact over time. This was relatively easy on fluid frontiers, where native authority was diffuse or low level. The Araucanos in Chile or the Comanche of the Great Plains learned to deploy cavalry and use firearms, rapidly closing the technology gap that favoured the invaders. They could not be subjugated; thus, they were able to negotiate a relationship with the Spanish monarchy on the basis of mutual respect, common interests, and, to some degree, mutual advantage. *Mutatis mutandis*, a comparable compromise prevailed in Japan. Having expelled or exterminated Portuguese and Spanish infiltrators, and having choked off the incipient conversion of the country to Catholicism, the shogunate used the artificial island of Deshima, constructed in 1634 in Nagasaki Bay, to host Dutch merchants in a sort of territorial limbo, because foreigners were not allowed to profane the 'sacred soil' of Japan.

Religion was instrumental. For conquerors it provided a providential explanation for the surprising successes, along with an evangelical justification, endorsed at an early stage by Christendom's highest arbitrator, the Pope. In 1455 in the bull *Romanus pontifex* Nicholas V handed dominion over West African lands conquered from Muslims and pagans to Afonso V, the Portuguese monarch, and his successors. In 1493 Alexander VI granted to Ferdinand and Isabella, of Aragon and Castile, other Atlantic lands, discovered and to be discovered, with the obligation of evangelizing them. For the indigenous subjects of new empires, on the other hand, religion offered scope to appropriate and exploit, to natives' advantage, what seemed, prima facie, an

THE SALVIATI PLANISPHERE, C. 1525. This world map shows the 'Tordesillas Line'—the meridian agreed, in theory, between Spain and Portugal as demarcating their respective spheres of navigation in the Atlantic. In practice, no means of establishing it accurately were available. Rather than include imagined material in unexplored areas—as was customary—the map leaves them blank, inviting future exploration.

imposition enforced upon them. For the status of a baptized Christian was very different from that of a pagan, as was apparent, for instance, to the African slaves who crossed the Atlantic unprotected by any rights save those consequent on the brotherhood of faith—irrespective of whether anyone asked their leave before sprinkling them with holy water at the foot of a slaving vessel's gangway, or offered them any prior catechesis.

Back in Europe, the designs of providence appeared, with varying degrees of obscurity, all over the place. The prosperity of the city-republics of the Mediterranean, especially Genoa, Florence, and Venice, grew after the Black Death, but seemed to nurture heresies and wayward cults. Corruption and division eroded papal authority and religious orders alike. In 1453, the fall of Constantinople to Muslim Turks extinguished the oldest and most venerable state in the Christian east. The Crusades waned in failure. Tricksters, false prophets, fake saints, and witches appeared, threatening to impose the Kingdom of Darkness, while wretched and selfish Christian rulers plunged into internecine wars in defiance of God's will. These were the perceived circumstances in which godly vocations or pastoral responsibilities impelled individuals to prepare the way of the Lord and make His paths straight.

Long before the Augustinian friar (as he was then) Martin Luther proclaimed his ninety-five theses against indulgences in Wittenberg in 1517, a providentialist and reformist—not to say apocalyptic—mood had gripped Western Europe. The spread of printing, the rise of what we might call bookishness, uncontrollable access to and re-interpretation of scripture, the multiplication of biblical translations, and movements in favour of vernacular liturgy: all these stimulated new forms of devotion. In the sixteenth and seventeenth centuries evangelizers focused on previously neglected targets: urban poor, spiritually deprived countryfolk, communities isolated and remote, and even slaves and neophytes in distant parts of the world. The re-Christianization of Europe was apparent in efforts, including those of the Inquisition, to 'hammer' witches (as persecutors put it), extirpate unbelievers, and combat ingrained features of popular culture, including astrology and fortune-telling, such as disclosed lack of trust in God or improper submission to superstitious or pagan priorities.

The growing power of rulers was part of the process: both a contribution and a consequence. But there was more to it than that. Princes favoured the objectives of the godly as long as they did not rival or impair secular authority. If states felt menaced, they were implacable and wielded all the power they could muster against the churches, Catholic and Protestant alike. In this connection, as in so many others, attitudes in Europe diverged after the Reformation much less than is commonly supposed. The way native elites in parts of the Americas and Asia debated whether to accept or reject Christianity can be compared with decision-making among German princes on whether to adopt Protestantism and on how to put the principle of 'cuius regio, eius religio' (the religion of the ruler was to dictate the religion of those ruled) into effect. In all cases, truth was easiest to recognize when it served power.

Spiritual experimentation became characteristic of the era—well exemplified in the widespread readership of *Imitatio Christi*, first in manuscript from 1471, and later in the printed version, by the Augustinian Thomas à Kempis, who became a member of one of the new communities of Brethren of the Common Life. Thomas's intended audience was of monks and friars but the book became popular among lay readers who wanted to develop an 'inner' spiritual life. A more incendiary case, in every sense, was that of the messianic friar, Girolamo Savonarola, burned to death and pounded to ash in the Piazza delle Signoria in Florence in 1498, after organizing his own bonfires of vanities, to which he consigned consumer luxuries, including cosmetics and purportedly unsuitable books. The services he had conducted attracted thousands of congregants to hear his fulminations against everything that learned humanism prized, along with the Medici dynasty, sodomy, and the Pope. A little later, in Spain, Cardinal Cisneros launched a searching reform of the clergy, imposing discipline and challenging moral

IN AN ANONYMOUS PAINTING OF 1498, children play and business continues as usual in Florence's main square, while Savonarola's pyre is heaped with fuel for his execution.

standards—some religious were so indifferent to their vows that they preferred to flee to Africa and live among Muslims rather than abandon their concubines; but the effect was to expose shortcomings as well as to achieve improvements. Social problems contributed to the religious temper. In a period of resumed demographic growth and growing disparities of wealth, the worldly distractions of many members of the Church hierarchy provoked scandal and discontent, as did the growth in the power of states with consequently aggravated burdens—fiscal, military, and bureaucratic—on their subjects. It is not surprising that some Protestants, like the Anabaptists who preceded and coincided with them in Germany, were drawn to such ideals as the abjuration of war, the abolition of money, and the community of property.

While there were uncatechized natives in America, there were plenty of Europeans at low levels of privilege and prosperity, who were equally uninstructed in the faith. The attempts of godly hierarchs and institutions to promote new religious thinking and practice were responses to the challenge of evangelizing the unevangelized and, for the under-evangelized, deepening their conversion. It is, indeed, tempting to argue that Protestant and Catholic reformations alike were aspects of a single, top-down movement among godly elites to confront and refashion, according to elite notions of order and discipline, a form of popular religion inherited from the Middle Ages. 'All superstition must be suppressed', the Council of Trent declared. Humanist theologians, accordingly, explained that the saints' role were limited to that of privileged intercessors. Every miracle came from God alone and claims of divine intervention had to be sparing and sceptical. Paganism, it seemed, could pop up anywhere. In 1553, a Jesuit in Bordeaux complained that in the adjacent countryside he had found people 'who have never been to Mass nor heard one word of doctrine'. In 1615 a member of the same order remarked on his bafflement at the large numbers of his confrères wanting to be missionaries in Asia or America, 'when there are so many people over here who neither know God nor even believe in His existence'. In 1693, the Swedish governor of a Baltic province ordered the destruction of certain stones and trees to forestall cultists and 'in order to leave nothing that might be superstitiously abused'.

Characteristically of organized religion in general, Catholic authorities enforced their monopoly over ritual by, inter alia, controlling the validation of miracles and relics, initiating a debate that continues to resonate. On 12 March 1622, for instance, at one fell swoop, Gregory XV canonized Isidro Labrador, Philip Neri, Teresa of Ávila, Ignatius Loyola, and Francis Xavier. Of these, the last two were Jesuits, respectively the founder of the Order and the bold missionary who died just as he was about to launch his mission in China. The first was a married layman who could make rain and locate water sources and whose many devotees in the town and court of Madrid, which became Spain's definitive capital in 1606, made him the local patron saint. St Teresa, who combined unusual traits as woman, writer, and Doctor of the Church, had reformed the Carmelite Order and developed an individualistic form of religiosity. In her *Life*, she explained her first steps in the faith:

We had a garden by our house, where we played at being hermits, trying to build little shelters for prayer by piling stones that tended to fall on top of us. So we could never put our desires into effect. I gave alms when I could—but that wasn't much or often. I sought solitude for my prayers, which were numerous, especially recitations of the Rosary. With other girls, we liked to play at being nuns in a convent.

The Florentine St Philip Neri shared Teresa's organizing mind. He founded the Oratorians, after rejecting the possibility of emulating St Ignatius's plans for a mission in Asia and deciding to remain in Rome to increase the faith there. Appropriately, he devised a pilgrimage route through the seven major churches of the city for seekers after plenary indulgence. Equally appropriately, the church in which his remains repose is called the 'New Church'. By accrediting some saints, the Church helped to establish popular models of exemplary behaviour; an ancillary effect, however, was to nourish cults of relics, which could channel pious sentiments and miracles, but which many commentators deemed superstitious or even magical. In any case, such cults were dubious from the point of view of a universal—which is to say, centralized— Church, ever more determined to promote the veneration of Christ and His mother at the expense of local devotions.

Poised between devotion and superstition, baroque relic-collections resembled 'engine rooms' of the Catholic faith, where popular and reformed religion rumbled together The Convent of La Encarnación in Madrid houses a fine example, begun in 1616, when the queen, Margaret of Austria, gave the nuns, as an object of curiosity, the bed in which she had given birth to one of her sons, the future Philip IV. Connected to the palace by a passageway, the treasury of relics is a big, square room, lined with sacred scenes and venerated remains, which include the arm of St Thomas of Villanueva, preserved in a glass column, and that of St Philip. A silver cross contains a fragment of *lignum crucis*—the True Cross—with some nails, a bit of the staff that supposedly bore the sponge that moistened Christ's lips, the cloth that wiped his face, and a stone from his tomb. Although the display includes, for public adoration, more than 700 relics of saints and martyrs from Italy, Germany, Spain, and the Low Countries, the most prized piece is the vial that contains the blood of St Panataleon, which liquefies 'miraculously' every year on 26 and 27 July.

Changes in public forms of worship affected private life. In the second half of the sixteenth century prosecutions for bigamy, breach of promise, adultery, and other wayward habits drew frequent attention from the Inquisition. Under the Spanish Habsburgs, in the Spanish and Portuguese monarchies, this institution maintained as its main task the unmasking of fraudulent claims of Christian conversion among crypto-Jews and Muslims. As time went on, however, inquisitors' focus shifted to the investigation of superstition and magic—activities in which mulatto and black domestics, both slave and free, attracted much suspicion as 'experts in enchantments and conners of love potions'. In England, meanwhile, Catholics endured equally systematic persecution, while in Geneva, for example, Calvin succeeded in exterminating opponents of his doctrines. Miguel Servet was condemned twice: burned in effigy by Catholics in France and in person by Calvinists in Geneva, where his denial of the Trinity and his advocacy of adult baptism led him to the stake in 1553.

Although Europe's elites were as committed to concerted and comprehensive evangelization as to the control of popular religion, a paradoxical outcome of Protestant secessions from the Church was that local and regional sects multiplied in parts of Germany, France, Switzerland, Hungary, Scandinavia, and the Netherlands, as well as in Scotland and England, where the Reformation took a distinctive course via the establishment of a peculiar national schism under royal leadership. Ironically, Henry VIII, who implemented the scheme, had been recognized as 'Defender of the Faith' by Pope Leo X in 1521. Nothing quite so radical happened in Catholic Europe, although, behind façades that proclaimed reigning monarchs in Spain, France, and Portugal as, respectively, 'Catholic', 'Most Christian', and 'Most Faithful', rulers kept up a state of constant friction with the temporal and spiritual power of the papacy, albeit without ever eliminating it entirely. In France, the shift towards an autonomous form of Catholicism culminated in 1682, when royal decree established the so-called 'Gallican Liberties' insisting that 'the pope is obliged to respect the rules, customs and laws of the kingdom'.

Paradoxically, perhaps the clearest symbol of conflict between duties of obedience to the rival majesties of church and state—the need to 'render unto Caesar the things which are Caesar's and to God the things which are God's'—was the special oath Jesuits swore to the pope. Ignatius of Loyola envisaged the Company as a projection of his own experience as a professional soldier, where such virtues as boundless comradeship and self-sacrifice would strengthen the Jesuits' schools and universities, as well as the missions to which the Jesuits turned increasingly and with great efficacy.

As soldiers of the pope and fully qualified representatives of global Catholicism, the Jesuits attracted much Protestant hostility. Partisan exaggerations, however, distorted the differences that animated confessional enmity. Most of the embittering debates on predestination, salvation by faith, and the nature of grace unfolded, for the most part, among theologians and jurists in academic settings. Almost everyone in Europe agreed that this world existed for misery in greater or lesser degree and that what really mattered in life only began with death. Even among Europe's 'other' Christians—the orthodox of the East—debate and reform echoed the travails of the Western Church. The patriarch of Constantinople, Cyril Lukarisch, who visited Venice and Poland and perhaps knew Geneva first hand, sought to displace 'beguiling tradition' in favour of guidance by faith and scripture—for which he was assassinated in 1638. Not long afterwards, a group of radicals persuaded Czar Alexei to ban popular devotions and pagan music from court. New vigour infused the old notion of Moscow as the 'Third Rome', while Orthodoxy's 'Old Believers' rejected reformist agendas in a schism that reflected fundamental features of the Reformation in the Latin Christendom of the previous century.

Global conversions

In Peru, after the death of Rosa of Lima in 1617, the viceroy's guard had to intervene repeatedly to guard her corpse against the depredations of excessively devout mourners who, if allowed, would have stripped her naked in their eagerness to seize scraps of her clothing as relics. She was canonized in 1671. Peru's black saint, Martin Porres, healer, carer, and protector of pigs and cats, who is usually represented with his broom in his hand, died in 1639, but was not beatified until 1837. For both, popular devotion grew with time. As with devotion for the Virgin of Guadelupe, who appeared to the native Juan Diego in Mexico in 1531, these American saints represented a new, globally aspiring dimension of Catholicism. Until the severance of the Spanish and Portuguese crowns in 1640, Philip IV of Spain merited his soubriquet as the 'Planet-king', using baroque spirituality to express his militant faith in Providence as he confronted, among other creedal and confessional enemies, Dutch Protestants in Brazil and Muslim proselytizers from the rich sultanate of Ternate, who arrived in the 1580s in the Philippine island of Mindanao, where their descendants are still known as 'Moors'.

OUR LADY'S parents embrace before the Golden Gate of Jerusalem in a depiction by Martín Alonso de Mesa and Juan García Salguero for the Church of Nuestra Señora de la Limpia Concepción in Lima in about 1620.

ST MARTIN DE PORRES, SANTA
PRISCA CATHEDRAL IN TAXCO,
Mexico, depicted as usual with his
black face and his broom in his hand
to recall how he began his service in
the Dominican Order as a servant
before being received as a religious
brother.

Save in some Dutch overseas ventures, most Protestant missions entered the field late.
But there were exceptions. John Eliot, who thought that the Algonquins were one of
the lost tribes of Israel, founded 'praying towns' in seventeenth-century New England,
under native pastors who read the Bible before variously attentive and uncompre-
hending congregations.

For a while, Franciscans and Jesuits achieved remarkable success in Japan, following
the old top-down model of converting lords in order to proceed to the Christianization
of their followers and subjects. By about 1630, more than 100,000 Christians had been
baptized, despite persecutions adjusted to the rhythms of the fears shoguns felt when
the progress of Christianity among provincial, and potentially separatist elites excited
understandable apprehensions of foreign infiltration. When Christian priests first
arrived, they seemed a potentially useful counterpoise, from an official point of view,
to the power of the Buddhist clergy; by the end of the sixteenth century, however, they
looked increasingly like the vanguard of an invasion. In 1597, 22 native Japanese martyrs,
including an elderly samurai, a carpenter, and a number of children, were put to death by

crucifixion, along with three Jesuits and a Franciscan. From 1639, Catholicism was outlawed and remained so until well into the nineteenth century.

In China, a conversion strategy of a similar sort proved impossible, since there were no local lords on whom to focus: on the contrary, the state was robust and highly centralized. Jesuits' initial optimism there was unfounded except on the basis of misleading success in Goa and other Portuguese enclaves in India, where faith followed the flag. When Francis Xavier died offshore in 1552, preparing to disembark in secret, he hoped that the conversion of China would be a divine portent of future success in Japan. But although the Jesuits' efforts among rural peasants achieved surprisingly large rates of conversion, the mission was always short-handed; successes among Mandarins and courtiers were rare, and almost unattainable in the ranks of the imperial family. Converts proved hard to wean from ancestor-worship, Buddhist devotions, polygamy, and sheer superstition, which they tended to regard as customs compatible with transformed beliefs. Matteo Ricci, the Jesuit mathematician and cartographer who launched the mission in earnest in 1583, adopted Mandarin attire and fascinated high officials with his mastery of Confucian learning, his lectures on Western science, and his artistic, astronomical, and cartographical skills (although his world map caused some ructions because his representation of China was too small and insufficiently central for Mandarin taste). He wrote intelligible introductions to Catholicism for Chinese enquirers and founded some Christian communities before his death in Beijing in 1610. But his patient strategy failed in the end. In 1644, Manchu invaders overthrew the reigning dynasty, elevating successors who, while admiring Western technology, eschewed barbarian religion. Suspicions in Rome clouded the Jesuits' efforts as the so-called 'Chinese Rites' controversy unfolded, in which critics accused the missionaries of unorthodox and opportunistic compromises with paganism: the Chinese word they used for heaven, for instance—did it signify a material place or a sublime principle? Was the veneration of ancestors, which some Jesuits were inclined to endorse as analogous to the cults of saints, compatible with Christianity? Pope Clement XI ended debate by condemning such doctrines in 1704. Twenty years later, the imperial authorities in China banned further Christian proselytization. This did not mean that cultural exchange or the controversy that accompanied it ended. On the contrary, thanks to Jesuits' reports, China penetrated European imaginations, representing for admirers a political and intellectual model, and for sceptics a model of what to avoid. While the Chinese experiment in Catholic evangelization faltered, Dutch Protestants launched efforts of their own in the Moluccas and Celebes, where they founded schools for the sons of local nobles, with scant success.

In the Americas, the diffusion of Christianity registered real progress, in a way typical of the Spanish monarchy, when cities began to function as centres of culture from which influence radiated across the land. In Mexico, where the conquest of former Aztec territory came to a close in 1521, the presence of zealous, militant clerics made a real difference. Franciscans baptized millions of natives. They issued catechisms and built hospitals and seminaries where they proposed to train native clergy. During the optimistic phase of the development of conversion strategies the most remarkable undertaking was the foundation of the College of Santa Cruz in Tlatelolco in New Spain for that purpose.

An atmosphere of providentialism and utopianism marked the beginnings of Christianity in Mesoamerica and other parts of the New World with long native traditions of religions organized on a large scale. Data compiled under the direction of clerics who wanted to know what they were converting natives from revealed instances of syncretic adaptation of old symbols and concepts, sacred spaces and cults, refashioned in Christian terms and forms. Debate was impassioned. For the Jesuit José de Acosta, the death of the Aztec paramount, Moctezuma, and the execution of the Supreme Inca, Atahualpa, had prejudiced the successful introduction of Christianity, as their conversion could have facilitated that of their subjects. Missionaries' first targets, he thought, should be chiefs and their families, whom it would be a mistake to strip of 'dignity and authority' or reduce to servitude. Debate on the proper status and means of conversion of indigenous nobility tacked between, on the one hand, openness to assimilation, which inaugurated marriages between conquistadores and wives of native lineage, and, on the other, fear of rebellion and disobedience, which sparked periodic uprisings.

Both sides shared some basic assumptions. Even if the natives were classifiable as fully human—as was not initially apparent to all observers—it was necessary to fit them into the panorama of humankind and to evaluate their civilization according to Aristotelian standards of rationality: the fewer the boxes ticked, the worse. No one in Europe wanted to exclude the Chinese or Incas from the ranks of the civilized. But the case of many peoples dispersed in forests and grasslands was less clear. Cannibals were at the low end of the scale and could be lawful victims of war and enslavement. In 1537, in the Bull *Sublimis Deus*, Pope Paul III pronounced Native Americans fully qualified to receive the faith of Christ: the task was to teach it to them 'by means of preaching and a good example of life'. A little earlier, Fray Juan Garcés, the Dominican Bishop of Tlaxcala, declared, 'Indio children are unafflicted with obstinacy or mistrust towards the Catholic faith, as are the Moors. They learn more readily than Spaniards.'

Even with general acceptance, at least in the Spanish monarchy, that natives qualified for the protection of natural law, and could not be lawfully harmed, the feeling persisted that they needed to transition towards the assimilation of Christianity. The result was the establishment of distinct communities—known as 'republics' respectively of 'indios' and Spaniards, with parallel laws and institutions. There was no apartheid or inequality in the system: the clergy's ingenuous aim was, rather, to preserve natives' supposed innocence from corruption by immigrants whose own Christianity—after generations of exposure to Jewish and Moorish influence—was itself imperfect. For good shepherds, it made sense to build pens for the security of the flock. The laws of the Indies were full of precepts against 'contagion'. Yet the interdependence and intermarriage of the two

THE JESUIT PRIEST JOSÉ SEGUNDO LAINEZ, who served as a missionary in Caquetá, attired as a native with feathered headdress.

communities was unimpeded. There were few European women and, especially in such frontier areas as Chile, the children of mixed marriages or contracts of concubinage, became their parents' unquestioned heirs.

The pace and circumstances of evangelization varied. Peru, for instance, was different from Mexico. In the former, civil wars between the conquerors disrupted early colonial society until 1550. It took longer for viceregal government to take hold. The clergy there did not share, on the whole, the utopianism of the Franciscans of Mexico. Yet the militant, missionary Church had to contend or coexist everywhere with the institutional Church that emerged from the Counter-Reformation. The religious orders took on ever more responsibility. The work of eradicating idolatry revealed the shortcomings of early methods of evangelization, based on mass baptisms supported by sketchy catechesis. Jesuits established model procedures. In cities like Mexico City and Lima, where the viceroys had their courts, the Order had universities, schools, and seminaries for the children of the nobles of both 'republics' and for the formation of Jesuit recruits. Elsewhere, they extended their influence by maintaining well-managed, productive estates. Further afield, on the frontiers of Brazil, from Paraguay to Venezuela, or in the remote northern marches from Sonora to Texas, they threaded a belt of missions that demonstrated both the length and the limits of evangelization's reach. Until they were expelled in 1767, the Jesuits manned the front line.

Buddhist and Muslim missions

Christianity's global expansion met other religions that were also escalating their culture areas and experiencing movements of reform. In Chinese and Japanese homes, thanks to the reformers Zhu Hong and Han Shan, Buddhism became a friendly religion, practisable in private and on a domestic scale, rather than the preserve of the religious. Lay devotees began to pray to Buddha, practise vegetarianism, and don saffron robes. In the eighteenth century, Peng Shaoshing promoted meditation and mental prayer as universally accessible techniques, rather as European reformers had done since the Renaissance. A little earlier in Japan, the monk Keishu re-edited the ancient indigenous poetical texts, the *Manyoshu*, to provide readers with spiritual guidance. Motoori Morinaga deployed the book as Protestants wielded the Bible, as a source book of morally improving readings. The proscription of Christianity in Japan facilitated the spread of Buddhism among nobles, merchants, and peasants.

The strongest Buddist missionary impulse came from Mongolia from about 1570. Altan Khan, founder of Koke Khota, the 'Blue City' and capital of a realm that extended from the Yellow River to the edges of Tibet, was committed to paganism, but even more to politics. To validate his power, and affect a civilizing mission in rivalry with other rulers on the western borders of China, he sponsored Buddhism, founded monasteries, and patronized the study of sacred text inscribed on exquisite tablets of Applewood. At his behest, the Dalai Lama, ruler of Tibet and tutelary genius of Buddhist institutions, visited Mongolia in 1576 and 1586. Some customs underwent radical reform. Human sacrifice and bloody rites were prohibited. The ongons, the traditional idols in which the spirits awaited shamanic arousal, were burned and replaced with statues of Buddha. The aristocracy hastened to receive Buddhism and in time young monks from noble families consecrated themselves to the task of translating scriptures. With the mission of Prince Neyici Toyin, who demonstrated the superiority of Chinese and Tibetan medicine over the arts of the shamans, Buddhism penetrated Manchuria in the 1630s. When the Manchu dynasty took over China in 1644, Buddhist expansion accelerated, for the rulers reckoned the missionaries as allies in the politics of pacification in their newly conquered empire. New gods and old superstitions fused, and the burning of ongons did not consume the nature-worship they had symbolized. As so often, syncretism ensued, with the displaced spirits inhabiting Buddhist shrines and artworks.

Meanwhile, Islam expanded in southeast Asia and Africa mainly by four means: trade, missions, holy war, and dynastic marriage. Merchants and missionaries—as had been the case since the foundation of Islam—combined to forge routes of proselytization, along which pious Muslims worked as agents, officials, vendors, and customs

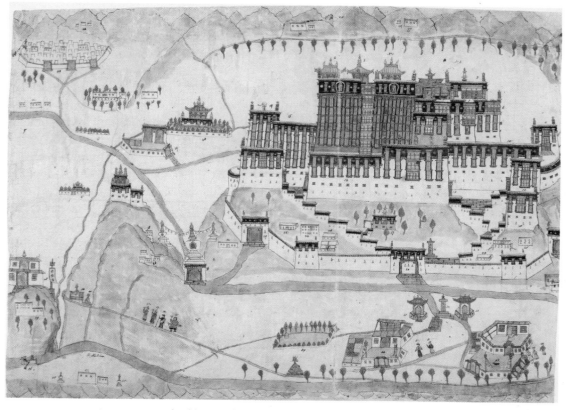

A VIEW OF LHASA'S most iconic buildings—the Potala Palace and the Jokhang Temple—drawn by a wandering lama in the late 1850s as part of the intelligence-gathering of a British border official, Edmund Hay.

officers for pagan rulers. Wherever they settled, sages and mystics followed, keen to spread the message of the Prophet and dissipate the darkness of unbelief or cauterize the blemishes of paganism by fire if necessary. Sufis played a prominent role, well adapted to appeal to pagan sensibilities because of their traditions of sensitivity to the power of feelings and the sacrality of creation. When Portuguese navigators explored the Indian Ocean in the sixteenth century, they found Sufis already well established in parts of Java and Sumatra. Later, in the face of the growing Christian presence in the region, the support of powerful sultans kept Sufis at work, especially in central Java. In West Africa in the same period, Muslim merchants married into local aristocracies, where polygamy helped them extend the range of their networks. Islamic sects with native leaders proliferated, as did teachers and scholars of the Quran. In 1655 a master living on the banks of the Niger advertised courses in 'law, interpretation of the Quran, the tradition of the Prophet, grammar, syntax, logic, rhetoric and prosody'. His fees were proportional to his pupils' resources and his methods were those of what we should now call comparative philology.

Syncretisms and mingled outcomes

From their places and cultures of origin, religions spread as an inescapable consequence of widening interactions in a globalizing age. Debate on how to preserve their 'pure' characteristics has continued ever since. If today we look conspectually at carnivals, say, in Rio, Goa, and Venice, we find that they happen simultaneously on the eve of Lent, but they seem to diverge in most details. Muslims preparing for the hajj, or pilgrimage to Mecca, all seek to re-enact the Prophet's original formula of ascetic self-denial, but do so in contrasting ways in different places. In every preserved rite, every conserved tradition, the seeds of change are present; and every community makes adjustments to reflect a sense of identity of its own. Hence the scholarly focus, in many recent studies, on institutions that mediated the religions in question to new constituencies in our period. Natives, mulattoes, and blacks in the New World, for instance, had their own confraternities, where their devotions reflected their peculiar hopes and frustrations. In England, from the torments of the civil wars of the seventeenth century, the Quakers emerged with their peculiar style of quietism in search of internal peace. Communities of fugitive slaves in Brazil or Cuba might preserve practices and beliefs recalled from their ancestors' African pasts, fused, in most cases, with Christian elements—the Yoruba deity Yemayá, for instance, with the Virgin Mary, or old gods with St Caleb (or Elesbaan), or St Basil. Millenarianism rippled through a lot of new religious developments, from radical Protestants eager for the world to end to Spiritual Franciscans awaiting the 'Last World Emperor' and Native American prophets who hoped that a similar consummation would restore their ancient power and freedom. Paradoxically, perhaps, the age of takeoff of Christianity, Islam, and Buddhism towards the status of global religions was also a period of secularization of many aspects of culture, when science—a new form of what we might call global intelligence—demonstrated more cultural adaptability and wider appeal.

Western science and enlightenment

According to the traditional explanation, modern science began with a Western, and specifically European, 'Scientific Revolution'. From a global point of view, both of the words that form the term are questionable. A new way of classifying nature, based on observation and confirmed by sources of previously marginal or unpractised methods of validation, could not emerge overnight: in that sense it was hardly revolutionary. Nor was what happened a 'revolution' in favour of science at the expense of something else. It took a long time for science to become secular, nor did scientists displace ministers of religion. The notion that science and religion are mutually independent—though often suggested—did not become current until the nineteenth century. What happened previously was a long process, in which possible responses to daring questions led gradually to dialogue between data derived from reason and experiment, on the one hand, and, on the other, verities proclaimed by revelation. Minds as remarkable as those of Nicolas Steno, Copernicus, Descartes, Leibniz, and Newton questioned the age of the Earth, its place in the solar system, the evidence for atomism, the physics of motion, the scope of calculus, and the workings of optics. None discounted the value of religiously derived truths. Rather, from the Renaissance onwards, the consistent thread that ran through all their thoughts and those of their scientific contemporaries was the conviction that nature, including humankind, could be known by means of observations from which universal laws could be deduced.

The emergence of modern science was both cause and effect of global cultural exchanges: a result of European expansion, in as much as it occurred in the course of a dynamic response to an avalanche of data—previously unknown, unclassifiable, and even unimaginable—that reached Europe from the early sixteenth century onwards. This amazing phenomenon, however, which generated a new consensus on how to tell truth from falsehood, occurred simultaneously and similarly on the far side of the world. In *An Essay Concerning Human Understanding*, John Locke told an anecdote—also related by Leibniz and Hume—of how the ruler of Siam once spent an entire afternoon in conversation with a Dutch ambassador. 'Sometimes,' the ambassador reported, 'water cools so much that people can walk on it. It freezes to a such a degree of solidity that even an elephant could walk on it.' Up to that point, the king averred, 'I have believed all the strange tales you have told me because I hold you to be a wise and honest man. Now I have no doubt that you have been lying consistently.' To him, the existence of ice was inconceivable: as in Europe, the intellectual climate in most of Asia was hostile to the reception of empirically unverified news. Cultural prejudices played their parts. The Confucian renaissance in China, Japan, and Korea made it difficult to form a favourable view of Westerners, who were classifiable, according to the Korean sage Yi T'Oegye, with beasts and birds. Mandarins who learned an ethos of self-effacement from their devotion to the ancient texts they studied found it hard to approve the relatively brash manners prevalent among late seventeenth-century Europeans.

At the time, debate between 'ancients' and 'moderns' was at its fiercest. For the former, virtue resided in the past and the only means to equal it was to imitate it. For the latter, progress necessarily made novelty superior. The quarrel, which began in the Renaissance or, in some respects, even earlier, suddenly grew in ferocity in 1688, when Charles Perrault, in his *Age of Louis the Great*, ventured to suggest that Homer would have exceeded his former greatness had he chanced to live in the refined era of the Sun King, Louis XIV of France. With this single example, he expressed the purported primacy in virtue of his own epoch over classical Greece and Rome. Determined defenders of Homer replied, but the moderns proclaimed the fall of the ivory towers of antiquity and published lampoons in mockery of their garrisons. The favourite riposte of the ancients—that the moderns were 'dwarfs on the shoulders of giants'— had first been uttered in the twelfth century, but was recycled in a new phase of the quarrel, when mutual hostility was fiercer than ever among practitioners of history, literature, science, and political thought.

Polemicists took up the theme in other European countries. In Spain, partisans of the need to innovate opposed those who insisted that 'whatever is new is noxious'. In England Jonathan Swift joined the debate in his satire of 1704, *The Battle of the Books*, in which he imagined volumes, respectively by ancient and modern authors, coming to life by night in the royal library and exchanging blows.

Swift's admonitions were ineffectual, to judge from the spirit in which the movement known as the Enlightenment began. In the eighteenth century, reason, science, and practical utility dominated most educated Europeans' values. Not by chance was this also an age of accelerated global travel and exploration, in which new ideas, techniques, technologies, and ways of organizing manpower were put to the test. Investigators studied nature with a conviction of their own infallibility and an expectation that all their questions were answerable. Advances in cartography transformed the map of the world by means of triangulation and mathematics, pure and applied, and of spectacularly improved instruments, not least of which was Harrison's marine chronometer that solved the problem of longitude. New ways of circulating news of inventions and discoveries—eagerly awaited in proportion to their extravagance and their power to arouse astonishment—took shape among the educated public in learned societies, academies of the initiated, and informal salons and cafés, where increasing numbers of men and women could take part. Increasingly numerous 'Gazettes', 'Mercuries', and similarly styled newspapers and periodicals stimulated diffusion and expressed the growing effervescence of public opinion.

Optimistic confidence in human perfectibility was fundamental to the Enlightenment, along with the assurance that wise policies could ensure 'public benefit and utility'. Humanity was on a progressive course from barbarism to civilization, thanks to enlightened principles asserted against those of obfuscation, identifiable, according to many commentators, with absolutist monarchs and obscurantist Christianity. In 1788, the year of the death of the great Spanish monarch, Charles III, the navigator José Vargas Ponce urged these opinions in his *Relation of a Voyage through the Strait of Magellan*. Frequent voyages, he explained, had improved shipping routes. Shoals and reefs were charted with certainty, and exact observations and measurements kept ships on course. Improvements in old techniques and inaugurations of new ones had made 'formerly constant dangers vanish'. Thanks to 'human ingenuity' it was even possible to foresee and elude terrible storms. Great explorers and their discoveries had, in the author's words, 'completed the system of geography'. The planet was so well known that significant modifications were improbable. The remaining task was to eliminate residual uncertainties. To perfect dominion over the Earth, humans needed to attain only 'one last apex of exactitude and rectify what our predecessors left unfinished'. In private, however, doubts abounded and rhetoric of Vargas's kind scarcely hid the problems of achieving definitive results. 'To supply by art the deficiencies of nature' was not as easy as Vargas made out.

PATAGONIAN GIANTS DEPICTED IN JOHN BYRON'S ACCOUNT of his voyage round the world, 1763. The mariner's relatively diminutive stature is an absurd exaggeration.

Nor, on the other hand, could anyone deny the impressive achievements of geography and cartography.

Manifest in the exact and ever more nearly complete representation of the real configuration of the surface of the planet, what we might call 'Enlightened geography', was the outcome of a long process of the development of scientific institutions that began in England and France. The Royal Society launched in 1660, at a meeting of a dozen savants under the chairmanship of Sir Christopher Wren, architect and professor of astronomy, 'for the promoting of physico-mathematical experimental learning'. The Horatian motto they adopted—*Nullius in verba*, or 'take nobody's word for it'—alluded to the superior credentials of experience over magisterium. The members were what we should now call scientific professionals. They met weekly to discuss topics as varied as natural history and alchemy, fossils and comets, spheres and stars. They started publishing proceedings in 1662 and three years later launched the *Philosophical Transactions*. Under the royal patronage that was conferred from the start, the society could articulate varied interests: academic, educational, and mercantile—including those of trading companies, which ensured that topics relating to exploration were always among those most favoured.

On the continent of Europe, signal events including the foundation in Paris of the Observatory in 1669 and of the Académie royale des sciences three years later, both of which focused on improving and correcting maps and charts under a degree of official control that set them apart from their English counterpart. One of the pioneers, Jean Picard, who allegedly started professional life as a gardener, was the prior of a monastery. In 1645, he had been working as assistant to the great astronomer Gassendi when an eclipse of the sun inspired him to devote himself to science. He used lenses to measure refraction and deployed the newly perfected pendulum clock to determine the intervals between meridian. In 1679 he began to publish his *Connaissance des temps*—a series of tables, arranged by date, of longitude and latitude. It remained unsurpassed until the appearance of the British *Nautical Alamanac* of 1766. Christiaan Huygens, the crafter of the clock concerned, was a Dutch disciple of Descartes. In 1655 he discovered the Orion nebula and examined the moons of Saturn, prior to proposing the theory that the Earth is a spheroid, truncated at the poles and bulging at the equator. In 1669 the French Academy recruited the Savoyard astronomer, Jean-Dominique Cassini, professor of astronomy in Bologna and successor of Kepler in the study of the variations in the apparent motions and size of the sun. He improved the method of calculating longitude from differences in the timing of eclipses.

As so often happened, however, in learned societies, rivalries ensued. Cassini confronted Picard and offended Huygens. Under his brilliant, egotistical leadership the Academy focused on gathering data on co-ordinates to map France and the world with unprecedented exactitude. On the third floor of the of the western tower of the Paris Observatory, Cassini laid out a world map seven metres wide, with lines of longitude and latitude inscribed at intervals of ten degrees. Whenever reliable reports came in of the co-ordinates of important places, the appropriate data were added to the grid. The results were distorted by the limitations of the Observatory and the impossibility of checking astronomical findings with measurements on the ground. Yet, as a quantifiable, verifiable project on empirical principles, the undertaking was of unparalleled importance for the history of science. Cassini issued instructions to expeditions bound for Guyana and Egypt, the Caribbean, and the remote Atlantic. Jesuit missionaries in Madagascar, Siam, and China sent him data. International co-operation was a prerequisite. The English astronomer Edmund Halley contributed from the Cape of Good Hope, and Jean de Thévenot's observations from Goa were called into use. When Louis XIV, the 'Sun King', visited to check up on the cartographers' progress, he strode across the map, aroused by curiosity, and pointed to various places with his foot.

Problems arising from cartography and exploration became political, as they excited competition of every kind between states. To solve those difficulties concerning the size and shape of the Earth, specialists turned from theory to practice, invoking new technologies in astronomy, mechanics, geophysics, and engineering. When Willebrand Snell, father of geodesy, set out to perfect the calculation of the size of the orb of the world in 1615, he assumed it was a perfect sphere. The work of the French Academy, however, raised the suggestion, on the basis of apparent discrepancies between the values of a degree on the surface of the world at different locations, that the planet might be distended towards the poles. Newton's laws of motion, meanwhile, predicted that it must, on the contrary, bulge at the equator, owing to outward thrust from a spinning axis. The consequent Anglo-French rivalry ended in Newton's favour as a result of laborious expeditions conducted under French leadership in the 1730s to measure the value of a degree in Lapland and Ecuador respectively, the former led by Pierre Louis de Maupertuis, the latter by Charles de La Condamine, Pierre Bouguer, Louis Godin, and Joseph de Jussieu, with the assistance of two Spanish scientific prodigies, the marine cadets Jorge Juan and Antonio de Ulloa. Hence arose an expression that seemed to encapsulate what had happened: a 'new geography' derived from proof that the Earth was not perfectly spherical.

Expectancy intensified. Towards the middle of the century everyone looked, for instance, for imminent solution of the enormously serious problem of how to determine longitude at sea. To safeguard shipping in a time of increasing seaborne trade in remote stretches of ill-known seas, it was vital for navigators to be able to locate their positions in relation to such hazards as were charted. Existing methods of measuring distance traversed yielded vague and inconsistent results. Since the sixteenth century, European monarchs had offered rich inducements for anyone who could crack the problem. In theory, it was possible to use horology as a simple check by recording the lag at, say, high noon, between the time at the point of observation and that at the port of departure or at an agreed meridian. But chronometers capable of achieving the perfect accuracy required and of resisting the motion of a ship seemed beyond the skill of clockmakers until the 1760s, when John Harrison, an English artisan of modest education, devised the requisite innovations. Henceforth, the dangers of malfunctioning chronometers bedevilled voyages, requiring constant vigilance and checks.

At the start of the eighteenth century, two further apparently unconquerable limitations hemmed science: scurvy and malaria, both of which impeded exploration by making long voyages and tropical expeditions deadly. Powders made of quinine bark were available to treat fever but no remedy or preventive for scurvy was known. Yet the disease lurked, often unseen, between the lines of many reports of maritime disasters ostensibly caused by violence, mutiny, or despair of duty. In 1569 Sebastián Vizcaíno, explorer of California and the Pacific, noted that 'no medicine or human help exists against this sickness and only abundant fresh food can avail to cure it'. Between 1740 and 1744, George Anson circumnavigated the world during the so-called War of Jenkins' Ear between Britain and Spain. He captured the Manila Galleon, but lost 1,400 of the 1,900 crew that sailed with him to scurvy, beriberi, blindness, 'idiocy, madness and convulsions.' The death rate excited alarm and stimulated systematic enquiry, in the course of which James Lind, a naval surgeon with Caribbean experience, tried twelve different remedies on a sea voyage, including sea water, sulphuric acid solution, and a mixture of garlic, mustard, horseradish, quinine, and liquid myrrh. All the subjects ate the same food: sugar-sweetened gruel for breakfast, mutton broth or pudding with ship's biscuit at mid-day, and, for dinner, barley with raisins, rice with currants, or meat stew. A sample of the sick got a pint of cider a day on an empty stomach with the sulphuric solution. Two others took only two spoonfuls of vinegar daily and the gruel. The worst afflicted drank sea water, and a pair of patients received two oranges and a lemon each every day. The remainder had the mustard mix. According to Lind, those fed on oranges and lemons recovered marvellously and could return to duty without delay. Even more miraculously, neither died. Lind had verified a preventive, which, in alliance with rigorous shipboard hygiene promoted by Captain Cook in the 1760s, helped to keep scurvy at bay.

Apart from scurvy, smallpox was the only disease that yielded to the ministrations of enlightened science—in consequence of the introduction of inoculation, an Asian folk practice, which Lady Mary Wortley Montagu learned to imitate when her husband was British ambassador to the Ottoman Porte. In other respects, despite a challenge in favour of empirical methods mounted by followers of the sixteenth-century physician known as Paracelsus, medicine remained mired in the ancient doctrines of Hippocrates and Galen, and a doctor was as likely to kill as to cure. Other sciences, however, continued to register advances, including, most notably, the isolation of oxygen by Antoine Lavoisier in 1783 and the observation by Lazzaro Spallanzani in 1768 that microbes germinate: by casting doubt on the theory of spontaneous generation Spallanzani seemed to rehabilitate belief in the divine creator and to anticipate the nineteenth-century development of germ theory.

Meanwhile, the celebrated *Encyclopedia* (*Reasoned Dictionary of the Sciences, Arts and Trades*), the great compendium of enlightened thought that appeared in seventeen volumes of text and eleven of plates between 1751 and 1772, condemned the 'zeal of discovery' as one of the excesses of the age. Denis Diderot, the French editor and mastermind of the project, insisted that 'long-range expeditions have given rise to a

INTERIOR VIEW OF THE LEVERIAN MUSEUM AT ALBION PLACE, Southwark, London. Until its dispersal in 1806, it was one of the most intriguing collections in Europe of curiosities from around the world. Ashton Lever, who founded it, gathered many of the objects and specimens from Captain Cook's explorations.

new generation of wild nomads—men who have seen so many lands that they end by belonging to none, amphibians who inhabit the surface of the seas', without roots or morals. Diderot was the acclaimed 'Lay High Priest' of the Enlightenment, spokesman of the movement's utilitarian values, secularism, and critique of the powers that be. His viewpoint therefore raises a curious problem: if European explorers had returned from all the calamities they endured in distant seas to decry the marvels they had witnessed, they would have been judged as obvious failures. Many of them therefore lied. That is how, from the Renaissance onward, the notion of the 'noble savage' became a figment in Western minds—a figure projected from an imaginary, supposedly vanished golden age of the past, whom Westerners thought they saw on the banks of the Orinoco, the beaches of Tonga, or the icefields of Alaska. In *Robinson Crusoe*, published in 1719, Daniel Defoe captured the notion and the narrative it inspired in his account of how his hero rescued Friday from the cannibals, made a servant of him, and reinvented him as a kind of alter ego. The desire to be 'the first to see', of which Captain Cook spoke before he died of stab wounds on a Hawaiian beach in 1779, was inseparable from the mystique that occluded travel literature from time immemorial by turning ill-focused eyes on supposed surprises. The explorers' veracity is always dubious, although to this day we continue to read their texts as if through a lens powerful enough, we think, perhaps delusively, to correct every distortion.

Eastern enlightenments

Until industrialization, the relationship between East and West remained unchanged: economies at the Eastern and southern edges of Asia remained richer, and states there more powerful, than those in Europe and America. Still, it is helpful to think in terms of a slow intermediate stage, when influences were exchanged and cultures converged. In the seventeenth century, for instance, Chinese Mandarins were fascinated with Jesuit astronomy and re-crafted accordingly the calendars of the sacred rites on which the harmony of Earth and heaven and, therefore, the success of the state, were held to depend. Jesuit reports reached Leibniz, who in 1679 published a work updating European readers on 'news from China' and declaring the superiority of the Chinese in values, morals, and politics, albeit not, any longer, in physics and mathematics. Voltaire shared a sinophile outlook, adapting *The Orphan of China* to a Parisian *mise-en-scène* and recommending Confucianism as a supposed alternative to the organized religions he detested. Chinese belief in the observable order, rationality, and intelligibility of the universe, together with Chinese respect for learning, seemed to him to embody obvious elements of civilization. Fascination with the polity of China also captivated François de Quesnay, who thought that Confucianism restrained despotism and that the benignity of Chinese rule could be measured in what mattered: the quality of life of an abundant and healthy populace. Opponents, however, of what came to be called 'enlightened despotism', lampooned his and Voltaire's preference for the absolutism of the celestial empire, where the judicial system was ruthless and torture even more general and brutal than in European jurisprudence. Montesquieu, who advocated the rule of law, the division of powers, and limited government, thought that, in contrast with Europe, east Asia readily spawned tyranny.

The Enlightened public in Europe also succumbed to taste for Chinese exotica— porcelain, tea, textiles, lacquers, fireworks, and even gardens, where it became highly fashionable to erect a tea-house or a pagoda. Porcelain-linings and wallpapers of Chinese inspiration enclosed dwellers in royal palaces and aristocratic mansions. Japan and India achieved comparable decorative influence. The Dutch envoy, Engelbert Kampfer, titillated curiosity about Japanese institutions by criticizing the severity of the penal code but praising the low levels of taxation. The latter element became an obsession in Enlightened economic thinking. For Adam Smith, taxation was 'more or less evil' because it infringed liberty and distorted the market. Montesquieu, for his part, thought Japan an object lesson in the vices of oriental despotism, whereas Voltaire noted that the laws of the Japanese state—thanks, perhaps, to the influence of a conducive environment—seemed to embody those of nature. India was, for him, an even better model, where the Brahmins were 'the foremost legislators, philosophers and theologians in the world'. Persia and the Ottoman Empire, too, supplied exotic images for European consumers and alternatives to European ways, in, for example, Montesquieu's *Persian Letters* or Mozart's *Abduction from the Seraglio*, which anticipated nineteenth-century orientalism by combining the critique of despotism with tributes to oriental generosity and acuity. The Ottomans also secured, in some Western scrutineers' opinions, religious tolerance, respect for law, and encouragement of trade. Overall, however, negative reflections on the sultans' despotism, their subjects' docility, and the depth of political corruption outweighed favourable judgements.

Europeans seemed, on balance, to have had more to learn from Asia than the other way around. Jesuits might instruct a Chinese emperor on the works of Euclid, but they hardly affected the self-absorption of the standard Chinese curriculum. Although Chinese emperors admired Jesuit astronomers, cartographers, painters, clockmakers, hydraulic engineers, and gunsmiths, reception of Western models was highly selective. A British embassy arrived laden with potentially awesome globes, chronometers, scientific instruments, and proto-industrial wares in 1793, but the Qianlong emperor chose to interpret as barbaric the ambassador's unwillingness to kow-tow. 'They have nothing China wants,' read the official judgement: 'permission to reside permanently at court denied.' Japan evinced more interest in some aspects of Western science, especially botany and anatomy, thanks to the presence of the Dutch—the only Europeans permitted, albeit with severe restrictions, to trade. Confucian revival prompted a kind of counter-culture that exalted empiricism and even, in the case of the master Ishida Baigan, a shadowy theory of the equality of all men. In Korea and Vietnam, too, empiricists reacted against preponderant Chinese influence, but direct input from Western influence was slight.

Enter the monsters: revolutionary and Napoleonic ideas

In one of his well-known reflections, Alexis de Tocqueville pointed out that, but for the destruction the French Revolution wrought, France might have preceded Britain in the forefront of the industrial era. From the perspective of this cultured provincial aristocrat whose world had vanished, the Revolution was a barbarian outrage that deprived society of useful people and necessary institutions.

The relationship between the Enlightenment and the French Revolution is complicated. Both terms cover uneasily compatible clusters of features and events. It is rash to assume that the one led to the other. There was a deistic, naturalist Enlightenment, with a fierce secular component. But there was another strand, too: Mediterranean and Catholic, deferential to the papacy, with sensibilities inherited from the baroque period, alert to magic and wary of the evil eye. Among its achievements were the abolition of torture, thanks in part to the classic, *On Crimes and Punishments* (1764) by the Milanese Cesare Beccaria, and the vision of the Neapolitan eccentric, Gianbattista Vico, who dreamed of a moderate, reasonable 'era of Man'. Even in the north, among mainly deist *philosophes*, along with unremitting optimists who confided in the unlimited possibilities of human agency, there were pessimists who withheld trust from the 'lights' and luminaries of the age. Jean-Jacques Rousseau was one of the most influential, living life to the full as he abandoned all his mistresses and broke with all his friends. In a prize essay of 1750, which brought him great fame, he denied that art and science had improved humankind and claimed that social change and civilization had corrupted primitive goodness. His followers cited the Huron of the North American Great Lakes as exemplary, or the 'savages' of the South Pacific, whom explorers and sailors had beheld in a state of natural felicity that included—let us not forget— free love. For Rousseau's followers, society was the sum of individuals linked as citizens in common fraternity, under the guidance of an abstract principle, the 'common good', in obedience to the 'general will'. Whoever refused to defer to the general will must be 'forced to be free'. Later thinkers would point out that an individual's freedom was illimitable save by that of others, but Rousseau's radicalism remained available to anyone who wanted to invoke it: first in political conflicts that dethroned absolute monarchies for injustice, ignorance, and corruption, and later in wider cultural struggles in which supposedly noble savagery confronted supposedly corrupt civility.

Meanwhile, a mob, which called itself the nation, stormed the Bastille in Paris on 14 July 1789 in what became the mythic start of a reputed great liberation. The influence of Rousseau's identification of the common man as a kind of noble savage, whose natural goodness could be set free by 'the nation' in pursuit of common good, was at work. In that gaol-house of errant aristocrats, where one of the most notorious inmates was the Marquis de Sade, there was a void as yawning as in the royal treasury, which maladministration had depleted, exacerbated by the costs of intervention in the US War of Independence and the penury induced by bad harvests. To confront the financial emergency, Louis XVI had summoned the Estates General, France's representative assembly, dormant since 1614. An experimental—and therefore unpredictable—political process began. It unfolded in four phases: a rebellion inside the elite was followed by moderate and radical phases, prior to a totalitarian climax. In the closing years of the eighteenth century, France introduced a new kind of narrative into the way human societies described change: revolution.

Its Latin root means 'the act of turning around or back on oneself'. But the deputies who arrived at the Estates General came equipped with memoranda of grievances and quickly proclaimed themselves a 'National Assembly' empowered to interpret the General Will of the nation. Short steps led thence to the proclamation of the sovereignty of the people, rather than of the divinely elected king, as the first three phases unfolded through the subjection of the Church under civil law, the persecution of the clergy and aristocracy, and finally the abolition of the monarchy, symbolized irreversibly when Louis XVI was guillotined before a fear-struck world, on 21 January 1793. A coalition of monarchies—Austria, Prussia, and Spain—declared war, while the final phase unfolded, in which revolutionary terror put a widening range of victims to death: nobles, priests, soldiers, artisans, peasants, men, women. Under a 'Committee of Public Safety' emergency, arbitrary tribunals dealt death without restraint, while the republic fought off invaders on every front. The police state, efficient censorship, and state terrorism were among the extemporizations of the moment, unprecedented in the West. In June and July of 1794 alone, the guillotine despatched 1,584 heads.

Science did not flag: researchers took the opportunity to establish that consciousness survived decapitation by seven seconds. In the same year the republic set up the École Polytechnique, which exerted enormous influence on the training of civil and military engineers. Among the products of the Enlightenment who emerged as revolutionaries was Napoleon Bonaparte, an artillery officer from Corsica, who became the 'strong man', self-detected to redeem the situation in fulfilment of destiny and history. A coup in 1799 made him military dictator. In 1804 he was crowned emperor, not 'by the grace of God', but by his own hand. His genius for land warfare had been apparent during his campaigns in Italy and Egypt. His understanding of naval matters, geopolitics, and global strategy, however, was equally evidently defective, and the limits of his charismatic style of leadership in politics and war gradually became apparent.

In the name of revolutionary ideals Napoleon mobilized huge armies, and in the lands he overran, he imposed a mix of administrative uniformity with martial discipline. He re-carved regions on geometric and rational lines, applied inflexible codes of laws, subordinated the Church and established bureaucratic organs of government to apply his propaganda in abject fashion, while systematically looting the cultural treasures of the conquered. He opened the final chapter in the long series of wars between England and France. In the French Caribbean he tried to re-impose slavery, which the revolutionaries of 1794 had abolished. He betrayed friends and allied states,

TOUSSAINT L'OUVERTURE, the best-known leader of the Haitian Revolution, shown in a popular engraving of 1802, such as made him a hero in France before his capture and imprisonment.

'THE CORONATION OF NAPOLEON', BY JACQUES-LOUIS DAVID AND GEORGES ROUGET. With characteristic swagger, Napoleon, having taken the regalia from the Pope's hands to crown himself, places the same crown on his wife's head.

including at various times Austria, Russia, and Spain, whenever it suited him. After his first defeat in 1814 he managed to escape confinement on the Italian island of Elba and resume control of France for a final 'Hundred Days'. On 18 June 1815, his luck ran out at Waterloo in Belgium. In the opening gambit of the battle he engaged the right flank of the opposing forces in an attempt to get the enemy commander, the Duke of Wellington, to commit his reserves. Next, the fearsome French cavalry made a frontal assault on British, Dutch, and German troops on the centre right. Finally, Prussian reinforcements appeared from the left, calling, 'No quarter!' to overwhelm the French reserves. William Leeke, a Cambridge graduate who later took Holy Orders, was just seventeen years old when he fought in the battle as an ensign of the 52nd Light Infantry. He recalled in his memoirs:

> The standing to be cannonaded and having nothing else to do, is about the most unpleasant thing that can happen to soldiers in an engagement. I frequently tried to follow, with my eye, the course of the balls from our own guns, which were firing over us. It is much more easy to see a round-shot passing away from you over your head, than to catch sight of one coming through the air towards you, though this also occurs occasionally.

He lived to recount the experience, as did Napoleon, who, instead of the placid retirement in the English countryside for which he hoped after a life devoted to glory, was forced to live out his days in remote exile on St Helena.

Romanticism

If there were such a thing as a law of history, it would perhaps be that of cyclical change, according to which everything in life ends up pretty much as it started. Accordingly, the question that obsessed the Renaissance—how to read the book of nature, including the doings and dynamics of human beings—recurred to challenge the Enlightenment. By the beginning of the nineteenth century, a new sensibility had taken shape, in which tradition and innovation, Renaissance and Enlightenment, blended, resisting enslavement to reason, deferring to feelings, responding to nature, finding beauty beyond humanity in wilderness and the savage state. This sensibility took on the name of romanticism, in linkage with arts and letters that exalted individual sentiment and the creative autonomy that goes with it. The sleep of reason, for all its optimism and assurance, as the great Spanish painter Francisco Goya, pointed

THE 'PRINCE OF TRAVELLERS', Alexander von Humboldt, with his exhausted assistant, Aimé Bonpland, in their 'Jungle Hut', beside the Orinoco, painted by Éduard Ender. The jumble of specimens and scientific instruments looks almost like plunder.

out, 'produces monsters'. The monsters may be political—such as revolutions, according to Edmund Burke who fearfully beheld events in France. They may be deformations of religion, such as deism and atheism. The beginnings of mechanization in the so-called industrial revolution also produced apparent aberrations. In the early nineteenth century, the Luddite movement destroyed spinning and weaving machines that threatened to deprive operatives of work and livelihood.

Reason came up against the buffers of emotion, checked by the return to nature and ideals of romantic sublimity. Romantics favourably revalued imagination, intuition, inspiration, and even passion as guides to free and worthy conduct. They upheld the works of nature as superior to those of man. In search of the picturesque—that which is worthy of depiction—they climbed mountains, peered into volcanoes, and explored the isles, wastes, forests, and remote interiors of the world. Their encounters with nature were inseparable from their attraction to irrational or supra-rational enthusiasms, such as worship of 'völkisch' spirit or devotion to essentialist nationalism, obsessed with assumed distinctions and imagined alterity.

Yet contrary tendencies persisted, universalist in values and attracted to the strange. The Prussian 'prince of travellers', Alexander von Humboldt, was a representative figure. To write his *Kosmos*—an attempt to describe the world in its entirety—he scoured the continents. The work appeared in print bit by bit, from 1845 to 1862, aimed, in its author's words, 'to recognize unity in diversity, to comprehend all the single aspects as revealed by the discoveries of the last epochs, to judge single phenomena separately without forgoing their entirety, and to grasp Nature's essence under the cover of outer appearances'. He was not concerned merely to observe but also to understand humankind's relationship with the rest of nature. The great legacy of his times was the acknowledgement of the wisdom of the principle of the inseparability of the one from the other.

CHAPTER 10

Connected by Emotions and Experiences

Monarchs, Merchants, Mercenaries, and Migrants in the Early Modern World

ANJANA SINGH

Introduction

IN 1325, Ibn Batuta left his home town Tangier on pilgrimage to Mecca. In much of the world of the time, pilgrimage for moral and spiritual reasons was a common practice. Ibn Batuta was exceptional because, after paying obeisance, instead of returning home he decided to go further, in unalloyed curiosity, to present-day Iraq, Iran, down the Swahili Coast in East Africa, as far south as Kilwa, up again to Arabia, and enter India overland. Visiting Delhi and Gujarat, he sailed across the Arabian Sea to the Maldives and Sri Lanka. Crossing the Bay of Bengal and South China Sea, he reached Beijing. Two decades and a year later he started his return journey to Morocco. He was in no hurry. He visited southern India, the Persian Gulf, Syria, and Egypt. He finally reached Fez, his homeland, in 1349. He had been travelling for almost a quarter of a century. Not having satisfied his zeal for travelling, the following year, he journeyed to Spain. In 1351 he crossed the Sahara Desert to reach the then-Mali Empire. After spending two years there, he crossed the Sahara again, on a different route to return to Morocco, where he put his experiences on a manuscript in Arabic titled *A Gift to Those Who Contemplate the Wonders of Cities and the Marvels of Travelling*.

Ibn Batuta's life is an example of how connected the Afro-Eurasian world was in the early modern times. Historians tend to be sceptical about travel accounts, especially when only the words of the authors are available as proofs. When details are checked, contradictions abound. Yet travellers' tales help to illustrate larger issues of life, an event, a time, and a space, across frontiers and between environments, physical and cultural. Ibn Batuta's display a world where men and merchandise crisscrossed the three continents that were connected by land. When difficult terrain, like the Syrian or Arabian Desert, the Hindukush, and the Himalayan Mountains, was impossible to cross, people took to sailing in order to continue the journey. Arabia was connected to east coast Africa and west coast India. Direct sailing across the Arabian Sea made it possible to move from Africa to India. East coast India was connected to Burma and the Malay Peninsula by sailing across Bay of Bengal. Voyagers went from Malabar to the Sumatra and Java directly; others navigated the South and East China Seas. Ports cities of Mediterranean Europe, Arabia, east coast Africa, west and east coast India, Southeast Asia and China were points of conjuncture—spaces for movements to start from and where cross-cultural encounters could happen. Seas have almost always connected people. When knowledge of the earth and larger universe was limited and technology only allowed small concessions, environment, especially wind systems and natural harbours, dictated routes and timings.

From the fifteenth century onwards, Ibn Batuta's world was extended so much that it became almost unrecognizably transformed. Via new routes, navigators reached across oceans to create unprecedented, world-girdling links. When Europeans, lured by gold, set out across the Atlantic, venturing to West Africa and the Canary Islands and, finally, crossed it in hope of finding a sea route to Asia, disease and technology altered

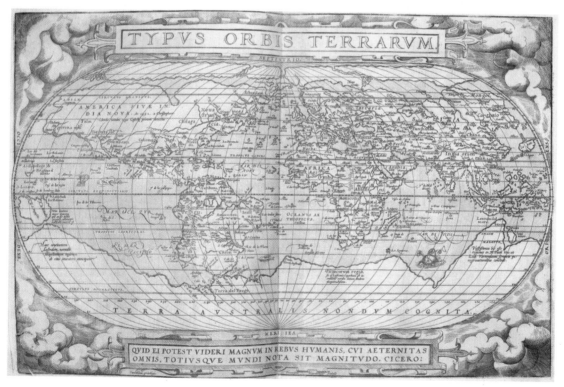

MAP OF THE WORLD FROM ABRAHAM ORTELIUS'S *Theatrum Orbis Terrarum* (Antwerp, 1570), one of the most widely reproduced images of the world as sixteenth-century Europeans pictured it. 'Can any human achievement seem great,' reads the legend from Cicero, 'when one knows the vastness and eternity of the world as a whole?'.

the dynamics of cross-cultural encounters. Commerce became routinely violent and its consequences routinely destructive. While people from West Africa were enslaved and brought to Europe, invaders crushed the cultures and identities of the native Canary Islanders, off the coast of northwest Africa. As Europeans expanded into the New World, the seas became a medium of far-projected death and destruction. Across the Atlantic, the Arawaks or Tainos of the Caribbean were almost totally destroyed. In 1498, Vasco da Gama reached India by sea. Because his ships were fitted with cannon, he could bombard native ports and ships when disagreements on terms of trade arose. Armed foreigners, invading by land, were not new to South Asia. Nor were pirates or maritime imperialists who sought to dominate selected routes or ports, but this was the first time that violence accompanied sea-borne commerce as a matter of course. When Vasco da Gama arrived in the Indian port of Calicut and later visited Cochin, he realized what a busy network of trade existed in the Asian waters. For centuries, Arab dhows, Indian ships, and Chinese junks crisscrossed and traded with the numerous ports in different corners of Asia. Cotton, silks, porcelain, precious stones, spices, sugar, grain, birds, and beasts were traded using monsoon winds that blew from southwest to northeast every summer, enabling sailing from Africa to India and beyond. Spices such as cloves, nutmeg, cardamom, cinnamon, and pepper were the world's most

ARAB DHOWS AT ANCHOR BY HENRY WARREN, with a monumental harbour entrance in the background and the crew relaxing in the foreground: a characteristic European image of the supposed fading grandeur and romantic idleness of the nineteenth-century 'Orient'.

valuable products by unit of weight. The barbarian arrivistes from Europe were poor suppliants in this enviably endowed region. According to a sixteenth-century Portuguese anecdote, when Vasco came back to Portugal after successfully reaching India by sea, the Count of Vimioso asked him what goods were there to be brought back, and what goods the people of India wanted from Portugal in exchange for them. Da Gama said to him that what was brought back from India was pepper, cinnamon, ginger, amber, and musk, and that what they wanted was gold, silver, velvet, and scarlets. The Count said to da Gama, 'So it is they who have discovered us!' In most of Asia, Westerners were more often clients than conquerors, at least until the second half of the eighteenth century. In most of the New World, they were collaborators with the indigenous people who remained masters of their own histories, even when they submitted to colonial rule.

Towards the end of the last millennium, the consensus among historians abandoned Eurocentrism, which represented the rise of the modern west in early modern times as

Naves e China et Iava velis ex arundine contextis et anchoris ligneis.

Schepen van China eñ Iava met rietten seylen eñ houten anckers

A WESTERN RENDERING OF A CHINESE OR JAVANESE JUNK from illustrations of Jan van Linschoten's pioneering late sixteenth-century Dutch study of the economies of maritime Asia—the richest in the world at the time and equipped with shipping that far exceeded European craft in tonnage. The fanciful engraver, who of course had never seen a real junk, misrepresents the shape of the vessel and gives it a tiller instead of a rudder.

an ideal model or 'miracle', to which other parts of the world had failed to conform. Instead, scholars began to reinterpret the rise of the West as a mere blip in an Asia-centred story. The centre of gravity of the world's economies—the region where the most productive and commercially active societies were located—did shift, eventually, from Asia to Europe, and from the Indian Ocean and maritime Asia to the Atlantic. But the rise of the West happened slowly and fitfully, at different rates in different areas of activity. The inruption of European traders and freighters into the Indian Ocean made it possible for Westerners to exploit the economic opportunities of the East, while the appropriation of New World resources by European powers hugely improved Westerners' access to wealth: to that extent, the rise of the West to global hegemony can be said to have started with the first establishment of Atlantic empires and trade routes in the sixteenth century. It was, perhaps, at least in retrospect, the most conspicuous feature of the history of the world in the period this chapter covers, while Westerners increasingly accumulated respect and exercised clout in much of the rest of the world. But the process was not complete until well into the nineteenth century, when new technologies and commercial and financial institutions made Western productivity, for a time, unmatchable, and Western might insuperable.

Empires of monarchs and mercenaries

In the western hemisphere, an important feature of the early modern period was the shift of traders, capital, and trading-hubs from the Mediterranean to the Atlantic. While Venice, Genoa, and Milan showed signs of decline, Lisbon, Amsterdam, and London were on the rise, attracting merchants and commodities from the formerly dominant South. The discoveries of routes back and forth across the Atlantic, coupled with Vasco da Gama's discovery of a sea route via the Atlantic to the Indian Ocean moved Europe's centre of gravity away from the Mediterranean.

Between 1492 and 1500, the path-breaking voyages of Christopher Columbus, Amerigo Vespucci, Vasco Núñez de Balboa, Pedro Álvares Cabral, and John Cabot took place. These pathfinders connected Europe to the New World, changing and connecting both sides of the Atlantic forever. Indigenous peoples occupied almost every habitable region of the Americas. Their encounters with Europeans and with the African slaves who soon followed were transforming for everyone involved.

European intruders appropriated the resources of the hemisphere by dazzlingly varied means. In some areas, where indigenous people were too divided or few or ill equipped to resist, violence—massacre, terror, genocide, mass expulsions—sufficed and settlers or slaves could replace the winnowed native labour. In most regions, however, especially among the rich and technically proficient peoples who submitted to the Spanish monarchy in the Andes and Mesoamerica, empire could work only with the help of native collaborators won over by negotiation and cajolery. The Spaniards were fortunate to operate in areas where cultures sympathetic to the stranger abounded, and where newcomers were welcome as allies, consorts, arbitrators, commercial partners, and holy men touched with the aura of a distant and divine horizon. Even where violence was least, losses of native population were stupendous, as diseases of European origin, to which natives had no natural immunity, wiped out up to ninety per cent of their number (except, for unknown reasons, in parts of what is now the US Southwest).

The intruders' most conspicuous rewards were in gold and silver. Aztec and Andean treasure mesmerized Europeans. When the newcomers exhausted the loot, they found that silver—the world's most useful medium of exchange at the time—could be mined in massive quantities, especially from deposits of unprecedented and unparalleled richness in Zacatecas, in what is now Mexico, and the 'silver mountain' of Potosí in Bolivia. But, even in regions unprivileged by silver and gold, the Americas flowed with other exploitable resources: vast reserves of timber, of furs and hides, of a new pharmacopoeia—including, most notably, tobacco and quinine—and a new fund of edible plants, especially in the forms of maize and potatoes. Above all, there was land adaptable for new activities, especially ranching and plantation framing, chiefly for sugar but also, increasingly, for tobacco and cotton, and for the support of settlers and slaves. The Tupi people of present-day Brazil suffered a severe decline in numbers, while Portuguese took over their forests and imported African slaves to set up sugar cane plantations. Trade between ports of Atlantic Europe, the west coast of Africa, and the Americas, where Latin America and the Caribbean played an important role, linked products with markets. Europe shipped arms, textiles, and wine to Africa,

IN PRE-COLONIAL MESOAMERICA, the forces that control nature were represented as clusters of divine attributes, to which personal names were given, as in this combination of solar, telluric, male, female, and shamanic components, known as Tlaltecuhtli, which missionaries, expecting indigenous religion to resemble Greek and Roman paganism, identified as a god or goddess of Earth.

THE OBA, OR RULER, OF BENIN
FLANKED by attendants in one of the
many bronze plaques that decorated
the palace walls and recorded scenes
of court life in the sixteenth century.
The inset figures are perhaps intended
as depictions of visiting Portuguese.

slaves from Africa to the Americas, and specie and raw materials from the Americas to Europe. Many made their fortunes, especially traders in sugar and slaves.

Despite the demographic disasters, new opportunities opened up for some, at least, of the indigenous survivors, if they eluded immiseration, servitude, or expulsion to marginal lands unwanted by white settlers. In the Spanish Empire, many native chiefs and communities took advantage of the new economic opportunities the Spaniards brought; some expanded existing production, especially of cacao or cochineal, for export to previously unknown markets; others engaged in new activities, raising livestock of European origin or honing manufacturing silks. Some threw in their lot with Jesuit or Franciscan missionaries in the construction of huge rural enterprises that sold surplus food and hides to settlers and traders. Others, such as the Mapuche in the southern cone and, in the eighteenth century, the Comanche of the northern plains, became imperialist entrepreneurs in their own right, exacting tribute from neighbouring peoples and payola or loot from the Spanish frontier.

The nationalist way that recorded the history of the so-called Age of Discovery and colonial empires in the nineteenth century, and for most of the twentieth, has completely changed in post-colonial times. Different perspectives and re-reading of archival material, sometimes between the lines and at others filling in archival silences with literary and visual records or oral traditions has helped us to better understand the

COCONUT-SHELL CUP, DESIGNED for chocolate and mounted in silver in seventeenth-century Mexico: a remarkable example of the economic and cultural transmutations that long-range trade effected—an artefact adapted to local taste and use but imported from across the Pacific.

nature, purposes, and shortfalls of history writing. We can now appreciate how much initiative natives retained and how much they contributed to the shaping of colonial history. Post-colonial historians analyse European efforts to negotiate with indigenous peoples the cession of their sovereignty through treaties, however fraudulent or unequal they were. An example from South Asia is the 'doctrine of subsidiary alliance', introduced by the British Governor-General Richard Wellesley between 1795 and 1805. By the late eighteenth century, power of the Mughal and Maratha Empires had weakened in the Indian subcontinent. There were many small and weak states that competed for territory and manpower. As a result, many rulers accepted the offer of British protection, which gave them security against attack by neighbours. Through a series of treaties signed by various princely states, the East India Company—the for-profit organization to which the British state devolved responsibility for India, greatly expanded its territories in the hinterland. The terms of 'alliance' forbade Indian rulers from maintaining armies. In return for 'protection' the princely states paid for the maintenance of Company's 'subsidiary forces'. When Indian rulers failed to pay, part of their territory was taken away as a penalty. In 1801, by force, rulers of Awadh and Hyderabad gave over half of their territories to the Company. Other states were forced to cede territories on similar grounds. Dutch, Spanish, Portuguese, French, and British Empires were created through comparable legal engagement with indigenous peoples, no doubt embedded in commercial and political opportunism. It was a more legitimate and economic means of appropriating indigenous sovereignties and acquiring land than were conquests or occupations.

Although indigenous collaborators could share the spoils of empire, the prevailing model of production was ruthlessly exploitative, creating racially defined underclasses, native and black, especially in regions where the colonial economy could dispense with native labour. Wherever the indigenous economy survived the conquest, Europeans tried to maximize wealth collection through brutal and excessive extraction of labour and tribute; elsewhere, expropriation was the starting point for reconfiguring the economy. Early Spanish America relied on the redistribution of native labour or tribute among Spanish 'encomenderos' for the maintenance of the settler elite, supposedly in exchange for military protection and instruction in the Catholic faith. Though the crown rapidly abandoned the system on the grounds that it depleted and discouraged the workforce, increasingly larger numbers of natives were reduced to effective peonage as land passed into the hands of Spanish and mixed-descent owners.

The political institutions of European empires overseas had to be extemporized, for want of existing models. At first, empire-builders drew heavily on the traditions of the seaborne empires of the medieval Mediterranean, which relied on viceroys and centrally appointed tribunals to balance patrician power in port cities and the ill-fettered jurisdiction of quasi-feudal palatines. Alternatively, from the end of the sixteenth century, especially in England and the Netherlands, aspects of government might be delegated to trading companies. For most European empires, which hardly expanded inland, but threaded together coastal strongholds, enclaves, and islands in an attempt to control selected trades, such methods sufficed until territorial expansion in the eighteenth century required suitable adjustments. The Spanish Empire, however, was different: a vast enterprise for controlling production as well as trade, incorporating, from the time of the acquisition of the Aztec *Grossraum* in 1521, enormous and almost ungovernably distant territories. After a period of what might be called emergency government, and always within the framework of collaboration with indigenous power-centres, a new kind of state gradually emerged: a bureaucratic state, where most offices were in the gift of the crown and where many were occupied by 'lettered' professionals; and a statute state, in which law, rather than jurisdiction, became the primary responsibility of government, as the crown churned out thousands of new laws to meet the requirements of an unprecedented society.

The seaborne empires that were a new feature of the period were lumbering giants, too big to be well articulated, stretching feeble fingertips towards their peripheries, with distant limbs ill controlled by inadequate information systems. They tottered or collapsed in the late eighteenth and early nineteenth centuries. In 1763, for want of settler-recruits, the French abandoned their attempts to create a land empire in North America. Slave rebels drove them from their Caribbean mainstay in Haiti in 1802. By then, the strain of war in Europe was beginning to weaken the Spanish and Dutch empires, which crumbled as war continued. Meanwhile, Britain, unable to sustain war against France and Spain simultaneously, lost most of its North American colonies.

A new age of what we might call industrially crafted European empires, forged with crushing industrial technology, was already beginning, but that story belongs in later chapters of this book.

In the Old World, meanwhile, empires (or states we now call empires) remained dominant: large states (in relation, at least, to those that preceded or followed them), forged by conquest and sustained at least in part by coercion, encompassing multiple communities and cultures in a single framework of allegiance or meta-identity, typically with unifying ideologies or, at least, universal pretensions. In some places, state systems were emerging alongside empires or even displacing them: in Europe, new doctrines of state sovereignty made it increasingly unlikely that anything like the Roman Empire could be resurrected. The nearest simulacrum, the Holy Roman Empire, which united much of central Europe in common but insecure allegiance to an elected overall arbiter, effectively dissolved, by stages or lurches, into its constituent parts. In Southeast Asia, where rulers aspired to a status comparable to that of a Chinese emperor, the balance of power between states centred in what are now Thailand, Myanmar, Laos, Cambodia, and Vietnam forestalled hegemony. But empires remained normative. The Ottomans, for instance, emerged at the crossroads of empire connecting the continents of Europe, Asia, and Africa. The Ottoman political formation operated in a rich and varied environment. Trade and political relations with eastern Mediterranean, central Asia, Egypt, and India became sources of wealth from which rulers created a vast and stable land and sea empire with multiple nodes that catered to long and short distance trade. The Ottomans were not an 'eastern' power that clashed with 'the west'. They had defeated and replaced the Byzantines and taken over as protectors of Christians in the Balkans. Although Ottoman notions of what an empire 'should' be owed much to their Mongol and Turkic predecessors, they also had Rome in mind—almost as much as European imperialists did. While the Spaniards were conquering the Aztecs, the Ottomans were expanding into Syria, Palestine, Egypt, and Arabia. By the mid-sixteenth century, the Ottomans had conquered one-third of Europe and half of the shores of the Mediterranean. They also considered increasing their influence on the Indian Ocean by digging what later became the Suez Canal. While the Spanish Empire moved strategically to consolidate power in the western Mediterranean and across the Atlantic Ocean, the Ottomans turned the eastern Mediterranean into a 'Turkish lake' and bade for power in the Arabian Sea. Fratricide substituted for a fixed rule of succession, as Ottoman Sultans produced rival heirs from different concubines. In Islamic law of the period, a man, depending on his resources, could have up to four wives and any number of slave concubines. Children from his marriages were legitimate and children with concubines could also receive legitimation and lay claim to the throne. If the method of succession was a source of weakness, the inconsistencies of governance were perhaps rather a source of strength: the Ottoman habit of devising a peculiar system for virtually every region or province of the empire—confiding some zones to family members or slave-nominees of the sultan, others to indigenous chiefs, and yet others to bandits or pirates—made the whole system flexible, while the universal role of the sultan as the ultimate source of justice, a complex range of tribute-levies, and the huge standing army they sustained, gave unity to the whole. In crucial ways, however, the empire adapted poorly to changing conditions. The Ottomans never sorted out the succession problem, or adapted printing as a means of making their commands known. Confined at sea by straits on every side, they could not share in the wealth European maritime empires garnered. Imperial systems of provisioning and settlement that defined Ottoman power in the 1500s could not cope with the pressures of climate change: extreme cold and drought led to the outbreak of the destructive Jelali Revolts (1519–1659). A combination of ongoing Little Ice Age climate events, nomad incursions, and rural disorder impacted the population, agriculture, animal husbandry, and economy; population stagnated, and usurpers eroded the empire at the frontiers. Slowly, in the eighteenth century the empire began to contract, forfeiting its status as the grand bogey of fear-struck Western imaginations.

While the Ottoman Sultans were Sunni Muslims, a Shiite state under the Ṣafavid dynasty (1502–1736) emerged in what is present-day Iran. The founder of the dynasty, Ismail I, was the head of the Sufis of Ardabil, and won sufficient support from local Turkmens and other disgruntled heterodox tribes to enable him to capture Tabriz from an Uzbek Turkmen confederation. In July 1501, Ismail was enthroned as Shah and he proclaimed Shiism as the state religion. In the ensuing decade he conquered the greater part of Iran and annexed the Iraqi provinces of Baghdad and Mosul. In the sixteenth century, both Ottomans and Uzbeks were constantly at war with the Safavid Empire, while Portuguese traders seized the island of Hormuz in the Persian Gulf and established fragile forts on the mainland coast. Under the rule of Shah Abbas, however, the Safavids experienced outstanding military successes and set up an efficient administrative system facilitating trade and political relations with European powers as well as the Mughal Empire. Isfahan emerged as centre of Ṣafavid art and architecture with several landmark buildings, comparable to the grandeur of neighbouring empires' capitals. As in the Ottoman and Mughal realms, Christian traders were welcome as long as they were remunerative, and, though all three empires relied on religion for legitimation, they tolerated non-Muslim communities.

Religious pluralism, however, was hard to sustain, as is clear from the case of the Mughal Empire in South Asia, east of the Safavids. Turkic-Mongol in origin, the Empire was established in 1526 by a Chagatai Turk, Zahiruddin Muhammad Babur. Babur, a native of the Fergana Valley in Central Asia and then ruler of Kabul, was invited by local nobles of Delhi to rescue them from Ibrahim Lodi, an Afghan ruler. In the ensuing 1526 Battle of Panipat, Babur, with the assistance of local people and firearm-wielding deserters from the crumbling Delhi Sultanate, killed Ibrahim Lodi. Babur was (or successfully claimed to be) a descendant of the Mongol conqueror Genghis Khan and the Turkic aspirant to world domination, Tamerlane. The Mughal Empire incorporated most of northern India and extended from the early sixteenth to the mid-eighteenth century.

The greatest of the Mughal emperors was Akbar, grandson of Babur, and to him goes the credit of consolidating the Mughal Empire. He not only annexed northern, western, and central India, but also present-day Afghanistan and parts of Bangladesh. He organized the administration and revolutionized the army. Through a system of hostage-taking and threatened vengeance, tempered by judicious appeasement and conciliatory policies, he maintained peace with conquered Hindu chiefs. The Mughal Empire had two major outlets to the sea: Gujarat and Bengal. Although maritime trade in the Arabian Sea, Indian Ocean, and Bay of Bengal had been going on for centuries, the contacts with Arabs, Africans, Burma, the Malay world, and Southeast Asia intensified owing to the peaceful situation in the hinterland. Akbar was not slow in realizing the advantages of maritime trade and port cities. After shifting court from Delhi to the newly constructed capital of Fatehpur Sikri, in 1571, he started to focus on creating pathways to the sea. One arm was Gujarat in the southwest, and the other was Bengal in the southeast. Through trade and taxation, he gained access to the riches of the traders from the Africa and Arab world as well as those from Southeast Asia. Chroniclers of the Mughal Empire maintained a narration about the grandest empire in the universe which could expand infinitely. Akbar's son Jahangir and grandson Shah Jahan furthered the empire building project and added territories as well as grand monuments like the Taj Mahal to mark their wealth and reign. Nur Jahan, one of the wives of Mughal Emperor Jahangir, was not only a beautiful and charismatic woman who used her personality, possessions, and position at court to gather power, but she also used family ties and networks, religious structures, and symbols to draw power into her hands when Jahangir became weak due to alcohol and opium addictions. Nur Jahan used religious resources for securing secular power. In the early eighteenth century, Aurangzeb annexed southern India, which brought the empire to its greatest geographic extent.

These achievements masked serious sources of weakness. Like the Ottomans, the Mughals never established rules of succession that would prevent rebellions and recurrent civil wars. They relied on ever renewed expansion to meet the costs of prior conquests—an ultimately unsustainable strategy. The stupendous growth of the elite, as native rajahs became subordinate rulers, imperilled the court aristocracy on whom the rulers relied. Above all, the contentions of the medley of religious and ethnic groups among whom the empire was divided were impossible to contain. Akbar tried to create a new, inclusive religion, but most of his successors reverted to Islam in order to secure elite adhesion, at the cost of alienating Hindus, Sikhs, Christians, and others. Climate change exacerbated the empire's difficulties. From about the seventeenth century, the Little Ice Age in the northern hemisphere that was creating problems for the Ottomans also started changing rainfall patterns in the Indian subcontinent. The substantially weakened Mughal Empire and other regional states struggled to deal with the droughts of the early eighteenth century, which the English East India Company could exploit to take over India. The subcontinent suffered devastating famines arising both out of the effects of the climate change and colonial maladministration. After Aurangzeb's demise, the empire stagnated. The region that once clothed the world started to de-industrialize, and by the mid-nineteenth century, when the British Raj took over the imperial role of the Mughals, had lost all its overseas market—partly as a result of British methods of exploitation, which were designed to favour British manufactures.

Historians commonly qualify the Mughals as 'Indian' rulers while the Portuguese remain foreigners. Factually, Portuguese Vasco da Gama arrived in 1498 and was befriended by the Raja of Cochin, after being rejected by the Zamorin of Calicut, whose port he had bombed and destroyed. Thus, the Portuguese had arrived in India a quarter of a century earlier than Babur. Both da Gama and Babur were outsiders; one came via the seas and the other overland. Both had limited manpower and financial resources, but the densely populated and rich agricultural Indo-Gangetic Valley that Babur's grandson Akbar managed to control yielded revenues and troops that helped to consolidate the Mughal Empire. At the coast, hard trade was necessary to make any profits. The Portuguese competed with Arabs and indigenous traders, and in time, they had to deal with other Europeans arriving in India.

The Portuguese, settling in littoral areas, eventually had to come to an understanding with Mughal power. From the early years of their settlement, the Portuguese sought to identify spaces of demarcation in coastal Gujarat, Bengal, and the Deccan, where dominion and frontiers were a matter of constant negotiation. Although on the fringes of the empire, the Portuguese were well aware of the contrast between Mughal imperial rhetoric emanating from the north and the actual turbulent frontier realities of the south. They relied on intriguing mechanisms of self-legitimacy, arguing that the northern white neighbours of the *Estado da Índia*, i.e. the mushrooming factories of Dutch, French, English, and Danish East India Companies, which besought the Mughals for concessions to set up factories and trade with India, were newcomers and foreigners.

Asia also housed nomad realms ruled by Mongols or Uzbeks, which maintained the traditions of medieval pastoral empires, albeit with diminishing prospects for the future, owing to the superior firepower of the sedentary states that surrounded them. In the seventeenth century, a new kind of indigenous empire—a maritime empire, not unlike those Europeans were forging at the time—arose in the Indian Ocean, where scions of the Sayyid dynasty of Oman took over outposts from the Portuguese and created their own network of loosely allied port cities. In the same period, the Japan of the Tokugawa shoguns at last began to take on the imperial character of which earlier Japanese rulers dreamed, incorporating the Ryukyu Islands and expanding by conquest into the northern extremities of the Japanese archipelago. The conquest of Khazan in 1552, and the slow, bloody, and in most respects superficial subjugation of Siberia in long campaigns from the 1550s to the 1690s, turned Muscovy into the Russian Empire. It was another in the series of vast Asian land empires, which, outside relatively small pockets of Russian agrarian settlement, was essentially a tribute-gathering enterprise, bludgeoning and extorting furs from indigenous trappers. Africa, meanwhile, though generally less stable than the empires of Eurasia, were as oppressive to their subjects and victims

MATO-TOPE, OR FOUR BEARS, DEPICTED BY KARL BODMER, the artist who accompanied Prince Maximilian zu Wied's pioneering ethnographic expedition across North America in 1832–34. Mato-Tope was a hero of Mandan resistance to Sioux imperialism in the 1830s, until the combination of smallpox and Sioux power forced the survivors out of their homeland on the Upper Missouri.

in their way as those of their Eurasian counterparts. Imperial Songhay dominated the Niger valley from its inception in the 1490s, until it was conquered in turn by one of the most spectacular imperial adventurers of the age: Mulay Hassan of Morocco, who sent armies across the Sahara, much as Spain sent them across the Atlantic. Ethiopia, Africa's oldest empire, survived Muslim challenges and clumsy (and ultimately subversive) Portuguese attempts to 'help'. Native states under Portuguese influence in the Zaire valley grew to imperial dimensions and shrank at intervals at alarming rates. Between the Limpopo and the Zambezi, the empire of Mwene Mutapa—adept at garnering salt, gold, slaves, civet, and elephants—resisted all attempts at conquest from outside, but gradually succumbed to enfeeblement at the centre and erosion at the edges. In the West African bulge, states materialized that were, if not imperial, militarized and predatory, dedicated to supplying white slavers with war-captives. In the Americas, where demand for native slaves was relatively small, indigenous empires responded to a different kind of European influence: the introduction of horses. The Comanche and Mapuche could literally mount expeditions over vast areas of their flatlands. The last great indigenous empire of the Americas rivalled white imperialism in the nineteenth-century North American prairie, when the Sioux moved out of their traditional woodlands and uplands on horseback to terrorize tributaries.

Impressive as some of these achievements were, in scale if not in moral worth, no empire of the early modern period could match China: the richest, the most product-ive, the most populous and—for other empires of east and southeast Asia—the most exemplary. The Ming dynasty, which succeeded the Mongol Yuan in China, were one of the most stable yet autocratic of all Chinese dynasties. They abandoned expansion in favour of Confucian quiescence; but in the first half of the seventeenth century, they forfeited the confidence of many of their subjects by mismanaging the effects of climate change, which racked the empire with famine and plague. The Qing or Manchu dynasty—unruly clients of the Ming who first made the emperors their dependants, and then their dupes—seized supreme power in the 1640s. Together, the Ming and Qing Empires shaped early modern China. In the sphere of state administration, the Ming perfected the civil service system. It became stratified with almost the entire top level of Ming officials entering the bureaucracy after passing a regulated competitive government examination called the *jinshi*, held at Beijing. The Yushitai, a censorate office designed to investigate official misconduct and corruption, was a separate organ of the government. Three agencies handled affairs in each province, each reporting to separate bureaux in the central government. The position of prime minister was abolished, and instead, the emperor took over personal control of the government, ruling with the assistance of the especially appointed Neige, or Grand Secretariat.

From Europe to Ming and Qing China, a common strand connected the early modern empires. They all went through what historians describe as the Military Revolution, caused by introduction of light and handy firearms. Since men had to be trained in the usage of these firearms, a system of maintaining developed. This was a major difference from the Turkic and Mongol empires of the Middle Ages, which disbanded armies once their conquests were accomplished. Standing armies put more power in the hands of monarchs; the armies repelled external enemies and supressed internal revolts. Their maintenance required a constant supply of money, creation of new organizational institutions, and bureaucratization of the administrative set-up. Increasing bureaucracy assisted by usage of paper also connected these political formations.

Courts, bureaucracies, and legislatures

Balthazar Gerbier was born in 1592 in Middelburg in the Dutch Republic to parents of Huguenot refugees. His life and times throw light on migration and political relations between early modern states as well as patron–client relations that crossed cultural or linguistic boundaries. Balthazar was an artist, and while trained as a calligrapher and engraver, he preferred to follow a political career. Gerbier worked as a skilled miniaturist and draughtsman, and won favour with Prince Maurits of Orange, under whose instructions he accompanied the Dutch ambassador, Noël de Caron, to London in 1616. There, he used his knowledge of art and expertise in penmanship, architecture, and drawing to further his political profession. George Villiers, Duke of Buckingham, appointed him curator of the ducal art collection in York House. He introduced his patron to Peter Paul Rubens, with whom he would later forge an informal partnership brokering diplomatic and artistic deals at the same time. With time, Gerbier received additional responsibilities for a variety of administrative and political tasks, and in his numerous autobiographical accounts, he summed up his heterogeneous offices as the duke's cultural and political agent. His skills of using his pen and knowledge, in his own words, included 'mathematics, architecture, drawing, painting, contriving of scenes, masques, shows and entertainment for great princes, besides many secrets which I had gathered from diverse rare persons'. Possibly a spy for his patron, Gerbier established himself as an influential artistic and political advisor in court circles. In 1631, King Charles appointed him as his official resident in Brussels. Thus, a Dutchman of French Huguenot birth represented the English in Europe. Later, Gerbier was knighted and called back to England to serve as Master of Ceremonies to the king.

A decade later in 1651, an anonymous 'authority' published a vicious attack on the late King Charles I of England: *None-Such Charles His Character: Extracted, Out of Divers Originall Transactions, Dispatches and The Notes of Severall Publick Ministers, and Councellors of State As Wel At Home As Abroad* claimed to enlighten its readers on the corrupt regime of the former monarch. This piece of work, although anonymous, was attributed to Balthazar Gerbier, who denounced his former life as royal favourite and sought favour with the new republican regime in England. Fluctuating empathies earned him few friends, but his skill and knowledge ensured that his contemporaries in the political arena could not ignore him. Many perceived him as untrustworthy, but Gerbier saw it differently: '[He] yields to nobody in the world in fidelity and disposition, which were born with him, and he has given signal proofs that in secrecy he yields to nobody in the world.' Balthazar Gerbier was not alone in his prudence.

Anthony Shirley is a further example of a life led in the courts of Eurasia by an individual who played roles and chose political partners based on pragmatism rather than ideas of nationality and patriotism. Educated at the University of Oxford, Anthony Shirley undertook various assignments in the Netherlands and France and expeditions along the west coast of Africa and across to Central America. In 1598, he led a group of English volunteers to Italy to participate in a dispute over the possession of Ferrara, from where he journeyed to Persia with the idea of promoting trade between England and Persia. He also aimed at provoking the Persians to undertake war against the Ottoman Turks. Well received by Shah Abbas, he received the title of Mirza, or prince, secured trading rights for Christian merchants, and helped in the training of the army. He returned to Europe as the Shah's representative, and visited Moscow, Prague, and Rome, among other cities. Thus, an Englishman was a representative of the Ottomans in European Courts. The English considered him a traitor. Anthony's imprisonment in 1603 by King James I caused the English House of Commons to assert one of its privileges, the freedom of its members from arrest, in a document known as *The Form of Apology and Satisfaction*. In 1605, when Shirley was in Prague, Rudolph II, the Holy Roman Emperor, gave him the title of Count and sent him on a mission to Morocco. The envoy then travelled to Lisbon and to Madrid, where the King of Spain welcomed him warmly and appointed him admiral of an exploratory fleet. Having worked for at least four different heads of states, he saw loyalty as part of the job. Men like Balthazar Gerbier and Anthony Shirley were loyal to any patron who paid them. Their changing allegiance, not limited by place of birth, cultural identity, religion, or language, was a direct consequence of their profession as a political agent or broker. Cross-cultural diplomacy increased between the fifteenth and eighteenth centuries among the states of Europe and Asia: e.g. Dutchman Joan Cunaeus visited the court of Safavid Shah Abbas II, and his countryman Dircq van Adrichem led an embassy to the court of Mughal emperor Aurangzeb; the English diplomat Sir Thomas Roe visited the court of Mughal Emperor Jahangir. Making use of elites who could cross borders and span cultures, exchanges of ambassadors and gifts took place with growing frequency among the Afro-Eurasian states.

Indian monarchs, like many rulers at that time, used to hold courts to meet ministers and ambassadors. Beginning with Humayun (Babur's heir), in order to connect with their subjects, Mughal Emperors used balconies, an old Hindu practice. Apart from that connection, their appearances in public, called jharokha darshan (literally, 'balcony audience') were also a way of abating rumours of sickness, fragility, coups, and deaths. Jharokha darshan usually happened in capital cities at forts and palaces, but if the monarch was expanding the empire or inspecting regions, two-storied portable wooden houses known as do-ashiayana manzil were used to display the monarch to subjects and armies. Several paintings of the Mughal School depict emperors

MAHARAJA BAKHT SINGH OF MARWAR AND JODHPUR at his palace window in 1737. He was one of the recalcitrant vassals whose rebelliousness and withholding of tribute helped to bring the Mughal Empire to virtual collapse, humiliated by Persian invaders in 1739 and reduced to dependence on the power of the British East India Company.

THE ARTIST JOHAN ZOFFANY WAS PROBABLY an eye-witness of the famous cock-fight in 1784 between Colonel John Mordaunt's British-bred bird and the indigenous champion, owned by the ruler of Oudh. The painting could be taken as an analogue of the conquest of India, but shared sports were a means for British and native elites to forge friendships and political collaborations.

during such epiphanies. At the Delhi Durbar of 1911, following the tradition, King George V and Queen Mary appeared in a balcony of the Red Fort, thereby etching themselves in the public memory of a very long list of rulers of the Indian subcontinent.

The early modern period also saw the emergence of legislatures, the branch of a government that concerns itself with law-making. While earlier the law was dictated by the monarch within an immutable body of tradition, the nature of law-making changed gradually from the fourteenth century onwards, as change accelerated and statutes multiplied to meet it. In the fourteenth and fifteenth centuries, in a development paralleled elsewhere in the West, English monarchs introduced law through royal charters, but members of parliament could also initiate legislation through debate and petitions, later called bills. More fundamental, however, than the growing role of representative assemblies in making and unmaking law was a shift in the very concept of sovereignty—definable in the Middle Ages as the absolute right to pronounce justice, but increasingly understood in the sixteenth century, at least in Europe, as the absolute right to legislate.

Conflicts over who should exercise the right became commonplace, as theorists squabbled over whether monarchs' power depended directly on God or was mediated through the people and their representatives. During the English Civil War, the

Parliament became a revolutionary body as well as the centre of resistance to the king, and emerged with powers that ranged from representing the population to passing laws, overseeing the government's budget, ratifying treaties, and impeaching members of the executive and judiciary, when needed. In 1776, when the union of the thirteen American colonies declared independence from Britain, the Patriot governments unanimously vested the powers to do so in Congress; afterwards, the United States of America was established under a presidential system in which law-making is, with marginal exceptions, the unique prerogative of the representative assembly. Broadly speaking, this model, which the Founding Fathers developed from French and English political theorists of the previous hundred years, has become a pattern for most of the world.

Along with fledgling constitutionalism, a new doctrine of rights began to transform political discourse in the West. In part, this was a development of a medieval doctrine of 'the community of mortals', bound by common moral obligations. But the practical effects of cross-cultural contacts that displayed the vast and varied panoply of human-kind before European eyes were alchemical, transmuting a vague criterion for estab-lishing membership of a moral community into a gold standard. Bartolomé de Las Casas, born in 1484, was the first to expose the European oppression of Latin American indigenous peoples. After a conversion experience, which led him to the priesthood as a Dominican and ultimately to a bishopric, he persuaded the Spanish crown to redouble efforts to enshrine in law the right of their indigenous American subjects to equality with Spaniards. His arguments were not primarily practical—though he did appeal to the monarchs' interest in conserving the lives of economically useful 'vassals'—but rather moral, based on the assertion that there were no inherent differ-ences of superiority or inferiority between manifestly human groups. Although his efforts led to only modest practical changes, in 1550 Las Casas represented the causes of the indigenous people in a debate held in Valladolid, Spain. He questioned the moral status of the Spanish conquest of America. He argued against the idea that the indigenous people were naturally inferior to Europeans and therefore must be enslaved and civilized. A prolific writer, in 1552, he published *A Brief Account of the Destruction of the Indies*, denouncing Spaniards who exploited or abused natives. Published in several editions in Spanish, it saw three editions in Latin, three in Italian, four in English, six in French, eight in German, and eighteen in Dutch.

Though often honoured in the breach, the notion that there are 'inalienable human rights' gradually permeated enlightened discourse. The discovery of 'noble savages' in the Americas and the South Seas disposed European thinkers to ennoble the 'common man' and even to entrust him with power (although when received in the French Revolution, the common man abused it, inducing reactions in favour of authoritarian politics in the nineteenth century). Meanwhile, individualism—a doctrine of disputed origin, according to which the rights of the individual precede and trump those of society collectively—increasingly contended with organic conceptions of the 'social contract', according to which individuals forfeited their rights to the ruler or to the state. In 1776, the US Declaration of Independence, drafted by Thomas Jefferson, embodied the language of individual rights; it became the model for revolutionary manifestoes all over the world.

In 1833, Great Britain outlawed slavery, after decades of struggle by British politician and philanthropist William Wilberforce, who had been publicly calling for abolition since 1787. Abigail Kelley Foster was an American feminist, abolitionist, and lecturer who is remembered as an impassioned speaker for radical reform. Popularly known as Abby Kelley, she was a Quaker from birth, educated in Quaker schools, and had a teaching career in a Quaker school in Lynn, Massachusetts. She became a follower of William Lloyd Garrison and in 1835–37 was secretary of the Lynn Female Anti-Slavery Society. In 1838 she joined Garrison in founding the New England Non-Resistant Society. She took part in the first and second woman's national anti-slavery conventions in New York City in 1837 and in Philadelphia in 1838. On 31 January 1865, the US Congress passed the thirteenth amendment, which abolished slavery in the United States; it was ratified on 6 December 1865, and provides that 'neither slavery nor involuntary servitude, except as a punishment for crime whereof the party shall have been duly convicted, shall exist within the United States, or any place subject to their jurisdiction'. Although Brazil had outlawed the slave trade in 1850, smuggling of new slaves into Brazil continued until the enactment of emancipation laws in 1888.

Empires also helped breed a new kind of politics, concerned with the management of what we should now call the environment—the sustainable exploitation of exotic Edens, the conservation of exploitable resources, including forests, soils, and the products of the hunt. Detailed and exact descriptions of natural things, like tides and eclipses, seasons and wind patterns, flora and fauna, circulated around the world. New information and insights poured into Europe from Asia, Africa, and the Americas. The mercantilist motivations of maximizing profits also enabled thorough examination of myriad plants, objects, etc., in hope of finding possibilities for profit. In the eighteenth-century field of knowledge, the science of ecology took root, which was different from nature, although linked to it. The eighteenth-century work of Carolus Linnaeus represented an 'imperial' view. He was the key ecological figure of the age and epitomized man's dominion over nature through reason and understanding. Nature was not God's puzzle, but rather something to be dominated by understanding its principles.

Rival attitudes contended on imperial frontiers. The thoughts of indigenous Americans on nature were quite different. One Native American scholar has summed it up in the phrase, 'The land is . . . not a means of survival, a setting for our affairs . . . It is rather a part of our being, dynamic, significant, real. It is our self.' Similarly, Australian aboriginals' environmental philosophy was related to their being observers, knowers, and users, rather than managers and interferers. This approach was the essence of their genius, enabling them to survive successfully for over 40,000 years. Their philosophy could be described as non-materialistic eco-centrism, expressed through totemism, dreaming, and the law, contrasting markedly with European materialistic anthropocentrism. The Quran, the sacred text of Islam, contains the affinity of nature and ethics: Marshall

G. Hodgson epitomized the Islamic commitment as 'the demand for personal responsibility for the moral ordering of the natural world'. The Islamic rationale for an ecological ethics rests on the Quranic notions of *khalīfa* (trustee) and *amānat* (deposit). Islam accepts Nature as a gift of God to man, and as an estate over which we have temporary control, but no sovereign authority.

None of these notions, nor comparable assertions of the sacrality of nature in Daoist and Shinto traditions, nor the practical arguments urged by conservationists in Europe and Japan who saw the need to ensure the sustainability of key resources, could halt the economic imperatives that drained marshes, felled forests, and hunted threatened species to extinction—a seemingly irreversible trend toward more intensive human control and use of land and the natural environment. Humans found access to previously unknown and unused natural resources that improved life and standards of living. Technological inventions and innovations, especially in maritime transport and later industrial production, raised economic output. But accelerating productivity came at an incalculable cost. Demands for natural resources, like coal and cultivable land, escalated as human population nearly doubled, from 400 to 500 million in 1500 to perhaps about 900 million in 1800. As numbers grew, so did the pressures on the natural world. In Afro-Eurasia and in the New World, states and private entrepreneurs aimed to maximize productivity of their lands. Early modern states protected and promoted those who brought increasingly more land and other natural resources under the control of the state. The state support, through capital investment and recognizing of pioneers as national heroes and entrepreneurs, led to biological invasions and shattering of regional ecosystems around the world. Intricate, complex, and diverse assemblages of vegetation and fauna were affected due to human intervention. Numerous species became extinct. Pioneer settlers, especially in America and Africa, encountered an abundance of wild animals, birds, and fish that could be readily slaughtered, eaten, or skinned for their hides. The idea of abundance and unlimited natural resources created a windfall mind-set in frontier societies. When settlers depleted the food, energy, and materials sources, they could simply move on to new, 'untouched' resources available merely by appropriation. For example, during the seventeenth century, the Netherlands shifted from wood to peat as its primary source of energy. The Dutch developed new methods for extracting, processing, carrying, and burning peat. Usage of canals for transportation meant low prices and high availability. But, by the late eighteenth century, the Dutch began to reach the limits of their domestic supply of peat. Coal burning proved to be the way out of the energy impasse. Britain was the first society in the world to substitute fossil fuel for biomass as its primary source of energy. By 1800, coal was the leading domestic and industrial fuel in the British Isles. The combination of coal, steam, and iron resulted in the Industrial Revolution; the increasing use of fossil fuels has damaged the environment, resulting in the challenge of how to boost economic growth without harming the planet permanently. The ultimate test, perhaps, of our emergent global society and its connectedness is how we manage ourselves and our biosphere.

Cultural contacts and social changes

Imperialism was not an exclusively white vice, nor was the abuse of religion to justify it. Only Christendom, however, produced a divided missionary class in which some zealots spearheaded or supported empire, while others challenged it in search of a peaceable kingdom. One consequence was the prevalence of martyrdom. Many Christian missionary workers left Europe for distant lands, hungry for self-sacrifice, well aware that they might never again see family and homeland. In Spanish Mexico, Friar Agustín Rodríguez accompanied two other priests into the upper Rio Grande region in 1581 to convert the Pueblo Indians to Christianity. The three men lived there for over a year without any military support or contact with Spanish authorities. Fearing harm would come to the priests, a rescue party, headed by Captain Antonio de Esteván Espejo, travelled down the Conchos River from San Bartolomé and then up the Rio Grande. Establishing contact with the Pueblo Indians of Zuni, Acoma (present-day New Mexico), Espejo later visited the Hopi at their settlements in present-day Arizona. In 1583 he reported that the Indians had killed three priests. He also brought back reports of gold and silver deposits in northern New Mexico and Arizona, which provided the basis for exploratory expeditions into the southwest in the late 1590s. Gold, glory, and God remained important incentives to move to different parts of the world. Leaving Europe was considered heroic and enterprising.

Zeal for martyrdom and the desire to outflank empire in pursuit of spiritual conquests were overwhelmingly Catholic ambitions. Outside Catholic contexts, when disease did not exterminate indigenous populations, religious rhetoric was used as a substitute. An extreme but not unrepresentative case was that of Cotton Mather (1663–1728), a Harvard-educated historian and church leader who argued in favour of Indian extermination. Born in Boston, he joined his father, Increase Mather, as minister at Boston's North Church. Father and son took to writing on historical and religious matters. Cotton Mather published in 1702 an ecclesiastical history of New England, *Magnalia Christi Americana*, where he argued that it was futile to attempt to Christianize and civilize Indians. Characterizing Indians as a manifestation of the Ten Lost Tribes of Israel, who had been led to North America by Satan, and their native rituals as displays of evil, Mather argued for their complete extermination on religious grounds. He shocked his milder contemporaries, but the prevailing attitude of white settlers to natives in North America remained frankly genocidal throughout our period.

A vital criterion for belonging to a community is the expression of willingness to play by its rules. In order to assimilate, it was necessary to incorporate the markers of dominant culture in a hybrid identity. In consequence, empires were at once destructive of existing traditions and creative of mixed communities, hybrid cultures, creole languages, syncretic religions, extemporized polities, and new ways of life. Meanwhile, in settler societies and in Europe, the public sphere expanded. More people than ever before discussed and analysed matters of state in clubs, coffee houses, salons, print media, and within political parties, and across an increasingly wide swathe of rank and education.

What people knew was related to where they lived. Europeans in the early modern period, if they thought about it, saw themselves in a moral community of Christian and civilized states which abided by the principles of *ius gentium*—the law of natural reason—which limited and regulated warfare. Although considerations of interest often overruled moral and legal principles of war, one thing was common to all wars within Europe (and, by a quirk of collective conscience, perhaps, all Spanish wars everywhere): the states involved always sought to prove publicly, verbally, and in writing, that they were waging just war. Printed pamphlets and brochures facilitated spread of information. Legitimations of war added to the formation of a European identity. In 1700, for instance, Peter the Great's campaign of public legitimation of Muscovy's attack on Sweden was part of his quest for gaining acknowledgement of Russia within the European moral, legal, and political community.

The public sphere grew in a globalizing world—in the sense of a world in which formerly sundered peoples learned ever more about each other, as trade and migration crisscrossed oceans and continents. Because Europeans dominated long-range shipping, the data banks of the age, so to speak, were concentrated in the West. It is estimated that 85 per cent of all migrants in the early modern period were Europeans; however, that figure overlooks coerced or enforced migrations, including vast, ill-documented movements of Chinese (mainly Fujianese) workers and sojourners into southeast Asia, Chinese peasants into Manchuria and Central Asia, Japanese exiles and economic migrants scattered from Burma to Borneo, Native American expulses and fugitives from white conquests, and great displacements of peoples in Africa and south and Southeast Asia as a result of war or at rulers' behests. Above all, slavery on an unprecedented scale to meet colonial labour needs transformed the early modern world's distribution of population. A Portuguese explorer who visited the west coast of Africa and ventured beyond Cape Bojador estimated that between 1434 and 1448, his compatriots had transferred around 927 men from Africa to Portugal to be sold as slaves: it was the first phase of a movement that removed about 20 million people from Africa by the time the trade subsided towards the end of the nineteenth century. Considerable numbers perished in the appalling conditions of the Atlantic passage. The autobiographical account of the West African Olaudah Equiano, published in 1789, is well known for its detailed descriptions of the sufferings endured on these transatlantic voyages. But, like oppressed indigenes who sustained continuities of their traditional civilization across the trauma of conquest, slaves did not surrender initiatives over their own lives. They developed new lifeways of their own devising on their plantations—including new institutions of self-government in the masters' shadows, new religions (which often combined fragments of Christianity with reminiscences of African deities), new music on extemporized instruments, and new languages (usually adapted from those of European owners to provide a means of communication among slaves of diverse provenance). Escapees founded maroon kingdoms, sometimes in alliance with native communities, and defended them for generations as independent enclave-states enclosed by or neighbouring white-ruled empires.

Individual contacts, animated by emotions as much as by impersonal economic forces, can in favourable circumstances have cultural consequences as great as those of mass migrations. In 1534, for instance, on the Gaspé Peninsula of present-day Quebec, Chief Donnaconna and a party of Huron, on a trip to hunt seals, met French explorer Jacques Cartier, who was seeking twin illusions: riches and a short route to Asia. Donnaconna was persuaded to allow his two sons to travel with the expedition as guides. They sailed with Cartier back to France and returned the next year, showing him the way to the Huron homeland. In 1535, the Cartier expedition was anchored in the St Lawrence River near the Huron village of Stadacona, present-day Quebec City, and Donnaconna was re-united with his sons. From Stadacona, Cartier continued up the St Lawrence to the Huron village of Hochelaga, present-day Montreal. Back at Stadacona, Cartier, who wanted Donnaconna to help him win patronage for further expeditions, had his men take the Huron chief forcefully on board. Although at first resisting, Donnaconna agreed to go with the expedition when Cartier promised to return him to his homeland within a year. Donnaconna made a speech from the deck of the ship to his warriors and sent them away before sailing with a few other men to France. He was presented to King Francis I. He and his men soon contracted European diseases and died. But before dying, they had done their job. Cartier received funding for future explorations. Cartier's three expeditions along the St Lawrence River would later enable France to lay claim to the lands that would become Canada.

Early modern European impact on Indian ports was most visible in the individual social connections established between Europeans and indigenous people. Several Europeans who migrated to India in early modern times assimilated into the Indian social milieu through marriage. Their life histories demonstrate that 'East' and 'West' did reconcile. They mingled as equals—as traders, but also through familial relationships that cut across cultural and linguistic barriers. In the Indian ports, over the centuries, the growing presence of Europeans and intermarriage between individuals of different communities led to the creation of new communities like the Indo-Portuguese, the Indo-Dutch, and the Anglo-Indians. The Portuguese freely married Indian women, be they Hindus or Muslims. Mixed marriages became a necessity as few European women undertook the long, harsh, and hazardous sea voyage to Asia. Portuguese became the lingua franca for cross-cultural communications.

The results of settlement overseas were at least as transformative—often more so— for European or African newcomers as for their indigenous neighbours. From the early decades of the sixteenth century until the early nineteenth century, European presence remained on the coastal regions of Asia. Their economic, political, and social existence was marginal compared to the hinterland political economies. Marxist and neo-Marxist historians play up the primary extraction of surplus that the companies could most efficiently extract without bothering about the expenses of administering the territories. Detailed research on various port cities of Asia as well as economic history of Asia and Europe has revealed that the Europeans actually underwent a protracted and often conflicting process of survival in Asian ports during early modern times. For most of our period they depended on local goodwill and when they forfeited it—as the Portuguese and Spaniards found to their cost in much of East Africa, the Persian Gulf, China, Japan, and much of southeast Asia—they could not continue. However, in the second half of the eighteenth century, European enclaves expanded inland via conquest in search of enhanced security or new revenues. The balance of military power was unresolved in Westerners' favour until the nineteenth century, when industrialization boosted white firepower, speeded white transport, and equipped whites with supplies and medication appropriate for the tropics. The best long-term strategy for survival, meanwhile, was to 'go native'. Dutchmen who arrived in the East as merchants, metamorphosed into rijstafel-eating landlords. In the Americas, 'creole' identities, unique to settlers and their descendants, were among the consequences. In Mesoamerica and the Andes, where eighteenth-century painters proudly displayed the racial and cultural heterogeneity of a hybrid civilization, an elite emerged consisting of individuals of diverse racial provenance in a shared identity—adorned in portraits with native plumage—to which Spain was foreign. Even in the British colonies, where fraternization with natives was rare, a new 'American' identity took shape, and stimulated the rebellion of 1776 that separated most of the mainland colonies from the mother country.

Meanwhile, as Islam expanded eastward from the Middle East to South and Southeast Asia, it was received by cultures vastly different from the region of its birth. From Arabia to India, Malaysia, Indonesia, and Philippines, a diverse global community came into being. Apart from religious belief, literature brought the community together. Between the sixteenth and twentieth centuries the *Book of One Thousand Questions* was translated and adapted from its Arabic original to Javanese, Malay, and Tamil. It uses a question and answer conceit between the Prophet Muhammad and the Jewish leader Abdullah Ibn-u Salam in seventh-century Arabia, and portrays the latter's journey from doubt to conviction that ultimately leads him to embrace Islam. The book connected Muslims across divides of language, distance, and culture. The history of the translations, reading, and circulation of this Islamic text demonstrates its varied literary forms and how processes of literary translation and religious conversion were historically interconnected. Texts became agents of connectedness—another form of globalization. The early modern characteristic of agents or brokers who transmitted or disseminated political, intellectual, and cultural ideas has, in recent years, received some scholarly attention, notably in the context of patron–client relationships.

By the late eighteenth century, Asian men started—or resumed—travel westwards in significant numbers. An Urdu couplet, translated into English, showcased ideas of that time: 'Let the Sheikh depart to Kaaba; I'd rather go to London; For he intends to see God's house, I God's glory.' One of the earliest Urdu travel accounts is that of Yusuf Khan Kambalposh, literally 'the one who wears a blanket', symbolizing mendicancy. He travelled through Europe and North Africa in the 1830s, not seeking fortune but driven solely by the urge to explore a world far removed from his own in north India. Comparing Lucknow with London, he wrote 'Lucknow is still fine as there is some innovation and craftsmanship here. But it does not even come close to the innovative abilities, trade and craftsmanship' that he had seen in England. Describing the Industrial Revolution, he stated, 'The British have machines to make iron canons, guns, swords, paper, cloth, and so on, and produce thousands of identical items in a moment. Here in India, no one has any clue about such inventions.' In November 1837, Kambalposh went to Baker Street to see Madame Tussaud's wax museum. He saw statues of Shakespeare, Lord Byron, Walter Scott, and the newly crowned Queen Victoria, as well as of Russian kings and pirates. Present-day travellers, insensitized to sensation, may find it hard to recapture the awe, astonishment, and disbelief that Kambalposh recounted. Other travellers to the west included Mirza Abu Taleb Khan, who lived between 1752 and 1806; his near contemporary, Dean Mahomed; Lutfullah, who undertook a voyage to Europe in 1765, and Munshi I'Tasamuddin, who travelled to Europe between 1766 and 1769. Through the broader reading of this genre of travel accounts, a sense of Occidentalism appears—an exoticizing image of the West, alive with emotions comparable to those of the Europeans who travelled eastwards.

Such reconfigured and enlarged accounts of the world fed a public sphere that was a largely male space. But it was open, so to speak, to female colonization. In the West,

'THE MARKET PLACE AT LUCKNOW', BY WILLIAM CARPENTER (1818–99), who travelled in India in the 1850s to take advantage of the English market for exotic scenes of the diversity and desirability of India.

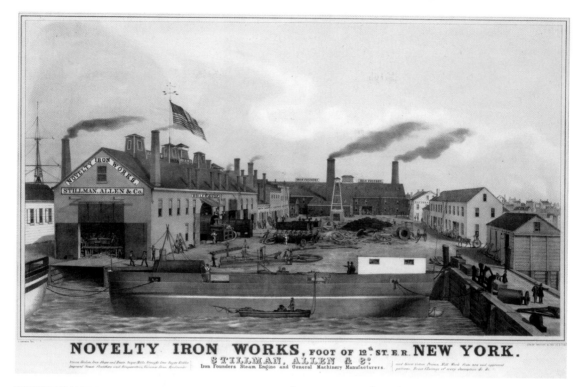

NOVELTY IRON WORKS, FOOT OF 12ᵗʰ ST. E.R. NEW YORK.
STILLMAN, ALLEN & C°.
Iron Founders Steam Engine and General Machinery Manufacturers.

INDUSTRIALIZATION IN THE WEST ACCOMPANIED the extinction of much traditional Indian industry. Outside Europe, only the US and, later, Japan seemed able to compete. John Penniman proudly depicted New York's Novelty Iron Works in 1841 in a painting on which this contemporary hand-coloured lithograph was based.

female status was transformed. In Padua in northern Italy in the 1550s, the anatomist Gabriele Falloppio sliced open female cadavers and found that they worked in unsuspected ways. Women were not just nature's bungled attempts to make males, as earlier medical theory claimed. Female rulers appeared in unprecedented numbers in Europe. Some, like the doughty Catherine de' Medici (1519–1589), Regent of France, used political arts to manipulate men, while others, like the flighty Mary, Queen of Scots (r. 1512–1567), re-enacted in their lives cautionary tales of the biblical Eve: submitting to lovers or favourites. To Mary's almost exact contemporary, the Scots Protestant preacher John Knox women in power were a 'monstrous' aberration. Most women rulers earned praise for what Elizabeth I of England (r. 1558–1603) called her 'heart and stomach of a king': in other words, men praised women for ruling like men. There were parallels beyond Europe. In the 1640s, Queen Nzinga of Ndongo, in the Zaire valley, announced that she would 'become a man'. Similarly, women ruled Aceh in Sumatra for most of the seventeenth century by dexterously juggling notions of gender.

ONE OF THE MOST REDOUBTABLE power-women of the early modern world, Catherine II, Empress of Russia, portrayed in imperious style—who could also look quirky, coquettish, and martial when she wished—by Vigilius Eriksen, the Danish court painter whom Catherine recruited in 1757.

In ordinary homes in Europe, struggles between different forms of Christianity gave new importance to women's traditional domain—as the guardians of household routine. Mothers were the hearthside evangelists who transmitted simple religious faith and devotional practice from one generation to the next. Their choices ensured, in some places, the survival of Catholicism, and in others, the rapid progress of Protestantism. In the interests of their own power, clergies enforced strict marriage discipline. A side effect was to protect women against male predators and secure their property when their husbands died. In late seventeenth-century Massachusetts, Puritan preacher Cotton Mather believed women were morally superior beings, because of their constant fear of death in childbirth.

There could, however, be no corresponding increase in what feminists today call women's 'options'. New economic opportunities on a sufficient scale were unavailable until industrialization. Widowhood remained the best option for women who wanted freedom and influence. The most remarkable feature of this situation, which might have tempted wives to murder, is that so many husbands survived it. In most of sixteenth- and seventeenth-century Europe, husbands committed more detected domestic murders than wives. And women, despite their improved status, were still often victims—beaten by husbands, scolded by confessors, repressed by social rules, and cheated by the courts.

Individualism helped. If all men are naturally equal, what about women? Montesquieu saw no reason to exclude them. The ideas we now call feminism—that women collectively constituted a class of society, historically oppressed and deserving of emancipation—appeared in two works of 1792, the *Declaration of the Rights of Woman and of the Female Citizen* by Marie-Olympe de Gouges, and *A Vindication of the Rights of Woman* by Mary Wollstonecraft. Both authors had to struggle to earn their living, led irregular sex lives, and died tragically: Wollstonecraft in childbirth in 1797 at the age of 38, and De Gouges in 1793 during the French Revolution—guillotined for defending the king and queen of France. 'Women may mount the scaffold,' she said, 'they should also be able to ascend the bench.' Both writers rejected the entire previous tradition of female championship, which praised women for their domestic and maternal virtues. Instead, they admitted women's vices and blamed male oppression.

Children, though ill qualified for equality, did assume a new status and importance while these changes were in progress. In Europe, those born with challenges lived in special institutions where the focus was on 'repairing' disabled bodies so that they may be 'useful to themselves and the community'. In the 1770s, the London Foundling Hospital initiated apprenticeships to understand and measure the possible potential of the disabled child. It was built upon the notion that any child, regardless of infirmity, needed to be afforded the opportunity to progress from the dependence of childhood to the independence of adulthood.

The effort to domesticate 'feral' children—self-reared orphans or foundlings nurtured by wolves—became an eighteenth-century obsession. Meanwhile, in South Africa, Indonesia, and Australia, Europeans were forcefully taking away children of the indigenous people to 'protect them from savagery' and give them basic education that included Christianity. There was presumed malleability and plasticity of native children which allowed the possibilities of educating and 'civilizing' them. The experiences of indigenous children in missionary infant schools demonstrate that education was vital to colonialism. The 'civilizing' mission was a means of disciplining 'othered' children and maintaining systems of colonial social power. Institutionalized colonial education was key in civilizing indigenous children and transforming their 'heathen', 'aboriginal' lives. It served the triple purpose of harvesting people educated in basic language of the colonizer in order to work in the lower levels of colonial bureaucracy, making Christianity global, as well as creating native missionaries who perhaps would have a better chance of converting the masses. These were gendered projects that focused on the participation of missionary wives, female teachers, wives of colonial administrators, and others aiming to forge uniform ideas of cultural, social, and political identities from childhood.

But moulding children did not necessarily lead to estrangement from one's own people. The great female warrior known as 'Woman Chief' is a case in point. She was born in the Gros Ventre tribe of the central American plains in the early years of the nineteenth century. At the age of ten, the Crow tribe captured her, and, following tribal custom, adopted her; her adoptive father encouraged her to use bow and arrow, shoot a gun, and hunt on horseback and on foot. She grew to be a tall and strong markswoman and a proficient buffalo killer. Her talents as a warrior and raider brought her wealth, fame, prestige, and power. Revered by the tribal elders, she served as the only female member of their council of chiefs representing the Crow. In 1851 the Treaty of Fort Laramie brokered peace between Crow and Gros Ventre. Perhaps wishing to meet relatives with whom she had had no contact for forty years, Woman Chief set out to visit her people and cement their tenuous peace with her adoptive tribe. Alas, she was killed en route by a large group of Gros Ventre warriors who had heard about her prowess and considered her a dangerous enemy.

Conclusion

We have followed monarchs, mercenaries, merchants, and migrants who were the agents through whom the early modern world connected and transformed. Sailing and shipping technologies brought new areas and people into a shared world, both mentally and physically. Lessons from slaves, indigenous people, and others whose histories and identities were lost in the shuffle of early modern globalization should help clarify survival techniques still necessary to today's people. Only by viewing the early modern world as inclusive and by appreciating the different societies in the eastern and western hemisphere as unique and transient cultures can we fully understand human histories, past, present, and future.

PART 5

The Great Acceleration

———

Accelerating Change in a Warming World,
c. 1815–c. 2008

CHAPTER 11

The Anthropocene Epoch
The Background to Two Transformative Centuries

DAVID CHRISTIAN

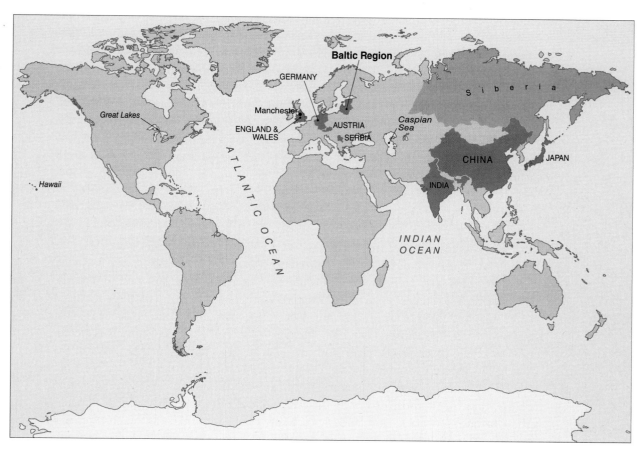

PLACES NAMED IN THE CHAPTER.

Introducing the Anthropocene: 1815–2015

SEEN through the conventional lenses of historical research, the last two centuries have been transformative. They have created a world radically different in its lifeways, technologies and politics, ideas, economics, and art and sensibilities from any earlier human societies. In the context of the biosphere as a whole, these changes look even more spectacular. They amount to a revolution that has no parallel in the 4.5 billion-year history of planet earth.

To get our bearings on today's world, we need to place it not just within the history of humanity, but within the history of planet Earth. For the first time in our planet's history, a single species (*Homo sapiens*) has acquired such control over the biosphere that it dominates change on the surface of Earth. In just 200 years, we humans have become a planet-changing species. Whether or not we understand what we are doing, the next few millennia will be shaped profoundly by human actions over the next few decades. This chapter describes the revolutionary changes that have made today's world.

Like many other scholars, I argue that the Holocene epoch, which began about 11,700 years ago at the end of the last Ice Age, has now ended, and we have entered a new geological epoch: the 'Anthropocene'. The word is based on the Greek root, '*anthropo-*' or 'human'. So, it means, roughly, the geological epoch dominated by human beings.

After a short history of the idea of the Anthropocene, this chapter offers some measures of the huge changes associated with the Anthropocene, because it is the *scale* and *pace* of change that are so striking. Then I describe the deep historical roots of the current epoch. In the second part of the chapter, I describe the major technological, economic, social, and environmental changes of the period from the late eighteenth century to the present day.

The idea of the Anthropocene

Most historians would agree that today's world is utterly different from the world of the previous few thousand years. We live differently; there are more of us; our societies, economies, ideas, and technologies are different; we experience life itself differently. Today's world is often described as the 'modern world'. But the word 'modern' has been used in so many different ways that it can no longer help us pin down what is most distinctive about the last two centuries. The idea of an 'Anthropocene epoch' is clearer because it makes more precise claims. Above all, it suggests that human power over the planet has increased exponentially, so that the crucial changes of this period arise from a new relationship between humans and the biosphere. We are now causing changes so huge that they match those driven by the great natural systems such as global climates, or the weathering of rocks and landscapes. Many of these human-caused changes will show up in the geological record far into the future, and that is why it makes sense to say we have entered a new geological epoch.

Some scholars recognized very early the growing impact of humans on planet Earth. In the late eighteenth century, the French naturalist, the Comte de Buffon, divided history into seven eras; the last was 'when the power of Man assisted that of Nature'. Charles Babbage, generally known as an early pioneer of computing, wrote in 1835 that modern industry was pumping huge amounts of carbon dioxide into the atmosphere, with consequences that 'are not sufficiently known'. In the 1870s, Italian scholar Antonio Stoppani argued that we had entered an 'Anthropozoic' era in which humans had become a 'new telluric force which in power and universality may be compared to the greater forces of Earth'. Two decades later, Swedish chemist Svante Arrhenius showed that the burning of fossil fuels on a massive scale would transform Earth's climate. Then, early in the twentieth century, Russian geologist Vladimir Vernadsky and French palaeontologist and Jesuit Teilhard de Chardin both described the emergence of a powerful new planetary sphere dominated by humans: the 'Noösphere', or the sphere of thought. (The Greek word, 'nous' means 'mind'.)

In the early twentieth century, the science was still too imprecise to justify the radical idea that we humans were transforming the biosphere. But the idea took hold in the second half of the century, after the rise of modern environmental movements and of new research fields such as ecology and environmental science. American biologist, Eugene F. Stoermer, who had been studying species change in the American Great Lakes, used the term, 'Anthropocene' in the early 1980s to describe the massive human impact he was observing.

The idea of an Anthropocene epoch took off after 2000, when it was used by the climate scientist Paul Crutzen. People listened because Crutzen had received a Nobel prize for explaining how human activity (in particular, the use of chemicals known as CFCs) had damaged the protective layer of ozone that surrounds the earth's atmosphere. At a conference in 2000, irritated by constant references to the Holocene, and aware of the massive changes caused by modern societies, he recalls blurting out: 'Let's stop it! We are no longer in the Holocene. We are in the Anthropocene.'

By 2000, the evidence for such a claim was difficult to ignore, and in 2002, a paper by Crutzen in the scientific journal, *Nature*, cited many revolutionary changes resulting from human activity. Most striking of all was the massive burning of fossil fuels, which threatened to transform the planetary climate system. The crucial measurements had been taken from 1958 by Charles Keeling in Hawaii. They showed that levels of atmospheric carbon dioxide (CO_2) were rising fast. But the full significance of Keeling's measurements became clear only after detailed studies of ice cores from Antarctica, which contain tiny air bubbles that allow us to tell the composition of the atmosphere in the distant past. Their analysis showed that the levels of CO_2 recorded by Keeling were higher than at any time in almost a million years. A 2016 study calculates that the current rate of release of carbon dioxide caused by human activity is 'unprecedented during the past 66 million years'.

As Arrhenius had argued in 1896, increasing carbon dioxide levels will inevitably lead to warmer climates because of the 'greenhouse effect', where carbon dioxide molecules (like methane, water vapour, and other similar gases) retain heat energy that would otherwise be reflected back into outer space. As carbon dioxide remains in the atmosphere for many decades, its warming effect will persist for generations. (Levels of another powerful greenhouse gas, methane, have increased even faster in the last two centuries, but methane breaks down more rapidly.)

Evidence of rising carbon dioxide levels persuaded Crutzen that humans began to transform the biosphere roughly 200 years ago, after the development of the James Watt steam engine, the machine that first encouraged the widespread burning of coal. 'The Anthropocene,' Crutzen wrote, 'could be said to have started in the late eighteenth century, when analyses of air trapped in polar ice showed the beginning of growing global concentrations of carbon dioxide and methane.' This chapter accepts Crutzen's starting date for the Anthropocene. In practice, of course, the Anthropocene arrived in different regions at different times, and its full, planetary, impact did not become apparent until the second half of the twentieth century, during what many scholars have called 'the Great Acceleration'. Nevertheless, it makes sense to link the beginning of the Anthropocene epoch to the fossil-fuels revolution.

Crutzen's 2002 article also listed other striking evidence of the growing human impact on the biosphere. Human populations had multiplied by almost tenfold in just 200 years; human energy use had multiplied by 16 times in the twentieth century; humans were now capturing atmospheric nitrogen faster than any natural processes, mainly for the manufacture of fertilizers; human activities had transformed up to 50 per cent of the earth's land surface; humans were now using half of all accessible fresh water supplies; deforestation was reducing the area of tropical forests; and, as humans used more and more of the planet's resources, other species (apart from domesticates such as cattle and wheat) were going extinct at rates not seen for tens of millions of years.

Since 2000, many other scholars have taken up the idea that we are living through a revolutionary transformation in planetary history. In 2009, a formal proposal to introduce a new 'Anthropocene epoch' began to be debated within the 'Subcommission on Quaternary Stratigraphy'. This is the scholarly body that decides on geological divisions in the last two and a half million years of earth history, the era dominated by regular ice ages. For geologists, the decision to introduce a new epoch means demonstrating that humans have caused changes on such a scale that they will show up in future geological strata. In other words, the task is to show that alien palaeontologists studying our planet many millions of years in the future will notice the changes we humans have caused. The evidence is accumulating that they will, indeed, notice the Anthropocene.

Measuring the Anthropocene: a statistical sketch, and lots of hockey sticks

To understand the scale of these changes, we need to measure. Therefore, this section measures some of the major recent changes and compares them to changes during the

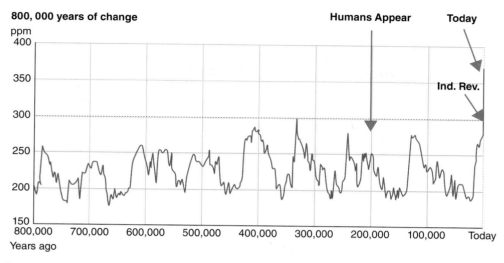

800, 000 years of change

800,000 YEARS OF CHANGE IN CARBON DIOXIDE LEVELS.

Holocene. When you do that, what you see is a series of 'hockey sticks': graphs that rise slowly for long periods then suddenly twist upwards.

The best known of the hockey sticks follows the rise in atmospheric levels of CO_2. The measurements of Charles Keeling and his successors showed that levels of atmospheric carbon dioxide rose by more than 30 per cent in just 50 years, from over 300 parts per million to about 400 parts per million today, while analysis of Antarctic ice cores showed that pre-modern levels of carbon dioxide had been below 300 parts per million for at least 800,000 years. Put the two measurements together—the sharp rise in modern CO_2 levels, and their earlier fluctuations around an average of about 250 parts per million—and you have the statistician's version of a hockey stick. Something very odd has happened to global climates in the last 200 years.

We now know of many other hockey sticks, some stretching over thousands of years. But to avoid overwhelming the reader with detail, I focus just on some of the most important ones and use figures from a single table, based mainly on the work of Vaclav Smil. (Different tables may give slightly different estimates of the scale of change, but it is the larger picture that matters.)

The first graph shows the astonishing increase in human populations that Crutzen noted in his 2002 paper. After rising very slowly for more than 100,000 years, and then slightly faster in the last 10,000 years, human populations rocketed upwards in the last 200 years, adding six billion more humans and raising human populations from 900 million to more than seven billion. These extra humans needed more resources, more food, more clothing, more goods, so it is not surprising that the energy needed to extract those resources increased as well. What *is* surprising is that energy consumption

TABLE 11.1 Statistics on human history in the Holocene & Anthropocene Epochs.

ERA	A: YEAR 0=2000 A.D.	B: POP (Mill.)	C: TOTAL ENERGY USE M. GJ/Yr (= B*D)	D: PER CAP ENERGY USE GJ/cap/Yr (1st 3 = max. est.)	E: LIFE EXPECTANCY (Years) 1st 3 = max. est.	F: LARGEST SETTLEMENT POP. (1,000s) 1st = max. est.
			B-G from based on Smil, *Harvesting the Biosphere*, kindle, loc. 4528, H based on Morris, *Why the West Rules—for Now*, pp.148–9 + 10,000 BP data interpolated			
ANTHRO-PHOLOCENE	−10,000	5	15	3	20	1
	−8,000					3
	−6,000					5
	−5,000	20	60	3	20	45
	−2,000	200	1,000	5	25	1,000
	−1,000	300	3,000	10	30	1,000
	−200	900	20,700	23	35	1,100
	−100	1,600	43,200	27	40	1,750
	0	6,100	457,500	75	67	27,000
	10	6,900	517,500	75	69	

The graphs based on the Table show several of the more important of the very large hockey sticks. Their handles fall within the Holocene Epoch, and their upturned heads within the Anthropocene. (The red arrows mark the start of the Anthropocene Epoch, about 200 years ago.)

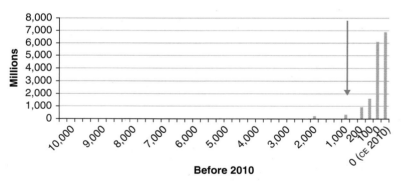

POPULATION GROWTH: Holocene and Anthropocene (Mill).

increased even faster than populations: by about 25 times in 200 years according to the data in this table, but by almost 100 times according to some estimates. The third hockey stick graph shows the result. The amount of energy available per person increased by at least three times in the last 200 years, and by almost 15 times in comparison with 2,000 years ago. Today, on average, humans have at their disposal

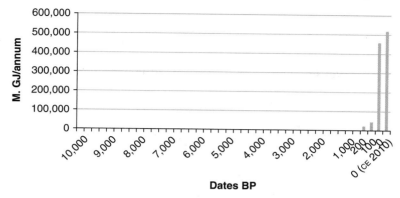

TOTAL HUMAN ENERGY USE: Holocene and Anthropocene: Mill. GJ/annum.

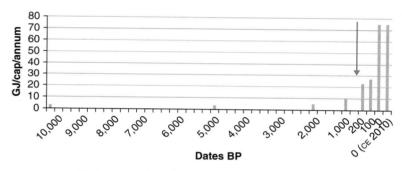

PER CAP. ENERGY USE: Holocene and Anthropocene: GJ/cap/annum.

15 times as much energy as was available for most of history. Though this energy wealth is distributed extremely unevenly, it has, nevertheless, raised material living standards for billions of humans. The fourth graph shows one of the most profound impacts of these changes: they have extended human life spans. For most of human history, average life expectancies at birth had hovered between 20 and 30 years, mainly because people were often poorly nourished, medical care for the sick and injured was rudimentary, and in most societies more than half of all babies died before they were five years old. In the 200 years of the Anthropocene, human life spans doubled, mainly because we learned how to better protect, feed, and heal the very young, the sick, and the aged. The final graph shows the size of the largest cities. It provides an indirect measure of the increasing complexity of human societies because, as Ian Morris has suggested, managing, provisioning, and policing large cities is a complex economic, political, legal, and logistical challenge. Here, too, we see a sharp jump in the last two hundred years, from settlements of just over 1 million, to settlements such as modern Shanghai, which is over twenty times that size.

Seen on the scales of human history as a whole, even on the 4 billion-year scale of planetary history, these are explosive and revolutionary changes. What caused them?

346   *David Christian*

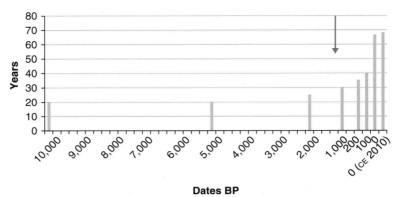

LIFE EXPECTANCIES: Holocene and Anthropocene: Years.

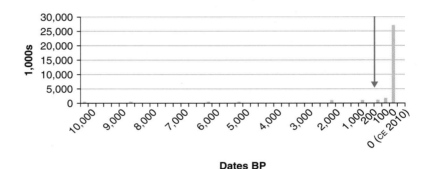

SIZE OF LARGEST SETTLEMENTS: Holocene and Anthropocene: based on Morris, p. 632.

The roots of the Anthropocene

Environmental historian John McNeill wrote, 'Several big shifts took place to nudge us into the Anthropocene, but the biggest of all was the adoption of fossil fuels and the leaps in energy use since 1750.'

To explain these changes, we need to see them within the context of human history as a whole. The Anthropocene was driven by innovations: new technologies and new ways of organizing human societies and exploiting the resources and energy flows of the biosphere. No other species can innovate like *Homo sapiens*; indeed, innovation is perhaps our most distinctive features as a species. We owe much of our technological creativity to human language. At some point within the last few hundred thousand years, our ancestors developed forms of language so efficient that, unlike their close relatives the great apes, they could share and build up stores of new ideas and information over many generations. As they accumulated, new ideas and new types of information gave humans new ways of managing their surroundings. As a result, despite many reversals and dead ends, the collective ecological power of our species has increased in the course of human history. No other species in the four-billion-year history of life on earth has shown this capacity for sustained innovation through collective learning. In these respects, the Anthropocene is intelligible only in the light of human characteristics that emerged, at the latest, with *Homo sapiens,* as much as 200,000 years ago (interested readers are referred to Chapters 1 and 2).

As they accumulated more information about their surroundings, our ancestors gained increasing control over the energy and resources flowing through the biosphere. Each of the migrations traced in Chapter 1 depended on innovations, because every time you entered new environments, you needed new technologies, new environmental knowledge, and new methods of survival. Humans in Ice Age Siberia, for instance, had to know how to hunt mammoth, to make warm clothes and dwellings from mammoth hides, to bury their meat in the permafrost, and to carve their tusks.

But the pace and consequences of innovation varied greatly. In some eras, innovation was so slow as to be barely perceptible; today, no one can miss it. Some innovations were minor; some were revolutionary. Improvements in bows and arrows or hunting techniques were important locally. But a few innovations were game changers; they set human history off on new pathways. They were the technological equivalents of striking gold. The appearance of human language was a change of this magnitude. So, too, were the technologies of agriculture, which appeared in many regions of the world within the last 10,000 years. Agriculture counts as a mega-innovation because it gave farmers access to much more of the energy flowing through the biosphere. Farmers transformed their environments so as to increase the production of species, such as cattle or wheat, which they could use, while reducing the production of those they did not need, such as weeds and rats. The energy they gained by doing this came, ultimately, from sunlight captured by plants through photosynthesis. Agriculture allowed humans to tap a larger share of the ancient flows of photosynthetic energy that powered the biosphere.

The change was revolutionary. Humans could produce more food, burn more wood, and manage more draft power from domesticated animals. With more energy, human populations grew, and with a greater number of humans living more varied lives, there were more ideas to be exchanged, so innovation itself accelerated. These changes generated the agrarian civilizations that dominated human history for much of the last 5,000 years. With increasing control over energy, populations grew, as did the size of cities, the strength of states and empires, the scope of organized religions, and the wealth and power of trading companies.

After 1500, humans began to exchange ideas, goods, and wealth across the entire planet, and the pace of innovation accelerated once again, as well as the willingness to *invest* in innovation. A recent estimate suggests that the value of global trade increased by more than 6,000 times in the last 200 years. But the acceleration was fastest in the Atlantic region, because European mariners and traders, searching for access to the huge markets of Asia and the Indian Ocean, were the first to discover how to sail around the world. Control of the first global trade networks gave European companies and governments privileged access to the huge flows of wealth and ideas generated by connecting regions that had been separated for most of human history. European scholars encountered new stars, new countries, new peoples, new religions. New information raised questions about traditional religion and knowledge, and planted the roots of modern science in new ideas about cosmology, geography, physics, and biology.

In all these ways, innovation accelerated in an increasingly globalized world. New wealth energized European science, engineering, and commerce, creating the intellectually and entrepreneurially vibrant societies that Karl Marx described as the first 'capitalist' societies. Global markets also generated fierce competition, encouraging governments and entrepreneurs to innovate in order to out-produce and out-sell their rivals. Among the results were the commercial and intellectual capital that pushed some European societies towards the industrial revolution.

And yet, despite accelerating innovation, there were reasons to think that growth would eventually stall, because there was a limit to the amount of energy that agricultural societies could tap. Agrarian civilizations depended on energy and food supplies captured through photosynthesis. Their energy came from the labour of humans and animals fed by the produce of farms, and from the burning of wood from woodlands. Much smaller amounts came from wind and water. Thus, managing energy meant managing the hard labour of humans or of domesticated animals such as horses and oxen; but the amount of work that could be mobilized in this way was limited (even with the addition of mechanical devices such as pedals and treadmills) by the amount of arable land and the size of the annual harvest.

A few centuries ago, some societies were already reaching these energy limits. Some economists, such as Adam Smith, argued that growth would stall as flows of energy dwindled. Eventually, wages would fall, and so, too, would populations, and societies would face the limits all other organisms face when they have filled up their niche.

1750–1900: breakthrough technologies of the Anthropocene

The Anthropocene, like the Holocene, began with game-changing innovations that released vast new flows of energy.

In the eighteenth century, entrepreneurs and inventors stumbled on innovations that tapped flows of energy accumulated and stored in fossil fuels over several hundred million years. The following graph of human energy use since 1850 indicates the transformative role of fossil fuels. In 1850, biomass (wood fuel and human and animal labour) still supplied most human energy needs. In 2000, biomass accounted for only about one-ninth of human energy use, and most energy came from fossil fuels: coal, oil, and natural gas. Remove fossil fuels and today's world is unimaginable.

The crucial breakthroughs did not come easily, because it was not at all obvious how to use fossil fuels efficiently. Coal, oil, and natural gas were familiar in many societies. Oil seeping through the soil around the Caspian Sea was used in the form of bitumen to caulk ships, or in liquid forms as a medicine or, occasionally, it was burnt for lighting, as was natural gas. Oil was probably an ingredient of 'Greek fire', the highly combustible material that Byzantine navies used in naval battles. In Song dynasty China, ironmongers running short of charcoal used coal on a vast scale to produce iron for weapons and

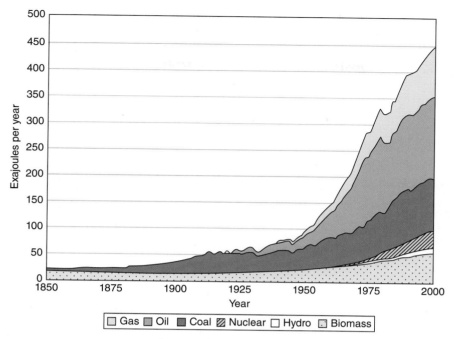

HUMAN ENERGY USE SINCE 1850 showing the transformative role of fossil fuels.

armour. But their reliance on coal proved temporary, because most coal came from the north of China, beyond the core territories controlled by the Song dynasty.

For a long time, fossil fuels remained unimportant, and with good reason. Most coal, oil, and gas was buried deep beneath the surface, and coal and oil were dirty and difficult to use with traditional technologies. However, as we have seen, governments and entrepreneurs in many parts of the world were searching for new sources of food and energy, either in lands over the seas or in their own more remote provinces. And this search, backed by entrepreneurially minded investors looking for cheap energy, would eventually generate the crucial breakthroughs.

Those breakthroughs came about in Europe, which was now the most commercially and intellectually dynamic region of the world. Britain was a small island off the north west of the Eurasian landmass, with ambitious governments, a dynamic economy, and trade links that spanned the globe. But it suffered from a shortage of wood and land as early as the sixteenth century, and the cost of firewood was rising fast. Trade with the Americas and the Baltic region made up some of the shortfall, while more efficient crop rotations, improved ways of breeding, and larger, more commercialized farms built by squeezing out smallholders, raised the productivity of the land. Meanwhile, England had a lot of relatively accessible coal, which had been used for heating since Neolithic times. By the sixteenth century, England's bakers and brewers and brick and glass makers began to use coal for heating, and so did increasing

THE SMOKESTACKS OF EARLY INDUSTRIAL SHEFFIELD, ENGLAND, in a scene that William Rideing, an American visitor in 1884, called 'a very clear day' by Sheffield's standards. Factories were 'the archetypal manufacturing institution of the early anthropocene'.

numbers of ordinary households in the cold winters, despite the foul smoke it produced. (Late in the seventeenth century, the diarist John Evelyn compared London to 'Mount Aetna, the Court of Vulcan, . . . or the suburbs of Hell.') Coal was accessible because north England was part of a geological belt stretching far into Germany, where coal seams approached the surface (the 'carboniferous crescent' as John McNeill calls this region). Many English coal mines were near rivers, so their coal could be transported cheaply around the coast to London.

By 1750, coal already supplied England and Wales with the energy equivalent of 4.3 million acres of woodland, or about 13 per cent of their total area; by 1800, it supplied the equivalent of 11 million acres, or around 25 per cent of the area of England and Wales. It had become the most important source of heating fuel for English manufacturers, making England, in the view of some historians, a 'proto-fossil economy'. London could not have grown into one of the world's largest cities if it had depended on energy from woodlands alone. Coal-fuelled industries provided employment, and that encouraged early marriage and raised fertility rates. Energy shortage, a dynamic and fast-growing population and economy, and easy access to coal ensured increasing investment in coal and related industries, creating powerful incentives to mine and use coal more efficiently. Combined with the increasingly scientific spirit that pervaded many European societies by the eighteenth century, these factors help explain why the critical breakthroughs occurred in eighteenth-century England.

The trick was to find ways of using coal not just to generate heat, but also to generate mechanical energy: to spin cotton or drive looms or pumps or pulleys, or even to power carriages or ships. In the early eighteenth century, many coal producers were already using coal-fired 'Newcomen' steam engines to pump out the water that filled coal mines as they were sunk deeper and deeper. But Newcomen engines were too inefficient to use anywhere except in mines, where coal was cheap. The Newcomen engine had a single cylinder into which steam was pumped from a coal-fired boiler, and then cooled to create a partial vacuum, which drew down a piston that worked a pump. The constant heating and cooling was extremely inefficient and required vast amounts of coal and water.

Many engineers tried to improve the Newcomen engine. The most successful was James Watt, a skilled Scottish instrument maker, well connected with the leading engineers, tinkerers, natural philosophers and entrepreneurs of the day. Watt encountered his first steam engine in 1760, when asked to repair a Newcomen engine. He was struck by its inefficiency. During a Sunday afternoon walk in 1765, he suddenly realized how to improve it: 'The idea came into my mind, that as steam was an elastic body it would rush into a vacuum, and if a communication was made between the cylinder and an exhausted vessel, it would rush into it, and might be there condensed without cooling the cylinder . . . I had not walked further than the Golf-house when the whole thing was arranged in my mind.'

Watt built a successful working model, but it took years, and much tinkering and financial backing, and much cutting-edge engineering, to build a successful full-scale version. He acquired a first patent in 1769, and news soon spread of a potentially revolutionary steam engine, a sign of the increasing demand in many countries for new ways of generating and using energy. In a globally connected world, Watt even got offers of work in Russia. In 1776, with the financial and engineering support of a Birmingham entrepreneur Matthew Boulton, he built an engine in which steam was released into and cooled in a separate condenser, so that the main cylinder could remain at a high temperature.

This was the crucial breakthrough. Watt steam engines were the first fossil fuel-driven machines that could provide cheap mechanical power anywhere, and he and Boulton knew there would be a vast market for them. In 1776, Boulton told Dr Johnson's biographer, Boswell: 'I sell here, sir, what all the world desires to have—POWER.' By 1800, about 500 Watt engines were at work in Britain, and steam was beginning to challenge water power as the most effective driver of Britain's rapidly multiplying cotton mills. By the end of the 1830s, steam was the dominant source of power in British industry.

With the possible exception of sailing ships, no prime mover this powerful had existed before. In 1750, a farmer ploughing with two horses controlled only about 1,000 Watts (W), and even a coach-and-four could generate no more than 2,500 W.

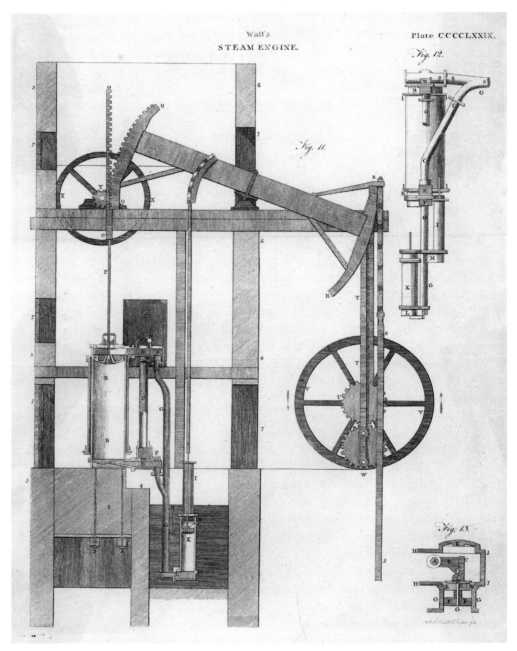

WATTS'S STEAM ENGINE: A TECHNICAL RENDITION OF WHAT, to the inventor, was the outcome of a revelatory, creative moment of insight.

TABLE 11.2 Chronology of power sources from 1800–2000, and corresponding power delivered.

DATE	SOURCE OF POWER	POWER DELIVERED (Watts)
1800	English peasant ploughing with 2 horses	1,000
1750	French coach-and-four	2,500
1780	Early Watt steam engine	7,000
1795	Improved Watt steam engine	10,000
1850	English steam locomotive	200,000
2000	Japanese bullet train	13,000,000
2000	Boeing 747 or Airbus 380	100,000,000

Statistics from: Vaclav Smil, 'A New World of Energy', *Cambridge World History*, VII, pt. 1, p. 173.

(It is no accident that this unit of power is named after James Watt, though he himself invented the unit of 'horsepower.') Horse-drawn ploughs and carriages represented the most powerful common prime movers before the fossil-fuels revolution. Even the earliest Watt steam engines delivered much more power—between 7,000 and 10,000 W (10–15 horsepower)—and improvements soon increased their power. In the next two centuries, the power of prime movers would multiply many times over. By 1850, the driver of an English steam locomotive controlled 200,000 W, and today the driver of a Japanese bullet train controls some 13 million W, while the captain of a Boeing 747 or an Airbus 380 is in charge of 100 million W. That is 100,000 times the power available to a peasant with two horses.

The fossil fuels revolution takes off: the nineteenth century

The fossil fuels revolution began in Britain and, even in the middle of the nineteenth century, Britain accounted for more than 50 per cent of global emissions of carbon dioxide. Yet so great was the demand for more powerful machines that the Watt steam engine soon spread to other countries and began to spin off many new technologies. Innovations came in waves as breakthrough technologies such as the steam engine stimulated and helped inspire for vast numbers of smaller innovations.

Steam dominated the first wave in the late eighteenth and early nineteenth centuries. Its effects were most apparent in Britain, but soon its consequences would ricochet back and forth across the planet. After the end of the Napoleonic wars in 1814, foreign engineers, officials, and entrepreneurs flocked to England to learn about and, if possible, purloin the new technologies. Steam engine technology spread quickly, particularly in northwestern Europe and the newly independent United States.

Used to pump water out of mines, steam engines gave access to deeper seams of coal, which increased the number of useable mines, cut the cost of mining coal, and encouraged engineers and entrepreneurs to develop ways of using coal in greater numbers industries that required cheap energy. When used to power cotton-spinning or power-looms, steam power vastly increased the output of textile factories. That increased the demand for raw cotton, which multiplied the number of cotton plantations in the southern States of the USA, and eventually stimulated cotton-growing in other regions such as Egypt and Central Asia. Increasing textile production raised demand for dyes and bleaches. That demand, combined with cheap heat energy from coal, and research into the rich chemistry of coal, laid the foundations for industrial chemicals production. Many of these innovations were introduced in France, Belgium, and Germany; German companies first began to systematically apply scientific methods to the challenge of exploiting fossil-fuels technologies more efficiently.

A second wave of innovations began when steam engines, mounted on wheels and in boats early in the nineteenth century; railways slash the cost of transporting heavy and bulky goods (including coal) by land and made land transportation as cheap as transportation by water for the first time in human history. Suddenly, it was economical to move people, produce, and goods across the prairies of the Americas or even (eventually) the steppes of Russia or the plains of India. Railways stimulated an investment boom on both sides of the Atlantic, and a whole new range of businesses, as they cheapened the cost of transporting cattle, produce, people, and coal, and increased demand for iron and steel to make rails and rolling stock. Steam engines also transformed transportation by water, increasing by orders of magnitude the scale of sea-borne trade and human sea-borne migrations. Steam engines powered river boats as early as 1807, installed by Robert Fulton (using a Boulton and Watt engine to drive paddlewheels), and at sea as early as 1822. Railways and steamships drove innovations in many other technologies, particularly in metallurgy. In the 1860s, William Kelly, an American iron-producer, discovered how to convert iron efficiently into steel by blowing air through molten pig iron. Henry Bessemer, an English entrepreneur, improved the process, which then advanced further with the Siemens-Martin method, using scrap metal and low-grade coals. Suddenly, steel was cheap enough for use in consumer goods such as tin cans.

The demand for coal soared. In 1800, the world produced 15 million metric tons of coal; by 1900 it produced 825 million metric tons, or 55 times as much. Cheap mechanical energy transformed the very nature of work. Eventually, it would replace both slave and animal labour on farms, plantations, and in transportation, as it became cheaper to feed machines with coal than to feed slaves with grains or grits, or horses with hay. Entrepreneurs who had invested in steam engines found that it often made sense to concentrate their workers in large factories, a form of organization already pioneered by late eighteenth-century cotton-manufacturers using water power. Factories would become the archetypal manufacturing institution of the early Anthropocene.

'RAIN, STEAM, AND SPEED - THE GREAT WESTERN RAILWAY', BY J. M. W. TURNER captures the romanticism of early industrialization.

By the late nineteenth century, cheap energy was encouraging experimentation and investment in many new technologies, such as electricity. The key discovery here was Michael Faraday's realization in the 1820s that you could generate an electric current by moving a metal coil inside a magnetic field; electricity generation on a large scale only became possible with the invention of the dynamo, credited to Werner von Siemens, among others. Electricity would eventually provide an efficient way of distributing the energy from fossil fuels over large distances to millions of factories and households. Thomas Edison and Joseph Swan invented the first workable light bulbs, which effectively extended the hours of daylight available for both work and leisure. Further transformations occurred in the communications technologies. Early in the nineteenth century, as it was two millennia earlier, the fastest way of sending a message was generally by horse courier. The invention of the telegraph in 1837 allowed communication at more or less the speed of light. By the end of the century, the phone and the radio allowed instant communication over large distances.

In the late nineteenth century, fossil-fuel technologies began to spread around the world. While agriculture had taken almost 10,000 years to reach all corners of the

'THE BESSEMER PROCESS FOR THE MASS PRODUCTION OF STEEL', BY FRITZ GEHRKE. The shower of sparks captures the feeling of transmutative performance that awed Bessemer's early audiences.

EDISON'S LIGHT BULB EXTENDED
the working day and provided an icon
of industrial inventiveness.

planet, the fossil fuels revolution circled the world in just two centuries, and it transformed the global distribution of wealth and power. Fossil-fuel technologies enriched many countries bordering on the Atlantic Ocean, countries that had been relatively unimportant for much of the agrarian era. But they undermined countries in other parts of the world that were slow to adopt them. Some of these regions, such as China, the Indian subcontinent, and the Eastern Mediterranean, had been major hubs of power and wealth as late as the eighteenth century.

In 1750, when most other societies in the world drew energy from human and animal labour, wood, wind, and water, coal already accounted for 40 per cent of Britain's energy consumption; a century later it accounted for over 90 per cent. By then, England and Wales consumed nine times as much energy as Italy, which still depended primarily on non-fossil fuels. On a global scale, the differences were even starker. As late as 1750, China and India had been two of the world's major producers, accounting, by some estimates, for more than 55 per cent of global production, while the UK and the US accounted for just a few percent. By 1860, China and India together accounted for just 28 per cent of global production, and the UK and the US together accounted for a similar proportion. By 1913, China and India accounted for only 5 per cent of global production, while the UK and the US together accounted for about

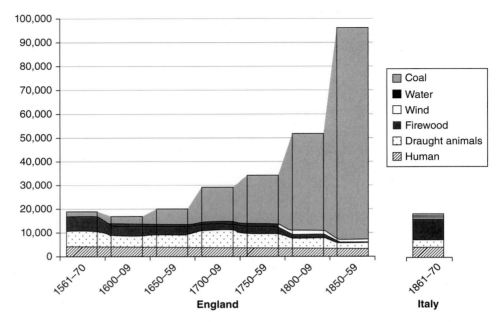

COAL USE ENGLAND COMPARED TO ITALY—SIXTEENTH TO NINETEENTH CENTURY.

46 per cent (the US for 32 per cent, the UK for 14 per cent). In human history, such sudden transformations in the global distribution of power and wealth were unique.

Contemporaries took notice. In 1837 Auguste Blanqui, a French revolutionary, argued that Britain was experiencing an 'industrial revolution', by which he meant a technological and economic transformation as fundamental as the French revolution. He was underestimating the magnitude of the change. By the time of the Great Exhibition at the Crystal Palace in London in 1851, the energy bonanza from coal had briefly turned a small island at the edge of Eurasia into the most powerful country on earth.

But other countries in Europe and North America soon began to catch up. As they did so, they were keen to control resource-rich regions, and this generated a new, global round of imperialist conquests. Seizing new colonies became easier through military innovations, including improvements in the power of explosives (Alfred Nobel invented dynamite, based on nitroglycerine, in 1866), the invention of improved hand guns and machine guns (first used on a large scale in the American Civil War— the first fossil-fuels war) and the building of steam-powered, iron-hulled warships. Railways made it possible to move troops, weapons, and military supplies faster and in larger amounts than ever before. These new weapons explain the speed with which European powers came to dominate the globe in the late nineteenth century.

Fossil-fuels weaponry was terrifying and appalling. The first iron-hulled gunship, the *Nemesis*, would play a crucial role in the Opium War of 1839–42, one of the first major wars between a fossil-fuels navy and a traditional navy. Britain's victory through its use of fossil fuels would force China to open its doors to British traders selling the

'QUEEN VICTORIA AND PRINCE ALBERT INAUGURATING THE GREAT 1851 EXHIBITION. The Crystal Palace' (detail), 1851, by J. McNeven. The building was a triumph of industrial engineering, housing thousands of other such triumphs.

poison of opium. The *Nemesis* had two steam-driven paddlewheels, and, with its two 32-pounder cannon and 15 smaller cannons, could sail in shallow river waters, sometimes towing other sailing warships. The English naval commander, Commodore Gordon Bremer, described how the *Nemesis* destroyed 'five forts, one battery, two military stations, and nine war junks, in which were one hundred and fifteen guns and [heavy muskets], thus proving to the enemy that the British flag can be displayed throughout their inner waters wherever and whenever it is thought proper by us, against any defence or mode they may adopt to prevent it.' Quite as appalling for traditional soldiers, such as the Zulu, armed only with spears, were machine guns that multiplied the killing power of a single soldier.

In the late nineteenth century and early twentieth centuries, there was a third wave of innovations. Increased demand for lighting (using kerosene) and the invention of the internal-combustion engine (for automobiles) kick-started demand for a second fossil fuel: oil. Oil was easier to transport and contained more concentrated energy than coal. It spawned a whole range of new technologies, from automobiles to tanks to the first heavier-than-air flying machines, and it transformed the geography of energy production. Oil fields became as strategic as coal fields, and once energy-poor

THE *NEMESIS* AND BOATS OF THE *SULPHUR, CALLIOPE, Larne,* and *Starling* destroying the Chinese war junks in Anson's Bay, 1858 by Thomas Allom.

regions from the Caspian Sea to Pennsylvania or, eventually, Persia and Arabia, became crucial suppliers. In this third wave of innovation, fossil-fuel technologies spread more widely. Most striking was their adoption in the Russian Empire and also in Japan, the first non-Western country benefiting from transformation thanks to Anthropocene technologies.

The new technologies exacted a price even in the first countries to adopt them. In the UK, Europe, and the US, industrial cities grew pell-mell, which encouraged the building of cheap, unsanitary tenements in environments where the air and water was fouled by smoke and industrial chemicals. In 1862, a visitor to Manchester wrote of the river Irwell that: 'whole wagonloads of poisons from dye houses and bleachyards [are] thrown into it to carry away; and drains and steam boilers discharge into it their seething contents . . . [until it becomes] less a river than a flood of liquid manure.' Fierce industrial competition encouraged brutal discipline in factories, the use of child labour, and the cutting of wages. Industrial accidents were common and victims rarely saw compensation. Such conditions prompted the rise of labour unions, and of a new revolutionary ideology, socialism, committed to overthrowing capitalism and building a society ruled by wage-workers.

Beyond the epicentres of the new technologies, their impact was even more destructive. Just as industrial weaponry destroyed the power of traditional empires, steam-powered textile production destroyed whole sectors of artisan production in India, which had been the agrarian era's leading textile producer. India's decline accelerated once Britain acquired enough control of the subcontinent to protect British markets from cheap Indian textiles. Even the building of India's major railways benefited Britain more than India. Britain manufactured most of the track and rolling stock, and the Indian rail network, which was eventually one of the largest in the world, was designed primarily to move British troops fast and cheaply, and to enable the export of cheap Indian raw materials and the import of (relatively expensive) English manufactured goods. In the Americas, Africa, and Asia, growing demand for sugar, cotton, rubber, tea, and other raw materials encouraged environmentally destructive methods of farming in plantation economies.

By 1900, it was already apparent that the Anthropocene brought both good and bad news, like all periods of revolutionary transformation. It was a planetary-scale example of what the economist Joseph Schumpeter had called 'gales of creative destruction'.

The twentieth century and the 'Great Acceleration'

The two halves of the twentieth century had very different histories. In the first half, wars between the leading fossil-fuel powers inflicted huge destruction on the European heartland and many other countries, and slowed economic growth and trade throughout the world. The outbreak of World War I reduced world exports by about a quarter, and in 1933 the value of global trade was still below the level for 1913. The civil wars of the industrial heartland also broke Europe's grip on its colonial empires. In the second half of the century, fifty years of relative peace allowed the most astonishing economic and technological boom ever. The fossil-fuel revolution spread around the entire world, and some scholars argue that this was when the Anthropocene really began.

The world of the late nineteenth century was the global equivalent of a gold rush, as the bonanza of fossil fuels and new technologies encouraged violent and chaotic competition for raw materials, labour, and energy. Eventually, that competition between the leading industrial powers led to hugely destructive wars within Europe, which spilled over into Africa, Asia, and the Pacific. These deployed all the devastating weaponry of the fossil-fuel revolution, including machine guns, high explosives, bombs dropped from the air, and early forms of rocketry.

By the late nineteenth century, Britain was losing its economic, military, and technological lead. While British GDP rose by more than six times between 1820 and 1913, that of Germany rose by nine times, and that of the US by an astonishing 41 times. By 1913, the US—a dynamic industrial society with vast resources as its growing populations exploited more and more of its huge territories—already accounted for almost 19 per cent of global production; Germany accounted for about nine per cent; and Britain for just over eight per cent.

A GERMAN MACHINE GUN UNIT DURING WORLD WAR I.

Early in the twentieth century, two other nations were also industrializing fast: the Russian Empire and Japan. Though Russia had an archaic government, it had vast resources, and some (including the German army's high command) feared that as it industrialized it would rapidly become an economic and military superpower. Japanese industrialization was managed largely by its governments, and by systematic borrowing and adaptation of western technologies. But Japan's problem was that it had limited resources to fuel industrialization; it would have to look for them elsewhere and that would drive Japan to seek its own empire in eastern Asia.

In this increasingly competitive environment, leading figures in many powerful countries began to see imperial conquests as the key to future power and wealth. In Britain, Lord Milner wrote in 1910: 'It is no small advantage at any time, and it may under given circumstances be vital, for a great industrial country to have the raw materials upon which its principal industries depend, produced within regions that are under its own control.' Joseph Chamberlain remarked in 1889: 'The Foreign Office and the Colonial Office are chiefly engaged in finding new markets and in defending old ones. The War Office and Admiralty are mostly occupied in preparations for the

KARL MARX, WHO ARGUED THAT GROWING INEQUALITY would eventually destroy capitalism, but that imperialism might provide a temporary safety valve.

defence of these markets, and for the protection of our commerce.' Cecil Rhodes argued that colonies were essential to survival because any slowing of economic growth might generate the sort of internal civil wars that socialists such as Karl Marx had predicted: 'The British Empire is a matter of bread and butter. If you wish to avoid civil war, then you must be an imperialist.'

With similar attitudes shaping policy in most of the world's industrialized powers, it is perhaps no surprise that eventually war broke out in 1914. Interlocking alliances ensured that a local conflict between Austria and Serbia would draw in all the major European powers within weeks. World War I was fought with the most advanced modern weaponry, and funded with the vast wealth of modern capitalist societies. Machine guns mowed soldiers down in their thousands, while modern medical services kept them alive in waterlogged trenches between battles. The needs of war also drove innovation; internal combustion engines were improved and installed in tanks and heavier-than-air planes. In Germany, the Haber-Bosch process, invented in 1909, was used to make explosives and artificial fertilizers.

When the war ended in 1918, few of the problems that had caused it had been resolved, and two decades later, after Japan invaded Manchuria and Germany invaded Poland, war broke out once more. World War II was both more global and more destructive than the first, as governments put together teams to design more powerful planes, ships, bombs, rockets, better ways of detecting enemy submarines and planes, better radios, more destructive explosives, and better mechanical calculators to break war-time codes. This war was fought in China and Manchuria, in Southeast Asia, and on the Atlantic and Pacific Oceans, as well as in Europe. With highly mobile armies and massive use of air power, civilian casualties were greater than those of the combatant armies. Global casualties may have exceeded 60 million people. In Europe alone, some 40 million people died, or four times as many as in World War I. More than six million people, most of them Jews, died in the industrial slaughter houses of the Holocaust. The war finally ended with the dropping of the world's first atomic weapons on Hiroshima and Nagasaki on 6 and 9 August 1945. Developed through a massive government-led research effort in the US, known as the 'Manhattan Project', the weapon dropped on Hiroshima killed 80,000 people almost immediately; within a year, radiation and other injuries had raised the death toll to almost 150,000. A decade later, the US and the Soviet Union had developed hydrogen bombs: even more terrifying weapons that used the power of fusion, the same mechanism that generated power in the heart of the sun.

The defeat of the Axis powers left a world dominated by the two largest and most resource-rich countries in the world, and the US and the Soviet Union became the world's 'superpowers'. The Soviet Union had replaced the Russian Empire after the 1917 Revolution. Under the guidance of its Marxist ideology, and with innovations mostly borrowed from the West, it had built a powerful industrial and military establishment using all the power of a brutal and highly centralized government. By 1950, despite colossal devastation during the war, the Soviet Union had rebuilt much of its industry and, with its armies occupying eastern Europe, it was now clearly the Unites States' primary rival. In 1949, the Communist armies of Mao Zedong took power in China so that, by the middle of the century, Communist governments ruled in both the world's largest country and its most populous.

By now it was apparent that, though the fossil-fuel revolution had brought great wealth and power to the first fossil-fuel societies, eventually, its main beneficiaries would be those countries with the largest resource base. Smaller industrial powers were weakened by war, the defeat of Japan ended its imperial aspirations, and the European colonial powers, having lost both the means and the will to defend their overseas empires, surrendered them within a little over two decades. Britain conceded independence to India and Pakistan in 1947, to Kenya in 1963 and, over the next decade, to all its African and Asian colonies. Eventually, France and the Netherlands would also surrender their Asian empires. By 1970, decolonization had created more than 70 new nations.

The US had suffered less than any of the other major combatant powers, and emerged as the richest and most powerful country in the world. By 1950, the US economy accounted for more than a quarter of global GDP. Learning from the lessons of World War I, the victorious powers did not impose punitive sanctions on West Germany or Japan, but encouraged them to re-build their economies, and soon both countries were growing rapidly.

The world was now divided into two large power blocks—one with capitalist economies, the other with Communist planned economies. New global institutions created after the war, including the United Nations and the International Monetary Fund, provided the framework for global negotiations and financial transactions, but real power lay with the superpowers and the blocks of powers they dominated.

Within this new global framework, economic growth would accelerate over the next few decades, and the fossil-fuel revolution would finally reach most of the world. The collapse of the Soviet command economy in 1991, and China's turn to a market economy from the 1980s, suggested that the market-driven societies of the capitalist world were better at introducing the innovations that made it possible to exploit the possibilities of fossil-fuel technologies. By 2000, capitalist economies dominated most of the world.

In the second fifty years of the twentieth century, humans became the most important single driver of change on the surface of the planet. This sudden increase in human power and impact, and their related changes, are what many scholars have called the 'Great Acceleration'. As with the whole of the Anthropocene, it is important to get a sense of the scale of the Great Acceleration. For the sake of consistency, I have taken many of the figures below from a single source.

Between 1950 and 2000, world populations more than doubled, rising from three to more than six billion within a single lifetime; this growth rate was unprecedented. In the past, such explosive population growth would have been a recipe for global famine, but food production increased even faster than populations, boosted by increasing irrigation (using fossil-fuel-powered earth-movers to build thousands of dams), the introduction of pesticides, the application of vast amounts of artificial

THE BURJ KHALIFA, IN DUBAI, UAE, completed in 2009, is the world's tallest building—the latest in a series of competitive hikes in building heights.

fertilizers, and the genetic engineering of more productive strains of wheat and rice. The production of artificial fertilizers illustrates the profound impact of fossil fuels even on non-mechanical processes. The Haber-Bosch process fixed atmospheric nitrogen in ammonia, and because nitrogen is unreactive, this process required so much energy that it only became possible in the fossil fuels era. In effect, it was a way of turning fossil fuels (mostly oil) into food.

The dollar value of global GDP increased even faster than populations, rising by 15 times in 50 years. In other words, increasing consumption was a much more significant driver of change in the Anthropocene than population growth alone. Combining figures for the growth of populations and GDP, we can estimate that wealth per person increased by more than seven times in the same brief period. World production of oil and natural gas also increased by at least seven times between 1950 and 2000.

Lifeways were transformed. During the Palaeolithic era, most humans lived in mobile family groups; during the 10,000 years of the agrarian era, most people lived as subsistence peasants in small villages. By 2000, more than half of all humans lived in large cities; in the second half of the twentieth century *Homo sapiens* became a species of city dwellers, and being a peasant ceased to be the dominant lifeway of human beings. Rapid urbanization was possible partly because cities had transformed from death-traps—with polluted air, insanitary dwellings, dirty rivers, and concentrations of disease vectors—to healthier, cleaner, and more productive places, thanks to improved transportation of food and other supplies, increased opportunities for work, the introduction of sewers and systems for water purification and distribution, improved medical care, and the introduction of new medicines, including antibiotics, which were mass-produced from the 1940s. Improvements in health care, nutrition, education, and sanitation have raised living standards for billions of people and doubled life expectancy across the world. Although many failed to benefit from these changes, billions did, and from their perspective the Anthropocene meant a sudden and profound improvement in living standards.

There have even been attempts to undo some of the harmful effects of the earliest stages of the fossil-fuel revolution by reducing air pollution, eliminating lead in petroleum, and forcing companies to limit what they pump into rivers, oceans, and the air. Particularly in the earliest fossil-fuel countries, legislation to protect local environments increased in the second half of the twentieth century in response both to growing human impact and to the emergence of environmental movements. Much of this legislation set limits to the permissible impact factories or cars can have on nearby rivers or on air quality, or to the fish catch of trawlers. Governments began to recognize that there were boundaries beyond which human impact on the environment endangered human beings as well as the natural environment.

New waves of innovations drove the 'Great Acceleration', some of which were pioneered during the wars of the early twentieth century. Rocketry, established for military purposes during World War II, enabled us to send a small number of humans to the Moon, and to send robotic vehicles to explore our solar system. Fossil-fuel-powered earth movers and diesel-powered pumps allowed the transformation of the earth's surface to build cities, dams, and roads, while diesel pumps made it easy and cheap to pump up the fresh water in the world's aquifers to quench the thirst of rapidly growing cities. Trawlers with more powerful engines, better navigational and sonar detection equipment, and massive nets, increased the catch of fish from 19 to 94 million tons between 1950 and 2000. Planes, trains, and ships moved more people and goods around the world than ever before. The discovery of the basic principles of digital computation and the invention of the transistor in the late 1940s laid the foundations for the electronic revolution, the spread of computers, mobile phones, and the Internet—changes that allow people to communicate at the speed of light around the world at tiny cost. But scientific knowledge in general has also increased faster than ever before, giving us new understanding of the history of the Universe,

THE EARTH AT NIGHT. A good guide to where you find the most energy.

how evolution works, and how the earth system works. Collective learning, the sharing and accumulation of new ideas, now drives innovation more powerfully than ever before in human history.

In the second half of the twentieth century, these changes spread to much of the rest of the world. Japan pioneered the fossil-fuel revolution in Asia, but in the second half of the century it was followed by South Korea, Taiwan, Singapore, Hong Kong, and, eventually, by the giant powers of China and India, both of which shifted towards more capitalistic economies in the last decades of the twentieth century. Today, China and India, with access to vast natural and human resources, are on track to become global superpowers again, after an era of decline lasting two or three centuries.

In the late twentieth century, a modest level of affluence never before achieved spread beyond elite groups to a rapidly growing global middle class, first in the Atlantic heartland, and then in the rest of the world. Increasing prosperity, and the fact that machines have taken on much of the burden of hard physical labour, may also help explain the remarkable changes in gender relations in many parts of the world, as women have taken on a greater number of roles traditionally assigned to men.

Many of the changes made possible by the energy and resource bonanza of the Anthropocene have been good to humanity. They have created better lives for more humans than ever before.

The 'Bad Anthropocene' and human impact on the biosphere

As in all periods of 'creative destruction', there is also a dark side to the Great Acceleration: while there is a 'Good Anthropocene', and all its gains, there is a 'Bad Anthropocene', which brings dangers that threaten those advances.

Some of these dangers arise from a failure to distribute the benefits of the Anthropocene more equally. Though more people enjoy modest affluence than ever before, larger populations and inequitable distribution means that the number living in dire poverty today is also much greater than ever before. In 2005, more than 3 billion people (more people than the total population of the world in 1900) lived on less than USD2.50 a day. While total wealth has increased, its distribution is now more lop-sided than ever before. In 2014, the wealthiest ten per cent of the world population controlled 87 per cent of the world's wealth, while the poorest 50 per cent controlled just one per cent. Many of those not yet benefiting from the bonanza of the fossil-fuel revolution suffer from the unhealthy, unsanitary, and precarious living conditions of the early industrial revolution. Modern travel means that new diseases can spread with terrifying speed once they appear, while bacteria and viruses can also travel, mingle, and evolve so fast that modern medicine cannot keep up with them. The worst pandemic of this kind so far was the outbreak of influenza at the end of World War I, which killed thirty million people—more than the war itself. Today, air travel means that such pandemics could spread around the world in days or weeks. Meanwhile, the stresses and complexity of modern life have created new forms of psychological suffering, particularly for those benefiting least from modern forms of wealth. Increasing inequality will exacerbate discontent of many kinds and, with modern weaponry added to the mix, such discontent may generate the sort of global class wars predicted by nineteenth-century socialists. Some of the dangers affect both rich and poor. The invention of nuclear weapons means that we can never discount the possibility of a nuclear holocaust, which would obliterate the gains of the Anthropocene along with much of the biosphere.

Harder to visualize, but even more dangerous overall, is the fact that human impact is now threatening to undermine the biospheric systems on which human well-being depends. To understand these dangers, we have to try to measure the effects of humans on the biosphere as a whole.

The 'Great Acceleration' turned humans into the most powerful drivers of biospheric change—more powerful than the natural drivers of the climate: erosion, biochemical cycles, natural selection, and plate tectonics. There are many ways of documenting this transformation. As mentioned, CO_2 levels rose well above the levels normal for the past million years, increasing by 30 per cent in just 50 years. Changes in the nitrogen cycle, mostly due to the manufacture of artificial fertilizers, are even more spectacular. In 1890, humans fixed about 15 megatons of nitrogen a year, while wild plants fixed about 100 megatons, or almost seven times as much. By 1990, the area of arable land had increased so much that wild plants only fixed about 89 megatons,

A POLAR BEAR STUDIES THE ANTHROPOCENE. Creatures of a self-endangered species look on.

while humans now fixed about 118 megatons. The danger here is that overuse of artificial fertilizers will create algal blooms that can poison both oceanic and freshwater systems and kill off fish and other aquatic organisms by depriving them of oxygen.

Humans have created numerous chemicals, and many are toxic. Radioactive substances from the testing of nuclear weapons will show up in the future, as will pure forms of metals such as aluminium, which normally exist as compounds. Plastic, a purely human creation, is now gathering as vast islands in oceans and in the landfills of cities and towns. Such a proliferation of new substances has not happened since the appearance of an oxygen-dominated atmosphere about 2.4 billion years ago. In the 1980s, Paul Crutzen and others showed that CFCs (chlorofluorocarbons, which had been widely used in refrigerators and aerosol sprays) were leaking into the high atmosphere and breaking up the thin layer of ozone (O_3) that shields the earth from harmful ultra-violet radiation. Fortunately, the impact of CFCs was soon recognized, and a global convention in 1987 sharply reduced their production and use. As a result, the ozone layer has stabilized and should eventually repair itself. Meanwhile, humans are now moving more earth for building, roads, and cities than is moved by all the natural forces of erosion and glaciation, and the many underground tunnels we have dug in search of minerals and fossil fuels will show up clearly in the remote future. We are removing freshwater from aquifers ten times faster than natural flows can replenish them.

Our impact on other organisms has been particularly profound. As humans use more of the earth's resources, fewer remain for other species. As a result, extinction rates are now 1,000 times greater than the rates of the last few million years. Vaclav Smil gives striking statistics that highlight the contrast between increasing human consumption of resources, and declining consumption by most other species. He estimates that the biomass of humans (measured as the total amount of carbon in all humans) overtook that of all wild (non-domesticated) mammal species early in the nineteenth century. By 1900, wild land mammals accounted for the equivalent of about ten megatons of carbon, and humans for about 13 megatons. In 2000, the biomass of wild land mammals had fallen to five megatons, while that of humans had risen to about 55 megatons. Meanwhile, the biomass of human domesticates, such as cattle and sheep, increased even faster. In 1900, they accounted for about 35 megatons, and by 2000 for 120 megatons of carbon. These figures mean that by 2000, humans and their domesticates accounted for over 97 per cent of the biomass of all land mammals. This statistic alone provides an astonishing measure of our sudden rise to dominance over the biosphere.

Warning signs

Human impact on this scale is dangerous. We know that the biosphere—the linked system of atmosphere, oceans, land, flora, and fauna that shapes the surface of our earth—is resilient. But we also know that parts of this complex system can suddenly

BOILING THE TOAD...

'BOILING THE TOAD': the acceleration of global warming can all too easily be ignored, but it seems to be a defining feature of the Anthropocene.

flip, and affect all the other parts. Almost 12,000 years ago, after several millennia of erratic warming, global climates suddenly stabilized at temperatures significantly warmer than those of the Ice Age that had dominated the last 100,000 years. The unusually stable climates of the Holocene were the background to the entire agrarian era of human history. Today, human impact threatens this stable climate system. The question is if human impact is likely to push the climate system across global (not just regional) tipping points, beyond which it may flip into new states that could be unpleasant for humans? For example, as glaciers melt, they leave large dark areas which, instead of reflecting heat (like white ice) will absorb it, thereby accelerating global warming in a dangerous positive feedback cycle. Similarly, forests preserve moisture, but with deforestation, the desiccation of the forests and the air above them can rapidly turn woodlands into grasslands or deserts. Finally, we know that the release of large numbers of nuclear weapons would have an immediate and devastating impact on the biosphere as a whole.

One of the most careful attempts to identify these tipping points comes from the work of the Stockholm Resilience Centre, which has been trying for almost a decade to define a 'safe operating space' for human activity. It has approached the task by trying to identify important 'planetary boundaries'. These are limits beyond which human activity threatens catastrophic breakdown, or transformations that will seriously undermine human societies. Currently, the Stockholm Resilience Centre identifies nine planetary boundaries that can be measured with varying degrees of precision.

They include various kinds of impact on the global climate system and on the ozone layer, on biodiversity, on forest cover, on the acidity of the oceans, on freshwater use, and on the circulation of phosphorus and nitrogen within the biosphere. Of these, they argue that climate change and declining biodiversity are the most critical, as each of these two systems 'has the potential on its own to drive the Earth System into a new state should they be substantially and persistently transgressed'.

Have any of these boundaries been crossed? Any answer involves large margins of error, because the biosphere is so complex that its workings are impossible to pinpoint with the certainty we would wish. Broad zones of uncertainty or increasing risk are associated with each planetary boundary. Beyond those zones, the probability of dangerous outcomes seems increasingly likely. Of the two core planetary boundaries, one—biodiversity—seems to have been crossed quite decisively, with current rates of extinction well beyond the zone of uncertainty. As for climate change, at 400 parts per million (ppm) of CO_2 in today's atmosphere, we are well into the zone of uncertainty, which ranges from 350 to 450 ppm.

Human impact on land use, and in particular on forests, has also taken us well into the zone of uncertainty. Currently about 62 per cent of original forest cover survives, while the estimated range of uncertainty ranges from 54 per cent to 75 per cent. The other danger area arises from biochemical flows, particularly flows of phosphorus and nitrogen, which are both now well beyond the zone of uncertainty, although their initial impacts are likely to be regional rather than global.

Conclusions

In the last two hundred years, a vast increase in the resources available to humans has transformed human history and human relations with planet earth. These remarkable changes have enriched billions of humans, creating levels of affluence that would have been unthinkable in the past. But many people still live in dire poverty. The huge flows of energy and resources that made these changes possible are now threatening to transform the biosphere as a whole in ways that will certainly harm many other species, and may also harm future generations of humans. This chapter has tried to describe these changes in the belief that understanding them is vital if we are to find methods of managing our astonishing power in ways that can benefit future generations.

But the Anthropocene epoch can also tell us important things about the nature of human beings and of human history. If the argument of this chapter is broadly correct, our collective capacity for sustained innovation ensured long ago that eventually humans would dominate the biosphere. But exactly when and how remained uncertain. Could the Anthropocene perhaps have begun first in China? Or perhaps, instead, in medieval Baghdad? If so, today's world would have been very different. Explaining the precise path that the Anthropocene took requires a sensitivity to both the long-term trends of human history, and its many unpredictable twists and turns over the decades that have led to where *Homo sapiens* is today.

CHAPTER 12

The Modern World and its Demons

Ideology and After in Arts, Letters, and Thought, 1815–2008

PAOLO LUCA BERNARDINI

FUTURISM, the French-Italian literary avant-garde of the early twentieth century, was probably the only artistic movement to provide a convincing, self-conscious, ambitious, complete, positive, and even mesmerizing image of modernity. Airplanes, trains, and skyscrapers were idealized as the symbols and soul of speed, of accelerating change, and of human achievement, exceeding apparently natural limitations. It comes as no surprise that Italian Fascism—a party and a dictatorship deeply involved both with the Roman classical past and with the purest expressions of modernity—had a certain penchant for Futurism. Some Futurists adhered in return, at least initially, but not without blind enthusiasm, to Fascism, while many of them were in favour of the Italian intervention in World War I. Futurism finally brought human agency to the centre of the scene; more than a century after the French Revolution turned atheism into political fashion, the arts celebrated the removal of God. In powerful images of Man, God was marginalized, and machines became the angels of the secularized world.

According to the materialist German philosopher Ernst Kapp (1808–1896)—who helped to found Sisterdale, a utopian settlement in remote Kendall County, Texas in the mid-nineteenth century, machines, tools, and mechanical equipment were but extensions of the human body: prosthesis, crafted to enhance otherwise restricted human abilities. Today's computers, iPods, mobile phones, and more are surely also additional 'artificial limbs', and meant to raise human capabilities to unprecedented peaks. Reading Kapp along with Charles Darwin who gave birth, or at least first expression, to evolutionary theory, it is easy to understand how modernity placed the individual, deprived of divine controls, quite alone, at the very centre of the universe—evolved to such a degree, that even machines were 'extensions' of his (more than 'her', so far) powers.

In the same period, ideologues placed the masses collectively in a key position overturning former systems of power. Many stressed that the French Revolution turned the world 'upside down', and its spokesmen for spiritual forces, at least in Europe, had to reflect on this literal 'revolutio': the radical subversion of the old regime.

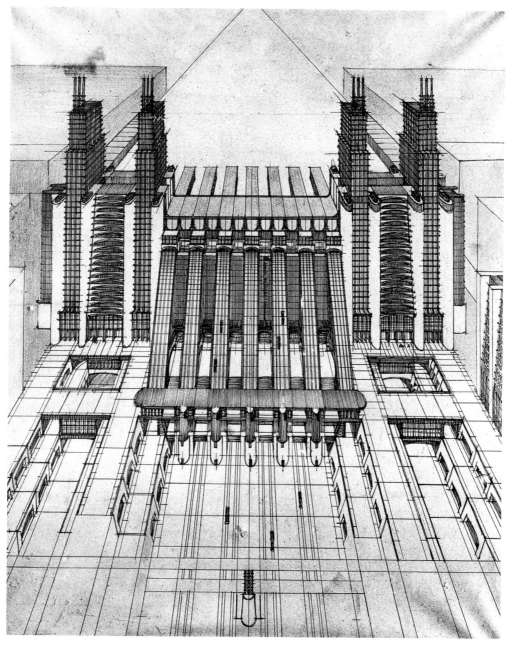

'PERSPECTIVE DRAWING FROM LA CITTÀ NUOVA', 1914, by Antonio Sant'Elia, the futurist architect who conceived a machine-like, systematic built environment.

Karl Marx based his own social and political ideas on multiple 'overturnings': in the political and social spheres he proposed to rectify capitalism by transferring wealth (i.e. power) from capitalists to the producers of goods; and in the philosophical realm he sought to overturn the 'philosophy of the spirit' of his master, G. W. Hegel, by instead placing 'reality' at the centre of whatever universe speculation disclosed.

Marx borrowed the concept of 'class' from eighteenth-century biology. The powerful rise of the individual, whom German Romantics promoted early in the nineteenth century, was mirrored in the countervailing rise of the masses, in the workers, armies, nations (and, later, voters), party members, women, and other 'classes' of individuals. The result was a mighty dialectic: *the one against the multitude*, a conflict that has continued to shape the spiritual life of the world since 1815. The individual lost the battle at the very beginning in political and social terms, but his or her role in the spiritual world, meanwhile, reached unprecedented heights.

It is as if the Romantic heroes of the early nineteenth century turned into the similarly embattled Hollywood heroes of today. In the interim, tension and reconciliation between the 'individual' and individualistic ideologies on the one hand, and the 'masses' and mass ideologies on the other, were among the most productive sources of art in the first half of the twentieth century. Futurism is a case in point. Filippo Tommaso Marinetti and others of the Italian Futurist movement emphasized technology, industry, and man's triumph over nature. Their links to the Italian National Fascist Party were strong at first but Futurism had anti-fascist and left-wing supporters, too: reconciliation failed, especially after Mussolini's defeat after World War II. The movement illustrates a powerful theme of the nineteenth and twentieth centuries: conflict between individual priorities and the needs of the masses stimulated interesting attempts to unify opposing views about Man and Machine.

In the end, neither the masses nor individuals have emerged as sole and indisputable victor. This is true for the Western world, but also for non-Western societies, which, especially in the last two centuries, have followed, imitated, amplified, and occasionally brought to a sort of 'perfection' Western values, attitudes, styles, trends, and fashions, as well as ambiguities, dilemmas, contradictions, and tragedies. Only in the post-modern, contemporary world, although firmly conditioned, once again, by the West, did 'local'—occasionally immense—cultures fully re-emerge in cracks and gaps between vast global tensions, and try to re-position themselves on the global world stage.

The four pillars of a disputed civilization

The idea of the four pillars amplifies four elements that the historian Fernand Braudel identified in *Le Monde actuel* (1963) as basic to the contemporary world and applicable to the study of all cultures: spaces, societies, economies, and collective mentalities. Over the last two hundred years or so, under the influence of accelerating globalization, they mingled, eventually resulting in the postmodern awareness of self-consciousness and uniformity. I attempt here to combine the four elements with what I call four 'pillars'. If we visualize the intellectual, spiritual, and artistic history of the world over the last two centuries or so as a lay temple, this fine high-rise tower or large compound features solid marble (or perhaps, for much of the period, ferro-concrete) pillars that confer stability, decency, and even beauty on the entire edifice.

The first pillar, **mass society**, is the birth of the 'masses', a mobile and powerful group able, without often being aware, to create its own destiny, apparently submissive to the word of dictators and television presenters. While the 'masses' have, in a sense, existed previously, they were either subject to millennial and mighty totalitarian states and rulers, as in ancient Egypt or until recently in China, or else they were part of mass migrant empires, like those of steppe-land invaders of sedentary lands (see Chapter 5 this volume). In both cases, deprived of autonomy, these masses normally remained confined to passive roles. However, after the eighteenth-century demographic revolution in Europe, they began to function as powerful agents within the settled, defined spaces of the states to which they were subject, without having to take part in vast disruptive migrations. They slowly became formidable. While the French revolutions of 1789 and 1830 were by no means 'rebellions of the masses', in those of 1848 and 1870 the hoi polloi played a substantial role, as well as in the 1917 Russian revolution. The mass of workers created by urban growth and, in some regions, by industrialization became more perceptible and identifiable than the millennial masses of peasants, who, incohesive and spread over immense territories, lacked the 'visibility' of their proletarian counterparts. No mere peasant revolt—not even the millions-strong Maitreya movement that helped bring the Ming to power in fourteenth-century China—ever involved the numbers and intensity of the nineteenth-century mass demonstrations in Europe and Asia.

Scholars, writers, and artists depicted the new power of the masses—a gigantic, sprawling, unbound Promethean hero, haunted Romantics, and Marxists alike. For example, the Italian painter Giuseppe Pellizza da Volpedo (1868–1907) fused peasants and workers—distinct 'estates' in traditional, vertically ordered societies—in his famous painting of the '*Quarto Stato*' (1898–1901). It provides what is still a visual icon of world socialism, although the image of Che Guevara (1928–1967) now rivals it as the ubiquitous image of this ideology. But instead of perceiving the 'masses' as the subject and object of history, most nineteenth-century scrutineers divided it into a number of classes; in partial consequence, entire new scientific disciplines were born out of the mass society, including sociology. Whereas, for instance, the Nobel Prize winner Elias Canetti (1905–1994) perfectly understood the unique, powerful, and irresistible new world force, in his *Mass and Power* (1960), sociologists like Gustave Le Bon (1841–1931) exemplified the contrast, writing manuals on how to condition the masses and make them serve dictatorships and political leaders, including Adolf Hitler.

While the 'masses' congealed in political minds, from the point of view of the spiritual world, the 'fold' transformed—or rather secularized—into 'the public'. As Jürgen Habermas convincingly demonstrated in his *The Structural Transformation of the*

'IL QUARTO STATO', C. 1901, BY GIUSEPPE PELLIZZA DA VOLPEDO. The masses resemble automata—the combination of grandeur and grind at the heart of the artist's idea of socialism.

Public Sphere (1962), at the start of the eighteenth century the formation of a 'public sphere' hitherto unknown or very limited in its agency conditioned authors and artists who increasingly sacrificed hopes of the perfect masterpiece to the needs and thirst of the 'market'. This is true for Johann Wolfang Goethe (1749–1832), who, as the world's first mass-market author, stripped the Bible of its long-standing primacy as bestseller. Concepts like 'mass', 'market', and 'public' were not present in early modernity, or at least not in a way that might condition intellectual production at every level. The more literate the masses—a process typical of our period—the more they can determine intellectuals' output, from poetry to commercials. At the same time, intellectuals and artists wrote both to please the public as well as to promote ideologically conceived forms of mass society with the aim of assuring what came to be called 'the greatest happiness of the greatest number'. Utilitarian utopians, from Jeremy Bentham (1748–1832) who coined the phrase, to his admiring adversary John Stuart Mill (1806–1873), tried hard to reconcile individualism with collective happiness. Mill's rather flawed and failed *On Liberty* (significantly published in 1859 the same year as Darwin's *Origins*) demonstrated all the difficulties intrinsic in this attempt. Depictions of the 'masses' grew increasingly disturbing, especially in popular culture. In 1818, Mary Shelley (1797–1851) published *Frankenstein* describing an individual creature born out of the deranged mind of an individual scientist, and modern fiction turned human masses to monsters, potentially destructive and unbound like a malign version of the Romantic Prometheus. George A. Romero's *Dawn of the Dead* (1978) began a horror saga that continues with today's filmmakers and writers, especially in eastern Europe.

The second pillar on which the temple of late-modern world rests is the **modern state**, born with the French Revolution, consolidated and occasionally mitigated in its intrinsic natural totalitarian aims in a number of guises and by a number of modifications and transformations, including the modern social democracies. The modern state, with all its features—including more or less complete *representative* democracy, and the relevant codifications, constitutions, and divisions of powers—and its formerly imperial projections in the wider world embodied unprecedented strength. It displaced rival sources of authority, monopolized violence within its borders, and could mobilize populations and resources with almost ineluctable completeness. Its power marks a large part of the cultural and intellectual productions of the last two centuries. First, scholars, writers, artists, and musicians celebrated its creation and achievements. At a further stage, other intellectuals impugned its nature and value by conceiving rival utopias, originally purely speculative, but realized later often in the most appalling way. No utopia is ever realized in the way it was conceived, and some were never realized at all. Thanks to their generally libertarian, anarchistic pedigrees, early Communists usually despised every form of states. But when Communists seized or built states of their own, such as now occasionally survive in various guises, the results more closely resembled the French Jacobin State of 1789–1795 than the utopias designed by the 'prophets of Paris'. Contemporary China, for instance, is an immense state in the Jacobin image, ruled by party members under a pale and frail masque of democracy, with an undeclared, but obvious, structure.

The birth and spread of the modern state, a typically European phenomenon in origin, deeply conditioned the intellectual, spiritual, and artistic history of the entire, not only during Europeans' ascent to global hegemony in the period 1789–1945, but also, lingeringly, for the decolonization period and up to the present. Its prevalence legitimates a Eurocentric view, for, as we will see, even the extra-European 'reaction' to the old European 'cultural hegemony'—or fertile concept—too often bears the marks of European culture: in terms of language, style, themes, and modalities of expression. The modern state has deprived world history of extra-European valid counterparts in a very rapid way. This is true also for those parts of the world, first North, and later Central and South America, that became politically independent in a long process from 1776–1898. As both North and South America shed their European rulers and struggled to find their own cultural identity, they remained powerfully related to European cultural and intellectual values and styles. Meanwhile, European powers conquered most of Asia, excluding Japan and Siam (but including strategic points in China, e.g. the crisis of late Qing China and the largely real 'Europeanization' of the empire). They seized almost all of Africa, minus Ethiopia (whose original cultures were still preserved at the time of the brief Italian colonization), and a few other spots. The intellectual production of these two centuries reflects their imperialistic nature, at least until the beginning of decolonization in the 1940s. Writers of the colonial era, along with anti-colonial or post-colonial writers, who are also products of imperialism, shaped trends in literature in most of the Western world, and almost entirely in Africa.

'THE SECOND OF MAY, 1808: The Charge of the Mamelukes', 1814, by Francisco Goya contrasts the alien invaders in their exotic attire, with the simply clad, poorly armed insurgents initiating 'war to the knife'.

The modern state, is and has been aggressive. Its intrinsically aggressive nature not only expressed itself in the colonial enterprise, but it also exploded in the French-Prussian war of 1870; from that time on, it expanded until (after an attempt at suppression by the League of Nations) the final holocaust of World War II. Unprecedented in human history, the level of violence caused devastation widely reflected in literature, the arts, and music. Pablo Picasso's *Guernica* (1937) is only one in a long series of depictions of human cruelty and destruction perfecting the ideal series inaugurated by Francisco José de Goya y Lucientes (1746–1828) with lurid descriptions of the cruelty perpetrated on both sides during the French invasion of the early nineteenth century.

A less obvious but genuine manifestation in art of state aggressiveness was the extension of the concept of 'the sublime', an eighteenth-century notion formulated by Kant and by Edmund Burke (1729–1797), which became in Europe, as well as in China and Latin America, a feature of the most daring and appealing as well as appalling art: the depiction of extremes, in all aspects of human life and death, from sex to violence. Indeed, as the state enforced a monopoly of violence, individuals appropriated its

A STILL FROM DIRECTOR PETER GREENAWAY'S FILM 'A ZED AND TWO NOUGHTS', 1985: 'self-conscious reflection on the depiction of horror'.

images, in an escalating way, that were the forerunners of movie directors like Quentin Tarantino, and artists such as Maurizio Cattelan and Damien Hirst. Others, such as British director Peter Greenway, self-consciously reflected on the depiction of horror in speculative art works such as 1985's *A Zed & Two Noughts*. The immense destructive power nurtured, accumulated, and finally released by the modern state begot this artistic trend. During the Cold War, when state power threatened global atomic destruction, cultural production became obsessed with this extreme option. Works like Nevil Shute's 1957 *On The Beach*, later turned into a blockbuster film by Stanley Kramer in 1959, revealed the widespread, almost universal anxiety, shades of which still haunt modern society.

The third pillar of the late modern world is the immense increase in power of ***science and technology***. Francis Bacon's Elizabethan dream of 'advancement of learning', thanks to both state agency as well as private entrepreneurship, came true in Victorian times, and continued to develop, through a number of 'scientific revolutions', into the twenty-first century. The so-called 'Fourth scientific revolution' and the communications tools at its core currently monopolize debate. The results on intellectual and artistic production were both direct and indirect. New paper-making and print technology shifted the world centre of the publishing industry to Britain. The mid-1980s advent of e-technology has transformed the way people access information formerly only found via printed material. Anyone can make any kind of information public, and access information from across the entire world via the Internet. It is the loss of Walter Benjamin's second 'aura' that once made artistic reproductions mysterious: today, not only can a work of art be reproduced—even made identical to the original—but it is available worldwide and available to billions of consumers.

New art forms have emerged, previously inconceivable without the aid of technology—such as those related to the Internet and its blurred, complex, articulated, and ever-evolving world—to challenge and change the status and very idea of 'art'. The invention of photography, first, and of the movie, towards the end of the nineteenth century, not only brought new art into the public eye, but also called into question the very meaning of 'art' and 'artwork'. While the Lumière brothers, the film industry's founders, saw films as entertainment, photography instead had a status as a form of 'art', although this difference has always been fiercely contested.

When photos of the Crimean war were first published, they were considered too crude for the public as documents, as well as too realistic for narratives which normally relied on the ornaments and rhetoric of writing. Eventually photography became an art like painting and sculpture, but even the status and concept of those 'traditional' arts

ENCAMPMENT, CRIMEAN WAR. Photography, for all its contrivance, transmitted real images of the wars of the second half of the nineteenth century to the home fronts.

were being widely challenged. Photography was a Western product, but immediately spread in regions of the world where 'modernization' was forcibly introduced by foreign rulers, as well as local elites, unhappy with their immense but static and fragile traditions. In the Ottoman Empire of the nineteenth century, for instance, photography spread slowly but brought about immense changes in mentality, anticipating the social media coverage of the ongoing civil wars of Egypt, Syria, and Palestine. The work of Italians artists-turned-photographers like Elisabetta Pante and Fausto Zonaro in the Ottoman Empire was fundamental. It was the same in China, during the late phase of the Qing dynasty, when photography—in its uncertain status between document and work of art—helped to speed modernization by spreading news of about the country and its customs, traditions, and problems. Photographic documentation of *lingchi*, the horrible torture of the 'death by one thousands cuts', sped up the process of abolishing such an abominable practice; the last *lingchi* execution took place in Beijing in 1904.

The new artistic tools and trends that science and technology produced included electronic music (from Karlheinz Stockhausen to Paul Lansky). A new interdisciplinary field, characteristic of modernity, was a further result, in which art and science mingle, and the very notions of genre and purpose for intellectual production fade. Thus, science and technology, by making old forms of communication obsolete, powerfully challenge the 'world as we know it' in its intellectual, spiritual, and artistic components. The nineteenth century extended the notion of human sciences, which eventually

RUINS OF THE MONUMENTAL ARCH destroyed by ISIS militants in Palmyra, a UNESCO world heritage site, 27 March 2016.

included the most typically bourgeois of developments in psychology (itself a new branch of medicine): psychoanalysis. It is probably true that the most valid ideas of Sigmund Freud were those concerning 'extremes'; certainly, his exploration of the intimate sphere of the Promethean individual brought to the surface all the complexities and traumas of the psyche. Gustave Courbet's 1866 painting *The Origins of the World*, depicting a woman's midriff, as if severed from the rest of her body, with exposed pudenda, seemed to anticipate the effect; psychoanalysis deeply influenced all the arts.

The fourth pillar of the late modern world temple is **secularization.** Of the four, secularization on a global level has most subtle effect on cultural, spiritual, intellectual, and artistic output, including China, where religion did not play the same role it traditionally played in the Western World, or in Africa. The emergence of the masses, of the modern state, and of science and technology could all happen in a world without 'arts and letters'. But the presence or absence of God is a key element in all spiritual, intellectual, and artistic work. The arts constantly gave their account of the clash between mutability and eternity as they relate to the human world and the eternal God; through these representations, they justify their practice and express their deepest meaning. These conditions of mutability and visions of the world in which the sacred space plays a fundamental role plead in favour of the divine dimension of art. They suggest 'divine inspiration', as a human response to the same mystery of existence. Therefore, what we might call the 'atheistic turn' after 1789 had an immense effect on all the intellectual, artistic, and spiritual life of mankind.

Nietzsche's famous assertion that 'God is dead' at least implied a previous existence, and up to life's natural end, death. In its origins, and very nature, the French Revolution was in large part a war of religion, in which competing faiths struggled for the mastery of a deeply religious, Christian France. In its frantic development, however, and rapid degeneration, the Revolution laid the foundation of an atheistic, secularized world. The pigs first brought into Notre Dame by the mob to desecrate the space and humiliate the clergy, are still roaming the world's intellectual spaces. Atheism was present but previously marginal, and many deists did not deny the existence of God, but instead the divine creation of the world; a number of scholars, including neo-platonists, warned about the dangers of atheism. Still, in the eighteenth century, atheism was mostly confined to Parisian intellectual circles.

The negation of God, however, became of paramount importance on the international intellectual scene from the early decades of the nineteenth century. Thereafter, it conditioned the intellectual growth of the world—from the 'invention of God' to the deification of man by Nietzsche and his followers—spreading devastatingly if compared to the atheism of the old regime. In the 'upside-down world' that the French Revolution bequeathed, God was labelled a human product. While still suspect and not so welcome in the new world, from the newly born US to Australia, and only falteringly influential in China or Japan, it triumphed in European philosophy, thus marking, *inter alia*, the spiritual atmosphere of a new creation of late modernity: the state universities.

It took a long time, however, to establish atheism as the equivalent of a new state religion: atheists were unwelcome in German universities when, in Berlin in 1810, the first truly 'modern' one was established by Wilhelm von Humboldt (1767–1835); atheists became numerous by the end of the century. In the meantime, secularization had appropriated almost the entire repertoire of concepts of the Church; *progress* was the new *providence*, social and moral *regeneration*, the new *baptism*, *resurrection* became 'Risorgimento'—re-appropriation, by the nations, of their own destiny made effective by the creation of *national states*. The concept of secularization, originally the violent act of forfeiture of Church property by the State, underwent major changes, or '*Aufhebung*' ('sublation', 'annulment'), denoting (with a term Hegel coined) the laicization of Christian ideas, ideals, and meanings. Atheism went well with the new cult of the 'deified' State, although occasionally, however, it could spread pessimistic ideas that convinced youths of the insignificance of human life, and thus of the goodness of suicide. Officials in Bismarck's Germany advised Eduard von Hartmann, a philosophy teacher, to reject the negative *Weltanschauung* he inherited from his master Arthur Schopenhauer, as students were killing themselves in despair. The Second German Reich needed soldiers, not sad, pale, melancholic youths prone to drug use and unable to fight, let alone lead normal, reputable lives.

Marx gave atheism its full political dimension, styling 'religion as the opium of the people'. The huge bulk of the intellectual, artistic, and spiritual output of the Communist world, from 1917 until 1992, from the USSR to China, from North Korea to Cuba, testified to a 'world without God', reflected in 'atheistic art' (and philosophy) whose ersatz divinity is the masses, the workers, worldly happiness, and nature at the service of modern civilization. The making of art became a 'collective' enterprise, apparently deprived of all individualism. The tragedy of the transition from rural society to industrialism, particularly from Orthodox Christianity to state atheism, is apparent in the work of many Russian artists, who, after a time of transition, were soon overwhelmed by the ideology and systematic censorship of Communist and Fascist regimes (which is still present in China). Typically, under totalitarianism the regime's cultural products, if any, are poor, while the most interesting works are those of persecuted, condemned, or exiled dissidents. In Communist Russia, novels revealed to the world the horrors of the Gulag. Mao's wife, Jiang Qing, tried to enter the world's cultural scene by promoting 'model opera', which failed to gain any attention, while the art sponsored by Franco, Hitler, and Mussolini had little intrinsic or extrinsic value, compared to the work of opponents and exiles. In Nazi Germany, destruction and censorship of works of art were done under the name of 'elimination of the degenerate'.

Secularization affected art beyond totalitarian and authoritarian regimes. Realism, an artistic movement born in France, focused artists on the '*hic and nunc*' of worldly reality while inspiring extreme reactions, such as *Decadenz*. Émile Zola (1840–1902) influenced writers like Giovanni Verga, from nearby Italy, to Japan's Takiji Kobayashi and Yuriko Miyamoto. Secularization was also evident in architecture and music—arts that were formerly dominated by religious traditions. Lay architecture came to embrace the radical 'rationality' of stark, angular geometry. The long repudiation of tradition is well exemplified in the work of recent leading architects, from the Genoese Renzo Piano, Catalan Enric Miralles Moya, Argentinian César Antonio Pelli, and the American Paul Rudolph.

Masses and *states*, *technology* and *atheism*: late modernity is both sustained and confined by these four pillars. In a world deprived of God and apparently open to endless possibilities, including pessimism and nihilism, not all the effects are negative. Atheism and materialism can foster a positive, joyful, truly Epicurean philosophy. Marx, a materialist, was not a pessimist, nor were Friedrich Engels or Vladimir Ilyich Lenin. The modern state needs masses and technologies, as was already clear to Francis Bacon well before mass society emerged, whereas, according to the doctrines of laïcité, traditional religion may be surplus to requirements. Religion, confined to the 'private sphere', might even increase its influence on human life, without interference from theocracies of the sort that already seemed obsolete in the middle of the nineteenth century, e.g., when the newly created Italian State occupied Rome and confined the Pope to a 'spiritual realm'. In the spirit and word of the Gospel, 'My Kingdom is not of this world . . . '.

To survive the waves of secularization, the old Catholic Church had largely to secularize itself as far as possible without denying the existence of God—its *'ratio essendi'*. The Church embraced doctrines of 'social renewal' first in France, and approached collectivist ideals. Since 1789, the Church's search for an identity intelligible in a secularized world has conditioned most of the work of Catholic intellectuals torn between the 'needs of modernity' and the 'tenets of the Gospel'. From sex to socialism, the battle involved supreme categories and mighty forces. Although it lost its temporal power, however, the Catholic Church has remained one of the most powerful spiritual driving forces in the world.

After the French Revolution, the marginalization of theology and religion brought about not only a widespread refusal of religion, but also a powerful return of God in mystical forms, fuelled by the encounter with the 'other God' of Eastern religions. This return was initiated at a 'mass' level, rather than in an academic context, by Friedrich and August Wilhelm Schlegel who were within that fertile intellectual cradle that was German Romanticism.

The four elements we have examined played a pivotal role in modernization in the West, but elsewhere in the world, the delay and violence with which they were introduced brought about an ambivalent phenomenon. Non-Western societies suffered from an overdose of spontaneous 'Westernization'. Specifically, in China they developed from an existing mass society in the throes of a belated but huge demographic explosion, and from long-standing but underdeveloped scientific potential. Yet, in the post-colonial world, they gave birth to intellectual, artistic, and spiritual trends and products still heavily dependent on Western canons, based on the needs of the market and current fashion. Meanwhile, Western approaches to Zoroastrianism,

AFTER THE FALL OF THE BERLIN WALL, Renzo Piano's technologically pioneering designs turned Berlin's Potsdamer Platz from a 'dormant wasteland' into the reputed 'largest building site in Europe' with 'stark geometry'. See p. 386.

Confucianism, Buddhism, and many other religions, were often a form of 'Orientalism' in a culturally exploitative sense of the 'other', which, in a sort of intellectual colonialism, was deemed 'inferior'.

Was the transition smooth, giving equal access for all to the spiritual, intellectual, and artistic 'universe'? Not at all. The Islamic theocracies that we see now as resurgent, for instance, proved that the links between secular and religious power cannot be easily and forever dissolved. Where post-modernity entered the picture before true modernity had made its mark, mass society, technology, state power, and atheism formed a complex and fragile system that was under constant challenge. The effect, moreover, seems unfavourable to creativity. While DAESH terrorists destroy monuments and entire historical cities in the Middle East—including the acknowledged seedbed of Western Civilization in what is now Iraq—the reaction to secularization and the return to blind faith brings about no work of art, nor any solid and convincing intellectual or cultural production. Their challenge to Western values includes a staunch, pervasive obliteration of the realms of the spirit. What is conceived as a mass reaction by the 'other' against the West has, in the Western world—especially among artists and intellectuals—found a parallel: rejection of tradition, establishment, and the mainstream. Those who reacted against the idolization of the masses and the power of the state fuelled the hyperinflation of individualism. The temple of late modernity may have strong pillars, but infiltrators have penetrated its gates.

The age of -isms

The combination of the emergence of the masses, the consolidation of the centralized state, secularization, and the technological revolutions brought about new conditions for living a spiritual life and, in general, for the arts and letters. By mobilizing immense, hitherto unknown energy, this combination created new entities: in a vast global market, artistic, literary, and intellectual products became commodities; taste and fashion functioned on a world scale; and, more recently, post-modernism led to parity across styles, ideologies, narratives, artistic products, and values, without regard for quality.

The notion of the 'masses' proved deceptive; it was not the proletariat that determined the course of spiritual and artistic life. Until at least 1945, the bourgeoisie became the arbiters by respecting the centralist state. Using technology, endorsing science, and adhering, often *à contre-coeur*, to the new atheist fashion fostered by governments eager to crown their conflicts with the Church in complete victory, the bourgeoisie was amply rewarded for its services.

Typically, even when cultures of origin challenged these bourgeois values, they were embedded in large post-colonial states. In India, for example, 200 million of its citizens live by standards the British middle-class left them; e.g., the Bollywood film *Monsoon Wedding* (2000) by Mira Nair displays the phenomenon clearly. The Nigerian movie industry, or 'Nollywood', similarly operates in a post-colonial, post-British setting, and is growing rapidly, challenging Hollywood and Bollywood alike. Post-colonial societies generally assimilate and magnify Western culture, from soccer to movies, from music to fast food.

This process of Western-initiated global cultural uniformity has, nonetheless, met with fierce resistance since its beginning. In the European context, resistance began when it became clear that the bourgeoisie had taken a leading role in the world at the expense of both the old nobility as well as the peasants and proletarians.

Among intellectuals, a characteristic form of resistance was to repudiate the Enlightenment—the source of prevailing ideas on the masses, the state, secularism and science. Anti-capitalists denounced the universal values applied by the use and abuse of reason as cold-blooded tools of exploitation. The nineteenth-century Western educational system was another target because, although states tended to leave entertainment to private actors, they controlled schools tenaciously. They maximized literacy, introduced compulsory schooling, constructed literary and artistic canons, and turned peasants and proletarians into citizens, soldiers, and ersatz bourgeois in a complex process involving numerous strategies of acculturation. I suggest that the creation of 'canons' was a mark of modernity, and one of the most destructive factors for culture in general. In my view, as the work of state-paid intellectuals, canons excluded true stars of world literature, arts, and thought, resulting in an impoverished learning process. I believe that, in order to enter the list of canonical literature, contemporary intellectuals often de-natured themselves and reached for major prizes, even ahead of major sales, rather than maintaining artistic integrity. The Nobel Prize is paradigmatic, and canonizes suitable writers while excluding potential disturbers of the mainstream.

Instead, opponents advocated the value of the absolutely peculiar—something not compliant with universal Enlightenment categories. Meanwhile, other prevailing or developing trends of thought favoured categorization, e.g. individualism, liberalism, and pluralism. Increasingly, throughout our period, '-isms' flourished irrepressibly. In the misnamed 'liberal century' (as liberalism implies the growth of the individual liberties and of the free market), a number of dissident ideologies attracted vast followings, primarily Romanticism. The need to re-discover a magical world, where nature, spirits, Gods, animals, and plants live together in a natural, unspoiled, but violent setting is exemplified in the work of Jean-Jacques Rousseau, who confronted modern civilization with the noble savage. Rousseau typified the theme inspired by nostalgia for a natural world and natural law. Romanticism, from the Brothers Grimm in literature to the Swiss composer Joachim Raff and his 1869 *Im Walde* symphony, revitalized the idea of untamed, and untamable, nature. In our technology-dependent world today, intellectuals respond with the formulation of individualistic utopias in the fanciful realms of isolation and renewed contact with 'mother Nature'. Nature takes a prominent position in the contemporary intellectual agenda, and a long line connects work from *Walden* (1854) to Jon Krakauer's *Into the Wild* (1996).

The next big '-ism', communism, or perfect collectivism, was, in origin at least, against any form of state. Along with communism, forms of anarchism sustained an even more radical challenge. The collectivist utopias of Marx and Proudhon, among many others, were strongly opposed, for instance, by the 'libertarian', or 'anarco-capitalist' school of thought. Originating in Austria with Carl Menger, it spread to the US, with the emigration of Ludwig von Mises, and his followers, including the American M. N. Rothbard. A major battle between the extremes of collectivism, embodied by communism, and the extremes of individualism, embodied by libertarians, is still taking place today. Both schools, however, have been so far defeated by history.

'Post-modernism', levelling every theory and abjuring the truth-quest in favour of interminable 'discourse', is, perhaps, the latest and the most placid '-ism' in the tradition. When young Hegel, in the aftermath of the French revolution that he was the first to hail as 'epochal', said, 'You will be not better than the present, but you will be the present in the best possible way', he might have been dreaming of post-modern philosophy. In the immense market of a world turned into a single 'global village', cultural industries multiply their products as never before. The end of '-isms', or at least of the prevalence, according to intellectual and cultural fashion, of one '-ism' on the other, is the result. They can all live together in relative peace: Marxism and existentialism, liberalism and libertarianism, feminism and transgenderism, realism and hyperrealism, anarchism, and collectivism, and possibly hundreds of others.

RIDLEY SCOTT'S *BLADE RUNNER*, 1982.

The cults of technology, the state and the masses, combined with the completion of the process of secularization, helped to bring about 'modern dictatorships' like those of Mussolini and Hitler, Lenin and Stalin. It seemed almost natural for intellectual tendencies before and after the dark decades of 1870–1945 to lean towards the idealization of other worlds, utopias of the past and of the future. Once again, the nineteenth century was their immense laboratory. Though most of 'the masses' stuck to ancien-regime religiosity there was now a huge constituency among them for substitutes for God. Intellectuals supplied 'supermen' as, say, Nietzsche conceived them—ersatz for God—or absolute, unbound individualists, like the sad Promethean in Max Stirner's 1844 *The Ego and Its Own*, who proved to be immensely popular. Even writers more interested in science than the state conceived negative, and pessimistic worlds. Science fiction, timidly inaugurated during the Enlightenment, was amplified, for instance, in a long tradition from the French sci-fi novelist Jules Verne to Ridley Scott's *Blade Runner* (1982), where the nightmares of the future are but the projection, on a bigger scale, of those of the present. It was sometimes hard to distinguish fictional travesties of the supermen from the cruel, robotic states they proposed and tried to create: utopias procured by the massacre of their enemies and enforced by extinguishing opposition.

Apologists were never wanting for the centralized, democratic, and welfare state. It took a long time to assume currently recognizable forms—in 1861 in Italy, for example, in 1870 in France and in 1871 in Germany—and powerfully re-emerged, after backtracking and interruptions, with new constitutions after 1945. It was and is in constant need of intellectual defence, theoretical legitimation, and recommendations for its betterment and 'perfection'. It saw off the supermen in wars hot and cold but the old Jacobin-style state, the enemy of the Marxists and of the libertarian alike, is still alive and well, with its lack of respect for private property, and its low esteem for human life. Now, with unprecedented intensity, 'mainstream' and 'marginal' thought oppose each other. Typical of modernity, the value and the primacy of the one, with respect to the other, is conferred upon not by intrinsic prevalence or coherence or validity, but rather by the acclaim and endorsement (or lack thereof) by the public. As never before, a great many antithetical and varied ideologies emerged, with 'collectivism' from the one side, and 'individualism' from the other.

The end of embourgeoisement

While the market, dominated by a solid bourgeoisie was the leading force of the world, that same market allowed and allows 'violations of the order'. In other words, to please the bourgeoisie the artist has to '*shock*'. Artistic production, in these circumstances, leans towards a difficult-to-identify 'left'—something as in Italy after 1945, where all the major publishers, intellectuals, and artists, from Turin to Rome, monopolized the cultural scene for decades. Art often becomes 'collective enterprise'—a means to promote the sales and enhance individual fortunes. For most of our period, while conservatism, 'reaction', or temperate nostalgia for the ancient regime lingers, in in the schools, universities, academies, and other state entities, avant-garde movements flourished. The avant-garde wanted to compete with institutionalized schools of thought. They, or the new product of modernity, the 'critic', gave their movements names terminating with '-ism', from Dadaism to Surrealism. The critic became the intermediator in the process of cultural production, between public and artists, although an unintended effect of the action of criticism typically isolated those movements in a politically neutral realm. It was what Adorno labelled 'cultural industry' before he died in a very modern way (a car crash), in 1969. The absolute 'anarchy', 'freedom', and 'peculiarity' of the artists, and the 'free' intellectuals in general, was a demand of the market, and was aptly defined as 'eccentricity', in order to promote the 'goods' produced by such intellectuals.

As Umberto Eco once said, 'apocalyptic' figures turned out to be the best integrated into the system, where they not only made money, but effectively validated the system by apparently challenging it. The death of David Bowie early in 2016 provided a retrospective of his career—from his inception as the champion of misfits and rebels to his acclaim and success as a capitalist (140 million records sold). Thus, the rebels appease capitalism. By criticizing dictatorships (from Peter Gabriel with South Africa to George Clooney with Sudan), they also endorse the 'powers that be' in the form of US-style 'liberal democracies'—'the most perfect government ever'—which will end all conflicts, poverty, and problems of the world through the extension of the American model to the entirety of the planet.

The 'eccentricity' of the producer of intellectual, spiritual, and artistic commodities had normally, at least until the emergence of post-modernity over the last four decades of the twentieth century, to be matched by the oddity of her or his work. From 1789

DAVID BOWIE, THE 'CHAMPION OF MISFITS AND REBELS', who became an exemplar of success in exploiting market capitalism.

onwards, the rise of eccentricity was constant, so that both the avant-garde and their output seemed to challenge current mentalities, all branches of the establishment, and even common sense. The fall of classical and neo-classical paradigms, tempered by taste and reasonability, gave way to extremes that almost immediately become institutionalized in their turn, and occasionally, when possible are exhibited in a museum or consecrated on a stage. The Tasmanian Museum of Old and New Art (MONA) opened in 2011, and is a perfect example of the 'institutionalization', and thus political neutralization, of the most extreme eccentricity. To be englobed in a museum was the 'foreseeable destiny of every form of avant-garde', and the MONA does that as it reconciles the public with the occasionally genuine revolutionary aims of the avant-gardes, behind a bullet-proof glass screen.

In the musical arena, Arnold Schönberg began to deconstruct classical music. Eventually, this deconstructive turn was pursued by his followers, from Luciano Berio to Tōru Takemitsu. American musician John Cage went a step further and wrote 4:33, a piece which was just silence, while in 1961 in *Merda d'artista*, sculptor Piero Manzoni encapsulated his own excrement, a 'multiple' which still commands high prices on the art market. Every 'excess' was depicted, sculpted, filmed, so as to eventually saturate the market.

However, in today's post-modern world, there is no longer any avant-garde, for everything is both acceptable and accepted, and the markets themselves are extremely diversified. At the same time, old sale strategies are still valid: the Italian poet Gabriele D'Annunzio famously made public his own death in order to sell more copies of his books: those entrepreneurial skills belong still to a number of artists, and intellectuals all over the world. They are magnified, and not at all limited, by the new technologies.

Furthermore, the new link between the individual speaker and the content of the spoken message, which marks modernity, completely alters the value of truth intrinsic to the statement. Who says what is immensely more important than what is actually said. This is the most powerful, and dangerous, device of mature modernity as well as of the post-modern world. While heresy was the problem in the early modern period, notwithstanding who the heretic was, mature modernity brought—with the attenuation of censorship—a new form of 'filtering' of thought. The more celebrated the person who speaks or writes is, the more heard and influential the message is, regardless if its contents are absurd or sensible. Both Oprah Winfrey and the pope are influential, regardless of how original or derivative their statements are. Political, social, and economic counsel from uncharismatic sources are marginalized not because of their contents, but rather because the system has astutely confined them to a marginal audience. This is true, for instance, for libertarian and religious spokesmen in Europe in general, although in the US, the fundamental liberal origins of the US Constitution and a federal form of government allow more scope to libertarian interpretations; at the same time, genuine adherence to religion and a spirituality richer than Europe's are still present in all the arts and disciplines, despite the Constitution's declaration of a separation of church and state. In other respects, a contrarian individual or 'think tank' will, no matter how credible and solid, forfeit visibility and influence. The 'think tank', by the way, is the heir, via the Enlightenment salon, of the Renaissance 'academy'. The most brilliant ideas are constantly formulated, but they are mostly inefficient, not applied, and even unheard if they come from sources unsanctified by celebrity.

Other worlds, and not-so-other

A Eurocentric vision of the world is legitimate, if not throughout the period from 1815 to 2008, at least until the 1960s, when a post-colonial world eventually emerged amid feelings, thoughts, and arts that now dominate the relevant markets. In the construction of Chinese literary canons, the 'Four Masterpieces', or Sìdàmíngzhu, play a major role, and none of them postdates the eighteenth century: two are of the fourteenth century, one of the sixteenth, and the last, The *Dream of the Red Chamber*, had its first edition in 1791. During the last phase of the Qing dynasty, artists and thinkers felt, more or less strongly, an 'alien presence' in growing European outposts and commercial enclaves. When the 'New Culture Movement' boomed after the tragic end of the Qing in 1912, which fostered Western ideals in all the spheres of learning and politics and decisively rejected Confucianism, the way towards modernization was already paved. When they were not looking for models outside the huge boundaries of China, intellectuals showed nostalgia for the old rules of truly Chinese dynasties. Their retrospection resembled that of some French conservative authors writing in the aftermath of the Revolution and of Restoration. Other writers, such as Gong Zizhen, who perfectly understood the danger of the Western acculturation, embodied the tendency in a time of the first massive translations of classical Western writers into Chinese. Gong lamented the lack and loss of the original Chinese spirit, tradition, and outstanding individual talents. The Meiji Restoration in Japan, and the urge of modernization, forcibly, and more rapidly than in China, introduced the Western world to the hitherto still relatively isolated islands of Japan. The end of the Shogun, powerfully depicted in Edward Zwick's 2003 The Last Samurai, brought to an end a millennial feudal culture. The Westernization of the Japanese Empire was, and is, a story of destructive internal conflicts, re-fuelled by the Japanese defeat in World War II. While mainstream popular culture leaned, sometimes cautiously, sometimes acritically, towards Western models, central figures of Japanese twentieth-century culture, from writer Mishima Yukio to movie director Akira Kurosawa, invoked the immense heritage of the Shogun, the Samurai, and the cult of honour, God, and homeland. This fragmentation of the Japanese culture scene still marks the cultural life of a country which bears a special historical significance, given the fact that it was never (not even partially, like China) politically conquered by the West.

Conquest, however, can take various forms. In a late arrival that sheds light on the conditioning power of Western civilization, staples of nineteenth-century Western culture seeped gradually and falteringly eastwards. They included newspapers and

AKIRA KUROSAWA'S *RASHOMON*, 1950, BASED ON A STORY BY RYŪNOSUKE AKUTAGAWA, recounts the unresolved story of a samurai's shameful murder. A simple woodsman is the only character to emerge with honour.

magazines of every kind, and later, on radio, television, and the Internet, as well as via the once-exclusive institution of the Western World, the modern university. Forms of universities existed well before Oxford, the Sorbonne, and Bologna, but they were normally religious schools like 'madrasas', or Buddhist seminaries like Nalanda in Uttar Pradesh, newly reopened in 2014 and probably the oldest college in the world. The model that spread all over the world derived from the most successful Western version of the nineteenth century: the German system. Johns Hopkins University in Baltimore established it as normative in the US. For the model's infiltration of the Pacific world the case of the now world-class University of Tokyo is enlightening. Established under the Mejii, 'Tokyo Daigaku' consisted in 1877 of four departments—Law, Science, Literature, and Medicine—and later incorporated three pre-existing institutions: Shoheiko ('Japanese and Chinese Literature' in 1789), Yogakusho ('Occidental Studies' in 1855), and Shutosho ('Vaccinations' in 1860). Vaccination, a landmark of Western civilization, spread systematically by the French troops after the Revolution, was made the subject of an entire school in Japan on the eve of the Meiji restoration. Tokyo University progressively introduced typical Western disciplines into its structure, even including 'nuclear studies' in 1955—a move typical of the new 'open' nature of Japanese mentality, while anti-nuclear forces started to be extremely active all over the world.

Not all exchange was unidirectional. The increasing presence of Chinese and Japanese artists, musicians, and writers in Europe and later on in the US, balanced the penetration of Western ideals, figures, ideologies, and cultural attitudes in the East. Artists like Katsushika Hokusai became immensely influential on European artists like Vincent van Gogh, Paul Gauguin, Egon Schiele, and Gustav Klimt, and on the Art Nouveau movement. Not only the style, but also some far-eastern themes entered into, and were transformed by, Western culture. For instance, the octopus in Hokusai's highly erotic 1820 painting *The Fisherman's Wife* became one of the themes dear to Western imagination, from André Pieyre de Mandiargues' marginally pornographic French fiction to Austrian Alfred Kubin's fascination with magic. The giant cephalopod became well known in the US as well, as it appeared in Herman Melville's 1851 legendary masterpiece *Moby Dick*. Even in Giacomo Puccini's unfinished opera *Turandot* (1926) there are hidden references to Hokusai.

'THE DREAM OF THE FISHERMAN'S WIFE', 1814, by Katsushika Hokusai, whose images—ranging from powerful eroticism, as here, to haunting landscapes and seascapes—helped promote the worldwide influence of Japanese art.

Meanwhile, the Far East adopted Western ideas and ideologies, and even Western philosophy became mainstream: the complete works of Martin Heidegger were translated into Japanese, while the theological basis of Eastern philosophy, until its recent rediscovery, progressively lost legitimacy, as well as audience. While the Far East, until Mao's cultural revolution—in itself inspired by some tenets of misinterpreted Marxism—adopted Western fashions, it also brought to perfection, and increased its relevant production, forms of culture belonging originally to pop cultures, such as cartoons. From the combination of two traditions, those of Western and Eastern old engravings, Japan developed a powerful production of cartoons, the manga, that are now identified as a 'peculiar' Eastern product.

At the same time, the post-1815 world saw the progressive growth of mutual interaction among cultures once completely unaware of each other. The globalization of culture included European outposts turned into powerful states, initially the US, then Canada, Australia, and Nigeria. In search of a much-needed cultural identity, the emerging US imported European ideas and intellectuals, the latter flooding from Germany and Italy after the rise of Fascism. In return, innovations in mass culture and mass production, heavily dependent on European contents and ideologies but related to new media—from cinema to television—transformed the US from an intellectual offspring of Europe into a powerful producer of art, and of free-market, individualist values. The magnetism of US popular culture helped to determine the cultural and intellectual scene worldwide after the end of World War II, and, even more profoundly, after the end of the Cold War.

Other parts of the world played a lesser role in shaping global culture. It took a long time for arts and thought from Latin America to break out of dependency and gain peculiar identities. Only after World War II did Latin American authors powerfully enter the world scene. Conquering a space for their reconstruction of a difficult colonial past, an ambiguous pre-colonial 'pre-history', and a precarious current existence, amid dictatorships and fragile democracies, novelists in Argentina and Colombia brought the Latin American intellectual and cultural sphere to the world stage.

The post-modern turn: mutability, uncertainty, pluralism, and their enemies

This last section of the chapter focuses on the most recent decades, which seem in consequence rather to anticipate, or even already to present, a 'world civilization' in which selective uniformity has displaced some differences, and differences, both cultural and intellectual, are best understood as self-conscious reactions to all-pervasive uniformity. Since World War II, with decolonization—and the fragmentation of big states, as well as the development of a surprisingly wide consensus in favour of capitalism and democracy, the world seems to have accelerated along the paths of globalization, peace, and prosperity. Many former dictatorships or post-colonial military regimes, are, at least on (constitutional) paper moving towards US-style liberal democracy, albeit without guarantees of success or even of sustained progress. The immense advance of science since the early 1980s, particularly in communications, has completely altered patterns, textures, form, and content in new fields like 'digital humanities', and in the old realms of music, literature, and the visual arts. The Internet in the official places of learning and scholarship has subverted censorship, at least in the Western world, while the screen presence of seemingly limitless content, from high literature to sheer and brutal pornography, makes it difficult for the ordinary audience to discern what is good or bad, original or plagiarized, fake or real. Now the boundary between what is 'art' and what is 'sheer commodity' is blurred as much as between 'ugly' and 'beautiful', or 'solid' and 'flawed', and so on. Cyberspace philosophers have begun to grasp and explain the huge amount of change brought about by the digital revolution in the realms of logic, philosophy of knowledge, ethics, and ontology. Finally, the Internet has virtually fulfilled the late nineteenth-century utopian dream of a 'single language'—a dream with precedents in the classical and Renaissance worlds. Naïve utopias of mechanical languages, like Esperanto and Volapük, conceived by nineteenth-century social engineers, died without having ever lived. English has a 'natural monopoly' as a language spoken globally, and will probably hold that status for a long time.

The book, in the form of the printed codex supreme since the Gutenberg bible, after almost 500 hundred years of glorious existence as one of the most controversial objects of civilization, is reproduceable; e-books retain a new kind of 'physical aura', a sort of beauty derived from their nature as artefacts, and from their solidity and transportability without need of the computer in all its different shapes. To read a traditional book is like driving an old car or riding an old bike: this fact, however, affects the very idea of 'culture' and 'knowledge', and applies largely to work in the humanities and creative literature, where almost all traditional readers are bibliophiles. In the sciences, paper is supererogatory. Readers of this volume might, for instance, still belong to the category of those who love the 'object-book', while at the same time OUP will probably make an electronic edition, to reach, let's say, the Catholic University of South Sudan, where traditional books are still expensive and hard-to-get, precious commodities.

Yet, at least in some large parts of the world, there is a growing, systematic, intense attention towards the past. Concepts like 'hope' occasionally re-surface, e.g. President Obama's 2008 presidential campaign, but the reins of the future, at least in the Western and Westernized world, are left to science and to 'liberal democracy'. As a concept, hope relates to a future still in the hands of theology and religion, which, once again, are conquering the souls of multitudes, in a variety of cults, sub-cults, and denominations hitherto unknown—thanks, once again, to the 'equivalence' of value conferred by post-modernity. In its secularized form (associated with Marx, or Bloch's *The Principle of Hope*), hope became a landmark of Messianic communism, and seems to be on the decline. Some of us live in a self-satisfied, rich present, and do not need to look upon the future with desires and ideals still to be fulfilled. For all of us, the future, on the other hand, is too crowded with menace to be welcome. Many constituencies—

BARACK OBAMA AT THE UNIVERSITY OF CINCINNATI during the 2008 US Presidential campaign.

the environmentally profligate, the ideologically reactionary, the economically spendthrift—seem to have repudiated it.

On the contrary, memory belongs exclusively to the past: no religion can be simply based on the cults of ancestors, without referring to some form of redemption and/or resurrection in the future. The prevalence of memory over hope, or of the relaxed, contemplative view of the past in a quiet, self-satisfied present, might be considered typical of stable societies—the Roman Empire at its peak, for instance, contemplating its Greek intellectual heritage and its own grand history. Post-modernity has brought about an intensified cult of memory, at the expense, among other things, of utopias for the future. In Europe and in the US the memory of the Holocaust, for instance, has become a powerful cultural industry, with a number of positive side effects, such as the intensification of the study of German history, but also a number of negative consequences, like the unwarranted self-legitimation of the liberal-democratic state as the unique preserver not only of freedom, but also of human life.

States moreover foster selected and sometimes distorted memories to legitimize their existence. Movies demonstrate this. In a world in which there are no longer arbiters of value, the market has become the ultimate criterion. So, as in every market, huge monopolies are strongest. Hollywood movies occupy the nearest thing to the role of monopolist in the cultural scene. They not only mirror the state-of-the-art of culture, but they also determine it in an extremely forceful loop. Typically adhering to liberal-democratic values, such as those embodied—at least in the eyes of the world—by the US, Hollywood movies make history alive by rendering it with extreme realism, conferring a perpetual value upon genuine sentiments and morality.

The cultural, artistic, and intellectual scenario of the world reveals more cracks than uniformity. Cultural globalization faces widespread resistance. The destiny of the book is emblematic of the contradictions. In 2001, before dying at the hands of a mob, Libyan dictator Muammar Muhammad Abu Minyar al-Gaddafi waved in front of the world cameras a book—the Libyan constitution, in a worn-out copy, as to defend his rights to dictatorship. The book, for an Arabic leader, has still the sacred value of the Quran, or the Bible for Jewish fundamentalists, or the New Testament for Christian ultras. In China, upon which financial and real economy largely depends, to find books that are prohibited by the regime, buyers must go to the few 'free' bookshops of Hong-Kong, which will all be shut down eventually. When the book is not hailed as sacred,

THE CONGRESS OF VIENNA, WHICH ENDED THE NAPOLEONIC WARS, was notorious 'more for waltzing than work', as Castlereagh (Britain's representative) quipped. Caricaturists often depicted it as a ball, none more savagely than in this Italian satire, which transforms it into the 'Dance of Death'—one of the favourite subjects of European artists during the plagues of the late Middle Ages and early modern periods.

nor forbidden as tool of diffusion of dangerous ideas, it is a hard-to-find commodity. Another large chunk of the world, Africa, apart from few free states, struggles to educate its people, and books are hard to find in all the sub-Saharan belt, from Ethiopia to Gambia, where, rather, meningitis and HIV triumph. It is therefore clear that the process of globalization is certainly not complete, and this incompleteness, for good or evil, refers also to the spiritual, artistic, and intellectual realm.

Religion, autocratic powers, class differences, and human and social inequalities seemed to evaporate with the French revolution, together with aristocracy, slavery, and legal incapacity for women and minorities. At a certain point, in 1815, the would-be restorers of the 'old regime' were depicted as 'ghosts' trying to rise from eternal graves. Those ghosts never rested in peace, and the despots and dogmatists still haunt the contemporary world, trying to eradicate progress and extinguish remaining glimmers of the Enlightenment by way of compromise or violence. Post-modernity, meanwhile, presupposes and fosters at the same time the equivalence of every ideology, turning every form of theoretical knowledge into discourse, and reducing every matter of taste to a personal option—a choice among others. At the same time, the apparently globalized, i.e. uniform, world, is far from real uniformity. From within the West, and more often from 'peripheries', powerful forces challenge the influence of Western cultural traditions. That influence preceded Western power but became dependent on once-formidable (but now diminishing) disparities of force and wealth to spread it around the world. In changed circumstances, will it survive?

CHAPTER 13

Politics and Society in the Kaleidoscope of Change

Relationships, Institutions, and Conflicts from the Beginnings of Western Hegemony to American Supremacy

JEREMY BLACK

AFTER 1815, hope and fear greeted the possibilities of change, influencing both social relationships and political definitions. This was a situation seen around the world from 1815 forward, but the local manifestations varied greatly. A focus on hope and fear moves historians' attention away from existing social and political structures and suggests that inherent volatility and dynamism in the human response were more significant than the degree to which the existing situation adapted to change. Given the extent of change across this period, the degree to which, nevertheless, elements of existing social conventions and political norms survived is surprising. However, ideological pressures demand due consideration. Many were conservative, notably attitudes to women among religious institutions and followers.

At the same time, the extent and pace of change are even more amazing than that of continuity. Futurologists were a growing group in 1800, but much of what happened in the following century would have astounded them. Their even more numerous counterparts in 1900 proved equally wayward in their predictions, as the pace of this change accelerated and its nature expanded. It is easiest, when assessing Futurology, to comment on technological change and its implications, which transfixed contemporaries, notably with powered manned flight from 1903 and, subsequently, when men first landed on the Moon, an achievement that was the earlier stuff of fiction. Nevertheless, to many, the changing relationships of men and women, or of the generations, would have appeared more remarkable still. The decline of deference, the rise of choice, and the individualism of norms, were all strikingly different to prior attitudes, and none was limited only to élite groups.

These changes were seen across the world, although there were major variations in large part because political and ideological strategies played a role in causing and

FRITZ LANG'S *METROPOLIS*, 1927, where the hero tries to overcome class antagonism in a cruelly engineered dystopia.

responding to change. In some countries, change was presented as a necessary response to the experience of foreign control, notably imperial rule, although less structured Western influence and control were also significant. The context was frequently one of resentment, notably in the Communist response to Western consumerist models in the twentieth century and in the Islamic response to Westernization, especially in recent decades.

Many other responses to foreign influences were, in practice, far more positive, and notably so at the individual level. Ruling groups might reject foreign influences and even seek to identify and empower themselves accordingly. Nevertheless, aspects of foreign models and practices were readily adopted, as with British influence in the nineteenth century and American influence in the twentieth. A key instance was that of language. People could adopt a language without the culture, appropriating the symbols and structures of English without accepting the meanings of the words or the values they expressed. However, the use of different languages brought a degree of relativism that very much challenged existing values and, thus, relationships, as well as encouraging openness to influences. As a result, the integration of the world and the consequent dissemination of ideas and images are key elements for the period since 1815.

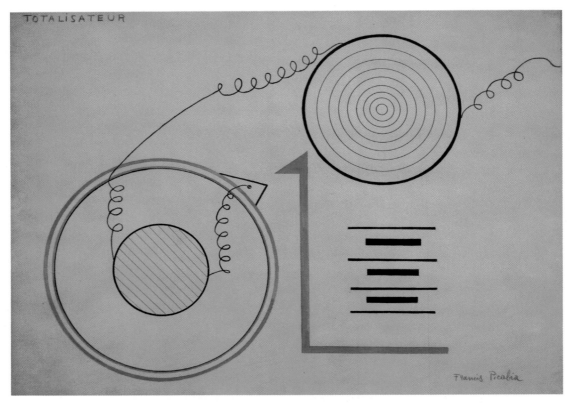

'TOTALISATEUR' (TOTALIZER), C. 1922, BY FRANCIS PICABIA, where the representation of the machine age seems poised between the service of totalitarianism and a quirky, imperfect humanism.

The transformations of empires

In this integration, the nineteenth century is most important because it entailed exposing, to pressures from afar, societies that had hitherto not generally experienced very distant influences (or, at least, at a sustained rate). Moreover, the pace of interaction increased greatly with the use of steam power and its application for shipping and railways. The context and consequences could be very different, as any discussion of, for example, China, Japan, New Guinea, and New Zealand would indicate: China 'modernized' patchily and falteringly; Japan systematically and comprehensively; New Zealand in contrasting ways for settlers and indigenes; and much of New Guinea, not at all. The character and identity of the existing society and culture were key elements. Moreover, impact were often traumatic, as exhibited in the cases of Tibet and northern Nigeria in the 1900s, which both suggest after exposure to British power (with force playing a key role). In 1904, British forces advanced to Lhasa, the capital of Tibet, and posed a cultural challenge different to that of the various forms of earlier Chinese presence.

Imperialism was very much a norm of world affairs in the nineteenth century, and was characteristic of ambitious states outside the West, e.g. in China, Egypt, Ethiopia, and Japan. Imperialism also occurred between neighbouring peoples, in the forms of

DEATH STAR. IN GEORGE LUCAS' STAR WARS EPISODE VI: *Return of the Jedi*, 1983. Imperialism reimagined as a revived threat in a dystopic but remediable future.

mission, historical destiny, triumphalism, racialism, and cultural arrogance. If these were indicative of modern Western powers, they were also on display in Egyptian attitudes to Sudan and those of Ethiopia to the Ogaden. Imperialism also exhibited competition between great powers, along with a search for economic opportunity. Britain became the most powerful imperial power, in part because of the strength of its economic, commercial, and financial systems, and its navy, but also because of the devastation of other Western empires in the French Revolutionary and Napoleonic Wars between 1792 and 1815. By 1900, when, in a largely pre-census age, there were about 1.6 billion people in the world, Britain had an empire covering one-fifth of the world's land surface and 400 million subjects, mostly in India; France's empire was mostly African, comprising six million square miles and 52 million people.

Ironically, it was thanks, in part, to the diffusion within empires, notably Britain's, of Western notions and Western practices (community in identity and political action, and politicization, specifically in democratization) that there was opposition to imperial control, although it was limited in scope. The Indian National Congress was founded in 1885, and the Egyptian National Party in 1897, but, simultaneously, there was a considerable measure of compliance with Western rule, in part reflecting the co-option of traditional local elites, as with the response in India, where rajahs complemented the Raj and the Brahmin *babus* who served it. This represented a continuation of long-standing responses to imperial control, which generally involved compliance as well as coercion, which interacted in a complex dynamic.

Yet, allowing for the global expansion of imperial power in the nineteenth century, and indeed up until 1919–20, it was the twentieth century that brought more comprehensive influences. In part, this was because of the more insistent and seductive nature of visual images in the world of film, colour photography, and the Internet, and in part because of wider practices of social and political participation and greater rates of literacy. Thus, the twentieth century (which experienced widespread decolonization) ironically proved far more significant for globalization than the nineteenth—the classic age of imperialism.

As so often, such a paradox is somewhat glib, not least because the twentieth century was also very much an age of imperialism, particularly by the Soviet Union—the Communist dictatorship that ruled the Russian Empire from 1917 to 1991. The Soviet Union seized control of areas that had been Russian until the Revolution, and that had then briefly won independence, such as Estonia, Latvia, Lithuania, Ukraine, Georgia, and Armenia, before making territorial gains from Poland, Romania, East Germany, and Romania at the end of the Second World War.

Moreover, in certain respects, globalization in the twentieth century was more insistent than hitherto because of attempts to reach out to the bulk of the population. Thus, 'hearts and minds' described reaching out to people not only in conflicts, notably the American efforts in the Vietnam War, but also, more generally, through the means and nature of policy. It suggested that alongside the apparent obsolescence of imperial territorial control, its replacement in terms of cultural influence was highly potent.

The latter point underlined the growing significance of ideological challenges to imperial rule and, more generally, to government. Communism presented itself as a universal cause, while subsequently, its Western rival became that of a global model—a matter of American influence—rather than the narrower one of European control of colonies. Generally understood and presented in terms of modernization, progress entailed searching for an alternative theory and practice to colonialism and imperial control. Americans (and British and French commentators, especially, but not only, on the Left) witnessed growth and social and political development through modernization. An explicit engagement with modernization theory took place in the US under President John F. Kennedy. Modernization was regarded in the US as a form of a global New Deal—an attempt to create capitalistic, democratic, and liberal states. This ideology led Kennedy to attempt to resist Communism in Vietnam.

Technology was also linked to modernization, notably with the use of electricity, which was encouraged by the introduction in the 1890s of alternating current (AC). Electricity was seen as a global means for beneficial change. The cult of the dam was an aspect of the iconography and ideology of electric power, because hydroelectric generation was regarded as cleaner than using coal, and as taming nature. Major dams, such as the Aswan Dam on the Nile in Egypt, presented clear means to modernity and were celebrated accordingly on film.

A key element on the global level was change in East and South Asia, the regions where the bulk of the world's population lived. In 1945, India was part of the British Empire and Japan was desperately fighting the US, while the rising Communist movement in China, which was to emerge victorious there in 1949, was anti-American. Indeed, under the Communist dictator Mao Zedong, the 'Cultural Revolution' of the late 1960s saw a frenzied attempt to ensure that all the means of information, discussion, and reflection served to legitimize and reiterate the nostrums of the Communist Party. Imperfect reality was to be brought under control.

CHINESE RED GUARDS DURING THE CULTURAL REVOLUTION.

In contrast, by 2008, Japan was to be securely in the American alliance system, while China and India vied to expand their trade with the US, having, to a degree, adapted their previous (different) systems of state socialism in order to welcome capitalism. This process of change was not without serious political difficulties, and part of it rested on the American ability to run debts and absorb imports, thus financing Asian growth, as the Europeans themselves had done for the New World—both the US and Latin America—in the nineteenth century. Moreover, in the 2000s, Chinese political assertiveness and cultural identity were increasingly directed against the US and in opposition to Western models of activity. Nevertheless, allowing for this highly significant caveat, these, whether in China or the US, were people essentially from the same material culture competing as how best to organize it and profit from it.

The city

Changes at the international level proved highly significant for those within individual societies. The term 'states' could be used instead of societies, but to do so implies that societies are best understood with reference to the different trajectories of states. While this is reasonable in some respects, notably the impact of war, and also most appropriate for the last century, it is less so for other respects and periods. As concerns people, personal experience is the key frame for political and social relationships. By its nature, experience changes with time. During the period post-1815, it is also a process that has gathered pace, notably because the context for experience has altered with the large-scale movement of people from the land to cities. In 1815, the bulk of the world's population lived by the land, but, in 2008, the majority lived in cities, and this process is set to accelerate. The combined dynamic of population growth, economic development, bureaucratization, and urbanization set the base context for these relationships. In Berlin, the population tripled to 870,000 between 1850 and 1870, even before it became the capital of imperial Germany. Cities showed their symbolic power by hosting great displays of technology, such as the Great Exhibition in London in 1851. They were also the centres of empire and displays for its iconography, e.g. Nelson's Column in Trafalgar Square in London.

Urbanization accelerated in the twentieth century. For example, the population of São Paulo in Brazil rose from one million in 1930 to 17.1 million in 1990. Across much of the world, the pressure on the urban infrastructure was acute. Issues included water supply, health, housing, and transport. The percentage of the population in the developing world with access to safe drinking water and sanitation was greater in urban than rural areas, but, even so, many urban areas lacked clean water, which encouraged epidemics of communicable diseases. Health provision was especially poor for recent migrants into cities, many of whom lived with squalor, disease, and great poverty, and lived in more marginal residential districts, especially squatter camps. Such urban areas proved difficult to police and, in a key indicator of political relationships, state authority

BRAZIL Madcap urbanization—here, for example, in São Paulo—surrounds what might otherwise be viable cities with monstrous, insanitary, ungovernable, gimcrack accretions.

in them was frequently limited. Gangs competed with each other, and with the police, in order to dominate large tracts of cities like Karachi in Pakistan, which led to high rates of urban violence. In greater São Paulo in Brazil, the number of murders rose above 8,000 in 1998. Another form of political relationship, corruption, was a key aspect of urban growth, especially with planning permission and land deals.

These were not the sole political aspects of an increasingly urban world. In addition, cities became major sites for conflict, notably in insurrectionary warfare, as in Brussels in 1830 and Paris in 1830, 1848, and 1870. This continued to be the case in the twentieth century. The urban fabric of cities posed problems for anyone seeking to maintain control. Cavalry and tanks could move along wide boulevards, but the complex warrens of narrow streets in old cities such as Aleppo in Syria posed serious problems. Cities continued to be epicentres of opposition to established order. Popular protests were suppressed, as in Budapest in 1956, Kuala Lumpur in 1969, Casablanca in 1981, and Beijing in 1989. However, demonstrations in key cities in the 1980s did much to overthrow Communist rule in Eastern Europe, including in East Berlin and Bucharest in 1989.

The West and the rest

The standard Western narrative and analysis of political development that prevailed in the twentieth century, when Western power, influence, and models appeared so dominantly, was less effective by the early twenty-first century. By then, the percentage of global wealth and population outside the West had risen, while there was a willingness to endorse non-Western political and economic models. The major rejectionist model of this type in the twentieth century had itself been European, namely Communism. Other models had looked to Western ideas. In China, the Fourth of May demonstrators of 1919 sought a 'new culture' that was at once scientific and democratic. In contrast, in the early twenty-first century, versions of a non-Western corporatist model were advanced in China, India, and Singapore, among other places.

It also appeared more pertinent in the twenty-first century to offer interpretations of history of the nineteenth and twentieth centuries that did not focus on the rise of the West. Whether these histories should focus on the response elsewhere to this rise of the West appeared plausible if the emphasis was on the material culture produced by Western technology, or on ideologies that derived from the West, including democracy and Communism. Yet such an approach not only failed to give due weight to the processes of adaptation and syncreticism that guided or, at least, influenced much borrowing. Moreover, the degree of agency enjoyed by non-Western cultures required emphasis, observed as Western influences slackened or came to co-exist. In particular, the vitality of Oriental social norms and of Islam both emerged in a prominent fashion in the late twentieth century, as did ethnic identities in African politics, in place of the class alignments that some commentators had anticipated.

Each of these significant factors drew attention to different elements in the fragility of the Western palimpsest across much of the world. Disguised first by Western military power and, subsequently, by the prevalence of Western consumerism, this fragility appeared in the US models of control and influence initially offered by the European colonial powers. However, the theme of self-consciously different routes to modernity became more common as part of what was a reaction to imperialism and to westernization. In practice, this was not new. Both the Meiji Restoration in Japan and the Self-Strengthening Movement in China offered such approaches in the late nineteenth century, and they were simply the most prominent instances of the ability to annex specific visions of the past to distinctive accounts of the future. In Japan, it proved possible to reconcile imperial legitimacy with radical change, but this combination was not sustainable in China, where the Emperor was overthrown in 1911–12 and replaced by a republic. If that indicated the range of the 'non-West', the same was also the case for the West.

The state, government, and politics

Much of the political history of the post-1815 period that attracts attention focuses on conflict within the 'West'. There are different narratives and analyses for such conflict. They include ideological, geopolitical, and economic rivalries, as well as the thesis of the conflict between rising and falling powers. Each of these has merit, but none works well as a total explanation. In part, this situation reflects the element of choice on the part of the governing elites of the major powers and, linked to this, the implementation of policy goals. In the nineteenth century, these processes involved relatively limited consultation with social groups outside the elite, but, in the twentieth century, there was both greater concern about these groups and a determination, even in authoritarian societies and autocratic political systems, to ascertain popular views. Indeed, public opinion became one of the considerations in judging political capability and effectiveness. The definition of the public varied, as did the understanding of its role. Nevertheless, concern about the public helped explain the interest in propaganda and the willingness to adapt consumerism to political messaging.

Whether elites responded to popular views or maintained a more distant approach to them, a common theme was that of the rise of the state, at least as measured in the development of bureaucracies, and the related ethos and pretensions. Eighteenth-century French economist Jean-Claude-Marie Vincent de Gournay, who coined the term bureaucracy, captured a sense of the potential of government. Already, then, many Western intellectuals and some rulers and ministers hoped that, by using and also transforming government, they would be able to reform and improve society.

These impulses developed in the nineteenth century, in part related to a utilitarianism considered in terms of scientific understanding and rational planning. Administration became more a matter of and governance for change than of preserving stability and administering justice. Linked to this, there was a slow eclipse of traditional elites. As administration became more bureaucratic, so administrators were increasingly trained and made to specialize. Information was a crucial adjunct, notably censuses and material for taxation.

'POPE PIUS IX BLESSING BOURBON TROOPS GATHERED ON ESPLANADE OF ROYAL PALACE, Naples, Italy, 9 September 1849', by Achille Vespa.

Government was not alone. The Western ethos in the nineteenth century was increasingly modelled on technological ideas and capabilities. The idea of the state gathered pace, as did a commitment to standardization. The mechanization of administrative work and, with it, the development of the office, was also significant. The use of the typewriter was linked to the mechanization of techniques.

A cult of modernity and progress had major political and social consequences, helping to boost values of efficiency over those of lineage. Greatly expanded institutions with meritocratic ethos—the civil service, military, professions, and education—were all highly significant in the creation of a new social and cultural establishment. There were significant consequences in constitutional forms. In particular, constitutionalism was increasingly understood in terms of democracy. The nature of this democracy was very limited by current standards, especially with the franchise (right to vote) being limited to men, and usually to men of property. Nevertheless, this democratization represented a legitimation of change and of the rights and wishes of the citizenry, or, at least, *a* citizenry. This led to the emphasis on nation-states and to growing interest in the nineteenth century in republicanism or, at least, in monarchies that were accountable to the public.

Linked to this, there was also a stress, in literature, music, architecture, statuary, and other arts, on forms and content that could be seen as national and distinctive. Moreover, a 'back-story' was fitted in with the presentation of what were regarded as suitably appropriate historical accounts and archaeological and anthropological researches. History was deliberately employed in order to serve the interest of governments seeking to encourage popular support as an aspect of public education, and textbooks and curricula present a workable past.

Militarization was a global theme that drove changes in the state. The sophistication and specialization of weaponry markedly increased with technological change, and this pushed up the costs of military preparation and war. Effective mass-production provided a major advantage over craft-manufactured firearms, however good the latter were on an individual basis. Mass production involved a major change in the production process, which required capital and organization. For example, much of the importance of the introduction of single-shot breech-loaders, followed by that of repeating firearms, stemmed from the ability to mass-produce rifling, sliding bolts, magazine springs, and chain-feeds to a high standard, and also to provide the large quantities of ammunition required.

This efficient mass production of new weaponry was a key stance of the process by which 'fit for purpose' ceased to be a state which changed episodically. Instead, change became both high tempo and continuous, challenging earlier practices and greatly driving up costs. Workshop space in Krupp's Essen works in Germany grew by an average of 5.2 acres per year in the five years to 1908, and thereafter up to 1914 by

THE MOBILIZATION OF GERMAN TROOPS IN WORLD WAR I.

6.4 acres per year. Even before the outbreak of World War I, Krupp was producing 150,000 shells of all calibres monthly.

Bellicosity was powerful in the background: a combativeness that reflected a belief that was could be a necessary aspect of national development and of individual masculinity, and, indeed, was a vital guarantee of both. The belief that the state had the right to the life of its citizens was very much seen with the widespread practice of conscription. A habit of military obedience took precedence over reasons for not serving, for example, religious feelings or international solidarity among workers.

The state in the twentieth century

The state became increasingly influential in social and economic matters. In part driven by international military competition and the determination to provide a fit population for conscript armies, 'welfare' also represented the would-be triumph of human agencies in society over spiritual responses to life. Thereafter, in the twentieth century, and expressed through a variety of political systems, egalitarianism, the belief that all people should have equal shares in society's rights, benefits, and duties, encouraged planning in order to ensure equality. Classically associated with the left, this belief led to authoritarian practices, notably the seizure of private property, including land. These goals and means encouraged totalitarianism and a brutalization of opponents. Examples include the Soviet, Chinese, and Cuban Communist regimes, but there are many populist left-wing ones as well. In contrast, in societies that had mixed economies, with much of industry outside state control, this aspiration created the problem of how best to manage the relationship between socialism and capitalism.

Irrespective of the ideology, the practice of government was frequently hostile to accountability. For example, in democracies, this hostility was demonstrated, albeit in an implicit and not overt manner, by the unwillingness of often self-defining elites employed by the state, such as judiciaries or town planners, to accept popular beliefs and pastimes as worthy of value and attention, and their self-satisfied conviction that they were best placed to define and manage social values and behaviour. The extension of the scope of government during the twentieth century exacerbated this controlling tendency, because much of it entailed social policing. Both in authoritarian societies and in democracies, behaviour deemed anti-social in the spheres of education, health, housing, personal conduct, and law and order all became a matter for scrutiny, admonition, and, in many cases, control by the agencies of the state.

State spending as a percentage of GDP in the wealthy Organization for Economic Co-operation and Development (OECD) countries rose from 25 per cent in 1965 to 37 per cent in 2000, when GDP was far greater. However, the expansion of the public sector, and notably of the welfare state, created a serious burden on the remainder of the economy. Across the world, the major expansion of government powers and agencies brought income and status to those who ran, or benefited from, government.

In many countries, state employees were able to negotiate their way into a relatively safe and comfortable position. This expansion of government often had a powerful class component, linked to the prestige of 'white collar' over 'blue collar' occupations. In addition, the continuation and spread of Western-style bureaucracies in states that gained their independence from colonial rule were important in the definition of new patterns of social ranking and behaviour. From the 1950s until 1985, Egypt provided bureaucratic jobs for all university graduates that sought them.

The local

In works of this type, it is all too easy, when space is at a premium, to forget about the local dimension and to focus, instead, on the global or, at least, national. This is a precarious move, as, for most people, the local defines much of their experience and influences how they respond to global developments and pressures. The direction of influence was generally from the global and national to the local, and not least in the case of government. Even in federal systems like the US, the central government became more powerful, in part due to World War II and the Cold War.

In India, the greater authority of the central government from the 1960s reflected not the response to external challenges, but rather a shift, also seen in many other countries, from politics and government understood as an accommodation of a number of interests and centres of power to a more centralized and less pluralist notion of authority. This owed much to a conviction of the value of government intervention and planning as a means to modernization and growth; it also reflected the difficulty of fulfilling goals for the latter. Ironically, local solutions, which inherently responded most to local circumstances, were generally best, but there was frequently great difficulty in securing attention at this level.

Egalitarianism, community, and prejudice

Egalitarianism as a goal or rhetorical strategy was not restricted to the left. Instead, right-wing populists, with their talk of the people or nation, advocated a notion of community. A number of views inspired paternalist conservatives, including a sense that a nation had an organic character (is like a body), and, therefore, that the health of one was the health of all.

The focus on the latter was linked to growing state concern with women and children, and, indeed, this concern was to be important to the development of human rights. In the late nineteenth and twentieth centuries, there was a profound series of changes for women, some shared with men and some not. The standard agenda, that of industrialization, urbanization, the decline of deference, secularization, and the rise of literacy, greatly affected women as well as men. Indeed, insofar as concerns female rights, the key right was that of girls benefiting as much as boys from the introduction and extension of the state provision of education. This led to a

WOMEN QUEUE TO VOTE IN CHENNAI, THE FIRST STATE in the Raj (in 1921) to admit women to the polls. Since 2016 female voters have outnumbered men.

marked rise in female literacy, and thus to the ability to consider circumstances, envisage options, and attempt social mobility.

At the same time, there were many respects in which women were far from equal with men. Some discrepancies were desirable: women were not conscripted and not expected to fight. As a result, although many women were victims and casualties of the world wars, they were not at the same rate, or generally in the same way, as men. Far less fortunately, women faced an unequal situation in terms of control over their bodies and in the workplace. Social and cultural trends and developments were also of great significance in undermining previous beliefs in the innate inferiority of women. An emphasis, instead, on socially and culturally encoded ideas of difference did not carry with it any notion that women were necessarily inferior. Equality with men in voting rights was one consequence, first at a national level in New Zealand in 1893, but not in the US until 1920 or Britain until 1928.

In the second half of the twentieth century, it became more common for all regimes, whatever their true character, to proclaim support for human rights. In practice, however, the situation was frequently otherwise. For example, although countries proclaimed equal justice for all as central to the state-supported rule of law, many people lacked access to law. Indeed, for much of the population throughout our period, the world of law was not that of the state and its agents, who frequently appeared either distant and unwilling to help, or too close and corruptly self-serving, but rather a searching after expedients, especially the help of local kinship networks, a key political means. Corruption by state agencies and agents was a major problem and remains one, undermining respect for government and, often, the state itself.

The law was important as a register and moderator of differing concepts of community. These, indeed, changed greatly as a consequence of social, economic, political, ideological, and religious changes, and the context varied enormously by state. The most successful countries were able to define a different basis for community and politics to that of ethnicity. In particular, the US, which took in nearly a million immigrants annually between 1901 and 1914 (and approaching double that number in some years of the 1990s), created an American culture that was more successful than most in overcoming sectoral differences, although this, like immigration, was not without serious difficulties. The position of African-Americans (or Blacks, or Negroes, as terms varied during the century, as did their acceptability) was a particular scar on American notions of opportunity and inclusion. Although no longer slaves, African-Americans were actively segregated, not just in the Southern states (where they were most numerous and had been slaves), but also at the national level, in, for example, the armed forces and sport. Moreover, the large-scale movement of African-Americans to work in northern and west-coast cities, especially as a result of factory opportunities during World War II, made this a more national problem.

The Civil Rights Movement, and eventual government action, made segregation illegal, which achieved considerable success in the 1950s and, even more, in the 1960s, especially with the Voting Rights Act of 1965. The Eisenhower presidency (1953–1961), with its concern that disaffection might be exploited by the Soviet Union, played a key role in the 1950s. Thus, desegregation was, in part, a product of a Cold War desire to strengthen the US, an aspect that has been less attractive to American public history than the idea of success as stemming from the Civil Rights Movement.

Reforms did not fully address the issue of social inequality, and a sense of anger at discrimination helped to fuel widespread disturbances, especially in the 1960s in Los Angeles, and some midwestern cities, such as Detroit. Nevertheless, black separatism and radicalism failed to develop as mass movements, and most black leaders pursued community interests through mainstream politics, especially the Democratic Party. The demographic shift in the second half of the century led to a multi-culturalism that was important to the nature of American public culture, although also contested, as seen with the election of Donald Trump in 2016.

Other states could find it more difficult to sustain a multi-culturalism, for example, in India, where Congress supported it, as the Party that governed for several decades after independence in 1947. It was then challenged by the Hindu sectarianism of the BJP. India had the largest Muslim minority in the world, and the long-term viability of its peaceful co-existence remains unclear.

Ideologies of hate

In many states, nationalism and the question for independence from imperial structures in the nineteenth and twentieth centuries, led to a political culture that in practice, whatever the theory, focused on one ethnic group. The result could be discrimination and brutality toward what were seen as outsider groups, a pathology of which was most clearly displayed in Nazi Germany under the rule of Adolf Hitler from 1933 to 1945. His messianic and, eventually, apocalyptic view of German destiny was accompanied by a particular loathing for Jews and an attempt to destroy them in what became known as the Holocaust. Hitler's conquest of much of Europe between 1939 and 1942 was followed by an attempt to wipe out Europe's Jews, and about six million were murdered, mostly in extermination camps, notably Auschwitz. Although the details of this policy were secret, the German public was fully informed of what was termed the 'war on the Jews'. Ultimately, Hitler was defeated by an uneasy coalition of America, the Soviet Union, and Britain.

It was not only Nazi Europe that witnessed the killing of millions. In a determination to remake society and to overcome what was regarded as an automatic conservatism, the Communists had a similar fate awaiting millions: particularly, in the Soviet Union, under Joseph Stalin, in power from 1924 to 1953, and in China, under Mao Zedong who ruled from 1949 to 1976. In each case, the combination of a dictatorial system with a belief in necessary transformation through the implementation of control by the Communist Party resulted in such an outcome. In particular, the collectivism decreed in the form of ownership of everything by the state proved highly unpopular in peasant societies where there was a strong sense of identity with particular plots of land. That

HITLER SPEAKING AT THE KROLL OPERA HOUSE, 19 JULY 1940.

collectivism also served for the enforced transfer of food from the countryside to the urban industrial workers who were the centre of Communist ideology and concern, contributed to the disruption and suffering involved in the expropriation represented by state seizure and the establishment of collective farms, as well as reflecting the politics of town–countryside relations that were important across the world.

Exacerbated by the poor management that such systems entailed, this situation led to mass famines, notably in Ukraine (at that time, as a result of conquest, a part of the Soviet Union) in the 1930s and in China during the 'Great Leap Forward' of 1958–62. The attempt to revolutionize agriculture was accompanied by large-scale killing and by the incarceration of many in concentration camps, for example, the Soviet gulags. Similar patterns of disruption appeared elsewhere, for example, in Cuba in the early 1960s, which led to large-scale emigration, and in Cambodia in the 1970s, resulting in the slaughter of much of the population—indeed probably over one-third—and the destruction of the Cambodian social and institutional fabric.

Divisions and divisiveness

All these points discussed need emphasizing because frequently ideology and politics are presented as somewhat genteel alternatives, as if in a debating society or a television panel programme. This view is misleading. It both underrates the issues at stake in those countries that managed to keep their politics largely peaceful, at least internally, and underplays the extent to which politics across much of the world were, in practice, violent, and remain so. This is readily apparent in Latin America, Africa, and Asia, but also in Europe where, in the period from 1960, there were coups, or attempted coups, in Greece, Portugal, and Spain, as well as the violent overthrow of a brutal dictatorship in Romania in 1989 and wars in the former Yugoslavia in the 1990s. The high level of military expenditure throughout the period is a powerful testimony to the significance of war and to the extent to which it creates anxieties for governments.

The legacy of earlier conflict remains significant in the politics and political culture of a range of countries from the US (civil war) and France (Vichy), to Ireland (war of independence against Britain and then civil war) and Spain (civil war). These conflicts have left divisive and often bitter memories at the familial, community, and national levels, and also helped to determine political alignments and relationships. Indeed, the role of perceptions of the past in the content of political relationships remains marginalized unless due weight is placed on the role of the past in senses of ideology and interest that go toward the identity and issues that comprise political relationships.

The Cold War

From 1946 to 1989, international power politics were defined by the confrontation between a Communist block led by the Soviet Union and an anti-Communist bloc led by the US. This confrontation was military, political, ideological, cultural, and economic.

The Cold War spanned the world and extended to include the Space Race to land the first man on the Moon (won by the Americans, although only after much difficulty and great expense). Totally incompatible ideologies and views about the necessary future for humanity both underlay the Cold War and gave it great energy. Communist commentators presented an image of Soviet-led equality as the means for, and guarantee of, progress, while anti-Communist commentators argued that Communism was inherently totalitarian and destructive to freedom.

The numerous confrontations and conflicts of the period, most prominently the Vietnam War and the nuclear arms race, but also conflicts in the Middle East, sub-Saharan Africa, and Central America, are usually considered through the lens of the Cold War. While valuable, notably in explaining foreign intervention and the provision of arms supplies, each of which was frequently crucial, this interpretation fails to allow for the distinctive and different nature of these struggles. In particular, decolonization, the cause of many of the conflicts in the period, had contrasting origins, causes, courses, and consequences, to the Cold War, and it is important not to run them together.

Separately, the Cold War dates to the Bolshevik revolution in Russia in 1917; it led to a civil war in which fourteen foreign powers, including Britain, Canada, France, Japan, and the US, intervened. This was the 'hot' stage of the Cold War, and, in practice, from 1921, there was the long echo, in terms of what is generally called the Cold War. Thus, the situation after 1945 was a revival of the earlier Cold War after the interval of Soviet-Western co-operation between 1941 and 1945.

The post-1945 Cold War first focused on Europe and East Asia. Post-war divisions between the areas of Soviet and Western advances in the closing stages of the World War II became the fault lines for confrontations, as each side entrenched their positions and sought further advantages. Initially, the Communists, although unsuccessful in gaining power in Iran, Greece, and the Philippines, made major advances. They took over Eastern Europe (bar Greece), won the Chinese Civil War (1946–1949, the largest conflict until now in terms of combatants and area fought over since World War II), and launched an invasion of South Korea in 1950. This expansionism led to a political and military reaction, notably the foundation of the North Atlantic Treaty Organisation (NATO) in 1949 in order to prevent further Soviet advances in Europe, and a large-scale military commitment that prevented the North Koreans from winning the Korean War of 1950 to 1953). America played the key role in the latter, as well as in NATO. The Cold War was well and truly launched, and military expenditure rose greatly in North America and Western Europe in the early 1950s.

The fall of the Western European colonial empires provided opportunities for competition, particularly in the Middle East, sub-Saharan Africa, and Central America. A large-scale American intervention in Southeast Asia, notably Vietnam, but also, to a lesser extent, in Cambodia and Laos, was unsuccessful. The analysis of the Vietnam War continues to be highly controversial and interacts with the debates about how best to conduct military operations since, notably, the viability of counterinsurgency

PILOT MAJOR 'KING' KONG (SLIM PICKENS) AS HE PREPARES TO RIDE THE NUCLEAR BOMB. From Stanley Kubrick's *Dr. Strangelove or: How I Learned to Stop Worrying and Love the Bomb*, 1964.

strategies. The Vietnam War also led to much discussion of the merits and limitations of air power, especially bombing.

The consequences for the Americans (though not the South Vietnamese) of failure in Vietnam was lessened by a diplomatic realignment in the early 1970s that led to America and China co-operating, thus greatly weakening the Soviet Union. This realignment arose from the earlier rift between the Soviet Union and China as each vied to lead the Communist bloc. The rift, which became significant in the early 1960s, was followed, later in the decade, by confrontation and by limited hostilities, and this situation provided President Richard Nixon with opportunities to win Chinese support. As a result, the Soviet Union had to fear war on two fronts.

The American idea of containment, a late 1940s idea that had appeared increasingly unsuccessful in the 1960s as Soviet influence spread, now seemed more durable as China became part of the system. Indeed, although North Vietnam conquered pro-Western South Vietnam in 1975 after American support had ceased, China attacked Vietnam in 1978–79, showing that alliance with the Soviet Union would not prevent such attack.

In the early 1980s, tensions between the US and the Soviet Union flared up again. Advanced new weapons were deployed by both sides, while Soviet military intervention in Afghanistan from 1979 and the suppression in 1981 of a popular non-Communist reform movement in Poland led to a rise in both anxiety and tension. In 1983, war was a prospect, with the Soviets believing that it was necessary to act as if war was imminent.

Nevertheless, from 1985, tensions eased under a young new Soviet leader, Mikhail Gorbachev. His reform policies, designed to strengthen the Communist bloc, inadvertently resulted, however, in the fall of Communist regimes in Eastern Europe in 1989 and to the collapse of the Soviet Union in 1991, where the attempt to create a modified Communist system of control did not work. The regimes in Eastern Europe were left without the strength and support they needed in order to resist popular pressure for change. Following large demonstrations, the Berlin Wall fell in November 1989, and the tottering of the East German regime communicated itself to the rest of Eastern Europe. Only in Romania was a significant, if ultimately unsuccessful, effort made to resist the process, at the cost of about 1,000 casualties. In contrast, in China, the Communist government retained control. The rapid collapse, without direct external pressure, of the Soviet bloc would have surprised commentators as late as the mid-1980s. This collapse serves as an instance of the unexpected character of history, of the play of contingency, and of the role of individuals in a roller-coaster decade that began with full-scale Soviet intervention in Afghanistan and ended with crises in the centres of Communist power.

Changing identities

The degree of change in identities over the last two centuries is not a topic that has attracted adequate research, and the neglect is notable. Nevertheless, the move of people to cities combined with the spread of literacy and the development of state education systems ensured, by the late nineteenth century, a greater focus on the nation than had been the case a century earlier. Yet that very statement is part of the politics of the situation because it assumes a 'vertical' alignment for society, one in which different social groups are bridged and incorporated into a nation. That interpretation was, and is, rejected by those for whom social structures are, and therefore were, the key element. This Marxist, or *marxisant*, approach was particularly influential in the twentieth century, but now appears somewhat limited. At the same time, the replacement analysis of choice by Western intellectuals was one based on identities—notably of gender, sexuality, and ethnicity. These identities were partial at best, and often presented in a doctrinaire fashion. The tendency to downplay religion was a serious flaw. So, too, was the unwillingness to engage with traditional themes of political and social identity and interest.

These, however, were descriptions of identities and relationships in Western terms. Categorization elsewhere is often different, and it is less convincing than in the past to employ Western concepts without qualification. In the second half of the twentieth century, for instance, it proved far harder than had been anticipated to ground democracy in states where Western imperial control ended. Commentators complained that tribalism was all-too-powerful when, in states like Nigeria during the Biafran War of 1967–70, ethnic division proved a basis for bitter internal conflict. The failure of newly-independent states to manage their economies was also a serious

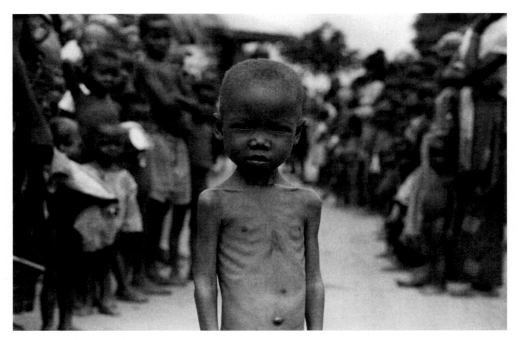

A NIGERIAN CHILD DURING THE BIAFRAN WAR OF 1967–70.

flaw. Moreover, there were questions about the social benefits of independence, not least as levels of corruption characterized the governments of many states. By the 2000s, the fallacy of Western assumptions was readily apparent as attempts to rebuild Iraq and Afghanistan as societies and political systems on the Western model totally failed despite initial optimism and considerable effort and expenditure. As with the 'discovery' to outside commentators of the strength of religious devotion in Eastern Europe and the Soviet Union when Communist rule collapsed in 1989–91, these failures indicated that earlier models of social and political relationships had been based essentially on ideology and hope. It is likely that a more general rewriting is required.

Religion

It became less credible toward the close of the period to leave religion out of discussions about political and social relationships and identities. Religion ranks as one of the most underrated factors of the period. This underrating in part reflects the hostility toward religion that was a novel aspect of the period, and notably so in the twentieth century. The public role of religion, as a source of ideology and morality, was widely condemned by self-styled progressives while, as a private source of meaning, hope, and faith, religion was treated in some circles as a delusion best clarified, like sexuality, by an understanding of anthropology, psychology, and sociology. As such, it was subject to the scrutiny of relativism.

Authoritarian states advocated secularization fervently, as they saw religion as a threat to popular loyalty. Thus, the Soviet Union and Communist China both made atheism their official creed and took major steps to extirpate religious customs.

Hostile governments were not the sole challenges to established faiths. There was also a widespread current of secularism and scepticism, as well as a marginalization of the role of religion, among many who considered themselves religious. General social currents, like the decline of deference, patriarchal authority, social paternalism, the nuclear family and respect for age, significantly undermined the established religions.

However, there were numerous signs of religious vitality throughout the period. For example, in the late twentieth century, the role of religion in US public life became more important and the overwhelming majority of Americans described themselves as religious.

Outside Europe, more generally, Christianity displayed a tenacious ability to retain support and to expand, continuing the long period of expansion that was coterminous with, but not confined to, Western imperialism. The experience of converted areas varied, but was an important aspect of the context and content for the subject of this chapter. Latin America, converted after Spanish and Portuguese conquest from the sixteenth century, remained very much a Catholic society, helping to ensure that Catholics made up the majority of Christians in the world. However, Protestant evangelicalism became increasingly important over much of Latin America.

In Amazonia and Patagonia, Christianity remained a missionary religion contesting tribal beliefs, and was linked to a more widespread assault on the Amerindian position and culture that included active discrimination.

In sub-Saharan Africa, the Middle East, and the Philippines, Christianity faced a major challenge from Islam. This contributed to violence, for example in Iraq, Nigeria, and the southern Philippines. Religious belief was linked to ethnic differences, for example, between Muslim Hausa and Christian Yoruba in Nigeria.

As with Christianity, Islam was not a united force. In addition to important ethnic, cultural, political, and economic differences in the Islamic world, there were major theological rifts. The most important of these divided the Shi'a, who predominated in Iran, from the Sunni, who predominated across most of the Islamic world and treated the Shia as schismatics, with consequent restrictions of public patronage, and, often, harsh discrimination. These divisions interacted with political strains, especially during the bitter 1980–88 war between Shia Iran and Sunni-ruled Iraq. The clash between Islam and Hinduism proved a major aspect of the political tension in South Asia that led to the bloody partition between India and Pakistan in 1947 and to subsequent clashes, especially over Kashmir.

Although Islam was frequently presented as a 'fundamentalist' creed, that greatly simplifies a religion whose manifestations are very diverse. As with Christianity, this diversity in part reflected the determination of individuals and communities to develop their own versions of faith, hope, and salvation. Some of these also reflected the pressures of events on patterns of belief and on the human capacity to bear misery and understand change.

Religion frequently served as a prime focus for identity, for example, with Buddhism in Tibet and Judaism in Israel. The varied manifestations of religion displayed the degree to which it was far from being an anachronism made redundant by scientific progress and marginal by secularism.

New world order, or asymmetric instability?

Talk of a new American-dominated world order followed the fall of the Soviet Union in 1991, and notably so after Soviet client states were defeated or intimidated: Iraq in 1991 and 2003, and Serbia in 1995 and 1999. American power appeared even more potent with the spread of American economic and financial models, especially those linked to free-market liberalism, particularly the liberalization of financial markets and the privatization of state-owned assets.

The confidence represented by this approach was dramatically challenged in the 2000s from a number of directions. The Islamic world, notably in Afghanistan and Iraq, resisted America and its allies via a range of opponents, including fundamentalists, most dramatically with attacks on New York and Washington, DC in 2001 using hijacked aircraft, when those opponents proved adroit at turning to terrorist methods. The fundamentalists were also able to exploit popular hostility to what was presented as Westernization; it was also frequently presented as a globalization that did down local people and challenged different values.

American power also suffered from the 2000s from greater assertiveness by both China and Russia and, more specifically, from a cooperation between the two powers that lessened American options. This marked a major reversal from the international alignment between America and China that had started in the 1970s. As a result of this reversal, America's ability to confront China in the East China Sea or Russia in Eastern Europe was greatly reduced.

This situation mirrored greater criticism of the United States around the world. As a linking factor, there was a more pronounced willingness elsewhere to look for other models, especially China. In turn, India, whose growth rate in 2015 passed that of China, presented itself as a model. These models were less liberal than the American one: the Chinese was that of a one-party state, while the Indian model was more corporatist.

Whether the situation amounted to a 'new world disorder' is unclear because such an assessment presupposes that there could be a world without strife. That is a utopian viewpoint, and not least because of the incessant pressures on resources, and of expectations, linked to a rapidly rising population.

Secondly, a focus solely on the tension between the US and other interests and models suffers from downplaying the extent to which there are separate, independent, or at least autonomous, sources of conflict. Insurrectionary conflict in a number of countries overlapped with both civil wars and a politics of force.

The use of violence to secure political outcomes was the common currency, and Afghanistan, Sierra Leone, Liberia, and Yugoslavia provided the clearest examples, in that

AKIHITO ANNOUNCES HIS PLANS TO ABDICATE. TOKYO, 13 JULY 2016.

levels of continuous violence were high. Ethnic tension and wider geopolitical rivalries also played key roles in the bitter civil wars in Central Africa, especially in Congo and Rwanda. The largest number of casualties in war arose from the conflict in Congo in the late 1990s and early 2000s. This complex conflict reflected the politicization of bitter ethnic differences and also the intervention of neighbouring African powers, especially Rwanda; there are similarities to long-standing conflicts within other African states. Indeed, from the perspective of the Central African Republic, Somalia, or Sudan, it is difficult to see any basis for a benign account of political developments. The regions affected by instability have a capacity to suck in neighbours.

There were competing accounts of what might happen in the future. In particular, it was unclear whether the focus should be the prospect of conventional warfare, notably between Russia and NATO or China and Japan, or rather on counter-insurgency warfare focused on resistance to insurrectionary groups like those in Afghanistan. By 2008, the optimism of the 1990s after the Cold War had ended appeared a far distant memory—both a product of a past age and naïve. The discontinuous nature of history emerged clearly, especially in the way in which trends are broken or reversed, and projections disproved. There is no reason to anticipate that the future will be any different.

New views of the world

While religious figures provided an account of the world in which political and social relationships were located with reference to divine intentions, new views of the world included not only the transforming ideologies already discussed, but also new spatial presentations. The most distinctive were those presented by the American Apollo space missions, which led to the landing of men on the Moon in 1969. They left as a legacy photographs of the Earth as a whole: a potent image of one world and one that accorded with the holistic views of environmentalists.

In the same period, different interpretations of the distribution of space on the Earth appeared, most controversially in a map projection devised in 1967 by the German Marxist Arno Peters, which was publicly presented in 1973. Capturing a different view of relationships between parts of the world, Peters presented the question as inherently political. Peters' equal-area projection contrasted the traditional Mercator worldview, which, instead, had put the emphasis on accurate bearings. Arguing that the end of European empires and the advance of modern technology made a new cartography necessary, Peters found a receptive international audience. His emphasis on the Tropics matched concern by and about the Third World, so that international aid agencies emphatically praised his projection, which offered a view of political and social relationships on the global level that was very different to that of governments. The Peters' world map became a politically correct (to use a new term reflecting new values) icon. It was both praised in, and used for, the cover of *North-South: A Programme for Survival* (1980): the 'Brandt Report' of the Independent Commission on International Development Issues that conflated globalist perspectives, social concerns, and redistributive strategies.

Although the Peters' projection was open to serious criticism, it dramatized the issue of how the world should best be presented. In the 1989 *Peters Atlas of the World*, he went on to produce all the maps at the same scale, ensuring that Africa, Asia, and South America received more, and Europe and North America less, coverage than in traditional atlases.

Less dramatically, the Robinson projection of 1963, designed to offer the least possible area-scale distortion for major continents in an uninterrupted format map, was more accurate in terms of area than the hitherto influential Van der Grinten projection devised in 1898, which had continued the Mercator projection's practice of exaggerating the size of the temperate latitudes.

Consideration of different projections offers a useful reminder that there is no single way to approach the treatment of the world's history. The sway of Western empire may have appeared as a clear theme, but in many states, for example, Chad, Myanmar, Nigeria, and Sudan, it lasted only for about sixty years, while, by 1825, European empires no longer controlled more than fragments on the American mainland south of Canada. In addition, from the perspective of the late 2010s, even imperial spans that were longer, such as that of Britain in India and France in Algeria, increasingly appear only as a period of world history. Once the British had renounced control over India in 1947, it was difficult to summon up much British popular interest in the retention of the remainder of the largest empire in the world, as the logic of that empire was largely gone.

Across much of the world, decolonization was not followed by a stable political system. In the Americas, it led to wars between and within states, most famously the American Civil War of 1861 to 1865, as well as persistent struggles in Mexico and much of Central America. It was the same in Africa and Asia, where there were a large number of coups. In many states, force was the normal means of politics, ubiquitously used to maintain their cohesion and especially in suppressing regional separatism. Post-colonial states frequently lacked any practise of tolerance towards groups and regions that were outside the state hierarchy. In turn, the use of state power encouraged a violent response.

Between states, the legacy of imperialism was frequently difficult as frontier lines paid no attention to local identities, interests, and views, and this led to much subsequent criticism: the practices of European imperialism were blamed for post-colonial ethnic conflict in Africa. More generally, the different values that were frequently advanced in neighbouring states ensured that frontiers could also mark important psychological boundaries.

If many post-colonial states found it difficult to make democracy work, it would be misleading to suggest that force and dictatorship supplied the post-colonial history of the developing state. The largest state, India, maintained the democratic system established at independence, albeit not without difficulties. Many authoritarian regimes, such as Malaysia under Mahathir Mohammad, Prime Minister from 1981 to 2003, often did so as a hybrid political form that included aspects of democracy and the rule of law.

Decolonization and conflicts between newly independent states were intertwined with the Cold War struggle between the Soviet-dominated Communist bloc and the American-led anti-Communist bloc. Intense in the 1950s and 1960s, this struggle became less serious in the 1970s due to closer relations between the US and Communist China, which had split from the Soviet Union. These closer relations gave the US a vital advantage in the Cold War, as did the resilience of the American economy and the ability of the Reagan government in the 1980s to use the state's capacity to raise money in the bond market. This was done to mobilize American resources for a military build-up that the Soviets could not match. They lacked the money, and could not raise the credit.

The collapse of Communism in the Soviet Union and Eastern Europe in 1989 and the integration of China and Vietnam into a global world economy led to a different world order in the 1990s. Initial optimism about a more stable, liberal world represented a resurgence of the high hopes held with the foundation of the United Nations in 1945, and a conviction that global multilateralism could work.

This confidence was quickly tarnished by the resurgence of ethnic and religious conflict across much of the world. Indeed, in the 1990s, local terms of ethnicity shaped and expressed identity and conflict, rather than the ideological divide of the Cold War. This situation gathered pace in the 2000s as the 'internationalism' of Islam came to offer a new qualification to liberal internationalism.

In many circles, this led to a crisis in confidence at the end of our period. The gaining of freedom following the fall of European empires and of Communism in Europe had not fulfilled liberal hopes. Rather than the progressive future envisaged, instead had come a menacing situation that, to many, represented a reversion to a dark past. Massacres in both Rwanda and Yugoslavia in the 1990s provided a clear indication of political depravity. As notable in the longer term was the resort to authoritarian solutions in newly independent countries such as Belarus and Kazakhstan.

The economic growth of the 1980s, 1990s, and early 2000s took a great number of people out of poverty, but the disruption it brought was also unwelcome to many groups. Hostility to globalization frequently meant suspicion of free-market economics. No viable alternative was on offer, but that did not prevent a widespread discontent, with which this period ended. The cohesion, co-operation, and unity of purpose at the international level that had inspired so many remained only a distant hope.

Epilogue

Historians, whose métier is the past, and whose inspiration is, all too often, revulsion from the present, are well advised to shun the future. But the future is only the past that has not happened yet. It will happen unpredictably, sometimes leaping or scraping suddenly out of its groove, like a bad gramophone needle. It is unlikely, however, that no continuities will bind it to preceding events. Except for prophets with a hotline to God, or magical diviners with privileged access to the secrets of stars, wrinkled palms, tea leaves, or what-not, there is only one way, good or bad, to tell the future: on the basis of the past. Historians are better qualified for the job than seers or soothsayers.

We can look back over the themes of this book and try to imagine what will become of them. Divergence and convergence will continue, perhaps in new or unaccustomed ways. Globalization is, in one sense, an intensified phase of convergence, in which cultures exchange traditions, notions, tastes, and techniques, and grow more like one another in consequence. We can expect, for instance, some religions to become increasingly ecumenical, inclusive, and mutually indistinct; for languages to infect each other; for mainstream music to become increasingly cosmopolitan; for fusion to characterize food; for the same brands and products to conquer every market; and for multiculturalism to get ever more dappled. It is tempting to think that convergence may displace divergence entirely—that we shall end in a culturally uniform world, in which everyone votes in democracies, counts on capitalism, speaks English (or some simulacrum of that once clear and precise language, now churned into formlessness), and thinks in Twitter-sized bites. But none of that will happen—or at least not to the extent of crowding out divergence, which will continue under the shell of globalization. Indeed, if we ever do get a single global culture, it will be one more culture added to the mix. Marginal cultures, tastes, and tongues will perish; but most will thrive, partly because cyberspace is riven into ghettoes of the like-minded, where members of minorities can nurture any eccentricity and treasure any tradition, and partly because every agglutinative process generates fissile reactions. Just as conservationists strain to protect endangered species, so they strive to preserve ailing languages, vanishing cuisines, abandoned arts, and apparently outdated customs. Nothing is more stimulating to the revival or invention of traditions than the fear of assimilation into some undifferentiated mega-culture.

Initiative—the power of some groups to influence others—will continue to shift around the globe along with the balance of wealth and might. China remains the next most likely halt for initiative, as the world enters a post-American century, in which US taxpayers no longer have the means or appetite to dominate the planet. China's prospects are clouded, however, by four main sources of obnubilation. First, the one-child policy per family has encumbered the country with an ageing population. Second, China lacks regional allies, and has disputes—ideological or territorial—with all neighbours. Next, internal articulation is poor: 'two systems' divide 'one country', owing to the unique autonomy of China's showcase region, Hong Kong; there are major secessionist movements in the east; and a big gap in economic interests cleaves privileged zones of rapid development from the vast, underdeveloped rural hinterland. Lastly, China's deepest structural difficulty is an apparently unsustainable mismatch between a one-party state, in which membership is an absolute condition of power, and a market economy, which concentrates wealth in the hands of a bourgeoisie that hardly overlaps with the party. If only for the good old Marxist reason that power follows wealth, the balance needs adjustment if political upheaval is to be avoided. Bad government has been, perhaps, the main reason for China's underperformance in global power politics for the last couple of hundred years. But with good government, courageous enough to make the required changes, the country is insuperably qualified to be a superpower, with vast manpower reserves, strong educational traditions and institutions, and rapid economic growth. The peculiar situation of the last few decades, in which one superpower has dwarfed all contenders, seems bound to yield. If Chinese hegemony does not take over, a multipolar world will ensue: major regional powers (including the US and China) will contend in a state of permanent tension and fluctuating equilibrium—a balance of power that is dependent on changing relationships of hostility, alliance, and entente.

Environmental stress will continue for the foreseeable future and will probably get worse, not only because climate change and disease depend on a distant sun and a volatile world of microbial evolution, but also because the main sources of anthropogenic damage are out of control. The biggest humanly generated source of environmental stress is consumption. Population increase is part of the source of the problem, but in the twentieth century, while global population rose by a factor of about four, average per capita consumption—most of it concentrated in the US and Europe—increased by a factor nearly twenty. If we had maintained constant rates of consumption, the world could have absorbed five times as many people without obliterating more biodiversity, or poisoning more soil, or emitting more carbons, or causing more desertification, or polluting more air and water, or exhausting more resources. Consumption, unsustainable at present levels, is bound to increase as previously underprivileged populations demand—not unreasonably—to enjoy the same amounts and quality of food, water, clothing, fuel energy, and goods generally as the Americans and Europeans who have gobbled up much more than their fair share in the past. We are in no position to control unbridled consumption, because we do not know what causes it: ingrained insatiability, according to some analysts, and the dynamics of a competitive economic system, say others; inescapable impulses from evolutionary psychology in rival assessments; or the delusive sense of striving for satiety in a zero-sum game. Two influences are inescapable. First, democracy boosts consumption, because economic growth buys votes, while electorates will not endure policies of austerity for long. Second, *l'appétit vient en mangeant*: prosperity encourages profligacy; abundance is there to be exhausted.

The irreversibility of increased consumption is a reminder that we are not likely to experience a slowdown in the overall rate of change any time soon, but there is no reason why change should continue to accelerate indefinitely. Circumstances that might ease or reverse it are imaginable: a mega-disaster that 'puts the clock back', an interruption in the exchanges of culture that stimulate changes. But there is no likelihood of such an eventuality for a while. Even a young Rip van Winkle would awake today, after a short nap, to a surprising world and a dislocating experience.

There will, therefore, be no escape from the ill effects: anxiety, 'future shock', fear, and the reactionary (and sometimes violent) responses of people who feel that change threatens their cultures, identities, jobs, or security. We lurch from one failed solution to its equal and opposite reaction: from over-planning to madcap deregulation and back; between despotism and democracy; between totalitarianism and anarchy; authoritarianism and libertinism; pluralism and ethnocentrism; ideological secularism and irrational religion. Deceptively simple and wickedly 'final' solutions attract electorates convulsed by fear of change. People's willingness to switch between the rival programmes of exploitative demagogues is, I suspect, a measure of their bafflement in the face of apparently uncontrollable change. One of the paradoxes of human values is that most of us combine restlessness for change with a strong conservative prejudice in favour of the familiar. Change may be good, but it is always dangerous. When people feel the threat of change, they reach for security, like a child clenching on a comforter; when they do not understand what is happening to them, they panic. *Grandes peurs* lash society like a flagellant's scourge. Intellectuals take refuge in 'postmodern' strategies: indifference, anomie, moral relativism, and scientific indeterminacy, the embrace of chaos, *je-m'en-foutisme*. In reaction against uncertainty, electorates succumb to noisy little men and glib solutions. Religions transmute into dogmatisms and fundamentalisms. The herd turns on agents of supposed change, especially—typically—on immigrants and on international institutions. Cruel, costly wars start out of fear of depleted resources.

Rapid change will continue to affect everything except wisdom and morals. To procure a better world, we need better people, but we have no means of improving them, except in rare individual cases of genuine sanctification, which is, in any case, impossible to engineer. In the past, three methods have been tried.

First, improving the system—tinkering with the configurations of state and society to create a social and political environment that can make people virtuous. Although this was the grand aim of most political thinkers for most of the last three thousand years, we seem to have given up on it. Such a long record of failure is unanswerable.

Every utopia seems distasteful or dystopic, deeply repellent, albeit advocated with impressive sincerity. All utopianists evince misplaced faith in the power of society to improve citizens. They all want us to defer to fantasy father figures who would surely make life wretched: guardians, proletarian dictators, intrusive computers, know-all theocrats, or paternalistic sages who do our thinking for us, overregulate our lives, and crush or stretch us into comfortless conformity. Every utopia is an empire of Procrustes. The nearest approximations to lasting realizations of utopian visions in the real world were built in the twentieth century by Bolsheviks and Nazis. Most people's ultimate utopia is a world without enemies and the quickest way to achieve it is to massacre them. The search for an ideal society is like the pursuit of happiness: it is better to travel hopefully, because arrival breeds disillusionment.

Secondly, is religion any better than social or political engineering as a means of improving mankind? It is a serviceable explanation for the goodness of good people, just as it is a useful justification for the evil of bad ones. But religion's record as a way of making people good is unencouraging, despite the fact that it should transform your life. Although people who declare that religion has transformed them often speak in terms of being 'born again', the effects appear minimal when you scrutinize their behaviour. Religious people, on average, seem to be as capable of wickedness as everyone else. The peccadilloes of tele-evangelicals, or the cruelties of fanatical suicide bombers, torturers, and decapitators seem compatible with sincerely embraced faith. Religion is more often abused to vindicate violence than wielded for peace. Even in lives susceptible to the effects of religious disciplines, or heedful of the call to salvation, holiness is usually long postponed. Popes—John Paul II, Benedict XVI, and Francis in their various ways—have been perhaps the most effective spokesmen for morality in the last fifty years, but their summons has been beyond the hearing of most of their followers, and beyond the reach of many of their clergy. Some religions serve the world by organizing practical charity, inspiring art, channelling devotion, forging community, nurturing family life, and comforting the afflicted. But to end moral stasis we need more than goodness—a miracle to which religions can only aspire.

Lastly, if society and religion cannot make better humans, perhaps science can. Plato's proposals for a perfect society rested, in part, on the assumption that it should consist of perfect individuals: the best citizens should be encouraged to reproduce, the children of the dim and deformed exterminated to stop them breeding. In nineteenth-century Europe and North America, eugenics revived under the influence of racism—which blamed heritable deficiencies of character for supposed racial inferiority—and a form of Darwinism, which suggested that the supposed advantages of natural selection might be helped along by human agency. The eugenic idea was most enthusiastically adopted in Nazi Germany, where its logic was fulfilled: the best way to stop people breeding was to kill them. Anyone in a category deemed genetically inferior by the state, including Jews, Gypsies, and homosexuals, was liable to extermination. Meanwhile, Hitler tried to perfect what he thought would be a master race by selective breeding. Children born of experimental copulation between big, strong, blue-eyed, blond-haired human guinea pigs did not, on average, seem any better or any worse qualified than other people for citizenship, leadership, or strenuous walks of life.

Nazi excesses made eugenics unpopular for generations. But the concept is now back in a new guise: you can now reproduce genetically engineered individuals. You can buy a designer baby by patronizing banks of supposedly superior sperm. The isolation of particular genes associable with various inherited characteristics has made it theoretically possible to filter presumably undesirable characteristics out of the genetic material that goes into a baby at conception. The results would surely be improving only by the standards—partial, partisan, and probably ephemeral—of those making the selection. A route to intellectual, if not moral, perfection lies, in some imaginations, through connecting human brains to the Internet, but the outcome would surely be robotic humans, glutted with data and deficient in wisdom.

In short, if we try to project into the future the probable development of the themes that have characterized the past, the resulting predictions are bleak. The crystal ball of futurology is depressingly cloudy. Two sources of consolation may be worth mentioning. First, pessimism is good: a means of self-indemnification against disaster. Second, the function of a prophet is to be wrong: to be right was Cassandra's curse, because no one heeded her warnings. As we face dangerous shifts of initiative, the continuing tensions of cultural divergence and convergence, and the accelerations of change without any corresponding improvements in morals or wisdom, our predictions may fail because they are false; but they may inspire successful counter-measures. Can anyone think of any?

FURTHER READING

Introduction

de Waal, F. B. M., and Tyack, P., (eds.), *Animal Social Complexity* (Cambridge, MA: Harvard University Press, 2003).

Fernández-Armesto, F., *So You Think You're Human?* (Oxford: Oxford University Press, 2004).

Jeeves, M., (ed.), *Rethinking Human Nature* (New York, NY: Eerdmans, 2011).

Lewis, M. T., *Cézanne* (London: Phaidon, 2000).

McGrew, W. C., *The Cultured Chimpanzee* (Cambridge: Cambridge University Press, 2004).

Whitehead, H., *The Cultural Life of Whales and Dolphins* (Chicago: Chicago University Press, 2015).

Wright, W. (as S. S. Van Dine), *The Bishop Murder Case* (New York, NY: Charles Scribner & Sons, 1929).

Chapter 1

Gamble, C. S., *Settling the Earth: The Archaeology of Deep Human History* (Cambridge: Cambridge University Press, 2013).

Gamble, C. S., Gowlett, J. A. J., and Dunbar, R., *Thinking Big: The Archaeology of the Social Brain* (London: Thames & Hudson, 2014).

Gellner, E., *Plough, Sword and Book: The Structure of Human History* (London: Collins Harvill, 1988).

Grove, M., 'Change and Variability in Plio-Pleistocene Climates: Modelling the Hominin Response', *Journal of Archaeological Science* 38 (2011), 3038–47.

Kelly, R., *The Lifeways of Hunter-Gatherers: The Foraging Spectrum* (Cambridge: Cambridge University Press, 2013).

Meltzer, D. J., *First Peoples in a New World: Colonizing Ice Age America* (Berkeley: University of California Press, 2009).

Mitchell, P., *The Archaeology of Southern Africa* (Cambridge: Cambridge University Press, 2002).

Oppenheimer, S., *Out of Eden: The Peopling of the World* (London: Robinson, 2004).

Pettitt, P. B., *The Palaeolithic Origins of Human Burial* (London: Routledge, 2011).

Potts, R., 'Variability Selection in Hominid Evolution', *Evolutionary Anthropology* 7 (1998), 81–96.

Shryock, A., and Smail, D. L., (eds). *Deep History: The Architecture of Past and Present* (Berkeley: University of California Press, 2011).

Smith, M., *The Archaeology of Australia's Deserts* (Cambridge: Cambridge University Press, 2013).

Stringer, C., *The Origin of Our Species* (London: Allen Lane, 2011).

Chapter 2

Arsuaga, J. L., *The Neanderthal's Necklace* (New York: Basic, 2004).

P. Bahn, P., and Vertut, J., *Journey Through the Ice Age* (Berkeley, University of California Press, 1997).

Chauvet, J. M., *Dawn of Art* (New York: Abrams, 1996).

Clottes, J., *Return to Chauvet Cave: Excavating the Birthplace of Art* (London: Thames & Hudson, 2003).

Cook, J., *Ice-Age Art* (London: British Museum Press, 2013).

Gamble, C., *The Palaeolithic Societies of Europe* (Cambridge: Cambridge University Press, 1999).

Hoffecker, J. F., *Landscape of the Mind: Human Evolution and the Archaeology of Thought* (New York: Columbia University Press, 2011).

Lawson, A., *Painted Caves: Palaeolithic Rock Art in Western Europe* (Oxford: Oxford University Press, 2012).

Lewis-Williams, J. D., and Clottes, J., *The Shamans of Prehistory: Trance Magic and the Painted Caves* (New York: Abrams, 1998).

Lindsay, J., *The Origins of Astrology* (Colchester: TBS The Book Service Ltd, 1971).

Marshack, A., *The Roots of Civilization* (Columbus, OH: McGraw-Hill, 1972).

Mithen, S. J., *Thoughtful Foragers* (Cambridge: Cambridge University Press, 1990).

North, J. D., *Stars, Minds and Fate: Essays in Ancient and Medieval Cosmology* (London: The Hambledon Press, 1989).

Renfrew, C., and Zubrow, E., (eds.), *The Ancient Mind: Elements of Cognitive Archaeology* (Cambridge: Cambridge University Press, 1994).

Sahlins, M. D., *Stone Age Economics* (London: Routledge, 1972).

Stringer, C., and Gamble, C., *In Search of the Neanderthals: Solving the Puzzle of Human Origins* (London: Thames & Hudson, 1993).

White, R., *Prehistoric Art: The Symbolic Journey of Humankind* (New York: Harry N. Abrams, 2003).

Chapter 3

Allaby, R., Fuller, D., and Brown, T., 'The Genetic Expectations of a Protracted Model for the Origins of Domesticated Crops', *Proceedings of the National Academy of Science* 105 (2008), 13982–9.

Barker, G., and Goucher, C., (eds.), *The Cambridge World History: Volume 2, A World with Agriculture, 12,000 BCE–500 CE* (Cambridge: Cambridge University Press, 2015).

Bar-Yosef, O., and Valla, F. R., (eds.), *Natufian Foragers in the Levant: Terminal Pleistocene Social Changes in Western Asia* (Ann Arbor: University of Michigan Press, 2013).

Bellwood, P., *First Farmers: The Origins of Agricultural Societies* (Oxford: Blackwell, 2005).

Cowan, C. W., and Watson, P. J., (eds.), *The Origins of Agriculture: An International Perspective* (Tuscaloosa: University of Alabama Press, 2006).

Cronin, T. M., *Principles of Paleoclimatology* (New York: Columbia University Press, 1999).

Denham, T., and White, P., (eds.), *The Emergence of Agriculture: a Global View* (London: Routledge, 2007).

Frachetti, M., *Pastoral Landscapes and Social Interaction in Bronze-Age Eurasia* (Berkeley: University of California Press, 2008).

Harlan, J., *Crops and Man* (Madison: American Society of Agronomy, 1992).

Jones, M., *Feast: Why Humans Share Food* (Oxford: Oxford University Press, 2007).

Jones, M., Hunt, H. V., Kneale, C. J., Lightfoot, E., Lister, D., Liu, X., and Motuzaite-Matuzeviciute, G., 'Food Globalisation in Prehistory: The Agrarian Foundations of an Interconnected Continent', *Journal of the British Academy* 4 (2016), 73–87.

Mei, J., and Rehren, T., (eds.), *Metallurgy and Civilisation* (London: Archetype, 2009).

Mithen, S. J., *After the Ice: A Global Human History, 20,000–5,000 BC* (Cambridge, MA: Harvard University Press, 2003).

Rindos, D., *The Origins of Agriculture: An Evolutionary Perspective* (Orlando, FL: Academic Press, 1984).

Ruddiman, W. F., *Plows, Plagues, and Petroleum: How Humans Took Control of Climate* (Princeton, NJ: Princeton University Press, 2005).

Sherratt, A., *Economy and Society in Prehistoric Europe* (Princeton: Princeton University Press, 1997).

Tanno, K.-I., and Willcox, G., 'How Fast was Wild Wheat Domesticated?', *Science* 311 (2006), 18–86.

Ucko, P., and Dimbleby, G. W., (eds.), *The Domestication and Exploitation of Plants and Animals* (Chicago: Aldine Press, 1969).

Vavilov, N. I., *Agroecological Survey of the Main Field Crops* (Moscow: Academy of Sciences, 1957).

Willcox, G., 'The Roots of Cultivation in Southwestern Asia', *Science* 341 (2013), 39–40.

Chapter 4

Broodbank, C., *The Making of the Middle Sea: A History of the Mediterranean from the Beginning to the Emergence of the Classical World* (London: Thames & Hudson Ltd, 2013).

Bryce, T., *The Kingdom of the Hittites* (Oxford: Oxford University Press, 2005).

Cline, E. H., (ed.), *The Oxford Handbook of the Bronze Age Aegean* (Oxford: Oxford University Press, 2010).

Crawford, H., (ed.), *The Sumerian World* (London: Routledge, 2013).

Earle, T. K., (ed.), *Bronze Age Economics: The Beginnings of Political Economies* (Boulder, CO: Perseus, 2002).

Fokkens, H., and Harding, A., (eds.), *The Oxford Handbook of the European Bronze Age* (Oxford, Oxford University Press, 2013).

Lloyd, A. B., *Ancient Egypt: State and Society* (Oxford: Oxford University Press, 2014).

Loewe, M., and O'Shaughnessy, E. L., (eds.), *The Cambridge History of Ancient China* (Cambridge: Cambridge University Press, 1999).

Pool, C. A., *Olmec Archaeology and Early Mesoamerica* (Cambridge: Cambridge University Press, 2007).

Trigger, B. G., *Understanding Early Civilizations: A Comparative Study* (Cambridge: Cambridge University Press, 2003).

Wright, R. P., *The Ancient Indus* (Cambridge, 2010).

Yasur-Landau, A., *The Philistines and Aegean Migration at the End of the Late Bronze Age* (Cambridge: Cambridge University Press, 2010).

Chapter 5

Abu-Lughod, J. L., *Before European Hegemony: The World System, A.D. 1250–1350* (New York, NY: Oxford University Press, 1989).

Angel, J. L., 'Health as a Crucial Factor in the Changes from Hunting to Developed Farming in the Eastern Mediterranean,' in M. N. Cohen and G. J. Armelagos (eds.), *Paleopathology at the Origins of Agriculture* (New York, NY: Academic Press, 1984).

Anthony, David W., *The Horse, the Wheel, and Language: How Bronze-Age Riders from the Eurasian Steppes Shaped the Modern World* (Princeton: Princeton University Press, 2007).

Bellah, R. N., and Joas, H., (eds.), *The Axial Age and its Consequences* (Cambridge, MA: Belknap Press, 2012).

Benedictow, O. J., *The Black Death, 1346–1353: The Complete History* (Woodbridge: Boydel and Brewer, 2004).

Benito i Monclús, P., (ed.), *Crisis en la Edad Media: Modelos, Explicaciones y Representaciones* (Barcelona: Editorial Milenio Lleida, 2013).

Biraben, J. N., 'Essai sur l'évolution du nombre des hommes', *Population* 34 (1979), 13–24.

Brooke, J. L., *Climate Change and the Course of Global History: A Rough Journey* (New York: Cambridge University Press, 2014).

Burger, R. L., *Chavin and the Origins of Andean Civilization* (London: Thames & Hudson, 1992).

Campbell, B., *The Great Transition: Climate, Disease and Society in the Late-Medieval World* (New York: Cambridge University Press, 2016).

Chang, C-s., *The Rise of the Chinese Empire: Nation, State, and Imperialism in Early China, ca. 1600-B.C.-A.D. 8* (Ann Arbor, MI: University of Michigan Press, 2007).

Cline, E. H., *1177 B.C.: The Year Civilization Collapsed* (Princeton: Princeton University Press, 2014).

Collins, P., *From Egypt to Babylon: The International Age, 1500–500BC* (Cambridge, MA: Harvard University Press, 2008).

Cunliffe, B., (ed.), *The Oxford Illustrated History of Prehistoric Europe* (Oxford: Oxford University Press, 2001).

Di Cosmo, N., *Ancient China and its Enemies: The Rise of Nomadic Power in East Asian History* (New York, NY: Cambridge University Press, 2002).

Elvin, M., *The Retreat of the Elephants: An Environmental History of China* (New Haven: Yale University Press, 2004).

Evans, S. T., *Ancient Mexico and Central America: Archaeology and Culture History* (3rd ed., New York: Thames & Hudson, 2013).

Gadgil, M., and Ramachandra G., *This Fissured Land: An Ecological History of India.* (Oxford: Oxford University Press, 1992).

Goldstone, J. A., 'Efflorescences and Economic Growth in World History: Rethinking the "Rise of the West" and the Industrial Revolution', *Journal of World History* 13 (2002), 323–90.

Harper, K., *The Fate of Rome: Climate, Disease, & the End of an Empire* (Princeton: Princeton University Press, 2017).

Harris, W. V., (ed.), *The Ancient Mediterranean Environment between Science and History* (Leiden: Brill, 2013).

Hoffman, R., *The Environmental History of Medieval Europe* (New York: Cambridge University Press, 2014).

Keys, D., *Catastrophe: An Investigation into the Origins of the Modern World* (New York, NY: Random House, 2000).

Landers, J., *The Field and the Forge: Population, Production, and Power in the Pre-industrial West* (New York: Oxford University Press, 2003).

Lieberman, V., *Strange Parallels: Southeast Asia in Global Context, c. 800–1830.* 2 vols. (New York, NY: Cambridge University Press, 2003, 2009).

Little, L. K. (ed.), *Plague and the End of Antiquity: The Pandemic of 541–750* (New York: Cambridge University Press, 2007).

Marks, R. B., *China: Its Environment and History* (Lanham, MD: Rowman and Littlefield, 2012).

May, T., *The Mongol Conquests in World History* (London: Reaktion, 2012).

McCormick, M., *Origins of the European Economy: Communications and Commerce A.D. 300–900* (New York, NY: Cambridge University Press, 2001).

McEvedy, C., and Richard J., *Atlas of World Population History* (New York: Penguin, 1978).

McNeill, J. R., and McNeill, W. H., *The Human Web: A Bird's Eye View of World History* (New York, NY: W. W. Norton, 2003).

McNeill, W. H., *Plagues and Peoples* (New York: Anchor Books, 1976).

Morris, I., *Why the West Rules—For Now: The Patterns of History, and What They Reveal About the Future* (New York, NY: Farrar, Strauss, and Giroux, 2010).

Moseley, M. E., *The Incas and their Ancestors: The Archaeology of Peru* (Rev. ed. London: Thames & Hudson, 2001).

Newfield, T. P., 'The Causation, Contours and Frequency of Food Shortages in Carolingian Europe, c.750–c.950', in Pere Benito i Monclús (ed.), *Crisis en la Edad Media: Modelos, Explicaciones y Representaciones*, pp. 117–72 (Editorial Milenio Lleida, 2013).

Newfield, T. P., 'Human–Bovine Plagues in the Early Middle Ages', *Journal of Interdisciplinary History* 64 (2015), 1–38.

Newman, J. L., *The Peopling of Africa: A Geographic Interpretation* (New Haven: Yale University Press, 1995).

Nur, A., with Burgess, D. *Apocalypse: Earthquakes, Archaeology, and the Wrath of God* (Princeton: Princeton University Press, 2008).

Quilter, J., *The Ancient Central Andes* (New York, NY: Routledge, 2014).

Rasmussen, S., Allentoft, M. E., Nielson, K., Orlando, L., et al. 'Early Divergent Strains of Yersinia pestis in Eurasia 5,000 Years Ago', *Cell* 163 (2015), 571–82.

Rosen, W., *Justinian's Flea: Plague, Empire, and the Birth of Europe* (New York: Viking, 2007).

Skillington, K., *History of Africa*, 3rd edn. (New York, NY: Palgrave MacMillan, 2012).

Thapar, R., *Early India: From the Origins to AD 1300* (London: Allen Lane/Penguin, 2002).

Van De Mieroop, M., *A History of the Ancient Near East, ca. 3000–323 B.C.* (Malden, MA: Wiley Blackwell, 2004).

Wertime, T. A., and Muhly, J. D., (eds.), *The Coming of the Age of Iron* (New Haven, CT: Yale University Press, 1980).

Wolpert, S., *A New History of India*. 8th edn. (New York, NY: Oxford University Press, 2009).

Chapter 6

Chadwick, H., *The Church in Ancient Times: From Galilee to Gregory the Great* (New York: Oxford University Press, 2001). Two masterful volumes.

Chadwick, H., *East and West: The Making of a Rift in the Church, from Apostolic Times to the Council of Florence* (Oxford: Oxford University Press, 2003).

Cochrane, C. N., *Christianity and Classical Culture: A Study of Thought and Action from Augustus to Augustine* (New York: Oxford University Press, 1957). A classic.

Esposito, J. L., (ed.), *The Oxford History of Islam* (New York: Oxford University Press, 1999).

Fagan, B., *From Black Land to Fifth Sun: The Science of Sacred Sites* (Reading, MA: Perseus Books, 1998).

Foltz, R. C., *Religions of the Silk Road: Overland Trade and Cultural Exchange from Antiquity to the Fifteenth Century* (New York: St. Martin's Griffin, 1999). An insightful study.

Garlake, P., *Early Art and Architecture of Africa* (Oxford: Oxford University Press, 2003).

Grant, E., *The Foundations of Modern Science in the Middle Ages: Their Religious, Institutional, and Intellectual Contexts* (New York: Cambridge University Press, 1996). Grant argues that the intellectual debates in medieval European universities led to the modern Scientific Revolution that propelled the West ahead of the Islamic world.

Gutas, D., *Greek Thought, Arabic Culture: The Graeco-Arabic Translation Movement in Baghdad and Early 'Abbasāid Society* (Abingdon: Routledge, 1998).

Jaspers, K., *The Origin and Goal of History* (London: Routledge & Kegan Paul, 1953).

Lapidus, I. M., *A History of Islamic Societies* (2nd edn., Cambridge: Cambridge University Press, 2002). A balanced and thoughtful overview.

Leff, G., *Medieval Thought: St. Augustine to Ockham* (Baltimore, MD: Penguin Books, 1958). A readable survey that gives Islamic influences their due.

Louth, A., *Greek East and Latin West: The Church AD 681–1071. The Church in History*, Vol. 3. (Crestwood, NY: St. Vladimir's Seminary Press, 2007).

Needham, J., *The Grand Titration: Science and Society in East and West* (Toronto: University of Toronto Press, 1969).

Needham, J., *Science in Traditional China* (Cambridge, MA: Harvard University Press, 1981). Two brief overviews by Needham, the great pioneer of Chinese science and technology.

Pelikan, J., *Christianity and Classical Culture: The Metamorphosis of Natural Theology in the Christian Encounter with Hellenism* (New Haven: Yale University Press, 1993). Lectures given on Natural Theology at the University of Aberdeen.

Provan, I., *Convenient Myths: The Axial Age, Dark Green Religion, and the World That Never Was* (Waco, TX: Baylor University Press, 2013). Critical thinking about categories of analysis.

Reat, N. R., *Buddhism: A History* (Berkeley, CA: Asian Humanities Press, 1994). A critical, lucid examination.

Ropp, P. S., *China in World History* (New York: Oxford University Press, 2010). A readable and interesting introduction.

Scharfstein, B-A., *A Comparative History of World Philosophy from the Upanishads to Kant* (Albany: State University of New York Press, 1998). Brilliantly daring, well-informed, and very readable.

Chapter 7

Benjamin, C. (ed.), *The Cambridge World History IV: A World with States, Empires, and Networks, 1200 BCE–900 CE* (Cambridge: Cambridge University Press, 2015).

Crosby, A., *Ecological Imperialism: The Biological Expansion of Europe, 900–1900* (Revised edn., Cambridge: Cambridge University Press, 2003).

Cunliffe, B., *By Steppe, Desert, and Ocean: The Birth of Eurasia* (Oxford: Oxford University Press, 2015).

Diamond, J., *Guns, Germs and Steel: The Fates of Human Societies* (New York: Norton, 1997).

Fagan, B., *The Long Summer: How Climate Changed Civilization* (New York: Basic Books, 2004).

Gellner, E., *Nations and Nationalism* (Oxford: Blackwell, 1983).

Johnson, A., and Earle, T., *The Evolution of Human Societies: From Foraging Groups to Agrarian States* (2nd ed., Stanford: Stanford University Press, 2000).

Kedar, B., and Wiessner-Hanks, M., (eds.), *The Cambridge World History V: Expanding Webs of Exchange and Conflict, 500 CE–1500 CE* (Cambridge: Cambridge University Press, 2015).

Maddison, A., *The World Economy: Historical Statistics* (Paris: Organisation for Economic Co-operation and Development, 2003).

Morris, I., *Why the West Rules—For Now: The Patterns of History and What They Reveal About the Future* (London: Profile, 2010).

Morris, I., *The Measure of Civilisation: How Social Development Decides the Fate of Nations* (London: Profile, 2013).

Morris, I., *Foragers, Farmers, and Fossil Fuels: How Human Values Evolve* (Princeton: Princeton University Press, 2015).

Renfrew, C., and Paul B., (eds.), *The Cambridge World Prehistory*. 3 vols. (Cambridge: Cambridge University Press, 2015).

Yoffee, N., (ed.), *The Cambridge World History III: Early Cities in Comparative Perspective, 4000 BCE–1200 CE* (Cambridge: Cambridge University Press, 2015).

Chapter 8

Braudel, F., *Civilization and Capitalism, 15th–18th Century*. 3 vols. (Trans. Siân Reynolds, New York: Harper and Row, 1979–1982).

Canny, N., and Morgan, P., (eds.), *The Oxford Handbook of the Atlantic World 1450–1850* (Oxford: Oxford University Press, 2011).

Cantor, N., *In the Wake of the Plague: The Black Death and the World It Made* (New York: Free Press, 2001).

Casale, G., *The Ottoman Age of Exploration* (New York: Oxford University Press, 2010).

Curtin, P. D., *Cross-Cultural Trade in World History* (New York: Cambridge University Press, 1984).

Eltis, D., Richardson, D., Behrendt, S. D., and Florentino, M., *Voyages: The Transatlantic Slave Trade Database*. Launched 2008. Available at: http://www.slavevoyages.org.

Fagan, B., *The Little Ice Age: How Climate Made History 1300–1850* (New York: Basic Books, 2000).

Frank, A. G., *ReORIENT: Global Economy in the Asian Age* (Berkeley: University of California Press, 1998).

Parthasarathi, P., *Why Europe Grew Rich and Asia Did Not: Global Economic Divergence, 1600–1850* (Cambridge: Cambridge University Press, 2011).

Pomeranz, K., *The Great Divergence: China, Europe, and the Making of the Modern Economy* (Princeton: Princeton University Press, 2000).

Russell, P., *Prince Henry 'the Navigator': A Life* (New Haven: Yale University Press, 2000).

Tracy, J. D., (ed.), *The Rise of the Merchant Empires: Long-Distance Trade in the Early Modern World, 1350–1750* (New York: Cambridge University Press, 1990).

Chapter 9

Bossy, J., *Christianity in the West* (Oxford: Oxford University Press, 1985).

Brockey, L., *Journey to the East The Jesuit Mission to China, 1579–1724* (Cambridge, MA: Harvard University Press, 2007).

Cohen, H. F., *The Scientific Revolution: A Historiographical Inquiry* (Chicago: University of Chicago Press, 1994).

Delumeau, J., *Catholicism between Luther and Voltaire: A New View of the Counter-Reformation* (Louisville, KY: Westminster John Knox Press, 1977).

Fernández-Armesto, F., and Wilson, D., *Reformations: A Radical Interpretation of Christianity and the World, 1500–2000* (New York: Scribner, 1997).

Gay, P., *The Enlightenment*. 2 vols. (London: W. W. Norton & Company, 1995).

Hodgson, M., *The Venture of Islam*. 3 vols. (Chicago: University of Chicago Press, 1977).

Israel, J., *Radical Enlightenment: Philosophy and the Making of Modernity* (Oxford: Oxford University Press, 2001).

Jacob, M., *Scientific Culture and the Making of the Industrial West* (Oxford: Oxford University Press, 1997).

Jardine, L., *Worldly Goods: A New History of the Renaissance* (London: W. W. Norton & Company, 1998).

O'Malley, J. W., (ed.), *The Jesuits: Cultures, Sciences and the Arts, 1540–1773* (Toronto: University of Toronto Press, 2015).

Rubiés, J., *Travel and Ethnology in the Renaissance: South India through European Eyes, 1250–1625* (Cambridge: Cambridge University Press, 2000).

Shapin, S., *The Scientific Revolution* (Chicago: University of Chicago Press, 1998).

Wakeman, F., *The Great Enterprise: The Manchu Reconstruction of Imperial Order in Seventeenth-Century China* (Berkeley: University of California Press, 1986).

Waley-Cohen, J., *The Sextants of Beijing: Global Currents in Chinese History* (London: W. W. Norton & Company, 1999).

Chapter 10

Alcock, S. E., D'Altroy, T. N., Morrison, K. D., and Sinopoli, C. M., *Empires: Perspectives from Archaeology and History* (Cambridge: Cambridge University Press, 2001).

Belmessous, S., (ed.), *Empire by Treaty: Negotiating European Expansion, 1600–1900* (New York: Oxford University Press, 2014).

Bently, J. H., *Old World Encounters: Cross-Cultural Contact and Exchanges in Pre-Modern Times* (Oxford: Oxford University Press, 1993).

Flores, J., 'The *Mogor* as Venomous Hydra: Forging the Mughal-Portuguese Frontier', *Journal of Early Modern History* 19 (2015), 539–62.

Mathisen, A., 'Charting Childhood Disability in an Eighteenth-Century Institution', *The Journal of the History of Childhood and Youth* 8 (2015), 191–210.

May, H., Kaur, B., and Prochner, L., (eds.), *Empire, Education and Indigenous Childhoods: Nineteenth-Century Missionary Infant Schools in Three British Colonies* (Farnham: Ashgate Publishing Limited, 2014).

Mazzaoui, M., (ed.), *Safavid Iran and Her Neighbors* (Salt Lake City: University of Utah Press, 2003).

Mosca, M. W., *From Frontier Policy to Foreign Policy. The Question of India and the Transformation of Geopolitics in Qing China* (Stanford: Stanford University Press, 2013).

Noldus, B., and Keblusek, M., *Double Agents: Cultural and Political Brokerage in Early Modern Europe* (Leiden: Brill, 2011).

Perdue, P., *China Marches West: The Qing Conquest of Central Eurasia* (Cambridge, MA: Belknap Press, 2005).

Piirimäe, P., 'Russia, the Turks and Europe: Legitimations of War and the Formation of European Identity in the Early Modern Period', *Journal of Early Modern History* 11 (2007), 63–86.

Ricci, R., *Islam Translated: Literature, Conversion, and the Arabic Cosmopolis of South and Southeast Asia* (Delhi: Permanent Black, 2011).

Richards, J. F., *The Unending Frontier: An Environmental History of the Early Modern World* (Berkeley: University of California Press, 2003).

Waldman, C., (ed.), *Biographical Dictionary of American Indian History to 1900* (Revised edn., New York: Checkmark Books, 2001).

Worster, D., *Nature's Economy: A History of Ecological Ideas* (Cambridge: Cambridge University Press, 1994).

Chapter 11

Christian, D., *This Fleeting World: A Short History of Humanity* (Great Barrington, MA: Berkshire Publishing, 2008).

Christian, D., *Maps of Time: An Introduction to Big History*, with a new Preface (Berkeley, CA: University of California Press, 2011).

Credit Suisse, *Global Wealth Report 2014* (Zurich: Credit Suisse AG, 2014).

Crosby, A. W., *Children of the Sun: A History of Humanity's Unappeasable Appetite for Energy* (New York: W.W. Norton & Company, 2006).

Crutzen P. J., 'Geology of Mankind: The Anthropocene', Nature, 415 (2002), 23.

Fernández-Armesto, F., *Pathfinders: A Global History of Exploration* (New York, NY: Norton, 2007).

Frederico, G., 'How has world trade changed in 200 years', January 2016, https://www.weforum. org/agenda/2016/02/how-has-world-trade-changed-in-200-years/?utm_content=buffera6-d34&utm_medium=social&utm_source=twitter.com&utm_campaign=buffer.

Headrick, D., *Technology: A World History* (Oxford: Oxford University Press, 2009).

Hobsbawm, E., *The Age of Extreme* (London: Weidenfeld & Nicolson, 1994).

Maddison, A., *The World Economy: A Millennial Perspective* (Paris: OECD, 2001).

Malm, A., *Fossil Capital: The Rise of Steam Power and the Roots of Global Warming* (London: Verso, 2016).

McNeill, J. R., *Something New Under the Sun: An Environmental History of the Twentieth-Century World* (New York: Norton, 2000).

McNeill J. R., and Pomeranz, K., (eds.) *Cambridge History of the World, Vol. VII* (Cambridge University Press, 2015).

Picketty, T., *Capital in the Twenty-First Century* (Trans. A. Goldhammer, Cambridge, MA: Harvard University Press, 2014).

Pomeranz, K., *The Great Divergence: China, Europe, and the Making of the Modern World Economy* (Princeton: Princeton University Press, 2000).

Rockstrom, J., and Klum, M., *Big World Small Planet: Abundance within Planetary Boundaries* (Sweden: Max Ström Publishing, 2015).

Rockström, J., Will Steffen, Noone, K., Persson, Å., Chapin III. F. S., Lambin, E. F.,...Foley, J. A., 'A Safe Operating Space for Humanity', Nature, 461 (2009), 472–5; updated in Steffen, W., Richards, K., Rockström, J., Cornell, S. E., Fetzer, I., Bennett, E. M.,...Sörlin, S., 'Planetary Boundaries: Guiding Human Development on a Changing Planet', Science 343 (2015), 1–15.

Smil, V., *Harvesting the Biosphere: What We Have Taken from Nature* (Cambridge, MA: MIT Press, 2013.

Steffen, W., Grinevald, J., Crutzen, P., and McNeill, J., 'The Anthropocene: Conceptual and Historical Perspectives', *Philosophical Transactions of the Royal Society A* 369 (2011), 842–67.

Steffen, W., Richards, K., Rockström, J., Cornell, S. E., Fetzer, I., Bennett, E. M.,...Sörlin, S., 'Planetary Boundaries: Guiding Human Development on a Changing Planet', Science 343 (2015), 1–15.

Uglow, J., *The Lunar Men: The Friends Who Made the Future: 1730–1810* (New York: Faber & Faber, 2002).

Wrigley, E. A., *Energy and the English Industrial Revolution* (Cambridge: Cambridge University Press, 2011).

Zalasiewicz, J., and Freedman, K., *The Earth After Us: What Legacy Will Humans Leave in the Rocks?* (Oxford: Oxford University Press, 2009).

Zalasiewicz, J., and Waters, C., 'The Anthropocene', in *Oxford Research Encyclopedia, Environmental. Science* (New York, NY: Oxford University Press, 2015). doi: 10.1093/acrefore/9780199389414.013.7.

Zeebe, R. E., Ridgwell, A., and Zachos, J. C., 'Anthropogenic Carbon Release Rate Unprecedented During the Past 66 Million Years', *Nature Geoscience* 9 (2016), 325–29.

Chapter 12

Aalavi, S., *Muslim Cosmopolitanism in the Age of Empire* (Cambridge, MA: Harvard University Press, 2015).

Adorno, T. W., *Critical Models* (New York, NY: Columbia University Press, 2005).

Bayly, C. A., *The Birth of the Modern World 1780–1914: Global Connections and Comparisons* (Malden: Blackwell, 2004).

Beiser, F. C., *After Hegel. German Philosophy 1840–1900* (Princeton: Princeton University Press, 2014).

Bell, U. J., Herberichs, C., and Sandl, M., (eds.), *Aura und Auratisierung: mediologische Perspektiven im Anschluss an Walter Benjamin* (Zurich: Chronos, 2014).

Black, J., *The Power of Knowledge: How Information and Technology Made the Modern World* (New Haven: Yale University Press, 2014).

Borthwick, M., (ed.), *Pacific Century: The Emergence of Modern Pacific Asia* (Boulder, CO: Westview Press, 2014).

Brook, T., *Death by a Thousand Cuts* (Cambridge, MA: Harvard University Press, 2008).

Buzan, B., *The Global Transformation: History, Modernity, and the Making of International Relations* (Cambridge: Cambridge University Press, 2015).

Chadwick, W., *Women, Arts and Society* (5th edn., London: Thames & Hudson, 2012).

Conrad, P., *Modern Times, Modern Places* (New York: Knopf, 1999).

Croce, B., *History of Europe in the Nineteenth Century* (London: Allen & Unwin, 1953).

Crossley, P. K., Hollen Lees, L., and Servos, J. W., *Global Society. The World Since 1900* (Boston: Houghton Mifflin, 2004).

Curry-Machado, J., (ed.), *Global Histories, Imperial Commodities, Local Interactions* (New York: Palgrave Macmillan, 2013).

Edgerton, D., *The Shock of the Old: Technology and Global History since 1900* (New York: Oxford University Press, 2006).

Fernández-Armesto, F., *A Foot in the River* (Oxford: Oxford University Press, 2014).

Fitzmaurice, A., *Sovereignty, Property and Empire 1500–2000* (Cambridge: Cambridge University Press, 2014).

Goodlad, L. M. E., *The Victorian Geopolitical Aesthetic: Realism, Sovereignty, and Transnational Experience* (Oxford: Oxford University Press, 2015).

Gordon, A., *A Modern History of Japan from Tokugawa Times to the Present* (3rd edn., New York: Oxford University Press, 2014).

Jones, G., *Beauty Imagined: A History of the Global Beauty Industry* (Oxford: Oxford University Press, 2015).

McGrath, A. E., *The Twilight of Atheism* (New York, NY: Doubleday, 2004).

Manuel, F. E., *The Prophets of Paris* (Cambridge, MA: Harvard University Press, 1962).

Morat, D., (ed.), *Sounds of Modern History: Auditory Cultures in 19th and 20th Century Europe* (New York: Berghahn Books, 2014).

Moyn, S., and Sartori, A., (eds.), *Global Intellectual History* (New York: Columbia University Press, 2013).

Nowell Smith, G., *The Oxford History of World Cinema* (New York: Oxford University Press, 1999).

Osterhammel, J., *The Transformation of the World. A Global History of the Nineteenth Century* (Princeton: Princeton University Press, 2014).

Readman, P., Radding, C., and Bryant, C., (eds.), *Borderlands in World History 1700–1914* (Basingstoke: Palgrave Macmillan, 2014).

Said, E., *Orientalism* (New York, NY: Vintage, 1978).

Stovall, E. T., *Transnational France: The Modern History of a Transnational Nation* (Boulder, CO: Westview, 2015).

Wenzlhuemer, R., *Connecting the Nineteenth-Century World: The Telegraph and Globalization* (Cambridge: Cambridge University Press, 2013).

Chapter 13

Beckett, I., *The Great War 1914–1918* (London: Routledge, 2001).

Black, J., *The Cold War: A Military History* (London: Bloomsbury, 2015).

Black, J., *The Holocaust: History and Memory* (Bloomington: Indiana University Press, 2016).

Clark, C., *The Sleepwalkers: How Europe Went to War in 1914* (New York: Harper, 2015).

Duara, P., *Decolonization: Perspectives from Now and Then (Rewriting Histories)* (New York: Routledge, 2004).

Ferguson, N., *The Pity of War: Explaining World War I* (New York: Basic Books, 2000).

Fussell, P., *The Great War and Modern Memory* (New York: Oxford University Press, 2000).

Gaddis, J. L., *The Cold War: A New History* (London: Penguin, 2005).

Gilbert, M., *The First World War: A Complete History* (New York: Holt, 1996).

Hobsbawm, E., *The Age of Extremes: A History of the World, 1914–1991* (New York: Vintage, 1994).

McCormick, J., *Understanding the European Union: A Concise Introduction* (3rd edn., New York, NY: Palgrave Macmillan, 2005).

Murray, W., and Millet, A. R., *A War to Be Won: Fighting the Second World War, 1937–1945* (Cambridge, MA: Harvard University Press, 2000).

Rostow, W. W., *The Stages of Economic Growth* (Cambridge: Cambridge University Press, 1962).

Rothermund, D., *The Routledge Companion to Decolonization* (New York: Routledge, 2006).

Sardar, Z., *Islam Beyond the Violent Jihadis* (London: Biteback, 2016).

Scott, D., *Marketing the Moon* (Cambridge, MA: MIT Press, 2014).

Short, P., *Mao: The Man Who Made China* (London: Taurus, 2017).

Slaughter, A.-M., *A New World Order* (Princeton: Princeton University Press, 2005).

Staley, D. J., *History and Future* (Lanham: Lexington, 2007).

Therborn, G., *The World: A Beginner's Guide* (Malden, MA: Polity Press, 2011).

Thomas, H., *Armed Truce: The Beginnings of the Cold War, 1945–46* (Sevenoaks: Sceptre, 1986).

Weinberg, G., *A World at Arms: A Global History of World War II* (Cambridge: Cambridge University Press, 1995).

Wesseling, H. L., *The European Colonial Empires* (New York, NY: Longman, 2004).

Westad, O. A., *The Global Cold War: Third World Interventions and the Making of Our Times* (Cambridge: Cambridge University Press, 2005).

Woods, N., (ed.), *The Political Economy of Globalization* (Basingstoke: Palgrave, 2001).

PICTURE ACKNOWLEDGEMENTS

The editor and publishers wish to thank the following who have kindly given permission to reproduce the illustrations on the following pages:

16	dieKleinert / Alamy Stock Photo
17	Wikimedia / hairymuseummatt (original photo), DrMikeBaxter (derivative work) / CC BY-SA 2.0
19	From L. Wadley, 'Recognizing Complex Cognition through Innovative Technology in Stone Age and Palaeolithic Sites', *Cambridge Archaeological Journal*, 2013
22	From C. Gamble, et al., *Thinking Big: How the Evolution of Social Life Shaped the Human Mind*, Thames & Hudson, 2014
25	From C. Gamble, *Settling the Earth*, fig 2.3, Cambridge University Press, 2013
28	Global landcover map © ESA – MEDIAS France / Postel
29	Courtesy Nick Drake
39	© The Trustees of the British Museum
43	© Bruno Compagnon / Sagaphoto / age fotostock
46	© Suzi Eszterhas / Minden Pictures / age fotostock
48	© CM Dixon / Heritage Image / age fotostock
50	Natural History Museum, Vienna. © De Agostini Editore / age fotostock
53	Ulmer Museum, Ulm. © Fine Art Images / age fotostock
54	Granger Historical Picture Archive / Alamy Stock Photo
55	Venus from Hohle Fels, Museum of Prehistory, Blaubeuren. Photo: Hilde Jensen. © University of Tübingen
56	Prof. C.S. Henshilwood, Evolutionary Studies Institute, University of Witwatersrand, South Africa
58	Anthropology and Ethnography Museum, Turin. © DEA / G DAGLI ORTI / De Agostini Editore / age fotostock
60	Museum of Anthropology and Ethnography, St. Petersburg. Photo: Thilo Parg / Wikimedia Commons / CC BY-SA 4.0
63	robertharding / Alamy Stock Photo
64	Wikimedia / José-Manuel Benito Álvarez
67	National Archaeological Museum, Saint-Germain-en-Laye, France. © DEA / G DAGLI ORTI / De Agostini Editore / age fotostock
74	Archaeological excavations at Sibudu by the University of Tübingen (direction Prof. N. Conard) during 2017
75	firina © 123RF.com
78	© DEA PICTURE LIBRARY / De Agostini Editore / age fotostock
80	Courtesy of the Oriental Institute of the University of Chicago
83	Phillip C. Edwards
85	(top) © CM Dixon / Heritage Image / age fotostock
85	(foot) INTERFOTO / Alamy Stock Photo
86	Photo: C. Jarrige, Mission Archéologique de l'Indus (M.A.I.)
88	Louvre Museum, Paris. © Werner Forman Archive / Heritage Image / age fotostock
91	© Hari Mahidhar / Dinodia Photo / age fotostock

INDEX

Note: Tables and figures are indicated by an italic *t* and *f*, respectively, following the page number.